REA

The Making of
Literate Societies

The Making of
Literate Societies

Edited by

David R. Olson and Nancy Torrance

BLACKWELL
Publishers

First published 2001

2 4 6 8 10 9 7 5 3 1

Blackwell Publishers Inc.
350 Main Street
Malden, Massachusetts 02148
USA

Blackwell Publishers Ltd
108 Cowley Road
Oxford OX4 1JF
UK

Library of Congress Cataloging-in-Publication Data

The making of literate societies / edited by David R. Olson and Nancy Torrance.
    p. cm.
  Includes bibliographical references and index.
  ISBN 0–631–22742–3 (alk. paper)—ISBN 0–631–22743–1 (pbk.: alk. paper)
    1. Literacy—Social aspects. 2. Literacy—Cross-cultural studies. I. Olson, David R., 1935–
  II. Torrance, Nancy.

  LC149 .M26 2001
  302.2′244—dc21

                                         00–065802

British Library Cataloguing in Publication Data

A CIP catalogue record for this book is available from the
British Library.

Typeset in Sabon on 10.5/12.5pt
by Kolam Information Services Pvt. Ltd, Pondicherry, India
Printed in Great Britain by MPG Books Ltd, Bodmin, Cornwall

This book is printed on acid-free paper

Contents

List of Contributors   vii
Acknowledgments   ix
Preface   x

Part I: On Being a Literate Society: Conceptual and Historical Perspectives on Literacy   1

1   Conceptualizing Literacy as a Personal Skill and as a Social Practice   3
   David R. Olson and Nancy Torrance
2   The Roles of Literacy Practices in the Activities and Institutions of Developed and Developing Countries   19
   Armin Triebel
3   Societal Literacy: Writing Culture and Development   54
   Georg Elwert
4   Literacy in Ancient Greece: Functional Literacy, Oral Education, and the Development of a Literate Environment   68
   Rosalind Thomas
5   Literacy in Germany   82
   Utz Maas
6   Literacy in Japan: *Kanji, Kana, Rōmaji*, and Bits   101
   Florian Coulmas

Part II: On Becoming a Literate Society: Literacy in Developing Societies   121

a) African Case Studies   123

7   Language, Literacy, the Production and Reproduction of Knowledge, and the Challenge of African Development   123
   Kwesi K. Prah

8   Literacy and Literature in Indigenous Languages in Benin
    and Burkina-Faso   142
    Joseph Akoha
9   Constructive Interdependence: The Response of a Senegalese
    Community to the Question of Why Become Literate   153
    Sonja Fagerberg-Diallo
10 Literacy for Gonja and Birifor Children in Northern Ghana   178
    Esther Goody and JoAnne Bennett

b) Central and South American Case Studies   201

11 Literacy and Intercultural Bilingual Education in the Andes   201
    Luis Enrique López
12 The Uses of Orality and Literacy in Rural Mexico:
    Tales from Xaltipan   225
    Elsie Rockwell

c) Asian Case Studies   248

13 Developing a Literate Tradition in Six Marginal
    Communities in the Philippines: Interrelations of Literacy,
    Education, and Social Development   248
    Maria Luisa Canieso Doronila
14 Issues of Literacy Development in the Indian Context   284
    Chander Daswani
15 Women and Empowerment through Literacy   296
    Malini Ghose

Part III: Conclusion: From Research to Policy   317

16 Literacy and Social Development: Policy and
    Implementation   319
    Ingrid Jung and Adama Ouane

Name Index   337
Subject Index   343

Contributors

Joseph Akoha Faculté des Lettres, Arts et Sciences Humaines, Université Nationale du Bénin, P.B. 526, Cotonou, Benin, West Africa.

JoAnne Bennett Department of Psychology, Queen's University, Kingston ON, K7L 3N6, Canada.

Florian Coulmas Gerhard-Mercator-Universität, FB3/Sprache und Geschichte/, Kultur des modernen Japan, Mühlheimer Str. 212 SV, 47057 Duisberg, Germany.

Chander J. Daswani UNESCO, UNESCO House, 8 Poorvi Marg, Vasant Vihar New Delhi 110057, India. Correspondence to: 157 Sahyog Apt Plot 3, Mayur Vihar phase–1, New Delhi GPO 110091, India.

Maria Luisa C. Doronila Education Research Program, Centre for Integrative and Development Studies, University of the Philippines, Diliman, Quezon City, 1101, Philippines.

Georg Elwert Institut für Ethnologie, Freie Universität Berlin, Drosselweg 1–3, 14195 Berlin, Germany.

Sonja Fagerberg-Diallo Associates in Research and Education for Development (ARED) and Centre d'Education, de Recherche et de Formation en Langues Africaines (CERFLA), Villa 8253, Sacre Coeur 1, BP 10737, Dakar-Liberté, Senegal.

Malini Ghose Nirantar – A Centre for Women and Education, B 64 Sarvodaya Enclave, New Delhi 110017, India.

Esther Goody Department of Social Anthropology, University of Cambridge, Free School Lane, Cambridge CB2 3RF, UK.

Ingrid Jung German Foundation for International Development (DSE), Tulpenfeld 5, 53113 Bonn, Germany.

Luis Enrique López Programa de Formación en Educación Intercultural Bilingüe para los Países Andinos (PROEIB ANDES), Calle Tomás Frias 1473, Casilla Postal 6759, Cochabamba, Bolivia.

Utz Maas Fachbereich Sprach und Literaturwissenschaft, Universität Osnabrück, Neuer Graben 40, 49069 Osnabrück, Germany.

David R. Olson Centre for Applied Cognitive Science, Ontario Institute for Studies in Education of the University of Toronto, 252 Bloor Street West, Toronto ON, M5S 1V6, Canada.

Adama Ouane Director, UNESCO, Institute for Education, Feldbrunnenstrasse 58, 20148 Hamburg, Germany.

Kwesi K. Prah Department of Anthropology and Sociology, University of the Western Cape, Private Bag X17, Bellville 7535, South Africa.

Elsie Rockwell Departimento de Investigaciones Educativas, Centro de Investigación y de Estudios Avanzados (CINVESTAV) del Instituto Politécnico Nacional, Tenorios 235, Tlalpan, CP 14330, México D.F., México.

Rosalind Thomas Department of History, Royal Holloway, University of London, Egham, Surrey TW20 0EX, UK.

Nancy Torrance International Centre for Educational Change, Theory and Policy Studies, Ontario Institute for Studies in Education of the University of Toronto, 252 Bloor Street West, Toronto ON, M5S 1V6, Canada.

Armin Triebel Institut für Soziologie, Freie Universität Berlin, Babelsberger Str. 14–16, 10715 Berlin, Germany.

Acknowledgments

Several persons and agencies contributed to the preparation of this volume. We thank in particular Min Wang for her editorial assistance in preparation of the manuscript, Sylvia Macrae for her preparation of the indices, and Anja Frings for the inspiring painting that appears on the cover of this volume. We also wish to thank the three funding agencies that contributed indirectly to the preparation of this volume, the Spencer Foundation, the Social Sciences and Humanities Research Council of Canada (SSHRCC), and the National Science and Engineering Research Council of Canada (NSERC).

Preface

This book is the product of two "rounds" of discourse, the first oral, the second in writing. With the leadership of Ingrid Jung and the sponsorship of the DSE, the German Foundation for International Development, a workshop was convened to address the problem that gives this book its focus: "What role does literacy play in social development?" Whereas there are by now several theoretical perspectives on literacy, perspectives that highlight the multiple roles that literacy currently plays or has played in personal and social development, much less is known about how these perspectives could contribute to policy and practices, especially those for developing countries and for marginalized segments of developed ones. As Triebel points out in his chapter, the literacy campaigns of the 1950s and 1960s are now seen as failures. Yet more enlightened theory and policy has been slow to develop.

The innovative step in the discussions aimed at developing a more enlightened view of the role of literacy in social development was to shift the traditional focus on personal literacy to a focus on what we may call "social literacy," that is, what makes a society a literate society. Contra Margaret Thatcher there is such a thing as a society, and it is not to be taken as just a collection of individuals. A literate society is not just a society in which a majority of people know how to read and write; it is a society in which important aspects of social life such as economics, law, science, and government are organized around texts and documents to form what we may call "textual institutions." Personal literacy allows one to participate in such institutions but personal literacy in itself does not guarantee the creation of such institutions nor their effectiveness. Literacy campaigns around the world failed, it was argued, because they focused on personal literacy but failed to come to grips with the problem of social literacy. Social literacy refocuses the problem on to the development of and participation in the textual practices of an increasingly bureaucratic society. An understanding of literacy must include how individuals and groups adopt

and utilize writing in the pursuit of their goals, whether organizing a cooperative, filing a land claim, or publishing a narrative. But it must also include how
individuals and groups come to terms with such textual practices of the dominant bureaucratic institutions of a literate society. A theory of literacy and social
development must bring into relief such facts as that being able to read and write
a contract is worthless unless there are institutions such as courts to enforce
them. Thus issues of literacy are not independent of issues of power. Such
considerations help to explain why literacy activities sometimes become self-
sustaining and why, more often, literacy programs in both developed and developing countries fail.

To bridge the personal and the institutional it is necessary to think of literacy
as an instrumental rather than a causal factor in social development. This
perspective focuses the question on how people can use literacy as an instrument
in the achievement of personal and collective goals ranging from forming a
personal identity to organizing economic reforms. Literacy is thus subordinated
to activities and goals without being lost as a decisive instrument in social
development.

The first of the two rounds of negotiation took place in the Villa Borsig, a
nineteenth-century mansion in Berlin, in June 1997. Some 30 participants were
invited to prepare and present papers which were then discussed by the group.
The novel feature of the program was that the goal was not merely the exchange
of views, although that is the major purpose of most workshops, but rather the
formulation of an agreed-upon statement of policy as to the role of literacy in
social development and the directions that governments and other agencies
should take in designing their literacy programs. This policy statement was
then presented and defended at the UNESCO conference on Adult Education
in Hamburg the following week. The attempt to bring extremely diverse theory
and activity into a common set of principles and recommendations was both
daunting and, in the end, extremely rewarding. It was rewarding in that it turned
participants away from the confrontational style common to academic discourse
toward formulating a statement with which all could agree. The statement
arrived at through these discussions both informed the Introduction to this
volume (chapter 1) and is summarized in the conclusion to that chapter. A fuller
discussion of these policy issues appears in the final chapter of the volume,
written by Jung and Ouane, co-hosts of the workshop.

The second round of negotiation occurred in turning these fruitful discussions
into a publishable volume. We solicited the papers which most usefully highlighted the many factors relevant to the role of literacy in social development.
The volume is divided into two major sections. The first examines literacy as a
social practice in societies in which it has become sufficiently established that we
feel comfortable in referring to them as "literate societies." These include not
only modern European societies but also classically literate societies such as
Classical Greece and Ancient Japan. As that section of the book makes clear,
literacy development reflects both the intrinsic structure of the society, the
economics of script, and the realignments of power in the society. But it also

makes clear that the consequence of adopting written documents as vehicles of social organization reshapes those activities and institutions in the direction of producing "document" cultures, cultures organized around texts.

The second part of the volume examines ongoing literacy projects, programs, and other initiatives in developing societies in Asia (India and the Philippines), Africa (Senegal, Ghana, Bénin, and Burkina-Faso) and Central and South America (Mexico and Bolivia). The countries were selected both to represent these widely diverse regions and to represent several types of literacy programs and activities so as to elucidate the factors involved in becoming a literate society. Here, the critical factors are even more diverse than the regional ones and include economic, educational, linguistic, and psychological dimensions. Economic factors play a critical role in literacy development in all societies but they are highlighted in the study of five Filipino communities examined by Doronila and in the Senegalese community examined by Fagerberg-Diallo. Educational programs play a critical role in all societies too, but their effectiveness depends on such factors as the educational resources available and the language of instruction, as pointed out in Goody's study of rural education in Ghana. Literacy issues are compounded by the complex relations to national languages, the languages of power, a problem examined in India by Daswani, in Bolivia by Lopez, and in Africa by Akoha. The relation of literacy to national identity is examined in the African context by Prah. And finally, the relation of literacy to personal identity and empowerment is examined by Ghose in the context of rural India and by Rockwell in rural Mexico. But above all, the papers in this section of the volume show how local and diverse are the interests and concerns people bring to literacy learning and the problems they encounter in, on the one hand, exploiting the resources of literacy for political, economic, or personal purposes and, on the other, of coming to terms with the demands of an increasingly bureaucratized and literate world.

Although the issues surrounding literacy are too rich to be summarized in a simple formula, there was sufficient agreement among the participants to allow the drafting of a policy statement for presentation to the UNESCO–CONFINTE V Conference as follows:

The Making of a Literate Society

Since its inception, UNESCO has recognized the importance of literacy for human and social development. Yet literacy programs and campaigns have often been constrained by a limited conception of literacy. In many of these programs literacy was seen as a quantitative and undifferentiated phenomenon creating the impression that the problem is of a monolithic nature with a uniform solution. On this understanding illiteracy was seen in terms of deficit or lack in the learner which could be remedied by ready-made packages of knowledge and skill, a marketable commodity with quantitative targets. Such programs have not succeeded as hoped.

Current research and practice has shown that in order to bring about cultural and social transformation, literacy must be seen as an activity embedded in social and cultural practice. Literacy and democratic participation become mutually reinforcing, enabling persons and communities to have influence over the factors that affect their lives. When empowering, literacy practices become self-sustaining. Literacy is not something which is delivered but something to be employed in order to explore their own language and the world on the learner's own terms, which allows them to create and engage in the diverse worlds of literacy.

One reason some campaigns have failed is that they have been carried out without proper regard to the language, knowledge, and learning needs of the individuals and communities involved. Linguistic diversity must be acknowledged by developing literacy programs in local languages. Research has shown that learning to read and write in the mother tongue not only facilitates the acquisition of literacy in that language but also the learning of a second language.

Thus we must acknowledge the fact of multiliteracies, literacies appropriate to the local as well as national and international contexts. Here the idea of societal literacy is crucial. It is this kind of literacy that fosters social networking, makes the rule of law feasible, complex economics viable, and formal education useful and worthwhile. The use of written language also enhances the exchange of ideas and the communication of innovations, technical knowledge, and individual and social creativity, in general. It enhances the rapid circulation of information. Written laws must be made accessible and transparent so that there may be accountability.

Literacy provision in the past has been characterized by centralized control, a one-way transmission of skills to the masses rather than an occasion for enhancing the competence needed for the empowerment of the individual and community. Literacy learning must reflect the specific and diverse contexts of acquisition and use of literacy. These include (1) what the learner already knows, wants and brings to the learning experience, (2) the mother tongue of the learner, (3) the cultural background of the learners, including family culture, local culture, oral traditions, and indigenous knowledge of the learners and their relation to the literacy being acquired, (4) the identity of the learner in relation to gender, class, religion, and race. The process of learning to read is itself an enjoyable and rewarding experience.

In order to contexualize literacy, diverse forms of provision need to be established in relation to the languages used, the content of programs, the producers of materials and the type of "textual community" at the personal, local, national, and regional level. These textual communities are groups of people who can read, write, interpret, and use textual materials whether working together or apart. Successful passage into literacy practices depends on pedagogy, teacher/facilitator education, and materials development which should reflect this diversity.

Sustainable literacy depends on publication at several tiers, ranging from local, nonpublished materials to professional publication. Professional publication requires a diversity of producers, including the readers themselves, as well as a greater variety of materials in history, poetry, modern fiction, folktales, and technical and scientific works, for information and enjoyment.

The learning and maintenance of literate practices depends upon the establishment of a political climate as well as institutional structures of accountability, particularly accountability to the learners and communities themselves, and which support local, national, and regional publication and training networks for the exchange of materials and information. Markets for providing an abundance of books and materials in local languages to meet the needs and demands of readers must be created, supported, and protected. These measures will allow a society to be informed about itself and thereby shape its future.

Part I

On Being a Literate Society: Conceptual and Historical Perspectives on Literacy

Chapter 1

Conceptualizing Literacy as a Personal Skill and as a Social Practice

David R. Olson and Nancy Torrance

The eighteenth-century Enlightenment provided the West with a legacy of hope, hope for the perfectibility of mankind and the perfectibility of social institutions. Behind both was the concept of progress. As the route to progress, the Enlightenment put a new emphasis on mass public education, a program made feasible by the relative availability of printed books and the universalizable knowledge books were assumed to contain. Access to that knowledge was through literacy and literacy along with schooling became the touchstones of the Enlightenment policy in the West. Philosophers of the Enlightenment, including Vico (1744), Condorcet (1802), and Rousseau (1754–91), provided a theory for the evolutionary views of culture, views which came into common use through such eighteenth-century writers as the philosopher Thomas Astle, who wrote, "The noblest acquisition of mankind is speech, and the most useful art is writing. The first eminently distinguishes man from the brute creation; the second, from uncivilized savages" (1784, p. 1). Of course, we now recognize such beliefs as hopelessly eurocentric, but the notion of human perfectibility, and the importance of literacy and education in its achievement, remain as strong today as in the eighteenth century.

There is simply no doubt that writing and literacy play an increasingly important role in the mental and social lives of people in modern bureaucratic societies, and that a legitimate aspiration of peoples everywhere is the right of access to the written word and to those institutional structures premised on writing and record keeping, on format and formula.

But when the significance of literacy to modern bureaucratic societies is put this way, it suggests that the developing countries of Africa, Asia, and Latin America, need only adopt such practices to become, well, like us. As many of the chapters of this volume point out, this assumption is both incorrect and in many cases harmful. Further, a number of Western historians and social scientists including Katz (1968), Gee (1990), Graff (1986), and Street (1984) point out that traditional encomiums to literacy as well as most psychological theories of literacy invite and sustain the inference that literacy and schooling were the *causes* of progressive cognitive and social change. Because literacy and schooling were seen as the causes or engines of social change, then the obvious means to producing psychological and social change was through imposing literacy and schooling on the ignorant and illiterate. The personal and social aspirations, interests, competencies and traditions of the learners could be ignored and overwritten by imposing literate standards and literate practices on them. More importantly, developing nonliterate cultures could be advanced by imposing on them the literate practices and literate institutions of the developed West, originally in the form of colonization. As the chapters of this volume make clear, these inferences are no longer seen as warranted; indeed such practices are now widely recognized as oppressive.

Theories of literacy advanced by Goody (1968; 1986), Havelock (1982), Ong (1982), Eisenstein (1979), and Olson (1994) examined in considerable detail the various roles that writing and literacy have played in the evolution of the dominant institutions in the West including law, science, religion, literature, economics, and politics, and indirectly in the evolution of a particular form of rationality, embedded in the elaborate bureaucratic procedures employed in the construction and evaluation of knowledge. Olson (1994, p. 282) concluded his treatment by claiming that "Our modern conception of the world and our modern conception of ourselves are, we may say, by-products of the invention of a world on paper." Critics such as Street (1984) and Prinsloo and Breier (1996) have criticized these theories for their lack of attention to context of use, proposing rather a "practice" theory of literacy more attentive to the activity of subjects in particular social and institutional contexts, a view first suggested by Scribner and Cole (1981). Triebel (chapter 2 below) contrasts these types of theory in considerable detail, referring to the former as "philosophical" and the latter as "practice" models.

What has become clear through these debates and what articulates a theme that runs through the present volume is that one must distinguish between "consequences of literacy" and the "uses and implications of literacy," or as we shall say, between *causal* and *instrumental* conceptions of literacy. Earlier theories were less sensitive to this distinction, allowing their findings to be used to justify "literacy policy," that is, the imposition of literacy onto people as a means of producing psychological and social change in them. What our new understanding requires is that we move away from the causal talk about what literacy does to people and towards the instrumental talk about what people do or can do with literacy. It is to put the learner and the social context at the center of the topic and to see the technology in an instrumental or functional role. It was the failure to clearly make that distinction that justified to some extent the charge of "technological determinism" leveled at such theories. Whether valid or not, it remains clear that not only theorists, but also policy-makers and the general public have uncritically adopted Enlightenment assumptions about the causal efficacy of literacy in social and psychological change. Indeed, even UNESCO, the most culturally sensitive of all institutions, had at an earlier period adopted the causal model, namely, that making everyone literate would produce valued social and personal goals. Triebel (chapter 2 below) suggests that two assumptions are most in need of revision, namely, that literacy generates social change, and that script changes mind. Literacy must come to be seen less as cause and more as instrument.

Nonetheless, one must not underestimate the instrumental role that literacy may play in psychological and social change in some cultural and institutional contexts. It will not do to simply revert to the credo that there are no "primitive" languages, minds, or cultures and hence to ignore the uses and implications of literacy altogether. Indeed, considerable research, including that reported herein, has been directed to examining the varied roles that literacy has played and can play in various cultural contexts. Such research allows us to revise our beliefs about the implications of literacy without downplaying its significance for either minds or societies. In this introductory chapter, we shall review seven of these issues while focusing particularly on two of them, pedagogy of literacy and literacy and social development.

The Evolution of Scripts

First, scripts as technologies were thought, ever since the Enlightenment, to have evolved from simple picture writing, through word scripts, to syllabaries and culminating in the alphabet (Gelb, 1963). On this view, non-alphabetic writing systems were seen as primitive and unsuitable for intellectual functions. However, it is now widely agreed that writing systems evolved, not in the direction of an ideal script, but rather in response to borrowing a script from one language for which it was reasonably suited to represent another language for which it was not. The product of the borrowing was, in several cases, the development of a writing system which could be taken as representing a more phonological level of the linguistic form (Sampson, 1985; Olson, 1994). Different scripts represent events and languages in different ways, thereby accomplishing different functions (Boone & Mignolo, 1994). Moreover, even children in the process of acquiring an alphabetic script explore alternative notions of how a script "represents" (Ferreiro & Teberosky, 1982). This is not to minimize the vast range of uses that the alphabet has come to serve, but rather to abandon the oft-assumed cultural superiority that earlier evolutionary theories sustained.

The Origins of Literate Societies

Second, historical studies (Clanchy, 1993; Lloyd, 1979; Thomas, 1989, and chapter 4 below) have shown that literacy played a less causal role in the development of modern forms of law, science, and government than has sometimes been assumed. Rather, literacy came gradually to play an instrumental role in preserving information and later in accumulating it. Only gradually did institutions come to bear the marks of a "document culture." Classical Greek society did indeed possess a writing system but its use was limited both to particular functions and to a small set of individuals. Many of the functions we now see as essentially literate, functions such as formulating laws, practicing democracy, constructing essentially modern forms of knowledge and argument, were carried out by essentially oral procedures (Thomas, chapter 4 below). Literacy came to subserve these functions but it did not bring them into existence. When recruited for a function such as law, it transformed the process in often unanticipated ways; written contracts, for example, coming to have more authority than oral ones even if, at the outset, the opposite was true (Clanchy, 1993; Johns, 1998).

Colonialism had a more complex impact on the colonized cultures. In some cases, such as the Philippines, Africa, and Central America, existing indigenous scripts were summarily replaced by Roman scripts, rendering significant parts of the population illiterate in the new script. At the same time the imposed scripts brought with them bureaucratic structures including organization of knowledge, economy, and law which, while instrumental to nation building, were often detrimental to indigenous culture. In other regions such as sub-Saharan Africa there was no previous literate tradition and the colonial language and colonial bureaucratic structures tended to be propagated, not only for reasons of monopolizing power, but also because the colonial language was adopted as a national language as a compromise between competing indigenous languages.

The Oral–Literate Distinction

Third, classical studies of the relation between literacy and orality (Finnegan, 1988) and developmental studies of the relation between oral and written language have found that rather than these being categorically different modes, there is a close interaction between the two. Carruthers (1990) found that in the late medieval period some of the most literate, Thomas Aquinas among them, were also the most gifted at oral memory and unprompted speech. This is not to deny the evolution and importance of more specialized written forms or registers tailored to the specific requirements of mathematics, logic, science, or literature (Kittay, 1991; Illich, 1993), but rather to say that literacy is built upon a strong oral tradition (see Doronila, chapter 13 below) and thrives only if a living oral culture sustains it (see Thomas, chapter 4 below).

Writing and Rationality

Fourth, the psychological studies designed to show the lack of logical powers in nonliterate subjects have come in for criticism and reinterpretation. Lévy-Bruhl (1926) attempted to explain the variety of cultural practices anthropologists described in terms of the psychological processes of nonliterate people, a form of explanation now seen as questionable (Moscovici, 1993). Luria (1976), on the basis of evidence collected in the 1930s in a remote section of Siberia, had found that nonliterate subjects often failed to solve syllogisms that were readily solved by schooled subjects. From this he, like Lévy-Bruhl, inferred that they were unable to reason strictly logically. For example, when told: "In the far North, where there is snow, all bears are white. Novaya Zemla is in the far north, what color are the bears there?" Subjects tended to reply that they had never been there so they did not know; literate subjects reported simply "White." Scribner and Cole (1981) repeated such experiments within a pretend format and found the subjects completely capable of drawing the appropriate inference. They concluded that not literacy, but rather a particular style of schooled talk, talk designed to provide reasons, was the source of the difficulty. It was that type of "schooled" talk that subjects lacked.

Olson (1994) interpreted these results quite differently, noting that the non-literates lacked a certain orientation to language, which he described as an unwillingness to "confine interpretation to the text," a strategy associated with reading and interpreting written texts in literate, bureaucratic societies and consequently taught in certain literate environments including schools. The ability to make inferences that we would judge as logically valid is universal (as writers from Locke to Goody have noted). What is associated with the evolution of the literary tradition in the West, and passed on through schooling, is a particular orientation to language, an orientation greatly aided by, indeed sponsored by, writing, namely, an orientation to such linguistic entities as phonemes, words, and sentences and their counterparts, word meaning and sentence meaning. Thus, it is necessary to distinguish reasoning skills, generally, from a textual orientation. People may improve their reasoning skills through involvement in the knowledge institutions of the culture. Literacy may, of course, play an instrumental role in such reasoning but it does not bring reason-ing into existence. Thus Bernardo, Domingo, and Peña (1996) have shown that the reasoning abilities of nonliterate adults in several Filipino communities were not essentially different from their more urbanized and schooled compatriots. What literacy adds is access to the specialized knowledge and bureaucratic structures of modern bureaucratic societies. An instrumental role that literacy may play is perhaps seen in the use of literacy by Freire (1972) as encouraging the development of vernacular, local literacies to promote "consciencization," that is, to help people use literacy for personal and social enlightenment, to reflect on their experience, and to see themselves as agents in their own lives rather than passively accepting the roles assigned to them by others.

Folk versus Bureaucratic Knowledge

Fifth, on the classical view, positive knowledge developed only by sacrificing what Francis Bacon called "the idols of the tribe," the common knowledge held as valid by ordinary people. The dichotomy between science and superstition like that between myth and history, marked one form of knowledge, scientific knowledge, as valid; the other, folk knowledge, as "ancient error." In modern bureaucratic societies, knowledge is taken to be the product of particular specialized methods and is accumulated archivally in books and records and a professional elite. Access to that knowledge is dependent upon the development of specialized competence and the assignment of professional rank. Clearly, such a view disparages all local knowledge and expertise by relegating it to the category of "folk knowledge." However, folk knowledge is often valid – aspirin, for example, was not invented by Bayer but is a traditional or "folk" medicine – and it is the knowledge that people have and trust. Doronila (1996) examined the relation between traditional forms and literate forms of knowledge in several Filipino communities and found that in some cases literate knowledge drove out traditional knowledge, leaving local populations feeling ignorant. In other contexts, literacy was assimilated to traditional ways of knowing and greatly enhanced and generalized those forms of competence that were already in place. Indeed, when seen as functionally relevant, indigenous literacy was easily acquired. Rather than simply eradicating local knowledge or overwriting it with the official knowledge of the dominant society, it must be acknowledged and employed as the basis of all further learning and development (Chi, 1992; diSessa, 1996; Robins, 1996, p. 127; see also Prinsloo & Breier, 1996).

Literacy and Learning to Read

Sixth, the classical view of learning to read saw the text as a map to be decoded. As Clanchy (personal communication) has noted, methods of teaching reading were first worked out for the teaching of a foreign language, Latin. Learning to read was a matter of teaching a code, letters and sounds, by means of which one could construct first syllables, then words, and finally full utterances in a foreign language. Only then could one become concerned with the textual meaning. Skill and drill methods copy this method unreflectively, ignoring to an important extent the fact that modern learners, unlike medieval ones, already know the language they are learning to read. Exploiting and reordering this "oral" knowledge is central to all modern theories of reading. Learning to read has come to be seen as relying on something that learners bring or fail to bring to the reading process. What the learner brings is much discussed in the literature (see Adams, 1990) but can be summarized by saying that the child has to bring his own meanings, understandings, perceptions, and knowledge to the encounter. In addition, the child has to bring a new consciousness to the implicit properties of his or her own language. To learn to read is to find entities in the print that the learner can recognize in their own speech. First, they find words that are recognized as known, later they find letter sounds that they can recognize in their own speech sounds. Throughout, the learner has to find in the print, meanings and ideas that he or she can recognize; hence, the emphasis on meaning and understanding in all modern pedagogical theories. One implication is the importance of first acquiring literacy in one's own language even if one is to subsequently also acquire literacy in a national standard language.

Additional insight into learning is provided by considering how adults learn and fail to learn to read and write. The mass literacy campaigns of the 1950s and 1960s that directly attempted to transplant literate skills, often in a foreign language, to members of an essentially oral culture, are now judged to have been largely a failure (see Triebel, chapter 2 below). They failed, presumably, because there was no reason to learn; literacy provided access neither to knowledge, literature, power, nor employment. Furthermore, literacy training did not involve the creation of literate institutions such as forms of government, economics, science, or literature in which developing literacy could play a significant role. On the other hand, adult literacy programs tended to succeed when they exploited an indigenous language (Fagerberg-Diallo, chapter 9 below) when the literacy being acquired had some functional role in the community (Doronila, 1996; and chapter 13 below), and when becoming a reader provided the learner with a new identity, namely, "one who reads" (see Fagerberg-Diallo, chapter 9).

The same may be true for children. Pedagogy, as mentioned, has traditionally focused on the mechanics of reading and writing. However, this focus has tended to lead to the neglect of those factors highlighted in the studies of adults, namely, that the learner has to see both what is going on in reading and why one would bother. This is part of the motivation for the "whole language" movement which places the mechanics of reading second to the uses and enjoyment of reading in the hope of making more beginners part of the "reading community" (Smith, 1994). Reading is important to the extent that it connects a reader with his or her own language and culture; if it fails to do this it will often be resisted or ignored. Consequently, when it is ignored, it is inappropriate to blame failure on the learner; it is a failure to find relevance.

The mechanics of learning, nonetheless, cannot be ignored. First, writing systems do relate or map on to speech in more or less direct ways. If children lack the oral competence with the language represented they will fail to grasp a fundamental fact about reading; to read is to see how what one says relates to the orthographic form presented. Consequently, learning to read is relatively easy if one is learning to read the language one already speaks (E. Goody, chapter 10 below).

Writing systems relate to speech and knowledge in quite different ways, ways which learners must sort out in the process of learning to read and write. First, for some types of writing, learners have to come to realize that graphic signs relate to language rather than to meanings or things. Further, for alphabets, they have to learn to analyze their speech into discriminable constituents represented by letters and words. Neither of these is automatic and many beginning readers are frustrated in their attempts because of a failure to grasp just what written marks represent. It is not merely that they must see that marks bear or relate to meaning, for the simple reason that most writing systems represent not meaning directly but the linguistic expression of meaning. Successful pedagogies, for this reason, find it useful to first make written transcriptions of the learner's own spoken utterances, thereby indicating how writing relates to words. And secondly, they encourage learners to "invent spellings" so they learn to interrogate their own pronunciation in order to discover in their speech the sounds which may be represented by written letters (Olson, 1996). Such activities are designed to foster knowledge about, or awareness of, one's own language – its sentences, words and sounds. Much of this metalinguistic knowledge is acquired in the course of learning to read, but it must be acquired if the learner is to see how the orthography works and if one is to become a skilled reader. Further, this linguistic awareness fosters the ability to think about the language and its properties, sentences, and statements, rather than thinking about things represented in those statements. It is this awareness which becomes the focus of prescriptive grammars and formal logic and which is at the basis of what we think of as "the standard language," the language of bureaucratic institutions (Lucy, 1993).

Although literacy can and has developed without national and institutional support, it tends towards universality only with publicly funded schooling. Literacy and schooling are essentially coterminous in modern societies. Overwhelmingly and unsurprisingly, the data show that literacy levels in a nation are closely tied to years of schooling (Statistics Canada, 1995). However, it should be noted that such statistics make a number of assumptions in their assessments. In using a universal and standard measurement, such statistics overlook more specialized and local forms of literacy (Barton, 1994; Levine, 1998). Schooling for children usually assumes a particular definition of literacy and a particular methodology for teaching it. Although calls for reform emphasize the importance of context and function, the literacy acquired in school tends to involve a general and transferable form of competence, reading and writing ability, which is then applied and elaborated in the acquisition of particular content domains. Nonetheless, learning to read and write is greatly fostered if children learn not only the "skills" but discover the utility of literacy in their day-to-day activities and, more importantly, recognize the significance of literacy for participation in the institutions of the larger society.

An important factor in a child's acquisition of literacy is the literate practices of the parents, a factor which has led to many attempts to persuade parents to read to their children, perhaps as bedtime stories. The school, though important, is not sufficient to guarantee literate competence; a literate environment is an important contributing factor. Part of the significance of adult literacy is the important role that adult literates can play in the literate development of their children; and, indeed, that provides the motivation for many adults to learn to read – the desire to read to their children.

All of these factors are amplified considerably in the growth or lack of growth of literacy in developing countries. Teachers may have a naive and inappropriate conception of just what literacy is, a conception which often leads to simple rote learning. Second, adults may provide little intellectual support for the acquisition of literacy in their children. Motivational support is often high, however. Bloch (1998) discovered that even in a tiny, remote rural village in Madagascar in which literacy had little or no functional significance, everyone, educated or not, was "absolutely convinced of the value of schooling and literacy" (p. 8). But the ability to turn that motivation into practical occasions for learning is limited by both resources and knowledge.

To achieve a high level of literate competence requires both sophisticated knowledge and sustained effort. Without parental support, learning is difficult. Without adequate resources for schools, such as teachers, and reading and writing materials, and without obvious and tangible rewards for sustained study, it is unlikely that literacy programs will have notable social impact. However, it is also the case that literate parents, in particular, have literate aspirations for their children, and that may have a bootstrapping effect over generations.

Literacy and Social Development

Seventh, and finally, literacy and social development. In the conventional view, literacy is taken as a central, causal factor in complex social organization and democratic forms of government. Writing is seen as essential to the formation of large social groups such as cities, states, or empires. Indeed, the earliest writing systems may be traced back to the formation of cities and the needs for inventories of goods, increased specialization of social roles, and other aspects of social management and social control of larger-scale societies. Further, it is an obvious fact that writing plays a central role in modern, bureaucratic societies in the formation of law and government, the advance of science, the production of literature, and more recently in the use of information technology. But whereas it is often assumed that literacy is the cause of such development, it is now clear that it rather plays an instrumental role. That is, writing does not create the idea of rules and laws, but through writing, the rules and laws may be public and universally applicable; writing does not create knowledge, but through writing and printing, knowledge can take the form of an archival tradition; writing does not create "literature," but writing can extend the range of exploration of the imagination in new and distinctive ways. Every society has, by definition, some social organization, some rules and traditions for the management of knowledge and power. Literacy is useful to those societies to the extent that it can make explicit, public, manageable, and achievable the goals and purposes of those social institutions.

Some forms of social organization, for example those involved in the management of debt, cannot be easily carried on without writing, computing, and written records. To supply this need, colonial powers often simply imposed the institutional forms borrowed from the "fatherland," disregarding the indigenous forms of social organization and social exchange already in place. The alternative is to "bureaucratize" existing social exchanges and social relations by incorporating literate practices into them, a theme of the present volume. While direct democracy can flourish without writing (see Thomas, chapter 4 below), large-scale social organizations depend upon written records, explicit procedures, and formal institutions responsible for carrying out those social functions. While literacy is relevant to participation in such functions as elections, for example, not everyone has to be a reader in order to be a voter (Prinsloo & Robins, 1996). The problem, much examined in this volume, is accommodating these two sets of concerns, the need to acknowledge existing language, knowledge, practices, and organizations in a society and the need, at least for some aspects of social development, to develop highly literate, bureaucratic national institutions and the competence to fully participate in them.

We should not forget, either, the middle ground, the role that literacy plays in local practices of employment, family, identity, schooling, and communication. These are important because they promise to provide the most fertile ground for the first and most important step towards the making of a literate society. Consequently, it is important to acknowledge the role of indigenous language, knowledge, and social organization in the acquisition of literacy. Literacy training in the language of the nation-state is often literacy in a second language with which learners have no competence; it advances a conception of knowledge which is out of step with traditional knowledge; and it assumes rules of power and authority discrepant from local understanding. Such training condemns a majority of children to failure. Goody (chapter 10 below) points out that in rural Ghana in the school she studied, the number of children enrolling in the first year, was some 130 whereas that had dropped off to some dozen by the sixth year. López, Prah, and Akoha (chapters 11, 7, and 8) all report similar failure rates for teaching literacy in the national rather than the indigenous language. On the other hand, studies by Fagerberg-Diallo and Doronila (chapters 9 and 13) show the conditions for success of indigenous programs of literacy in places as diverse as Latin America, Africa, and the Philippines.

In order to understand and participate in the modern world it is increasingly obvious that one must have access to writing and other notational systems. Speech is what allows the growth of local culture but writing is critical to the functioning of complex bureaucratic societies. Writing is not confined to the alphabet, and knowledge is not confined to that in books. Writing is important to the extent that it finds a place in the personal and social life of individuals. To understand how writing relates to social development we must broaden our understanding of the many forms and functions of writing and reading, and examine the factors associated with its teaching and learning.

To understand the role of literacy in society it is never sufficient to consider only the interests, goals, and activities of individuals. A literate society is not made by turning everyone into readers and writers. Something more is required, namely, the invention or development of literate institutions, what with Elwert (chapter 3 below) we may call "societal literacy." In the simplest case, there is no point in being able to write and read a contract if there are not, in place, legal institutions for guaranteeing the interpretation and enforcement of such contracts. Such institutions are conveniently thought of as bureaucratic structures – courts, banks, universities, and the like. These institutions also include the host of conventional, mechanical rules and procedures for carrying out the variety of social functions we sometimes describe as "infrastructure." All cultures have procedures for dealing with routine events such as birth, marriage, death, trade, war, etc. What literate institutions do is to make these and other procedures, so far as possible, purely mechanical, such that they can be carried out "object-ively" by specialists without regard to the individuals who carry them out or the local contexts in which they occur. A contract may be written by one scribe and interpreted by another without loss of knowledge or meaning. Further, these activities are carried out within clearly defined structures of authority. Only those authorized have the right to determine the innocence or guilt of an individual or to decide whether a claim is valid or invalid. Science is one such institution; law another. Both have rules, norms, and procedures and the authority and power to enforce and maintain them. Schools, too, are such institutions. They have the means and the power not only to educate but the authority to say if one passes or fails, and ultimately to say if one is literate or illiterate.

Societies become literate by creating opportunities for people to see how literacy can be instrumental in their lives. But they become "literate societies" only when a significant majority of the people come to use their literacy in the context of the powerful institutions of the society. These two are different but not incompatible. The challenge is to find ways of mediating the relations between them. In these ways, we may contribute to a coherent picture of the roles of literacy in contemporary culture and offer some new directions for research and public policy.

Conclusions

The study of literacy inherits from the study of language a distinction between structure and use, semantics and pragmatics. Both are needed for an under-standing of the cognitive and social implications of literacy. The problem is working out the details of the relation between them, and then extrapolating from this understanding useful suggestions for public policy. We shall conclude with a summary of those suggestions:

1. Literacy is not the solution to a host of social ills including poverty, mal-nutrition, and unemployment. It is not, in most cases, even relevant to the solution of those problems, and to blame those problems on illiteracy deflects attention from the more basic social causes such as political oppres-sion, injustice, political and economic disenfranchisement, that is, the lack of political representation, and sometimes absence of needed land reform. Participatory democracy is impossible without a sharing of wealth and resources.

2. The direct imposition of a foreign literacy on an indigenous, traditional culture dramatically undermines both the existing social organization and modes of thought. Proposed change must respect existing forms of social organization, local knowledge, and local language, and build on rather than replace them.

3. It does not follow that literacy should play no role in social development and cultural change. Literacy can play an enormously transformative role in a society by providing a means for the development of the specialized forms of competence and specialized social roles that are useful in local activities and practices as documented in several chapters in this volume (Doronila; López; Fagerberg-Diallo). Furthermore, these more specialized competencies are essential to the functioning of a bureaucratic, literate society in two ways. First, they are essential to the establishment of the explicit processes, including rules and procedures, as well as principled means for the formation and interpretation of records and documents required for the development of bureaucratic institutions such as law, government, science, and economics. Secondly, they are essential if people are to play a role in these institutions, as opposed to being manipulated by them. Institutional structures and specialized competencies are mutually sustaining (see Elwert, chapter 3 below).

4. While literacy is a useful skill, it is useful only if it is tied to the literate resources of a society. These resources range from purely technical matters to higher-level social structures, and include:

    a) a suitable orthography as defined by the functions it is to serve (see Coulmas, chapter 6 below).

    b) an orthography which reflects the oral competence of the readers; learning to read a language they do not speak fluently often consigns the vast majority of the learners to failure and early withdrawal (see Prah, Doronila, and Goody, chapters 7, 13, and 10 below, but see Coulmas's chapter 6 and Burnaby, 1998 for counterexamples).

    c) a suitable pedagogy, including pedagogical materials, which allows the reader to understand how the script serves the learner both as a reader and as a writer (see Goody, chapter 10 below). Even then, literacy programs for children as provided by the school tend to have limited effects unless supported by parents or other adults. But it is also a truism that literate parents want their children to become literate. Hence, even limited acquisition can multiply over generations. Many nonliterate adults seek help in learning to read and write just so they can help their children learn. Adult education has, at least in many cases, reoriented itself by distinguishing child education from adult education programs and by attempting to meet the needs and demands of the learners rather than prescribing and imposing some generic solution. Similarly, traditional pedagogies based on classroom lessons are now seen as inappropriate and are being replaced with study groups and cooperative learning (Prinsloo & Breier, 1996; Boyarin, 1992).

d) a rich array of reading materials to meet both functional and literary interests. It is not uncommon for the only written materials to be those provided by government or other institutions that want to convey specialized information. Readers are unlikely to invest the effort required to learn to read merely to have contact with official information. Consequently, the establishment of authors, publishers, and distributors of written materials, designed to meet the needs and interests of readers, is essential if literacy is to be self-sustaining (Fagerberg-Diallo, chapter 9 below).

e) institutional contexts, including large-scale social institutions, in which reading and writing can play a role of perceived significance, and thereby provide a social and economic return that compensates for the years of study and learning required.

f) communities or institutions to which access is given by virtue of being literate so that learners are socially empowered by their participation.

As can be seen, literacy is important, but it is important because of the instrumental roles reading and writing can play in the planning and execution of functions perceived as significant by the newly literate themselves, rather than as being seen as important by those who would impose literacy policy and literacy standards on them. The contributions to this volume show just how literacy, while not the solution to the world's evils, can play an important instrumental role in social development.

The mass adult literacy programs which flourished in the 1960s attempted to induct nonliterates more or less on the model of a religious or military campaign. These programs had extremely low return and are now seen as a failure. Literacy, unlike mass immunization, cannot simply be imposed on adults. Quality public education for children, on the other hand, is now recognized as a human right, and it is the responsibility of governments everywhere to see that this opportunity is provided. Education is not to be identified with literacy, although here too literacy should be seen as an important instrument of both knowledge and social organization.

Policy formation is the deliberate attempt to achieve at least some of the goals we identify with the Enlightenment, the improvement if not the perfectibility of people and their institutions. What role does literacy play in the deliberate attempt to change a traditional society into a bureaucratic one? Perhaps we must resist the temptation to make a deliberate attempt to produce such a general change. On the other hand, governments and other agencies can nonetheless support the efforts of individuals, cultures, and subcultures to pursue those social changes they recognize as essential to their goals of justice and empowerment. It is here that literacy and literacy programs may play an important role (see Jung & Ouane, chapter 16 below).

References

Adams, M. J. (1990). *Beginning to Read: Thinking and learning about print*. Cambridge, Mass.: MIT Press.

Astle, T. (1784). *The Origin and Progress of Writing*. London: Author.

Barton, D. (1994). *Literacy: An introduction to the ecology of written language*. Oxford, UK and Cambridge, Mass.: Blackwell.

Bernardo, A. B. I., Domingo, M. S., and Peña, E. L. F. (1996). *Cognitive Consequences of Literacy: Studies on thinking in five Filipino communities*. Manila: Education Research Program and Department of Education, Culture and Sports, University of the Philippines.

Bloch, M. (1998). The uses of schooling and literacy in a Zafimaniry village. In B. V. Street (ed.), *Readings on Literacy*. Cambridge: Cambridge University Press.

Boone, E. and Mignolo, W. D. (eds.) (1994). *Writing Without Words: Alternative literacies in Mesoamerica and the Andes*. Durham, NC: Duke University Press.

Boyarin, J. (ed.) (1992). *The Ethnography of Reading*. Berkeley: University of California Press.

Burnaby, B. (1998). Literacy in Athapaskan languages in the Northwest Territories, Canada: For what purposes? *Written Language and Literacy*, 1(1): 63–102.

Byrne, R. M. and Whiten, A. (1988). *Machiavellian Intelligence: Social expertise and the evolution of intellect in monkeys, apes, and humans*. New York: Oxford University Press.

Carruthers, M. J. (1990). *The Book of Memory: A study of memory in medieval culture*. Cambridge and New York: Cambridge University Press.

Chartier, R. (1995). *Forms and Meanings: Texts, performances, and audiences from codex to computer*. Philadelphia: University of Pennsylvania Press.

Chi, M. (1992). Conceptual change within and across ontological categories: Examples from learning and discovery in science. In R. Giere (ed.), *Cognitive Models of Science: Minnesota studies in the philosophy of science*. Minneapolis: University of Minnesota Press.

Clanchy, M. (1993). *From Memory to Written Record: England 1066–1307*, 2nd edn. Cambridge, Mass.: Blackwell.

Condorcet, M. de (1802). *Outlines of an Historical View of the Progress of the human Mind: Being a posthumous work of the late M. de Condorcet*. Baltimore: G. Fryer.

deFrancis, J. (1989). *Visible Speech: The diverse oneness of writing systems*. Honolulu: University of Hawaii Press.

diSessa, A. (1996). What do "just plain folks" know about physics? In D. Olson and N. Torrance (eds.), *Handbook of Education and Human Development*. Cambridge, Mass.: Blackwell.

Doronila, M. L. (1996). *Landscapes of Literacy: An ethnographic study of functional literacy in marginal Philippine communities*. Hamburg: UNESCO Institute for Education.

Eisenstein, E. (1979). *The Printing Press as an Agent of Change*. Cambridge, Mass.: Harvard University Press.

Ferreiro, E. and Teberosky, L. (1982). *Literacy Before Schooling*. Exeter, NH: Heinemann.

Finnegan, R. (1988). *Literacy and Orality: Studies in the technology of communication.* Oxford: Blackwell.

Freire, P. (1972). *Pedagogy of the Oppressed,* trans. M. B. Ramos. New York: Herder and Herder.

Gaur, A. (1987). *A History of Writing.* London: The British Library.

Gee, J. P. (1990). *Social Linguistics and Literacies: Ideology in discourses.* New York: Falmer Press.

Gelb, I. J. (1963). *A Study of Writing,* 2nd edn. Chicago: University of Chicago Press.

Goody, J. (1968). *Literacy in Traditional Societies.* Cambridge: Cambridge University Press.

Goody, J. (1986). *The Logic of Writing and the Organization of Society.* Cambridge: Cambridge University Press.

Graff, H. (1986). *The Legacies of Literacy: Continuities and contradictions in western society and culture.* Bloomington: Indiana University Press.

Havelock, E. (1982). *The Literate Revolution in Greece and its Cultural Consequences.* Princeton: Princeton University Press.

Illich, I. (1993). *In the Vineyard of the Text: A commentary to Hugh's Didascalicon.* Chicago: University of Chicago Press.

Johns, A. (1998). *The Nature of the Book: Print and knowledge in the making.* Chicago: University of Chicago Press.

Katz, M. (1968). *The Irony of Early School Reform.* Boston: Beacon Press.

Kittay, J. (1991). Thinking through literacies. In D. Olson and N. Torrance (eds.), *Literacy and Orality.* Cambridge: Cambridge University Press.

Levine, K. (1998). Definitional and methodological problems in the cross-national measurement of adult literacy: The case of the IALS. *Written Language and Literacy,* 1(1): 41–61.

Lévy-Bruhl, L. (1926). *How Natives Think.* London: George Allen & Unwin. (First published 1910.)

Lucy, J. (1993). Reflexive language and the human disciplines. In J. Lucy (ed.), *Reflexive Language: Reported speech and metapragmatics.* Cambridge: Cambridge University Press.

Luria, A. R. (1976). *Cognitive Development: Its cultural and social foundations.* Cambridge: Cambridge University Press.

Lloyd, G. E. R. (1979). *Magic, Reason and Experience.* Cambridge: Cambridge University Press.

Moscovici, S. (1993). *The Invention of Society: Psychological explanations for social phenomena,* trans. W. D. Halls. Cambridge: Polity Press.

Olson, D. R. (1994). *The World on Paper: The conceptual and cognitive implications of writing and reading.* Cambridge: Cambridge University Press.

Olson, D. R. (1996). Towards a psychology of literacy: On the relations between speech and writing. *Cognition,* 60: 83–104.

Ong, W. (1982). *Orality and Literacy: The technologizing of the word.* London: Methuen.

Prinsloo, M. and Breier, M. (1996). *The Social Uses of Literacy.* Amsterdam: Benjamins.

Prinsloo, M. and Robins, S. (1996). Literacy, voter education and constructions of citizenship in the Western Cape during the first democratic national elections in South Africa. In M. Prinsloo and M. Breier (eds.), *The Social Uses of Literacy.* Amsterdam: Benjamins.

Robins, S. (1996). Cultural brokers and bricoleurs of modern and traditional literacies: Land struggles in Namaqualand's Coloured reserves. In M. Prinsloo and M. Breier (eds.), *The Social Uses of Literacy*. Amsterdam: Benjamins.

Rousseau, J.-J. (1966). Essay on the origin of languages. In J. H. Moran and A. Gode (eds.), *On the Origin of Language: Two essays by Jean-Jacques Rousseau and Johann Gottfried Herder*. New York: Frederick Unger. (First published 1754–91.)

Sampson, G. (1985). *Writing Systems*. Stanford: Stanford University Press.

Scribner, S. and Cole, M. (1981). *The Psychology of Literacy*. Cambridge, Mass.: Harvard University Press.

Smith, F. (1994). *Understanding Reading*, 5th edn. Mahwah, NJ: Erlbaum.

Statistics Canada (1995). *Literacy, Economy and Society: Results of the first International Adult Literacy Survey*. Ottawa: Statistics Canada (in cooperation with the OECD).

Stock, B. (1983). *The Implications of Literacy*. Princeton: Princeton University Press.

Street, B. (1984). *Literacy in Theory and Practice*. Cambridge: Cambridge University Press.

Thomas, R. (1989). *Oral Tradition and Written Record in Classical Athens*. Cambridge: Cambridge University Press.

Vico, G. (1984). *The New Science of Giambattista Vico*, eds. T. Bergen and M. Fish. Ithaca: Cornell University Press. (First published 1744.)

Chapter 2

The Roles of Literacy Practices in the Activities and Institutions of Developed and Developing Countries

Armin Triebel

Introduction

Literacy has become a major problem globally in recent years for several reasons.[1] Three of them, at least, deserve closer inspection.

First, the conquest of the Western industrial nations by electronic media since the early 1980s has fueled the interest in pictograms and the language of pictures as well as reflection on the consequences of visualization of a culture *per se*. Since Marshall McLuhan predicted the fall of the book age and the rise of the pictoral era a quarter of a century ago, the decline of literary culture in the developed and strongly literary industrial countries is increasingly being dreaded (Postman, 1982; Lüsebrink, 1990, p. 2; McLuhan, 1962). The question is provoking: Is there a future in writing? (Flusser, 1992).

Second, the problem of literacy cannot be restricted to the Third and Fourth Worlds. The discovery of a crisis in literacy, as measured by the distribution of reading and writing skills among the population in the most highly developed countries, was shocking (Nascimento, 1990; the UNESCO extrapolation of numbers of adult illiterates 1980–2010 is reported in Müller, 1996). In these countries low literacy is seen as a drag on societal development no less than illiteracy is in the developing countries. In the US at least 5 percent of 21- to 25-year-olds could not read or write; but almost 25 percent had problems in reading texts that "required inferences and understanding *across* sentences" (Wagner, 1995, p. 351, citing findings from the *US Young Adult Literacy Survey* and the *National Adult Literacy Survey*; cf. Kirsch & Jungeblut, 1986; Kirsch et al., 1993; Kozol, 1985). In Europe, the 1995 International Adult Literacy Survey

(OECD, 1995; Jones, 1995; cf. Gläss, 1990) revealed that over 20 percent of adults in some rich European countries have low literacy or numeracy skills. The estimates for Germany vary between 0.75 and 5 percent; in 1990, the German UNESCO Commission concluded that 3 million German citizens in the Federal Republic of Germany could be labeled as "habitual illiterates" (UNESCO aktuell 1990; press reports by the German UNESCO Commission are in: Deutsche UNESCO-Kommission, ed., 1991, pp. 9–20). Deficiencies in literacy skills in Western countries take on a particular shape, though. Literacy skills become deficient and remain so because of a lack of commitment and agency within the person. German schoolboys answered, when asked by their teacher why they did not avoid misspelling a word by looking it up in a dictionary, that "looking things up was not their thing." Furthermore, it was discovered that infant school children are undernourished because their parents would not acquire the basic nutritional knowledge.

Third, today, the success of literacy campaigns like UNESCO's Experimental World Literacy Program in the 1960s, or efforts like the Education For All or "Literacy For All" policies (Lockheed & Verspoor, 1990; for final report see World Conference, 1990), are viewed suspiciously. First, the example of Senegal (Lüsebrink, 1990) shows that colonial experiments with basing a culture of literacy on the colonial culture and language only had a marginal effect. In Senegal, only a small francophone upper class was produced; very low alpha-betization rates were coupled with very low economic performance (Wiegelmann, 1998). The majority of the population was not affected by these programs and more recently Senegalese is reestablishing ties to its own oral traditions. The following pattern can be observed in all countries: there is a growing number of drop-outs from formal schooling, so-called secondary illiterates, "aliterates," semi-literates, functional illiterates, or people who simply never were successful in becoming literate (Harman, 1976; Nascimento, 1990; Rogers, 1993 ; Elwert, 1997; Ouane, 1996). What troubles experts is that "most literacy campaigns rarely produce more than minimal literacy." The "number one problem" is that participation in literacy campaigns drops off rapidly after the first weeks or months of program execution (Wagner, 1995, pp. 344, 354). People "left class when they felt they had learned enough for what they needed in daily life" (Mueller, 1996, p. 2). The notion of *aliteracy* was coined in order to describe the ubiquitous fact that literacy and reading skills while being latent are not put in practice.[2] The consultant for nonformal education in the German Education, Science and Documentation Center concluded that analphabetism was unlikely to be overcome by formal education (Müller, 1991, p. 48; see also the reports in *Norrag News* 19 (1996), which for the most part have a pessimistic tone).

Setting aside for the moment the experience of development workers, even statistical evidence on illiteracy is not very detailed. Wagner gives the aggregate figures registered by UNESCO. The numbers of illiterates extracted from the Human Development Reports published by the UNDP complete the statistics furnished by UNESCO (Wagner, 1995, table 1, p. 342; Human Development Reports 1993–6, especially 1994, tables 3, 4, and 5; 1996, tables 4 and 6).

Daniel Wagner estimates that there were a billion illiterates in the world in 1993. This is the same figure the Jomtien Conference agreed on in the 1980s (960 million adults: World Declaration, 1990, Preamble; 872 million: Mueller, 1996, p. 1). Illiteracy rates have been dropping over the last decades, but the successes reached are not expressive even in developing countries. There are signs of stagnation or even regression (Weltentwicklungsbericht, 1998/9: Mali, Niger, Senegal, table 2, pp. 236ff). Major gains seem to have been made in the years 1970 through 1985. In many cases the real numbers of illiterates showed an increase while illiteracy rates dropped (the sub-Saharan and southern Asian countries or the average of all developing countries) or illiteracy rates and numbers increased (Mali). A more general feature is the relative ineffectiveness of literacy campaigns in the female part of the populations.

The actual cause for reviewing the theoretical landscape is the apparent failure of 25 years of struggle for alphabetization. The reports on the Regional Policy Review Seminars at the International Consultative Forum on Education for All in Amman 1996 (Issues Paper for Discussion prepared for the Policy Review Seminar for East and Southeast Asia & the Pacific, Paris, 1995, pp. 15ff, quoted in Mueller, 1996, p. 10) according to UNESCO hinted at "the need to give *greater relevance* to literacy activities," they deplored the high drop-out rate and the relapse into illiteracy, but failed "to get to the root of such failures or to suggest how these difficulties might be overcome or reduced." The "challenge of illiteracy" is all the more pressing as research seems to linger on futile debates and experts in the "field" are demanding to get "from reflection to action" (Morsy, 1994, quotation p. xviii). In the face of researchers forever repeating that "we know little," it is tempting for the experts in the field to try anything.

Any report on the state of the art of research on literacy in the last 40 years cannot overlook the close link between the role of the individual in the community and his literacy practices. Literacy has to be seen as an element within a web of practical activities and community commitments (Selznick, 1992; Etzioni, 1993). Further, there is ample evidence from history that literacy is embedded in a system of social functions and cultural processes whereas alphabetical competence is only a technical skill. Finally, I shall argue that the discussion on the role of literacy in developing a society has been, to this very day, hampered first by the belief that literacy generates social change, and second by the belief that script changes mind.

There are many important questions regarding literacy and orality and social change which are not touched on in the following pages (see e.g. the research program of the German Science Foundation DFG at Freiburg University, Sieben Jahre 1992, p. 18). Further, the whole complex of language didactics is set aside along with the problem of undertrained teaching personnel in the developing countries. To what extent is illiteracy the result of underpaid and poorly motivated teachers, wrecked school buildings, and shortage of teaching aids? There is a big literature of reports and case studies on basic education and literacy in the Third World. None of this is included here.

The aim of this paper is to regain the broad perspective on the subject and possibly to give fresh stimulation to discussion. Here the focus is literacy as an alleged instrument of social development and modernization which has become acute in the discussions on development policy since the 1970s. Generally, two approaches hold their ground in the scholarly discussion. Both of them deal with variables which, following a totally unpretentious convention, we may divide into four clusters: (i) the economic sector, (ii) the world of symbolization, meaning and belief systems, (iii) the relations of social inequality, and (iv) the realm of political power and interest groups. The question is which role literacy plays as an agent of change either in each of the four systems or in their interrelation. Different approaches to literacy emphasize different factors.

Apart from the consideration of different approaches to literacy three main questions will be touched on in diverse contexts: (a) Do literacy programs for a total population make sense? (b) What is the relation between alphabetization and literacy? (c) What was, in European history, the relationship of development, alphabetization, and literacy?

In the context of this paper, for two reasons, it seems promising to glance at Europe and the Western model of development. First, the European path of industrialization has turned into a global model. However much criticism it may provoke, it is a model of modernization that needs to be taken into consideration. In addition, it is the Western capitalist countries that have become committed to the problem of literacy and to the question of how to make literacy development part of sensible developmental policy.

Literacy in Practice

Even a superficial glance at the bibliography at the end of this chapter shows that quite a range of different disciplines have made contributions to the question of literacy. There are few fields of research or politics where interdisciplinary work is more pressing than literacy. Barton (1994) follows this idea and brings together, with much insight from personal experience, the view of various disciplines. The failure of alphabetization campaigns is a case in point. Anthropological research is forced to acknowledge the fact, but declares itself at a loss to explain it (Probst, 1991, p. 19). Consequently, the following survey willingly transgresses established boundaries between academic disciplines. It is to be hoped that this overstepping does not violate professional standards but rather stimulates the production of some new ideas.

There are very few, if any, cultures that have not been influenced by literacy. Hence the contrast between literate and oral cultures posited by the well-known "Toronto School" is of only limited value to the matter-of-fact interrelation of literacy and development. Development policies since the end of the Second World War have followed one of three paradigms. First, there was the time of new departures after the demise of fascist rule. There grew a sense of mission to bring democracy to the world, and its vehicle was to be the written word.

Afterwards literacy was seen as one of the factors of modernization. In the end, the emerging profession of teachers proclaimed literacy as being the ideal route to rationality. This interest group readily referred to a culture-and-thought paradigm which upheld and stuck to the notion that rationality of thought has to do with the acquisition of literacy. This educational exuberance led many to overlook what was commonplace to historians and what was being devised by sociologists.

These three ideas, then, had a determining influence on practical action for literacy in the last four decades: modernization, democracy, and the paradigm of enlightenment. Education, such was the commonly held belief, should contribute to social and economic development, and literacy was one element in education. The aim of transforming society swung between two extreme strategies, one being a top-down approach of a socialist shade. The second was the "liberal" approach of modernization that would not do more than give incentives to endogeneous change.

The politics of education

The ways in which an institution or society defines literacy implies a definition of the culture's "collective identity" more generally. Literacy is an expression of cultural and political aims, and it is used to designate social roles in the society. In this respect literacy is always an essentially normative notion and an instrument of politics. This is true also with respect to classifications of literacy levels (e.g. Wagner, 1990). Definitions of literacy are not innocent. They are subject to renewed political evaluation. Thus, if literacy is defined as to be "the reading ability comparable to that of the average child entering fourth grade," this could lead to a policy that would divert resources away from community services aimed at more sophisticated levels of literacy. Or, from a definition that declares literacy being the ability to perform reading and writing tasks needed in everyday life, "a vision emerges of a citizen who should not aspire beyond the modest rounds of getting a job, going to work, and coming home in the evening to read the newspaper" (the point made by Winterowd, 1989, pp. 4 ff.; on the political consequences of different definitions of literacy see Street, 1990).

After the Second World War the building of a new and better world was on the agenda. The paradigm of fostering the values of democracy, human rights, and social justice put emphasis on political action for democracy. A political commitment of a slightly different sort appeared in the 1970s when the pedagogy of political empowerment sought to bring emancipation to the oppressed. Illiteracy was then realized to be injustice *per se*; it was said to "threaten the very fabric of democracy. It undermines the democratic principles of a society" (Freire & Macedo, 1987, p. vii). Numerous books were written to proclaim the beneficial effects of literacy programs in the developing areas. These reports revealed, however, that in many cases the most noteworthy outcome was not increased levels of literacy but rather solidarity and self-confidence. A successful outcome was construed less as sustainable literacy and more as a joint effort to recon-struct a hut after a blaze (Curtis, 1990, p. 6). This is not to discredit such initiatives, but to observe that the development of literacy and self-help activities are different things. The latter may result in community-based initiatives but not lead to a lasting sense of community or to sustainable literacy. What did distinguish the literacy-for-social-change approach, however, is the notion of agency being linked with literacy.

The normative content of literacy is once again being activated in programs executed by developmental agencies. In this context literacy is seen as serving as a means of overcoming traditionalism and promoting modernization (see e.g. the writings of H. S. Bhola; also UNESCO & UNDP, ed., 1976; Schwöbel, 1982; Lockheed & Verspoor, 1990; Haggis, 1992; Delors, 1996).

The economics of modernization

The opening statement of Olson's *grand résumé* – "there can be little doubt that a major feature of modern societies is the ubiquity of writing" (Olson, 1994, p. 1) – brings back the third driving force behind the policy of education and alphabetization, i.e., the concept of modernization. The link between literacy and modernization in developing countries at the end of the twentieth century was first worked out in the late 1950s. From the outset, the comparative approach connected literacy to three dimensions to which it attributed equal relevance: economy, inclusive of "urbanization" and "widespread literacy," mass communication, and participation (the definition by James Coleman, in Almond & Coleman, eds., 1960, p. 532). This is substantiated by Daniel Lerner's comparative study of modernization processes on the basis of UNESCO and UN data and survey data from Greece and some Near East countries. It was crucial to Lerner's model that "the conditions that define modernity form an interlocking 'system'" (Lerner, 1958, p. 55). Compulsory education as well as literacy levels, i.e., "the proportion able to read in one language," functioned as the two primary indicators of the transition process from traditional to modern society. Table 2.1 shows the ideal types at the beginning and at the end of this transformation process.

Language and education were given the function of inclusion within the concept of the political development theory. Therefore, literacy was an im-portant step on the way to the integration of a society and to nation-building. Lerner considered the transformation process as a regular sequence of three phases (Lerner, 1958, p. 60):

> Urbanization comes first . . . Within this urban matrix develop both . . . literacy and media growth. . . . historically, literacy performs the key function in the second phase. The capacity to read, at first acquired by relatively few people, equips them to perform the varied tasks required in the modernizing society. Not until the third phase, when elaborate technology of industrial development is fairly well advanced, does a society begin to produce newspapers.

Table 2.1 Transition from traditional to modern society

		Oral systems	Media systems
		→→→ *time* →→→	→→→ *time* →→→
Historical systems of public communication	Channel	Personal (face to face)	Broadcast (mediated)
	Audience	Primary (groups)	Heterogeneous (mass)
	Content	Prescriptive (rules)	Descriptive (news)
	Source	Hierarchical (status)	Professional (skill)
		→→→ *time* →→→	→→→ *time* →→→
Sector in social system	Socioeconomic	Rural	Urban
	Cultural	Illiterate	Literate
	Political	Designative	Electoral

It became manifest that literacy did not seem to grow in proportion to urbanization; instead typical threshold ratios were found. The comparison of UNESCO data for 73 countries showed that the "'critical minimum' of urbanization appears to be ... one may say 10 percent":

> Only after a country reaches 10% of urbanization does its literacy rate begin to rise significantly. Thereafter urbanization and literacy increase together in a direct ... relationship, until they reach 25%, which appears to be the "critical optimum" of urbanization. (Lerner, 1958, p. 59).

In empirical research work since the late 1980s, the relation between modernization and economics has continued to take precedence. A close link-up between a society's economic efficiency, its modernity, and the literacy of its culture influences the politics of international development agencies like the World Bank and the OECD to this day. The very title of the 1995 OECD survey, *Literacy, Economy and Society*, demonstrates this (for a painstaking critique of this survey see Graff, 1996, p. 4 ff.). It was claimed that, for example, an 80 percent national adult literacy rate would be necessary for rapid economic development, whereas a 40 percent literacy rate would do for a minimal amount of economic development (Anderson, 1966; cf. Fagerlind & Saha, 1983). Although this connection has been denied recently, "The economic rationale remains an article of faith among advocates of literacy programs, at least in part due to the belief that industrialized countries are more prosperous primarily because they are more educated and more literate" (Wagner, 1995, pp. 343, 345). What Wagner calls into question with regard to the whole of a society definitely does not apply to the lives of individuals – as observation of everyday life shows. There is "virtually no evidence," said Wagner, for the assumption that adult literacy programs have resulted, so far, in visible economic gains for the participants of these programs. We might add that even in the developed countries, the correlation between "cultural capital" (Bourdieu, 1983), and economic prosperity is a despairingly intricate matter. In the Western countries at the moment we are experiencing a serious setback in the rates of return of higher education. What are, then, the reasons in favor of the "economic rationale"? (For a summary of recent research and further references see World Bank, ed., 1995, pp. 19ff.) At the core of the argument are the human capital theory and the rational choice theory. "Investment in education leads to the accumulation of human capital," that is, improvements in the quality of the labor force ("together with technological progress and economies of scale") which result in reduced poverty, improved living standards, self-sustaining economic growth, and political stability (strengthening of the institutions of civil society). The incentive for investment in education remains on the individual level, a decision for delayed gratification, i.e., the weighing up of present-day sacrifice and future monetary yields.

These premises pass over a number of arguments that will be addressed below. It may be argued that an institutional framework, such as the existence of regular rules and procedures in a society – the "rule of law" – results in a level of trust and confidence in individuals which in turn encourages more personal investment in long-term goals; this may be at least as important as the improvement of the quality of labor. Religion can be a factor of similar relevance and may have influenced a type of rational behavior which has been prevalent in Europe and in North America (Weber, 1920)

The economics-of-education model draws much of its support from the finding that rates of return in education are very high in low- and middle-income countries (International Bank, ed., 1995, table 1.1). Such findings are misleading. In poor countries there is little demand for highly trained labor and a considerable part of the population is illiterate. In this case it is hardly surprising that those who have *some* skills will realize high returns. For it is their attainment level which will be best adapted to the economy. If a country has gone through a first phase of economic takeoff, the value of this modestly trained workforce will be reduced and there will be a greater demand for higher levels of skill. So high rates of return for educational investments could well be the outcome of a specific degree of economic development rather than its invigorating input. This method of correlation does not permit conclusions on the logic of causal connections.

The beliefs in the symbiotic connection between modernization and economy (insofar as economy was understood in terms of economic welfare) were dashed during the 1970s on the global level. One had to realize that the politics of modernization often ended in mass poverty, that economic growth, if it appeared, did not lead to a proportional increase in employment, and the result of literacy training turned out to be a disappointment. The Jomtien Declaration made reference to the "mounting debt burdens, threat of economic stagnation, widening of economic disparities and rapid population growth." In 1993 the world-famous Verein für Socialpolitik felt obliged to constitute a work group on poverty.

Since 1990, the link between literacy and economic development has been abandoned, but literacy came to be embedded within a comprehensive concept of modern society. Rather, "alphabetization" came to be seen as instrumental in effecting humanistic values, and of giving individuals more power and self-esteem (see World Declaration, 1990, art. 1), of bringing about participation through literacy training. As literacy of course requires the basic skills of reading and writing, alphabetization comes to be considered the prime mover of modernization. So it is understandable enough that currently interest in literacy *per se* and the cognitive difference between orality and literacy is high on the agenda.

The strategy of schooling

Literacy is conceived of as part of educational politics that are to bring about emancipation and well-being through a broad understanding of the world. The oft-repeated keyword is "to make the world a better place to live in." "Primary education and struggle against illiteracy," i.e., literacy training, was always UNESCO's special policy. This was proven, at the time, by the foundation of the International Institute for Adult Literacy Methods (IIALM). On the occasion of the International Literacy Year in 1990, the UN, UNICEF, UNDP, and the World Bank adopted these policies. They made alphabetization part of a world-wide campaign they called "Education For All." This program is intended to bring about equal opportunity and participation in society for children and adults in the developing countries through "Basic Education." Thus, these policies readopt the aim of political mobilization that was central to development policy after the end of the Second World War in a radical form (see the Universal Declaration of Human Rights in the Preamble of the World Declaration, 1990). Radical it is because the policies take a one-eyed look at education. Taking education and alphabetization as the keys to economic and social progress (Ryan, 1981) is mere reverie, as generally available evidence showed. In practice, knowing how to read and write is often of minor use to ordinary folk in developing countries. Glück (1987, p. 155) contradicts the popular opinion that literacy is progress by calling to mind fascist Italy, which fought fiercely for alphabetization in the 1920s and 1930s.

The Jomtien conference was a landmark in the readoption of the idea of opportunities opened up by education, but it was not a "fresh approach" as Delors defiantly insisted. He articulated the shift from the political development theory to educational policy-making when he said policy-makers "cannot leave it to market forces or to some kind of self-regulation to put things right when they go wrong" (Delors, 1996, p. 29).

In order to prevent things from going wrong the World Declaration on Education For All recommended undertaking a global educational campaign. The aim was to meet "basic learning needs" which should, according to the definition, "comprise both essential learning tools (such as literacy, oral expression, numeracy, and problem solving) and the basic learning content (such as knowledge, skills, values, and attitudes) required by human beings to be able to survive, to develop their full capacities, to live and work in dignity, to participate fully in development, to improve the quality of their lives, to make informed decisions, and to continue learning." In this respect, the strategy of schooling meets the old politics of education. It is only in paragraph 8 that economic power relations are referred to, though in a rather fuzzy way: "Suitable economic, trade, labour, employment and health policies will enhance learners' incentives..." (World Declaration, 1990, pp. 3, 7).

At least this definition brings into relief the social quality inherent in both learning and literacy. UNESCO, too, emphasizes the impact literacy has in the group context: "A person is literate when he has acquired the essential knowledge and skills which enable him to engage in all those activities in which literacy is required for effective functioning in his group and community, and whose attainments in reading, writing and arithmetic make it possible for him to continue to use these skills toward his own and the community's development."[3]

The Philosophy of Literacy

For years the debate about the great divide between oral and literate cultures diverted attention from the varied functions and institutions literacy has in every single society. What it succeeded in doing was to make clear that preliteral orality and literacy bring forth different concepts of understanding the world and that the concepts pertaining to the former have to be translated into the latter by means of a metadiscourse. But it missed the mark insofar as in developmental politics neither oral communication nor the epistemic difference between orality and literacy was the crucial issue. What the great-divide approach[4] was interested in was the difference between types of society without any writing system and those with a literate culture. When explaining the transformation from one to the other it gave preference to the mediating forces of poetry and religion.

The technology of literacy

The approach which was to become famous for introducing mass communication was, in the beginning, a reading of the history of mankind and an interpretation of the great civilizations, their role, and their characteristics in history. All of the keywords that later played a role in the comparison of literate and oral societies had already been brought up in Innis's works in the 1940s (Innis, 1951, pp. 95 ff.): the development of characters beginning with Egyptian pictograms, the alleged magical properties of the hieroglyphics and the religious functions of early script, characters as auxiliary tools for memory, the conceptual link between orality, religion, time, music, and poetry, and finally the crucial role of the printing press for modern communication.[5] Innis, an economist with strong historical interests, was occupied not so much with the sequence of historical events, as with the *imagery of cultures*; he termed these their *technology*. He did not shy away from daring generalizations in drawing a straight line from the democratic reforms under Solon and Cleisthenes, to Protestantism, the printing press, and industrial culture. Even today we are confronted with this style of argument in the debate over orality and literacy. Another classical scholar, Eric A. Havelock, in his pioneering work *Preface to Plato* (1963),[6] spelled out the idea that oral poetry was an integral part of oral culture and qualitatively different from literal culture.

Though it makes general assertions on the whole of a society, the communication approach is directed, principally, to the individual. Texts only get a meaning when someone reads them – or: The text *is* the message (cf. Flusser, 1992, p. 36). Goody spoke of the "'individualizing' tendency of a literate technology" which, as he saw it, linked up with division of labor and the greater emphasis literate religions placed on individual paths of righteousness. While they put much emphasis on the individual communication act, most definitions of literacy are rather unsophisticated with regard to explaining literacy in terms of an individual quality. Instead, particular qualifications such as the inability to decipher and interpret a bus schedule, or fill out an employment form, or lists of "What Every American Needs To Know" are enumerated in a rather arbitrary way (Hirsch, 1988; cf. Curtis, 1990, p. 10 on cultural literacy).

If writing becomes understood as a technique rather than a social practice it is apt to acquire a dynamic or "logic" of its own: literacy shapes the human mind, as Havelock put it, and the "technologizing of the word" is said to *restructure* thought (Havelock, 1963; Ong, 1982).[7] The theory of the two cultures worked itself into broad public consciousness. Flusser characterized oral culture as the circular thinking of magical societies and literal culture as the linear thinking of societies which have a history. He asserted the idea that a culture of images cannot draw conclusions and produce abstract ideas; that this is a world of emotions and irrationality (cf. Postman, 1982; prior to that, McLuhan, 1962). He drew a pessimistic three-stage picture of the history of mankind progressing from the prehistoric times of oral societies through the times of literacy and logical ("linear") thinking into the *post-histoire*, the age of the picture, when binary logic would prevail and enlightenment come to an end.

The "great divide"

The communication approach and the great divide model are closely related even though they differ diametrically in their evaluation of the oral. Innis declared bluntly: "My bias is with the oral tradition, particularly as reflected in Greek civilisation, and with the necessity of recapturing something of its spirit" (Innis, 1951, p. 190) – back to good old orality. In a later model that was put on the agenda after Goody and Watt's epochal essay, there was no doubt that orality was contrary to progress (Goody & Watt, 1968, p. 27; cf. Olson, 1977, Saenger, 1982, Ong, 1982, Olson, 1991):

> Looked at in the perspective of time, man's biological evolution shades into pre-history, when he becomes a language-using animal; add writing, and history proper begins.

A long-established tradition has tied alphabetization to democracy, rationality, and modernity (e.g., Lilley, 1966; Lefevre & Martin, 1976; Eisenstein, 1979; Oxenham, 1980; Goody, 1968, p. 3; Lüsebrink, 1990, pp. 7 ff.). So ancient Greece became the paradigm for all research into the consequences of literacy. According to this view the Greek invention of the alphabet was crucial for the emergence of literacy because only the Greek 24-letter system with vowels and consonants would provide a medium for communicating economically. Additional support came from experiments made by Luria (1976).[8] The Russian psychologist and anthropologist found in the early 1930s in central Asia that illiterate persons were unable to comprehend syllogisms. This approach when adapted to a historical perspective would become a theory of the cognitive development of the human species. According to this theory a watershed separates the oral, say primitive or "savage," mind from modern, "rational" thinking.[9] It is the dichotomy of additive versus subordinative, aggregative versus analytic, redundant versus rational, conservative versus innovative, and situational versus abstract thinking. The oral culture was said to have been empathetic, close to the human lifeworld, and agonistically toned. "For an oral culture learning or knowing means achieving close, empathetic, communal identification with the known, 'getting with it.' Writing separates the knower from the known and thus sets up conditions for 'objectivity,' in the sense of personal disengagement or distancing" (Ong, 1982, pp. 45 ff.). It was a commonplace that in preliteral cultures remembering, instead of logic and rationality, played an all-important role that was to become more or less obsolete with literacy (cf. Epskamp, 1995, p. 19, table 3). Preliterate cultures were declared prelogical as well as prehistoric, a view that amounted to the claim that history only begins with writing (e.g. Illich & Sanders, 1988, p. 7). "Before writing was invented nothing happened, things only 'came to pass'" (Flusser, 1992, p. 12). Flusser was one of the last scholars who elaborated the idea that linear thinking, made possible by the Greek alphabet, was the logical form of modern societies. The never-ending circularity of magical thinking was to come to an end, but not before writing was invented.

The distinction between preliterate and literate cultures, according to this line of thinking, had practical consequences on developmental policies:[10]

> The illiterate man's thought...is, in fact, a series of images, juxtaposed or in sequence, and hence it rarely proceeds by induction or deduction. The result is that knowledge acquired in a given situation is hardly ever transferred to a different situation to which it could be applied. (UNESCO Regional Report, 1972)

Literacy versus orality?

The philosophy-of-literacy approach magnifies the distinction between orality and literacy into two different stages of cognitive capability. The "great divide" model was so immensely plausible that it brought on the danger of creating a myth of literacy (this criticism is in Probst, 1991, p. 18). Thought, lies, memory, translation, and, above all, *the self* were considered as constructs "that could not exist independently from the alphabet" (Illich & Sanders, 1988, pp. 16 ff., pp. 83 ff.; Flusser, 1992, pp. 33 and 139 ff.). The myth of literacy chiefly took two shapes. First, the model promoted a shortened antithesis of "primitive" and "developed" societies which was subject to being fitted out with the criterion of the occidental concept of rationality (Goody, 1986, p. xii).The approach took up the humanities fundamentals that all members of the educated classes in the Western world were familiar with. The high esteem for tradition and culture which was common among the educated public as opposed to humble everyday life (Assmann & Assmann, 1983) paved the way for the belief in the Great Divide. Plato's *Symposium*, classical rhetoric, the library of Alexandria – all this was wheeled out.

Secondly, there was the temptation to overlook the dynamics of human interests and social inequalities and to bestow on technology – the technology of writing and printing – a dynamic of its own. The reification of the writing materials in Mesopotamia and east Asia is a point in case. The modernization of writing technology indeed made it possible to write faster, but does it follow that the goose quill was the motor of progress?

Script and literacy are, in a broadly generalized and literal sense of the words, political instruments. On the other hand, even in literate societies where strings are pulled without any words being written, the exertion of personal influence, connections that work in totally oral ways, continue to be a medium of politics. So the outcomes of both literacy and orality depend on the social context. A particular and very understandable aspect of the connection between literacy and politics was emphasized in the political climate of the 1960s and 1970s, when it was supposed that there existed a direct connection between cognitive development, script, and the introduction of democracy (Schlaffer, 1968, p11). Another political aspect of literacy, however ambivalent, is that efficient administration needs literacy (see Elwert, 1987, p. 257). In fact, literacy does not only have benign aspects. Revolutions were generally preceded by the liberation of literature and an upsurge of texts.[11] Literacy by itself does not make a society democratic or authoritarian. Literacy lends itself to all sorts of purposes, enlightenment and democracy being only one set of them, political education and propaganda another. History is full of examples of literacy destabilizing a society and resulting in rebellion, oppression, civil war. The power function of literacy was salient to Lévi-Strauss both from his observations of Indian life and his knowledge of European history (1974, pp. 299 ff.).

David Olson's latest book (Olson, 1994) marks the threshold of the modernization of the great-divide model and its opening up to fresh approaches. Child psychology (Piaget), speech-act theory (Austin, Searle), and anthropology (Evans-Pritchard, Rosaldo, Duranti, McKellin, McCormick) were his points of reference. Some years ago he argued a quite radical position (Olson & Torrance, 1991, p. 1, Olson, 1994, p. 19; cf. Olson, 1991, pp. 157 ff.):

> it is misleading to think of literacy in terms of consequences. What matters is what people do with literacy, not what literacy does to people. Literacy does not cause a new mode of thought, but having a written record may permit people to do something they could not do before – such as look back, study, re-interpret, and so on. Similarly, literacy does not cause social change, modernization, or industrialization. But being able to read and write may be vital to playing certain roles in an industrial society. Literacy is important for what it permits people to do – to achieve their goals or to bring new goals into view.

His core argument is that writing is, in some respects, a seriously inefficient and restricted medium compared with oral communication (cf. Elwert, 1986). Oral face-to-face communication has a variety of ways to express meaning. A tiny gesture may indicate a whole gamut of ideas without words. Texts do not represent them, nor does electronic communication, we may add. So a literal context calls for functionally equivalent tools for expressing what writing cannot capture – "reading such texts calls for a whole new world of interpretative discourse, of commentary." Literacy therefore produces illocutionary expressions: "once the illocutionary force of a text is recognized as the expression of a personal, private intentionality, the concepts for representing how a text is to be taken provide just the concepts necessary for the representation of mind." Here is the origin of metalinguistic discourse and – such is the argument – the prerequisite of metaphysical thinking; "what writing provides is consciousness of the implicit structure of speech" (Olson, 1994; the quotations are from pp. 260 ff.).

The Practices of Literacy

The philosophical approach to literacy elaborated the general difference between oral and literal communication. However, it did not offer a history of the development of literacy. It did not descend to questions concerning writing in multilingual societies and the pedagogy to be followed in writing and reading classes; or those concerning the function of institutions such as religion, the family, and the administration in the diffusion of writing skills; or, the other way around, the impact of writing on the functioning of these institutions; or even the role of literacies in the construction of identities. The philosophical approach did not investigate the function of literacy under specific conditions, or the function of oral forms in a literate context, which is the normal case in present-day societies. Its concern was not to be led astray by the appearance of a world of things which may look the way it looks just because the observers are literate. Its aim was to discover the epistemic preconditions of our perception of the world. Its concern was not to take the objects of observation for granted. In principle, the philosophical view adopted for its model the human mind, be it orally restrained or literately refined, and generalized to society.

The philosophical approach remained within the confines of the Platonic-Aristotelian alternative – what is primordial: the ideas or the necessities? The counterpart within this dichotomy looks at literacy as dependent on society.[12] Here, mind is the dependent variable and the "real world concerns" (Scribner & Cole, 1981, p. 14) the independent one (Eisenberg, 1996, p. 26). On the one side there is the promise of the modernization of mind being the prerequisite for changing the world; on the other is the skeptical attitude that conditions and society provide the scope and constraints for action. There are various approaches that promise a way out from this stalemate.[13]

One possible approach is to study how literacy developed in specific societies in the past and attempt to explain the course of events on the basis of the concept of social change. This is the historian's job. Anthropologists, psychologists, linguists, and sociologists can examine how literacy functions in contemporary societies. All would try to draw generally applicable conclusions from historical or current data. Whatever the approach taken, literacy should not be understood as an individual cognitive term. That means, secondly, that literacy is linked to social practices, an "emic perspective" (Wagner, 1991, p. 12; cf. Pike, 1967). The third consequence, apropos of a point made by Street (in Maybin, 1994), is that social practices are constitutive of collective identities. If investigated in such a manner, literacy turns out to be so multiplex a phenomenon, dependent on historical tradition, everyday-life routines, and functional requirements of the social community in question, that it is advisable not to think of literacy as a common competence of the human mind but rather in terms of literacies, in the plural form.

Cognition theory and literacy

The main problem in investigating literacy is its covariation, and hence the necessity of controlling its interaction with other variables. The aim is to differentiate methodically between (i) the influence of script, its requirements and use, as well as (ii) the practice of writing, and (iii) the effects of other economic, cultural, social, and political influences. The question is whether the effect of writing and reading skills on complex mental operations such as memorizing, logical thinking, comparison, etc. comes about not through literacy *per se*, but through the uses to which it is put in a social situation.

Scribner and Cole found near-laboratory conditions for such a study in the people of the Vai in Liberia. A considerable number of the male population had mastered the Vai script. However, they did not acquire this knowledge in a school but in the practice of everyday life. Besides this vernacular script there was Arabic and English, which were taught in schools. This setting of three parallel script languages offered the opportunity (i) to differentiate between the effects of script and those of formal schooling on cognitive competence, and (ii) to examine literacy in a cultural context. Instead of focusing "exclusively on the technology of a writing system and its reputed consequences," the authors approached literacy "as a set of socially organized practices which make use of a symbol system and a technology for producing and disseminating it. Literacy is not simply knowing how to read and write a particular script but applying this knowledge for specific purposes in specific contexts of use." Every "context of use" is connected to another: "inquiries into the cognitive consequences of literacy are inquiries into the impact of socially organized practices in other domains (trade, agriculture) on practices involving writing (keeping lists of sales, exchanging goods by letter)" (Scribner & Cole, 1981, p. 236 ff.).

The cognitive capacities in nonliterates in Vai society turned out not to be inferior to those in literate people, nor did formal education prove the only way to literacy. The authors identified only three skills that were clearly linked with Vai literacy. The "true literacy effect" was in constructing meaning from graphic symbols ("encoding skills": Scribner & Cole, 1981 , pp. 131 ff., 184 ff., 234, 243 ff., 251). The authors concluded that, on balance, "Vai script does not fulfill the expectations of those social scientists who consider literacy a prime mover in social change" (Scribner & Cole, 1981, p. 239). What then, if not literacy, is the push factor? The question put the other way around – what are the reasons for the system of Vai society not pushing the Vai script to become an elaborated standard language? – points to some basic social, political, and economic pre-requisites for the emergence of literacy. In Liberia, the Vai remained largely a subsistence agricultural group (Scribner & Cole, 1981, p. 241) while, apart from Vai script, there were other strong competitors like Arabic. Also, the question of language was a question of political power between ethnic groups.

The culture-cognition model puts literacy in the context of social practice (Scribner & Cole, 1981, p. 252). What is "practice"? "By a practice we mean a recurrent, goal-oriented sequence of activities using a particular technology and particular systems of knowledge" (Scribner & Cole, 1981, p. 236). For literacy as "a set of socially organized practices" letter writing is a case in point. Literacy involves a set of activities, some of them social, some economic. Some are the outcome of long-range civilization processes, either on the technological level or on the social one. Civilization involves teaching people how to cope with con-ventional rules which govern the representation of a particular script or make possible social agreements of any sort. Conventions of form and style appro-priate to personal correspondence and patterns of behavior towards strangers or persons who are not present have a long history. Literacy demands a high level of technological development, knowledge of processing natural products in order to furnish materials to read and write – the invention of eye-glasses and the spread of domestic lighting are likely to have been major technological innov-ations in modern times (Zboray, 1993). It demands means of transmitting messages and the organization of geographic mobility. In this way, literacy turns out to be the result of a complex civilization process not unlike that of the emergence of a "fire regime" in the history of mankind (cf. Goudsblom, 1992). Yet, there are some practices that Scribner and Cole brought into play that will not be accepted by scholars of the philosophy-of-literacy approach, who are likely to argue that it is only the written word which makes them possible: to classify information, to know how a language is represented in the syllabary, to be able to retrieve the representation of an individual word from memory, to succeed in planning and organizing a message, to take into account the informational needs of the reader, to be able to separate *ego* and *alter*, they argue, depends on the experience of writing.

Even the scrutiny employed in the observation of a single African society failed to explain the triggering factors which are likely to make literacy work. Anthropological and psychological fieldwork, though having elaborated the social embedding of literacy, did not manage to answer the question – what comes first: mind or practice? Carrying on from the old bicamerality model of the brain (Jackson, 1874; Jaynes, 1977; Ong, 1982, pp. 29 ff.; van Lancker, 1987) linguistic and neurolinguistic theory forges links to the embedding approach. Script is thought to facilitate cognition by forming segments like syllables and words.[14] For the brain to be able to operate with symbols requires the existence of symbolic systems in the outside world, i.e. the existence of script. How, then, did script grow and evolve? The emergence of external symbolic systems like script presupposes the existence of everyday-life routines. Research shows that script was the result of a flourishing economy between the Euphrates, the Tigris and the Zagros Mountains, and of an expanding administration. The purpose of the first notations was mnemonic, making registers of crop and livestock and lists of office-bearers. The earliest traces of these types of writing systems date back to a point of time when "the organizational structures of the Sumer economy and government had taken shape already" (Nissen, Damerow, & Englund, 1991, p. 56; cf. Schmandt-Besserat, 1978; Scheerer, 1993, pp. 176–81).

Historical findings

The research results reported on in this chapter do not deal with the transition from primary orality to literacy but with the decisive expansion of literacy in the self-modernizing societies of Europe in contexts that were already molded by literacy. History qualifies the simplistic contrast between the oral and literary worlds. In reality, the transformation from one to the other was a protracted one. The concept that script had its own potential to change society needs to be revised in the light of historical experience. A reliance on script must be seen rather as the result of specific social processes of change. Social change in Europe, including processes of economic change, created nuclei of modernization around which other centers of literacy could develop.[15] It took a very long time for these insular centers of literacy to grow so much and branch out so extensively that one could speak of literacy having taken hold of all society. This was the case in Europe but not before the nineteenth century. On the whole,

Table 2.2   Estimated percentage of the population of Middle Europe (over 6 years old) who might have been able to read

	Year				
	1770	1800	1830	1870	1900
Percentage	15	25	40	75	90

historical research provides an abundance of proof of the social and institutional embedding of the processes of literacy.

In Europe, writing permeated the business dealings of the more important merchants in the commercial centers in the thirteenth century. This is in line with the first urban grammar schools being founded in the second half of that century. During the fourteenth century more and more people came to expect literate abilities of their rulers, even though many important sovereigns continued to be nonliterate: for instance, the founder of Heidelberg University. After about 1400 most priests could read and write, although up to that time few priests could. Still, four centuries had to pass after the world-famous invention by a certain Mr. Gutenberg before significant parts of the population actually started reading.[16] It goes without saying that the figures in table 2.2 are estimates from various times and places and must not be interpreted as a time series.

In Germany, even the work of the representatives of the Enlightenment movement, such as the famous educators Basedow and Pestalozzi, as well as the circulation of innumerable pamphlets that pointed out the advantages of reading abilities to the public, were to a large extent futile up to the beginning of the nineteenth century. The first accounts that simple folk could read turned up during the industrial age (1769 marked the invention of the steam engine in England). The call for mass education rang out only when, in the nineteenth century, industrial society was in need of a skilled workforce and emerging national armies were short of adequately trained recruits. For mass literacy to be realized in the eighteenth century it was necessary to have the printing press, which had been invented long before; but the technology was not the vital cause.

Historical research shows that literacy did not permeate whole populations at one time but commenced in scattered areas at different times. The needs of society produced readers and at the same time texts for these readers. When one studies the results of empirical research, one is always struck by the image of insular centers of literacy from which it spread out. Centuries passed before the widespread networks of a literate culture evolved from the many different and scattered types of literacy centers. This happened in Europe only in the nineteenth century. It took considerable time for a standard written language to evolve in Europe. For a long time, beginning in the early modern era, literacy was coupled with a multitude of vernacular or regional languages. In the German Empire, until late in the nineteenth century, the national standard language competed with the various local vernaculars. This is understandable if literacy is assumed to be embedded in social practices. The success of the top-down implementation of a standard language (*lingua franca*) is debatable. On the one side, it succeeded in Europe in the nineteenth century; on the other, the Somalian language policy had some positive effects, yet all attempts at creating a novel language from parts of existing vernaculars failed (Reh, 1981, pp. 548, 550). Language planning cannot be easily forced upon a society in contravention of its demands (Elwert & Giesecke, 1987); a case in point is the decline of Esperanto in Europe (see Aspects of Internationalism, 1992).

Certain occupational groups, social classes, or bearers of special functions were considered forerunners of literacy long before general agencies of basic education and elementary schooling developed.[17] In Mesopotamia, these were obviously scribes, administrators, bookkeepers, and senior officials (Nissen, Damerow, & Englund, 1991; Rix, 1992). In Europe, reading and sometimes writing were by and large the business of religious (priests) or worldly (civil servants) employees and the propertied urban entrepreneurial classes or landed gentry. Nowadays there are still certain professions that possess an individual complex of behavior patterns and cognitive conventions which can hardly be separated – one could think of the subculture of programmers and other administrators of specialized knowledge. Literacy was indigenous to certain places, such as temple areas and convents. In Europe, the courts and seats of government were predominant, e.g., the language of the court in Prague and the chancellaries in Cologne and Erfurt before Luther standardized the language and script by translating the Bible. The academies and universities also had a great effect in the making of a literate society, for instance the Sorbonne and, in Italy, the University of Bologna. Finally, literacy took root in the cities where merchants and artisans were concentrated. In Italy, commercial schools were founded very early on. These specialized in the needs of entrepreneurs and great merchants, but were also open to the general urban public.[18] In England and Germany literacy concentrated on the husbandmen heading households in town and country. It was for these that a type of literature consisting of manuals and encyclopedias developed whose aim it was to teach technical skills such as bookkeeping and meteorology, as well as handing down information on medical aid and health and traditional moral norms and values (Brunner, 1956; Giesecke, 1983). Literacy found its way through special genres, in the Europe of the late Middle Ages and early modern period, through religious texts, picture books (*imageries populaires*), that is, single sheets which were dominated for the most part by a picture, often of a saint, "pin-ups," depictions of spectacular events with a small or no caption, and fliers that could also be illustrated. Furthermore, there were song books and instructional books, for example, on letter writing.[19] In Germany, during the seventeenth and eighteenth centuries a special genre of philosophical-political literature disseminated manners and values to the middle classes and bourgeoisie by way of standard reading material. Thus a typical middle-class identity developed which was still perceptible in the early twentieth century (Engelsing, 1974; Kocka, 1995). Leaflets and booklets soon formed a market for a *petit* capitalism (Schenda, 1970, pp. 270 ff.; Zboray, 1993, p. 40).

Under scrutiny, one must admit that literacy covers a far wider range of skills than the command of a technique ("clerical literacy": Illich, 1992). Being literate means mastering a grid of semantic relations that connect a reader and the text and which go beyond the individual (Illich's "lay literacy"). In early modern times, when children were sent to school they often did not understand what they read; rather, as critical contemporaries noted, they recited mechanically (Engelsing, 1973, p. 66 *et passim*). Such was the sad fate of the well-read miller Domenico Scandella, called Menocchio, in northern Italy in the sixteenth century (Ginzburg, 1982). He was proficient in the technique of basic literacy skills but he was not cognizant of the general knowledge and semantic cross-references which make up a literate culture. All his basic reading skills earned for him were, first, the Inquisitional court, and, in the end, the stake (see Feldman, 2000).

When making diachronic and geographic comparisons, one can distinguish between the factors that supported the processes of making *social life literate* (Giesecke, 1992, pp. 73–121) and the spread of literacy, and factors that rather obstructed them (Cipolla, 1969; François, 1989). Low population density in a region without dense centers of urban life, scattered settlements, and the predominance of diverse dialects and regional languages (vernaculars) were negative factors. The *social restrictions* on alphabetic literacy, according to Goody, were religious ones in the first instance, the secrecy of magical books that were not intended to be read, the existence of the authorized teacher who had the monopoly on reading from the holy script ("the Guru tradition"). In these contexts literacy is a mere aid to oral communication. Historical evidence shows that positive starting conditions for literacy proved to be the integration of local urban commercial centers into distant markets, mercantile development, and a well-developed traffic system. Social historians emphasize that, in regions of relative wealth, commercial activity is the factor which especially furthers the expansion of literacy in a population. Luther's "innovative education program" (Engelsing, 1973, p. 34) consisted in coupling the ideal of accumulating wealth through one's own work with the accumulation of knowledge. However, providing for the uneducated through church agencies or the prebends and sinecures of mundane agencies, was in his view adverse to the spread of literacy. In modern times general literacy occurred in conjunction with "the institutionalization of citizenship through the democratic revolution" (Parsons & Platt, 1974, p. 3). Lévi-Strauss emphasized that urbanization and integration of society were, throughout history, the only processes that accompanied the spread of literacy unequivocally (Lévi-Strauss, 1974, p. 299). We may add some other favorable factors: the institution of a written language common to the various ethnicities in the developing nation-states; the expansion of a school network, however loose; a newspaper culture after the second half of the eighteenth century, even if it initially reached only a small portion of the enlightened public. The emergence of a public sphere, the praise of the "common good," and the call for "good governance" and development of the polity accompanied, in Europe, propaganda for reading and writing abilities (Giesecke & Elwert, 1982, p. 12; Giesecke, 1992; cf. Wagner, 1995, p. 347: the "endogenous rationale").

The experience of discontinuity, social conflicts, or interruptions in the life-course, possibly even religious pluralism, were emphasized by many authors as being stimuli for the demand for literacy and its dissemination among the public. It was no coincidence that theological dispute produced a great number of written texts that were widely distributed and debated heatedly by the public. The experience of discontinuity could be found in the socialization process as well. Within early American society it was family life and the common school – both very much in a radical Protestant spirit – that "tied the youthful mind down to a restrictive reception of texts, monitored through mechanical recitation" (Zboray, 1993, p. xix). In contrast, private experiences of literary acquisition, libraries, youth improvement associations, maternal associations, a public lecture system, proved even more promising. The emotional sustenance the personally-made text, the letter, procured to those "shaken by the winds of economic circumstance" (Zboray, 1993, p. xx) was a prerequisite of economic development, which is a phenomenon often overlooked.

It is common to the approaches opposing the great-divide model that they recognize the substantial role orality has even in literate cultures. "Oral structures must be embedded in literacy practices and serve these by being based on them" (Elwert, 1986, p. 76). Writing is by no means the most economical mode of communication, nor does it enhance understanding under all circumstances (Elwert repeatedly points to this fact; see e.g. 1987). There are, even in literal cultures, areas of symbolic use that cannot be put down in writing. The approval of a person's judgment, in academic life, is dependent on the social status one acquires by his oral abilities (Parsons & Platt, 1974, p. 59; Latour & Woolgar, 1986). It was not only in modern Europe that oral traditions and literal elements coexisted in one and the same culture (Schlieben-Lange, 1983; Raible, 1998, p. 23). The legal system is a specific field that is strongly dependent on literacy on the one hand. Yet elements of oral communication are firmly institutionalized in it – forms of oral proceedings have established themselves across a wide range in the Anglo-Saxon legal system. Vollrath, who analyzed English legal texts which were copied into vernacular languages, even thinks that legislation worked in reality without the written word and that frequently the writing down of it ensued much later (Vollrath, 1979). "Protoliteracy," the restriction of literacy to a small proportion of the total population, is another instance of the coexistence of orality and literacy. The introduction of Islam in west African societies from the thirteenth century resulted in the formation of *protoliteral* societies (Goody, 1986). There are certain circumstances under which oral forms are resurrected, even in a literate culture: contemporary Senegalese literature, literary productions in Latin America in the second half of the nineteenth century, the debating public during the French Revolution, the culture in Italy around 1500 all are examples (Lüsebrink, 1990, pp. 273 ff.). It could be argued that oral tradition flourishes primarily in a written culture. Traditional culture often has serious constraints on what can be talked about and to whom.

The question of whether the oral elements are relics within this mixture or are newly created elements within the literate is subject to discussion. The observation of the long-lasting coexistence of oral traditions and literate elements has relevance in the question of how to cope with illiteracy in a pragmatic way. The historian raises the objection that it is necessary to allow for many levels of competence in both reading and writing in one society at the same time (Goody, 1968, pp. 4–20; Goody & Watt, 1968, p. 36; Clanchy, 1979; Stock, 1983).

> It should be remembered that one can learn to read without being able to write. …Writing…comprises several levels of competence, ranging from the ability to copy an existing text to a capacity for literary composition in both the vernacular and in the common language. (McKitterick, 1990, pp. 3, 5)

The story historical research on literacy tells us, in McKitterick's opinion, is that "literacy in any society is not just a matter of who could read and write, but one of how their skills function, and of the adjustments – mental, intellectual, physical and technological – necessary to accommodate it." It is the story of the close association of orality and literacy, the story of a pluralism of literate practices which are embedded in a variety of social contexts and behavior patterns and which are closely linked with specific institutional arrangements in the society.

The sociology of writing

Historical research digs deep into the specific circumstances of a society. Sociological theory is a good antidote against getting lost in the variety of directions social change may take. The historical experience of literacy reconsidered from a sociological perspective leads to some general insights into the nature of literacy. The common denominator of historical and sociological research is the concept of embedding (Street, 1987; Elwert, 1997; cf. Barton, 1994).

Historians have shown literacy to be embedded in a social context, and it has largely been associated with concepts of social change, modernization, the emergence of new social groups, the functional diversification of society, or the evolution of new ways of life. The concept of modernization had already been modified to represent a process which takes on a different form and speed dependent on region and milieu (Heath, 1983). At the same time, in order for script and writing to become both a factor and an agent of development, an opposite process had to be effective: the standardization of a social system or *lifeworld* (Elwert, 1986).

The second general feature of embedding is that literacy is tied to institutional arrangements. Giesecke employs the term "domain of experience." Each domain has its (i) typical structures of time and space, (ii) rules of segmentation, and (iii) rules of connection. Standardization, according to Giesecke, is the means for coordinating these three systems. Coordination poses no major problems if the communication scene clearly lies open, which is the case in face-to-face communication. If this is not so, five functions must be developed in order to secure understanding: a common stock of knowledge, a shared stock of symbolic patterns for representing the real world, a shared medium of communication, and a shared set of communication conventions (Giesecke, 1992, pp. 76, 86), resulting in a reciprocity of perspectives in the participants. These functions seem to be exactly the achievements reached within the above-mentioned islands of literacy.

On balance, the meaning of "institution" is twofold (Olson, 1994, p. 273). The process of becoming literate takes place, first, within a "domain." Other terms meaning roughly the same have been used by other scholars instead: "institution," lifeworld, societal subsystem, domain of knowledge, *Bildungswelt*, etc. Literacy is combined, secondly, with a new way of conceptualizing the world. To become literate a person must become familiar with a network of conventional arrangements. He has to be subjected to a socialization process which provides answers to questions such as the following: What is an argument? What is "legitimate" (Bourdieu) knowledge? What are the legitimate ways of learning something? Ubiquitous literacy requires a shared world of meaning, interpretation, and collective identity. The whole "philosophical approach" dealt with that theme.

What kinds of institutions did sociological analysis distinguish? Several institutions require attention, primarily economic, legal, political, and religious.

An institutional arrangement of outstanding influence which gave vigor to literacy was market capitalism. It was one of the most powerful forces of standardization. The concept of capitalism has to be qualified, though. Braudel's model of three forms of capitalism in history is fruitful in this respect (Braudel, 1985, introductory remarks). The social context of literacy has not been, in most cases, the global capitalism of big business and finance empires of the kind which prevails today. To say this is to deliberately ignore that there were very few "global" companies of the early modern period which gave indirect incentives to urban literacy. The social context where literacy flourished was what Braudel called the small capitalism of the marketplace and the workshop.

A special institution that has been repeatedly referred to in research on literacy is law. Legal texts, statute books, and contracts spear-headed written culture. Law is the trustee of another institution that is less conspicuous, namely the regularity of procedure. Elwert repeatedly touches on this point (once again: Elwert, 1997, p. 11, and this volume). Regularity, in other words the sequentiality and iteration of events, is a cornerstone of the cognitive theory emphasizing the emergence of script. What is needed is a theory of action, social change, and the necessary persistence of explicit rules. Siegenthaler puts forward a theory of individual action and economic development. His main concern is the connection between social rules and individual decision-making. Social procedures and standards make up the institutional framework that constitutes the background structure for rational information processing in the individual. In the nexus of law and economy, property rights are central to inspiring confidence and, historically, operated in the takeoff into literate culture and a modern economy in Europe (Siegenthaler, 1993; North & Thomas, 1973).

Another institution that creates and employs literacy is political power. So the nation-state comes to be a prominent social context of literacy. The example of nationalism shows that literacy is closely connected with the emergence of collective identity (see Street, in Maybin, 1994). Collective identity defines a public in a society and may articulate itself in the policy formation process. The public is, in a way, a type of imagined community with shared values and standards which have been shown (see above) to be a corollary to literate culture. A public and literacy are concomitant. Elwert and Giesecke even argued that the latter is a prerequisite of the former (Elwert & Giesecke, 1987, pp. 422 ff.). The example of Zaïre can be understood, however, in the opposite way – a democratic public life has been a prerequisite to literacy. In the end, the possibility cannot be ruled out that both, literacy and public life, are dependent on a specific phase of development of society.

So far, both from historical evidence and from sociological conception it is clear that literacy and the process of becoming literate is more than alphabetization on the level of the individual. Literacy cannot be separated from politics, social structure, culture, or economy. In order to cope scientifically with this complex interdependence and to derive rational action based on a thorough understanding of it a consistent theory is needed. The general theory of action may be perceived as a comprehensive variant of an embedding approach (Parsons & Platt, 1974, pp. 18ff., 313). Indeed, the theory presents a rather complicated nest structure of systems and subsystems. Parsons did not apply it to writing and literacy, but much of his argument concerning the academic social system is to the point. It is not possible to integrate literacy into a broader picture of social action here (but see Triebel, 1997). Suffice it to say that writing is a type of social action: *Action*, here, *means human behavior insofar as it is symbolically oriented*. Script is part of cultural meaning systems: "Symbolic systems are organized in terms of codes similar to linguistic codes in that they constitute sets of norms regulating processes of communication" (Parsons & Platt, 1974, p. 8).

The general theory of action provides a basis for connecting the numerous isolated aspects of literacy which I have discussed. The concept of rationality, instead of being reduced to a historically contingent "Western" form, is made a function of social interaction. This makes an emic perspective on literacy imperative. Neither is rationality conceived of as an individual quality, but as a societal exigency. Symbolic practices are not tied to individual achievement, but are seen as being integrated into social contexts within a nest-structured theory of action.

The Future of Literacy

Upon closer inspection, article 4 of the the World Declaration on Education for All (1990) is more enigmatic than elucidating. The question of how to get literacy under way still remains open.

> Whether or not expanded educational opportunities will translate into meaningful development – for an individual or for society – depends ultimately on whether

people actually learn as a result of those opportunities, i.e., whether they incorporate useful knowledge, reasoning ability, skills, and values.

Obviously the "medical model," which treats illiteracy like some disease that
will come to an end as soon as the germs of illiteracy are wiped out (Wagner,
1987), is not appropriate.

The question of the particular stimulus required for the emergence of literacy
has loomed large in the preceding sections. In the field of the economics of the
industrial revolution the once-famous theory of Rostow answered this question
by laying down the magical figure of 10 percent of the proportion of net
investment to national income. This increase was thought to raise real output
per capita and in doing so start a chain reaction that would result in self-
reinforcing industrial growth (Rostow, 1956). Is education the key to sustainable
development in the same way as the rate of productive investment was thought
to be to industrialization? The human-capital argument runs along the same
lines as the model of takeoff into self-sustained growth. The criticism has been
that the evidence of aggregate rates and of their coincidence does not rule out the
possibility that education (or literacy) investment and economic development,
while being independent from each other, are both the result of specific elements
of social change, or, put even more radically, that a certain type of economic
performance or a specific stage of rationalization of behavior is the determinant
of literacy rates. This was Parsons' explanation of the modernizing of American
society (Parsons & Platt, 1974, p. 45).

The field of study of literacy, then, is structured according to two main
approaches. They are in fact clusters of theories, and, while being different in
their purport, they do not contradict each other. The first we have termed the
"philosophical" one. Its merit is in having made clear the principal difference
between oral and literate cultures and in making us aware of the fact that these
cultures are congruent with specific modes of perceiving the outside world. This
is its concern with epistemology. But this implies a narrowing of literacy down to
its technical aspects. This is the deeper sense of talking about *skills* and of the
question of the "media" of communication.

The second main approach refers more directly to real-world concerns. The
main goal of this cluster of theories is to understand literacy as embedded in
social contexts. According to this approach the emergence of literacy and the
acquisition of literacy abilities is a complex social process which takes place in
diverse historical situations and entails more than learning to read and write.
Like a substance that crystallizes in a solution, literacy crystallizes into various
literacies in the course of social change.

Behind the debate on how to manage the takeoff into self-sustained literacy
there seems to lurk the principle question of whether and how alien authorities
should interfere with social processes which are, as history has shown, first and
foremost processes on the local and community levels. Only to the extent that
local markets expanded and that social integration increased did reading and
writing become ubiquitous tools in the hands of their users. Much of what has

been said about literacy gives the impression that becoming literate is not the result of learning to read and write but depends on underlying institutional arrangements that are closely related to policy. The kind of economic system employed is one instance of this underlying institutional social structure. Research has also indicated the relevance of power relations and social inequality; the creation of a responsive public; the linkage between community development and a sense of the common good; the commitment of religious communities and private organizations; and the institutionalization of citizenship. Unlike the "takeoff" of industrial revolution, literacy may not be self-sustaining. Institutional arrangements are the groundwork to support it.

The concerns of article 1 of the Jomtien Declaration, such as the quality of life, empowerment, tolerance, morale, community sense, and humanistic values, will have to be made "profitable" for both the individual and the polity. By acknowledging this, politics will return – not, however, with the idealist emphasis of former days – with a more pragmatic look at the real interests of people and the "habits of their hearts."

Notes

I am indebted to Catalina de Laczkovich, who, thanks to her native speaker's competence, skillfully translated some difficult passages and quotations from German, and in general kept a watchful eye on the linguistic standard of the text. Nonetheless, I am responsible for any confusion and foreshortening that might have occurred. Many thanks to Ivan Illich who provided me with a copy of his "Plea for Research on Lay Literacy."

1   The research literature on literacy is immense; see the comprehensive bibliographies furnished by the German Foundation for International Development, Bonn. The bibliography in Triebel, 1997 contains more than 350 titles. Any work on literacy cannot do without Glück, 1987; Olson, 1994; and the research done in the Interdisciplinary Research Group 321 of the German Science Foundation DFG – see Raible, 1998. See also Graff, 1981; Hladczuk et al., 1990; Giese, 1993; Barton, 1994; Günther & Ludwig, 1994.
2   Aliteracy was a special topic at a 1982 conference sponsored by the American Enterprise Institute for Public Policy Research, Washington, DC.
3   Selden Ramsay, Education. Fifth Report of the National Council on Education Research (Washington, DC: NIE, fiscal years 1978–9), p. 32, cited in Winterowd, 1989, p. 7.
4   What is referred to here as the philosophy of literacy or the great-divide approach, Street (1993) calls the *autonomous model of literacy*.
5   Innis's paramount sources were Ernst Cassirer and Gotthold E. Lessing, Henri Frankfort and Salomon Gandz, W. F. Albright (*From the Stone Age to Christianity: Monotheism and the Historical Process*, 1940) and M. Cornfeld (*From Religion to Philosophy: A Study in the Origins of Western Speculation*, 1912).
6   The title alludes to a learned book written by a German philologist, Friedrich A. Wolf, *Prolegomena ad Homerum* (1795). Havelock elaborated on ideas put forward by two anthropologists who in the 1930s took their empirical data from the venerable

region of ancient Greece and some traditional societies of the contemporary Balkans. See M. Parry, "Studies in the epic technique of oral verse-making: Homer and Homeric style," *Harvard Studies in Classical Philology* 61 (1930), and "Studies in the epic technique of oral verse-making: The Homeric language as the language of an oral poetry," *Harvard Studies in Classical Philology* 63 (1932); Albert B. Lord, *The Singer of Tales* (Cambridge: Cambridge University Press, 1960). Fresh research on archaic Greek poetry refuted Havelock's theory of early Greek epic poetry as a sort of collective oral encyclopedia; see e.g. Kullmann & Reichel, 1990.

7   Even Elwert & Giesecke (1987, p. 433) do not abandon the comparison of standard languages and high-tech systems. The influence of the philosophical approach manifested itself, now 10 years ago, in their insistence that literacy is the condition of mathematical reasoning and other forms of meaningful behavior, while their basic argument was that a standard national language is dependent on social structure and social practice.

8   A. R. Luria, *The Working Brain: An Introduction to Neuropsychology* (New York: Basic Books, 1973); Luria, 1976.

9   Introducing this line of argument to a wider German audience: Schlaffer, 1986.

10   UNESCO Regional Report (1972), quoted from Scribner & Cole, 1981, p. 14; other quotations to the same effect.

11   Koselleck, 1976; Markoff, 1986. Stone, 1969, p. 138, puts forward the idea that a range of 30 to 60 percent illiterates in the population is the critical quantity; the Swiss Society In Medio, the Akademie 91 Zentralschweiz Foundation (Luzern), and the Zürich University Sociological Institute (Dept. for the Sociology and History of the Mass Media) form a circle of scholars whose interest is in the investigation of the interrelation of revolution and mass media. The theory is in Imhof & Romano, 1996.

12   The social context ("scene": Burke, 1957). Cf. recent anthropological work that makes a plea for literacy being embedded in activities, institutions, and social settings or domains: Grillo, 1989; Heath, 1983; Hymes, 1974.

13   Street, 1993, lumps research of this type together as *the ideological model of literacy*. But the term "ideological" is open to misunderstanding; therefore I prefer to use more precise terminology.

14   Research along these lines has been pursued at Oldenburg University by Eckart Scheerer in the Dept. of Psychology. Another center of neurophysiology research is the newly founded Hanse Wissenschaftskolleg und Delmenhorst, Germany (Director: Gerhard Roth). On domains of mental functioning see Scheerer, 1990; Scheerer, 1993; Ehlich, 1993. Scribner & Cole, 1981, pp. 146ff., make some remarks regarding the segmenting capacity effectuated in Vai literates.

15   I find a similar idea in Scribner & Cole, 1981, p. 236 ("spheres of activity") and in Giesecke, 1992, p. 75 ("*kulturelle Systeme*").

16   There is abundant empirical evidence on the continued existence of analphabetism in large parts of the population in Europe until far into the nineteenth century in Engelsing, 1973. See also: François, 1989; Schenda, 1970, pp. 37, 49, 443–67; Wehler, 1987, vol. 2, pp. 458–546.

17   A nationwide elementary school system started in Europe, especially in Germany, not earlier than in the nineteenth century. See Leschinsky & Roeder, 1983.

18   Braudel, 1986, p. 445. Cf. the merchant society of the *Hanse* which founded schools in some trade cities of northern Germany in the thirteenth century: Giesecke, 1992, pp. 75 ff.

19   Collections of model letters were in use with some educated classes as early as the sixteenth century; see Engelsing, 1973, pp. 34 ff. And even today in Germany; see e.g. Bruno Horst Bull (ed.), *Die schönsten Glückwünsche. Texte und Gedichte für jeden Anlaß* [Congratulations. Prose and Poems For All Occasions] (Niedernhausen: Bassermann 1996).

References

Almond, G. A. and Coleman, J. S. (eds.) (1960). *The Politics of Developing Areas*. Princeton: Princeton University Press.

Anderson, C. A. (1966). Literacy and schooling at the development threshold. In C. A. Anderson and M. Bowman (eds.), *Education and Economic Development*. London: Frank Cass.

Assmann, A. and Assmann, J. (1983). Schrift und Gedächtnis [Script and memory]. In A. Assmann, J. Assmann, and C. Hardmeier (eds.), *Schrift und Gedächtnis*. Beiträge zur Archäologie der literarischen Kommunikation, München: Fink.

Barton, D. (1994). *Literacy: An introduction to the ecology of written language*. Oxford: Blackwell.

Bhola, H. S. (1984). *Campaigning for Literacy*. Paris: UNESCO.

Bhola, H. S. and Bhola, J. K. (1984). *Planning and Organization of Literacy Campaigns, Programs and Projects*. Bonn: Deutsche Stiftung für internationale Entwicklung; DOK 1240 C/a.

Bourdieu, P. (1983). Ökonomisches Kapital, kulturelles Kapital, soziales Kapital [Three forms of capital: Economic, cultural, and social]. In R. Kreckel (ed.), *Soziale Ungleichheiten*. Göttingen: Schwartz.

Braudel, F. (1985). *Sozialgeschichte des 15. – 18. Jahrhunderts. Der Alltag* [Social history. The structures of everyday life]. München: Kindler.

Braudel, F. (1986). *Sozialgeschichte des 15. – 18. Jahrhunderts. Der Handel* [Social history. Trade and markets]. München: Kindler.

Brunner, O. (1956). Hausväterliteratur [Books on husbandry]. *Handwörterbuch der Sozialwissenschaften 5*. Stuttgart/Tübingen/Göttingen: Fischer/Mohr/Vandenhoeck & Ruprecht, pp. 92 ff.

Burke, K. (1957). *The Philosophy of Literary Form*. New York: Vintage.

Cipolla, C. M. (1969). *Literacy and Development in the West*. Baltimore: Penguin.

Clanchy, M. T. (1979). *From Memory to Written Record: England, 1066–1307*. Cambridge/London: Harvard University Press/Edwin Arnold.

Curtis, L. R. (1990). *Literacy for Social Change*, foreword by Hanna Arlene Fingeret. Syracuse: New Readers Press.

Delors, J. (1996). Education: The necessary utopia. In UNESCO (ed.), *Learning: The treasure within*. Paris: UNESCO.

Deutsche UNESCO-Kommission (ed.) (1991). *Die Alphabetisierung geht weiter – Pressestimmen am Ende des Internationalen Alphabetisierungsjahres 1990* [The alphabetization goes on: A press report at the end of the international year of alphabetization]. Bonn: UNESCO-Pressespiegel.

Ehlich, K.(1983). Development of writing as social problem solving. In F. Coulmas and K. Ehlich (eds.), *Writing in Focus*. Berlin/New York/Amsterdam: Mouton.

Eisenberg, P. (1996). Die Schrift ist zum Lesen da. Orthographiereform und historisch gewachsener Sprachbau [Script is good for reading: The reform of orthography in Germany versus the natural development of language]. *Wirtschaft und Wissenschaft* 4(4): 22–9.

Eisenstein, E. L. (1979). *The Printing Press as an Agent of Change: Communications and cultural transformations in early-modern Europe*. Cambridge: Cambridge University Press.

Elwert, G. (1986). Die Verschriftlichung von Kulturen. Skizze einer Forschung [Making cultures literal. An outline of research]. *Sociologus* 36(1): 65–78.

Elwert, G. (1987). Die gesellschaftliche Einbettung von Schriftgebrauch [The social embedding of writing]. In D. Baecker et al. (eds.), *Theorie als. Passion*, Frankfurt a.M.: Suhrkamp.

Elwert, G. (1997). Pas de développement sans culture écrite: Réflexions sur la persistance de la pauvreté dans les pays moins avancés d'Afrique. In *D+C. Développement et Coopération*, 1: 11–13.

Elwert, G. and Giesecke, M. (1987). Technologische Entwicklung, Schriftkultur und Schriftsprache als technologisches System [Written language and literacy as technologies: The role of technological change]. In B. Lutz (ed.), *Technik und sozialer Wandel*. Frankfurt a.M.: Campus Verlag.

Engelsing, R. (1973). *Analphabetentum und Lektüre. Zur Sozialgeschichte des Lesens in Deutschland zwischen feudaler und industrieller Gesellschaft* [The social history of reading in Germany in the transition period between feudal and industrial society]. Stuttgart: Metzler.

Engelsing, R. (1974). *Der Bürger als Leser. Lesergeschichte in Deutschland 1500–1800* [The Bourgeois – a reader. A history of the reading public in Germany, 1500–1800]. Stuttgart: Metzler.

Epskamp, K. (1995). *On Printed Matter and Beyond: Media, orality and literacy*. The Hague: Center for the Study of Education in Developing Countries (CESO). CESO Paperback no. 23.

Etzioni, A. (1993). *The Spirit of Community: Rights, responsibilities, and the communitarian agenda*. New York: Crown Publishers.

Fagerlind, I. and Saha, L. J. (1983). *Education and National Development: A comparative perspective*. New York: Pergamon.

Feldman, C. (2000). The sociability of meaning: Olson's interpretative community. In J. Astington (ed.), *Minds in the Making: Essays in honor of David R. Olson*. Oxford: Blackwell.

Flusser, V. (1992). *Die Schrift. Hat Schreiben Zukunft?* [Script. Does writing have a future?]. Frankfurt a.M.: Fischer. (Fischer Wissenschaft, 10906.)

François, E. (1989). Alphabetisierung und Lesefähigkeit in Frankreich und Deutschland um 1800 [Alphabetization in France and Germany and the development of true reading capability]. In H. Berding, E. François, and H.-P. Ullmann (eds.), *Deutschland und Frankreich im Zeitalter der Französischen Revolution*. Frankfurt a.M.: Suhrkamp.

Freire, P. and Macedo, D. (1987). *Literacy: Reading the word and the world*. South Hadley: Bergin and Garvey.

Giese, H. W. (1993). "Geschriebene Sprache" 1981–1991. Eine Zusammenstellung von Arbeiten der Studiengruppe "Geschriebene Sprache" bei der Werner Reimers Stiftung, Bad Homburg [A report by the research group "Written Language" at the Werner Reimers Foundation, 1981–91]. In J. Baurmann, H. Günther, and U. Knoop (eds.),

Homo scribens. Perspektiven der Schriftlichkeitsforschung. Tübingen: Max Niemeyer. (Germanistische Linguistik no. 134.)

Giesecke, M. and Elwert, G (1982). Literacy and emancipation – Conditions of the literary process in two cultural-revolutionary movements (16th Century Germany and 20th Century Bénin). Paper given at the World Congress of Sociology, Universität Bielefeld, Sociology of Development Research Center. (Working Paper no. 26.)

Giesecke, M. (1992). "Rezepte" im Mittelalter und in der Neuzeit. Der Funktionswandel eines Informationsmediums [Recipes in the Middle Ages and in early modern history: The changing functions of a specific media]. In Giesecke, 1992 (see the entry below).

Giesecke, M. (1992). *Sinnenwandel, Sprachwandel, Kulturwandel: Studien zur Vorgeschichte der Informationsgesellschaft* [Desire changes, language changes, culture changes: Studies in the prehistory of the information society]. Frankfurt a.M.: Suhrkamp.

Ginzburg, C. (1982). *The Cheese and the Worms: The cosmos of a sixteenth-century miller.* Markham: Penguin.

Gläss, B. (ed.) (1990). *Alphabetisierung in Industriestaaten? Europäische Probleme beim Umgang mit den Kulturtechniken Lesen und Schreiben* [Problems of alphabetization in the industrial countries of Europe], 2nd edn. Bonn: Deutsche UNESCO-Kommission.

Glück, H. (1987). *Schrift und Schriftlichkeit. Eine sprach- und kulturwissenschaftliche Studie* [Script and literacy. A study in linguistics and the humanities]. Stuttgart: Metzler.

Goody, J. (1968). Introduction. In J. Goody (ed.), *Literacy in Traditional Societies.* Cambridge: Cambridge University Press.

Goody, J. (1986). *The Logic of Writing and the Organization of Society.* Cambridge: Cambridge University Press.

Goody, J. and Watt, I. (1968). The consequences of literacy. In J. Goody (ed.), *Literacy in Traditional Societies.* Cambridge: Cambridge University Press.

Goudsblom, J. (1992). *Fire and Civilisation.* London: Penguin.

Graff, H. J. (1981). *Literacy and Social Development in the West: A reader.* Cambridge: Cambridge University Press.

Graff, H. J. (1996). The persisting power and costs of the literacy myth. *Literacy Across the Curriculum,* 12(2): 4–5.

Grillo, R. (1989). Anthropology, language, politics. In R. Grillo (ed.), *Social Anthropology and the Politics of Language.* Cambridge: Cambridge University Press.

Günther, H. and Ludwig, O. (eds.) (1994). *Schrift und Schriftlichkeit. Writing and its Use. Ein interdisziplinäres Handbuch internationaler Forschung* [Script and literacy. Writing and its use. A handbook of interdisciplinary and international research]. Berlin: de Gruyter.

Haggis, S. (1992). *Education for All: Purpose and context.* Paris: UNESCO.

Harman, D. (1976). Nonformal education and development. In D. Harman (ed.), *Expanding Recurrent and Nonformal Education.* San Francisco: Jossey-Bass.

Havelock, E. (1963). *Preface to Plato.* Cambridge, Mass.: Harvard University Press.

Heath, S. B. (1983). *Ways with Words: Language, life and work in communities and classrooms.* Cambridge: Cambridge University Press.

Hirsch, E. D., Jr., et al. (1988). *The Dictionary of Cultural Literacy: What every American needs to know.* Boston: Houghton Mifflin.

Hladczuk, J., Eller, W., and Hladczuk, S. (1990). *General Issues in Literacy/illiteracy: A bibliography.* New York/Westport/London: Greenwood Press.

Homann, K. (1995). *Gewinnmaximierung und Kooperation – eine ordnungstheoretische Reflexion* [Maximization of profits or altruism? Some thoughts on state and society]. Kiel: Institut für Weltwirtschaft.

Hymes, D. (1974). *Foundations in Sociolinguistics: An ethnographic approach.* Philadelphia: University of Pennsylvania Press.

Illich, I. (1992). A plea for research on lay literacy. In I. Illich (ed.), *In the Mirror of the Past: Lectures and addresses (1978–1990).* Special guest lecture at the American Education Research Association General Assembly, San Francisco, Aug. 1986. New York/London: Marion Boyars.

Illich, I. and Sanders, B. (1988). *ABC: The alphabetization of the popular mind.* San Francisco: North Point Press.

Imhof, K. and Romano, G. (1996). *Die Diskontinuität der Moderne. Zur Theorie des sozialen Wandels* [The discontinuities of the modern age. A theory of social change]. Frankfurt/New York: Campus.

Innis, H. (1951). *The Bias of Communication: Introduction by Marshall McLuhan.* Toronto: University of Toronto Press.

Jackson, H. (1915). On the nature of the duality of the brain [1874]. *Brain* 38: 80–103

Jones, S. (1995). The practice(s) of literacy. In Organization for Economic Cooperation and Development (ed.), *Literacy, Economy and Society: Results of the first International Adult Literacy Survey (IALS).* Paris/Ottawa: OECD.

Kirsch, I., et al. (1993). *Adult Literacy in America.* Washington, DC: Dept. of Education.

Kirsch, I. and Jungeblut, A. (1986). *Literacy: Profiles of America's young adults. Final report of the National Assessment of Educational Progress.* Princeton: Educational Testing Service.

Kocka, J. (1995). Das europäische Muster und der deutsche Fall [The European Pattern of middle-class lifestyles and the German case]. In J. Kocka (ed.), *Bürgertum im 19. Jahrhundert. Deutschland im europäischen Vergleich. Eine Auswahl,* vol.1. Göttingen: Vandenhoeck and Ruprecht.

Koselleck, R. (1969). *Kritik und Krise. Ein Beitrag zur Pathogenese der bürgerlichen Welt* [Crisis in society and social criticism], 2nd edn. Freiburg/München: K. Alber.

Kozol, J. (1985). *Illiterate America.* Garden City: Anchor Press/Doubleday.

Kullmann, W. and Reichel, M. (ed.) (1990). *Der Übergang von der Mündlichkeit zur Literatur bei den Griechen* [The transition from orality to literature in Ancient Greek history]. Verhandlungen des Symposiums vom 11.–14.10, Tübingen: Narr.

Latour, B. and Woolgar, S. (1986). *Laboratory Life: The construction of scientific facts.* Princeton: Princeton University Press.

Lefevre, L. and Martin, H.-J. (1976). *The Coming of the Book.* London: New Left Books.

Lerner, D. (1958). *The Passing of Traditional Society: Modernizing the Middle East.* Glencoe, Ill.: The Free Press.

Leschinsky, A. and Roeder, P. M. (1983). *Schule im historischen Prozeß. Zum Wechselverhältnis von institutioneller Erziehung und gesellschaftlicher Entwicklung* [The history of elementary schools in nineteenth-century Germany]. Frankfurt a.M./Berlin/ Wien: Klett-Cotta.

Lévi-Strauss, C. (1974). *Tristes Tropiques,* trans. John and Doreen Weightman. New York: Atheneum.

Lilley, S. (1966). *Men, Machines and History.* New York: International Publishers.

Lockheed, M. E. and Verspoor, A. M. (1990). *Improving Primary Education in Developing Countries: A review of policy options*. Draft prep. for limited distribution to the participants at the World Conference on Education for All, Bangkok, March 5–9, Washington, DC: The World Bank.

Luria, A. R. (1976). *Cognitive Development: Its cultural and social foundations*. Cambridge: Cambridge University Press.

Lüsebrink, H.-J. (1990). *Schrift, Buch und Lektüre in der französischsprachigen Literatur Afrikas: Zur Wahrnehmung und Funktion von Schriftlichkeit und Buchlektüre in einem kulturellen Epochenumbruch der Neuzeit* [Reading and literacy in francophone Africa]. Tübingen: Niemeyer.

Markoff, J. (1986). Literacy and revolt: Some empirical notes on 1789 in France. *American Journal of Sociology* 92(2): 323–49.

McKitterick, R. (1990). Introduction. In R. McKitterick (ed.), *The Uses of Literacy in Early Mediaeval Europe*. Cambridge: Cambridge University Press.

McLuhan, M. (1962). *The Gutenberg Galaxy: The making of typographic man*. Toronto: University of Toronto Press.

Morsy, Z. (1994). Introduction. In Z. Morsy and International Bureau of Education (eds.), *The Challenge of Illiteracy: From reflection to action*. New York/London: Garland.

Müller, J. (1991). Alphabetisierung im Rahmen des integrierten Grundbildungsansatzes der UNESCO [Alphabetization on the basis of UNESCO's approach on integrated basic education]. In I. Neu-Altenheimer and B. Sandhaas (eds.), *Grundbildung. UNESCO-Schwerpunkt der neunziger Jahre*, Bonn: Deutsche UNESCO-Kommission.

Müller, J. (1996). *Literacy and Non-formal (Basic) Education – Still a donor priority?* Education for Development, Occasional Papers; Series I, no. 3. London: Education For Development.

Nascimento, G. (1990). *Illiteracy in Figures*. Geneva: UNESCO, IBE.

Nissen, H. J., Damerow, P., and Englund, R. K. (1991). *Frühe Schrift und Techniken der Wirtschaftsverwaltung im alten Vorderen Orient. Informationsspeicherung und -verarbeitung vor 5000 Jahren* [The role of early script in the management of agriculture in the advanced civilizations of Mesopotamia]. Bad Salzdethfurt: Franzbecker.

North, D. C. and Thomas, R. P. (1973). *The Rise of the Western World: A new economic history*. New York/Cambridge: Cambridge University Press.

Olson, D. R. (1977). From utterance to text: The bias of language in speech and writing. *Harvard Educational Review* 47(3): 257–81.

Olson, D. R. (1991). Literacy and objectivity: The rise of modern science. In D. R. Olson and N. Torrance (eds.), *Literacy and Orality*. Cambridge: Cambridge University Press.

Olson, D. R. (1994). *The World on Paper: The conceptual and cognitive implications of writing and reading*. Cambridge: Cambridge University Press.

Olson, D. R. and Torrance, N. (1991). Introduction. In D. R. Olson and N. Torrance (eds.), *Literacy and Orality*. Cambridge: Cambridge University Press.

Ong, W. J. (1982). *Orality and Literacy: The technologizing of the word*. London: Methuen.

OECD (ed.) (1995). *Literacy, Economy and Society: Results of the first International Adult Literacy Survey* [IALS]. Paris/Ottawa: OECD.

Ouane, A. (1996). *Literacy for the Twenty-first Century: The future of literacy and literacy of the future*. Hamburg: UNESCO Institute for Education.

Oxenham, J. (1980). *Literacy: Writing, reading and social organization*. London: Routledge and Kegan Paul.

Parsons, T. and Platt, G. M. (1974). *The American University*, 2nd edn. Cambridge, Mass.: Harvard University Press.

Pike, K. (1967). *Language in Relation to a Unified Theory of the Structure of Human Behavior*, 2nd edn. Den Haag/Paris: Mouton.

Postman, N. (1982). *The Disappearance of Childhood*. New York: Delacorte.

Probst, P. (1992). *Schrift, Staat und symbolisches Kapital bei den Wimbumi: Ein ethnographischer Bericht aus dem Grasland von Kamerun* [Script, the state and symbolic capital in Wimbuni society. An ethnographic report from the grasslands of Cameroon]. Münster/Hamburg: LIT.

Raible, W. (ed.) (1998). *Medienwechsel. Erträge aus zwölf Jahren Forschung zum Thema "Mündlichkeit" und "Schriftlichkeit"* [Twelve years of research on orality and literacy]. Tübingen: Gunter Narr.

Reh, M. (1981). Sprache und Gesellschaft [Language and society]. In B. Heine et al. (eds.), *Die Sprachen Afrikas*. Hamburg: Buske.

Rix, H. (1992). Thesen zum Ursprung der Runen [On the origin of the runes]. In L. Aigner-Foresti (ed.), *Etrusker nördlich von Etrurien*, Akten des Symposions von Wien – Schloß Neuwaldegg, 2–5 Okt. 1989, Wien: Verlag der Österreichischen Akademie der Wissenschaften.

Rogers, A. (1993). The world crisis in adult education: A case study from literacy. *Compare*, 23: S.159–75.

Rostow, W.W. (1956). The take-off into self-sustained growth. *The Economic Journal* 66: 25–48.

Ryan, J. (1981). Analphabetentum – eine globale Herausforderung [Illiteracy – a global challenge]. In F. Drecoll and U. Müller (eds.), *Für ein Recht auf Lesen. Analphabetismus in der Bundesrepublik Deutschland*. Frankfurt a.M./Berlin(West)/München: M. Diesterweg.

Saenger, P. (1982). Silent reading: Its impact on late medieval script and society. *Viator* 13: 367–414.

Scheerer, E. (ed.) (1990). *Domains of Mental Functioning: Attempts at a synthesis*. Based on a conference at the Center for Interdisciplinary Studies. Berlin: Springer.

Scheerer, E. (1993). Mündlichkeit und Schriftlichkeit – Implikationen für die Modellierung kognitiver Prozesse [Orality and literacy. On the modeling of cognitive processes]. In J. Baurmann, H. Günther, and U. Knoop (eds.), *Homo scribens. Perspektiven der Schriftlichkeitsforschung*. Tübingen: Max Niemeyer.

Schenda, R. (1970). *Volk ohne Buch. Studien zur Sozialgeschichte der populären Lesestoffe 1170–1910* [A people wothout books. Studies in the social history of popular reading, 1170–1910]. Frankfurt a.M.: Klostermann. (Studien zur Philosophie und Literatur des 19. Jahrhunderts; 5)

Schlaffer, H. (1986). Einleitung. Historische Bedingungen der Erkenntnis über Schriftkultur [The historical fundamentals of literate cultures]. In J. Goody et al. (eds.), *Entstehung und Folgen der Schriftkultur*. Frankfurt a.M.: Suhrkamp.

Schlieben-Lange, B. (1983). Schriftlichkeit und Mündlichkeit in der französischen Revolution [Literacy and orality in the French Revolution]. In A. Assmann, J. Assmann, and C. Hardmeier (eds.), *Schrift und Gedächtnis. Beiträge zur Archäologie der literarischen Kommunikation*. München: Fink.

Schmandt-Besserat, D. (1978). The earliest precursor of writing. *Scientific American* 240(6): 38–47.

Schwöbel, H. (1982). *Erziehung zur Überwindung von Unterentwicklung. Curriculumentwicklung emanzipatorischer Alphabetisierung und Grunderziehung zwischen Tradition und Moderne. Das Beispiel Somalia* [Education to overcome underdevelopment: Creating a curriculum for alphabetization towards emancipation. Basic education between tradition and modernity (the case of Somalia)]. Frankfurt a.M.: Verlag.

Scribner, S. and Cole, M. (1981). *The Psychology of Literacy*. Cambridge, Mass.: Harvard University Press.

Selznick, P. (1992). *The Moral Commonwealth: Social theory and the promise of community*. Berkeley: University of California Press.

Siegenthaler, H. (1993). *Regelvertrauen, Prosperität und Krisen: die Ungleichmäßigkeit wirtschaftlicher und sozialer Entwicklung als Ergebnis individuellen Handelns und sozialen Lernens* [Agency and the confidence in predictability. Economic prosperity, crises, and uneven social change]. Tübingen: J. C. B. Mohr (Paul Siebeck).

Stock, B. (1983). *The Implications of Literacy: Written language and models of interpretation in the eleventh and twelfth centuries*. Princeton: Princeton University Press.

Stone, L. (1969). Literacy and education in England, 1640–1900. *Past and Present* 42.

Street, B. V. (1987). Literacy and social change: The significance of social context in the development of literacy programmes. In D. A. Wagner (ed.), *The Future of Literacy in a Changing World*. New York: Pergamon.

Street, B. V. (1990). *Cultural Meanings of Literacy*. Geneva: UNESCO, IBE.

Street, B. V. (1993). Introduction: The new literacy studies. In B. Street (ed.), *Cross-cultural Approaches to Literacy*. Cambridge: Cambridge University Press.

Street, B. V. (1994). Cross-cultural perspectives on literacy. In J. Maybin (ed.), *Language and Literature in Social Practice*. Milton Keynes: the Open University.

Triebel, A. (1997). *Cognitive and Societal Development and Literacy*. Bonn: German Foundation for International Development.

UNESCO/UNDP (ed.) (1976). The experimental world literacy programme. Paris: UNESCO.

van Lancker, D. (1987). Non-propositional speech: Neurolinguistic studies. In A. W. Ellis (ed.), *Progress in the Psychology of Language*, vol. 3. Hillsdale, NJ: Lawrence Erlbaum.

Venezky, R., Kaestle, C. F., and Sum, A. M. (1987). *The Subtle Danger: Reflections on the literacy abilities of America's young adults*. Princeton: Educational Testing Service.

Vollrath, H. (1979). Gesetzgebung und Schriftlichkeit: Das Beispiel der angelsächsischen Gesetze [Legislation and literacy. Law in the English-speaking world]. *Historisches Jahrbuch* 99: 28–54.

Wagner, D. A. (1987). Literacy futures: Five common problems from industrialized and developing countries. In D. A. Wagner (ed.), *The Future of Literacy in a Changing World*. Oxford: Pergamon.

Wagner, D. A. (1990). Literacy assessment in the Third World: An overview and proposed schema for survey use. *Comparative Education Review* 33: 112–38.

Wagner, D. A. (1991). Literacy as culture: Emic and etic perspectives. In E. M. Jennings and A. C. Purves (eds.), *Literate Systems and Individual Lives*. Albany: State University of New York Press.

Wagner, D. A. (1995). Literacy and development: Rationales, myths, innovations, and future directions. *International Journal of Educational Development* 15(4): 341–62.

Weber, M. (1920). Die protestantische Ethik und der Geist des Kapitalismus [The protestant ethic and the spirit of capitalism]. In M. Weber (ed.), *Gesammelte Aufsätze zur Religionssoziologie*. Tübingen: Mohr.

Wehler, H.-U. (1987). *Deutsche Gasellschaftsgeschichte*, vol. 2 [The History of German Society]. Munchen: Beck.

Weltentwicklungsbericht. Entwicklung durch Wissen. Mit ausgewählten Kennzahlen der Weltentwicklung 1998/9. Frankfurt: Frankfurter Allgemeine Zeitung 1999 [World Development Report 1998/9. Knowledge for Development, ed. by the World Bank, Oxford: Oxford University Press, 1998/9].

Wiegelmann, U. (1998). *Alphabetisierung und Grundbildung in Senegal* [Alphabetization and Basic Education in Senegal]. Ein empirischer Vergleich zwischen modernen und traditionellen Bildungsgängen und Schulen. Münster: IKO.

Winterowd, W. R. (1989). *The Culture and Politics of Literacy*. Oxford: Oxford University Press.

World Bank (ed.) (1995). *Priorities and Strategies*. Washington, DC: the World Bank.

World Conference on Education for All (1990). *Final Report*, New York: World Declaration on Education for All and Framework for Action to Meet Basic Learning Needs, Adopted by the World Conference on Education for All . . . Jomtien . . ., edited by the Inter-Agency Commission (UNDP, UNESCO, UNICEF, WORLD BANK). New York: UNICEF House.

World Symposium on Family Literacy (1995). *Final Report*, 3–5 Oct. 1994. Paris: UNESCO.

Zboray, R. J. (1993). *A Fictive People: Antebellum economic development and the American reading public*. New York/Oxford: Oxford University Press.

Chapter 3

Societal Literacy: Writing Culture and Development

Georg Elwert

Literacy continues to be defined as one of the most important goals of development. On the other hand there can be no doubt that no other developmental goal has a comparable record of failure. Literacy campaigns in those least developed countries which had no widespread tradition of written laws and/or holy books routinely failed (Wagner, 1995). Conversely, in some contexts – as in Asian countries – where a literate tradition and administration existed, the spread of writing increased.

Judging the success of literacy campaigns is not a straightforward matter. One criterion is that people remain literate even 10 years after the last campaign. It is only in respect of this last criterion that we can declare most literacy campaigns as failures.

The new criterion for judging adult literacy, the one advanced herein, is even more demanding. Literacy, herein defined as societal literacy, is associated with basic social transformations (cf. for similar approaches: Goody, 1986; Prinsloo & Breier, 1996; Street, 1995; Triebel, 1997). There are three such social transformations which have to come into the foreground: First, respect and control of social norms including respect of laws, rules of associations, and contracts; this is most important especially in the sector of a market economy where contracts have to be respected. Second, societal literacy requires the diffusion of technical knowledge. And third, it requires a society's communication about itself, which includes the development of political discourse. The attainment of these goals shall be defined as the development of societal literacy or written culture.

It is the thesis of this chapter that only the development of a writing culture stabilizes the use of literate tools. If a society does not aim at the ambitious goal of societal literacy, basic literacy will never be stabilized.

The Limitations of Functional Literacy

New proposals for adult literacy tend to repeat the old ones; in the initial phases of a program it is the community or social impact which is sought. Yet there has been a conceptual shift from a focus on basic literacy, the ability to read and write, to a focus on functional, that is, useful, literacy. When programs for the development of literacy concentrate primarily upon the communication of one body or type of information, they may be termed programs for functional literacy. This includes functional literacy in the sense employed by UNESCO (1973), which combines literacy with instruction in simple technical skills, especially in agriculture. This concept can, however, be applied as well to the literacy of religious education which has the purpose of training people in order to be able to read a standard set of texts. Such functional literacy is not equivalent to societal literacy.

Functional literacy programs succeed with only a minority of around 10 percent of the former pupils if tested after a longer period. This applies to the pupils of Islamic schools as well as to the pupils of UNESCO functional literacy campaigns. This contrasts sharply with the historical evidence of those countries which attained a general literacy with a general writing culture. Historically, there have been at least four functional fields of communication which provided a motive for written communication (cf. Triebel, 1997). The first is moral teaching involving religious texts or normative texts. Second is technical information, from information on products to information about procedures for agriculture or health. Third is the normative use of documents for the affirmation and control of contracts, including marriage contracts, land registers, and credit letters. Finally, one may also acknowledge the importance of emotionally binding texts such as fiction or love letters. The number of well-documented cases is, however, limited.

It should, however, be clear that at least three of these forms of communication had to be developed concomitantly in order to create the broad front needed to overrun "stubborn illiteracy." That this is so, can be explained by anthropological studies which show the high efficiency of oral culture (Malinowski, 1923; Powdermaker, 1933; Elwert, 1986). The development of *literate* culture has to be viewed as in competition with a highly performing, well-integrated, and highly complex oral system of communication. Oral culture is very difficult to emulate in *literate* culture.

The strengths of oral culture are several. First, there are institutions guaranteeing the validity of information. Information can be checked by one's own experience and by communal discourse. Second, communication takes place on several channels in parallel: the words are accompanied by gesture, mimes, varied speed, varied pitch, and intonation. Third, oral communication can easily carry several meanings simultaneously: text, ironic subtext, and emotional appeal. Fourth, oral communication is parsimonious: a direct physical demonstration is more precise than words. Thus many things do not need specific words. The concepts are saved as visual or sensual knowledge and are repro-duced by deictic gestures. The shared context of speaker and audience contri-butes to parsimony and unambiguity. If the context is unambiguously defined, then words can be given a specific sense in relation to this very situation. Thus fewer words are needed, but they are much more often relational (changing sense according to context) and polysemic (loaded with several meanings) than in literate languages.

Finally, oral dialogue allows for direct reference. One does not have to browse through a bulk of paper to get access to the information sought for; neither does one have to watch hours of radio or TV broadcast (which are orally transmitted *literate* communication). The lack of this possibility of direct reference causes literate languages to include the references. This created or expanded a specific element of syntax: the hypotaxis. Oral language can do without this complica-tion.

To sum up. Oral communication is less costly, less complicated, it can make better use of relational meanings (defined by context), it can use direct reference in the dialogue as a very parsimonious means of information transfer, it produces information fit for direct absorption by memory, it can use personal presence as a means for validation and creation of trustworthiness. *Literate* culture, seen from the perspective of a functioning oral culture, is very complicated, clumsy, untrustworthy and elitist.

Does Writing Alone Introduce an Intellectual Transformation or Does it Require a Specific Institutional Environment?

Havelock (1963) and Ong (1980; see Glück, 1987 for a critique) argue that the development of logical reasoning, of structurally complex intellectual systems and the differentiation between power discourse and truth-seeking discourse, is linked to literacy. There are many cases, beginning with Greek culture, which are wonderful illustrations of this thesis. But since this is a general statement we should rather look for possible falsifications than for illustrations. And there are falsifications. There are many cases where writing is used without producing the social consequences often associated with it (Scribner & Cole, 1981). There is the Tuareq culture in the Sahara where writing is used for love letters and street signs (writings on rocks in order to show the way) (Renell of Rodd, 1926); there was the culture of Easter Islands and there were many African cultures where writing was continuously translated by a minority of specialists for just one religious or political purpose; there are cases of a so-called Islamic decadence where, for example, in the Marabu system of north Africa, religious authorities use writing only as a means for legitimation (Elwert, 1987a, 1988) – they use their personal authority in order to create a trustworthiness which goes beyond the text, and in some cases openly contradict the text, the Holy Koran, they are reciting. Writing may even be reduced to the role of pure symbolic reference to transcendental or political power excluding any communication (Goody,

1968; Probst, 1990). The Koran verse may be choked but not read (Lambek, 1996).

If the introduction of writing in some contexts is followed by the development of flourishing markets, powerful states, or fertile science and in other contexts not, then there must be a second factor in the environment which causes this difference. In older theories the climate and genetic factors were held to be responsible. Both claims, however, have been disproven. In order to search for this environmental factor we compared two extremely different fields of empirical research as distant in time and space as sixteenth-century Germany and twentieth-century west African Bénin (Elwert & Giesecke, 1983). In both cases it appeared that the presence or absence of specific institutions made a difference. Institutions can create frames of reference, they can stabilize meanings, and they can thus disable idiosyncratic communication. That is, they can generalize meaning, understanding, and trustworthiness. Institutions channel the stream of communication into conventional forms, creating a societal embedding for the multiple uses of literacy.

The argument concerning the institutional embedding of literacy is related to similar arguments concerning the functioning of markets (Elwert, 1987b). Those markets which privilege investment into means of production seem to be characterized by institutions guaranteeing the fulfilling of contracts. This environment itself is not organized as a market but as a moral economy. An analogy is, however, not a sufficient intellectual argument.

The argument is, that there is a need for institutions which do something for and about writing, more so than just increase the use of writing.

Societal Conditions for Literate Culture

Standard form

There are prominent cases where the success of literacy is consecutive to the development of standardizing and prestige-conferring state institutions, such as the "Académie Française" for the French language. There are, however, other cases such as the expansion of the English language that show us that such a state-organized institution is not a *conditio sine qua non*. The forces of the market together with the prestige system can create alternative and equally powerful institutional forms. The King James Bible and later the daily newspaper *The Times* had standardizing effects equal to those imposed by the French Academy, but did so more flexibly. What was achieved in both cases was a standardization of the alphabet, orthography, and meaning and interpretation.

Trustworthiness

Even more important than standardization seems to be trustworthiness as a requirement for literate culture. If we compare the success or failure of some subcultures in differentiated societies, we can find clear grounds for distinguishing the development or nondevelopment of a writing culture. In the Middle Ages in Europe the Jewish subculture was one which created within itself a very dense form of social control including a respect for contracts and testaments. It is not surprising that, within this subculture, literacy was much more widespread than among the majority population. This is not the only subculture using special writing. Another had been the Eastern Christians (the "people of Mosul"), who played an analogous role to that of the Jews but whose institutional network was weaker. In Black Africa today we find Islamic minorities actively reading the Koran, just like the Lebanese or Haussa traders in west Africa or Bible-reading Christian minorities such as the Kitawala in southern Africa, who all operate in a "heathen" environment and who respect contracts among themselves just as they respect the Holy Word.

Technological development requires textual communities. How far is techno-logical development connected to literacy? There is a level of technology that works with an illiterate workforce – repair shops in African cities provide evidence for that. A look at orally transmitted local knowledge (Elwert & Séhouéto, 1999) can tell us something about the conditions for technological development. In any system, oral or written, there is a need for feedback. Information has to be controlled for its validity. Valid sources of information have to be reinforced and invalid ones have to be dismissed. Knowledgable persons, experts in their local environment, never rely only upon tradition; they all operate these control and selection processes. If one can no longer determine whether promised technical information is really more accurate – and that is the case in some written and printed communication – then chains of oral communication have to assure that the meaning of concepts has not been altered in the process of transmission. This is relatively easy to achieve in local communication where the empirical references are "at hand." Once we enter into written communication with partners we do not know and who do not know us, certainty of meaning and conceptual stability become a major problem (Johns, 1998). This problem is aggravated if a specialized jargon is needed which is locally mastered only by few people, or just one. Such specialized languages require for their stabilization a "community of communication" or a "textual community" (Olson, 1994; Stock, 1983) which is continuously checking the language for its consistency and assessing conceptual innovations. These func-tions of control, stabilization, and change require that such a "community" take an institutional form. Institutions of reading and research and professional organizations as well as courts of law can provide for this. They create an "embedding" (Elwert, 1987a) for these specialized segments of written language.

There is a need for institutions which control validity. To eliminate error and lies, a continuous process of selection must be available for two reasons. First, material interest and the quest for reputation, the two major sources for new discoveries, work against the admission of error and disinformation. Secondly, the truth of yesterday may become today's error in the light of new perspectives and new information. To select positively in favor of better information so as to produce an increase of knowledge under these conditions is therefore a rather paradoxical enterprise (Luhmann, 1984). It requires a self-organizing institutional net, such as universities and academies, which receives prestige and reputation from the society and which distributes and creates further prestige while enhancing the quality of information. This processing of information has to be shielded from interference by power relations. If a power-holder can make false true, credibility decreases. This need for an institutional embedding of technological information follows as well from linguistic imperatives. If every expert communicates in his/her private language, the medium loses its transport capacity. However, because of the generative linguistic capacity of human beings, we have to stress the social factors: if one cannot trust technical norms, if vanity and power interests protect disinformation, if people get their knowledge from sources in a local environment that they personally control – or from a charismatic leader whom they trust – instead of relying upon information from an anonymous world, the institutional order needed as an infrastructure for a literate society will fail to develop.

The Sandwich Structure of Efficient Technological Communication

So far this chapter's arguments might be read as if it were merely a transition from oral to written communication that is needed for economic technological development. Although there is a need to elaborate a technical written language in order to stabilize it, it is important to underline that a change of the channel of communication is not at all sufficient for economic-cum-technological development. In a recent study we contrasted the diffusion of agricultural knowledge in west African Bénin and western Europe (Elwert & Séhouéto, 1999). The factors which make the difference between rapid and slow development of agricultural knowledge are not only the use of writing but also specialization, feedback, and a non-economic motivation. Among the five factors which are partially or totally absent in the rural west African context, are those relating to institutions, motivation, and specialization which require the social organization of communication in both oral and written forms. These factors are made productive through an intertwining of oral and written communication.

Specialization: This implies not only the selective accumulation of knowledge but also the development of special registers of language able to cover fine details of the production process. Even producers who specialize in a minority product in the respective region require a special set of concepts. It is, therefore, a problem if diverging directions or specialization cause producers to be in a minority in a region. Written communication can link these minorities and allow them to improve their specialist language and accumulate knowledge.

Feedback structures: Positive feedback is no problem in oral communication. It is even required to keep social relations going. However, the selection of knowledge also requires negative feedback. The plant breeder should know it, if a new seed does not grow. Only special social relations allow for this. Under certain conditions written communication can pave the way for negative feedback. Wrong information can be corrected by a letter to the editor, by the publication of scientific research, and by reports about failure in distant markets. Indirect feedback works as well in oral as in written communication. Irrelevant or misleading information reduces the audience for oral presentations or the market for respective publications.

Writing is a powerful means for storing information over time and for making it accessible to isolated individuals who specialize in a field not covered by other people in the same locality. The modernization of European agriculture is linked to published books by Estienne (1567), Coler (1665), and Thaer (1810–12) which compared methods from different regions of Europe.

In the case of western Europe the strength of oral and written communication is combined. In an innovative process one can observe chains of written invitations to visits on the farm site, oral discussions there, written reports about these discussions, oral information about a report's contents which leads other people to read it, letters between peasants and owners, phone calls, etc. (Box, 1986; Elwert, 1988). In this sandwich structure it is orality which provides for the quick selection, for rapid feedback, and for the specification of information in dialogue. The contribution of written communication is the stabilization of information and the capacity to make it available over long distances at a low price.

Motivation by commercial and prestige interests combined: That information can have a market value is evident. This is the basis for information media. It is much less well known that the Western idea of "publication" does not reflect a pure market logic for publishing new ideas and sharing them with the public. The prevalent individual motive is the acquisition of prestige. Someone who helps other people, someone who is an explorer or inventor, earns a high reputation. The rewards for sharing information can, therefore, partially offset the rewards for monopolizing information for economic advantage. The goal of building a reputation frequently causes the sharing of knowledge where individual motives might lead to hoarding and secrecy.

Any writing culture requires introduction, explanation, and comment in oral form. Written communication provides for further oral communication. It gives new content to oral communication. Some of this oral communication may be informal, but some requires new organized forms. Any elaborate writing culture has "parascriptural" oral communication as one of its firmly organized elements (Elwert, 1987a, 1988; Horowitz, in preparation).

The Need for Elaborated Languages and Embedding Institutions

So far my arguments seem to be geared only towards institutions, such as the norm-creating bodies or patent offices as described by Weber (1922). These are, indeed, very important means for making the use of writing consequential. But much more important and much more general is the need for a language which can effectively convey technical information. This capacity is not something natural which could be found in every language. The diffusion of technical information on a large scale is only possible with a language defined by the parameters of context-indifference, differentiation, and internal referencing, which differs from oral language. This language requires some degree of standardization (something which can be acquired through regulating institutions or the selective force of markets). Its basic feature has to be an *elaborated code* which transforms logical thinking into the conditional and causal clauses of language (Giesecke, 1992; Elwert, 1987a; see also Bruner & Olson, 1974; Bernstein, 1964).

There should be no doubt that every population of this world has the same capacity for logical reasoning. The old argument that illiterate groups have a less logical way of reasoning has been invalidated (Elwert & Séhouéto, 1999; Scribner & Cole, 1981; Triebel, 1997). Older studies were flawed by not taking into account the silence of politeness when confronted with tests and the differences in the cultural encoding of categorization and logic. Anthropologists can point out both historical and contemporary examples of people who orally develop impressive logical arguments. But oral language transports this logical information through means of dialogue rather than through hypotaxis. Hypotaxis means that there are part-sentences which answer an argument potentially related to the main sentence. They are linked by a logical clause, such as in the case of "if–then" arguments. This contrasts with the "then-and-then-and-then" strings of argument that are predominant in narrative in oral culture. Dialogue is more efficient in the direct transmission of logical arguments. Hypotactical sentences are, however, easier to reproduce and transport information at lesser expense through chains of communication, in the absence of dialogue with persons present.

Another requirement is that information becomes freed of the context in which it was given: it has to be context indifferent. In oral communication there is seldom a need to use precise spatial arguments because one can use one's index finger to point at something; the reference to the actual context is an integral part of most arguments and explications. In *literate* cultures this has to be changed. Words to differentiate relative positions and directions of movement have to be developed (diagonally behind, cylindrical spiral, etc.) and their meanings have to be standardized.

Every human being has knowledge of what one "has in front of his eyes" or what one has a "grip" on but cannot express in words. We call it visual (or iconic) and motoric (or enactive) knowledge (Bruner & Olson, 1974). This knowledge can be transformed into words. But in an oral culture there is no need for it; dialogue and visual demonstration are less onerous, more precise, and allow for feedback. Communication with absent persons by means of writing requires that this knowledge be translated into words. Visual and motoric knowledge has to be transformed to verbal knowledge. Therefore language has to be extended and these extensions or elaborations have to be standardized. Language is enriched especially by concepts for space, number, and logic which are basic for technical communication. This does not make people more "intelligent." But intelligence is more easily shared.

Every language has the capacity to produce such an elaborate code. But in some cases the use of such an elaborate code is so clumsy that it automatically becomes ridiculous (Elwert, 1987a). Thus there is a need for institutions which convey prestige to this use of an elaborate code and which produce some degree of standardization and training for these special means of communication. Religious institutions (churches, mosques, synagogues, convents, temples), institutions for higher learning (special schools, universities, academies), or established media institutions (elite newspapers, literary societies) are such "parascriptural" institutions constructed around the written language. In these institutional contexts people have to learn to use the language of writing in its oral form!

Literacy research in the majority of cases concentrated on didactics, had a short-term perspective, and paid little attention to its institutional contexts. But there are some very explicit studies of literate cultures which show that, without such embedding institutions, elaborate codes of language are unable to exist (Elwert, 1987a; Giesecke, 1994; Triebel, 1997). Standardizing written language, teaching it, and attributing prestige to its use and teaching are second-order activities which are not themselves byproducts of writing. These activities which make the use of writing efficient require an institutional framework. Functional literacy alone – without the development and institutional stabilization of the elaborate code of written language – can, in the long run, only create deception. Only a minority of people will adopt the new skill. Functional literacy cannot succeed in creating the "elaborate language," that is, the linguistic features associated with literate culture, nor cause them to be sedimented in the mental routines of the majority. The developmental dynamics of literacy is produced only if there is a specific institutional embedding.

Literacy with Societal Impact

It cannot be denied that most of the least-developed countries recurrently invite foreign donors to spend money on literacy programs, and sometimes even contribute some money from their own budgets devoted to this noble goal. These efforts serve to underline a declared wish for "development." But without a societal base there is no driving force to transform literacy into a self-sustaining activity (Brice-Heath, 1980; Goody, 1986; Humbert, 1975; Prinsloo & Breier, 1996; Street, 1996).

It is uncontroversial that literacy offers access to information. However, it is important to distinguish between individual and societal literacy. Informing an individual has an impact other than infusing information into the social system. Traditionally much attention has been focused on the opportunities for individuals to learn to read and write. But there is still a long way to go, and one strategy that should be emphasized is the development of a literate environment, and the transformative potential of literacy for society (Jung, 1998).

Here the idea of societal literacy is crucial. It is this kind of literacy that fosters social networking, makes the rule of law feasible, and formal education utilitarian. Societal literacy means that written communication is consequential in economic and power relations. The use of written communication and written language enhances the exchange of ideas and thus both individual and social creativity. It enhances the creation of a stable framework for the rapid circulation of information and for economic activity.

The rule of law and growing literacy rates are correlated. The rule of law requires the written text in order to create realms of foreseeablility, what we may call pre-vision spheres. Organization of family life – kinship, marriage, heritage, etc. – as well as economic activity – production and investment – profit from foreseeability. One knows what is forbidden and what is possible. The rule of law implies that the forgery of texts – including those of the laws themselves – is ruled out. Thus agreements and other forms of written communication with partners, including anonymous partners who cannot be controlled by personal presence, can have consequences. Such forms of communication include contracts, information on prices, patents, employment instructions, legal norms, etc.: the necessary tools for administering social life.

A serious problem for the development of societal literacy is constituted by a type of government and administration which we call a "command state" (Elwert, 1999). It resembles Max Weber's concept of a "patrimonial state" (Weber, 1922). In the command state present authority orally transmitted stands above written contracts, bylaws, laws, and the constitution. Demands to the bureaucracy find an answer only if one follows personally (or through friends, patrons, or clients) every administrative step. Orders given by someone no longer in power are invalid. Appeals to legal guarantees are valueless. Everything not formally authorized is potentially illegal. The administration may use written texts, but they have a practical meaning, only if they coincide with present authority or represent a consensus. Important economic transaction with the state is unlikely to be covered by a written form. This has important consequences. Without a receipt no one can control whether the money given to a policeman is a fine, a bribe, or a tribute to a disguised street robber. Without a land register, state administrators or their clients can bypass the mandates of the states and, in effect, transform land rights into floating power relations. In such societies, foreseeability, pre-vision realms, can only be created outside the state apparatus.

Literacy strategies aimed only at individuals do not evolve into sustained societal literacy. Individualized or restricted literacy does not create a demand for literacy in the whole society, nor create the social development that is hoped for. The few cases in which literacy campaigns have been successful indicate that for literacy to take root community involvement and community acceptance are required (Doronila, 1999; Humbert, 1975).

If information can reach anonymous persons, and if this is achieved at low cost by means of printing, it can have a strong effect not only on activity but also on the understanding of the society itself and its potentials. In itself this can produce unwanted consequences, such as the spreading of rumor and prejudice (cf. Glück, 1987, p. 157 on the concern for literacy in fascist Italy). If the increased density of information is perceived as chaotic, then any reduction of complexity – be it oversimplification, dogma, or prejudice – is welcome. Only if the validity of information can be checked by experience, if this check has a positive influence upon the market, and if there is normative control which sanctions false information, can written communication then create effects of societal learning and anticipation of the future. The ability of the society to gain information about itself is one of the main factors explaining the rapid social and economic change in industrial countries. In other words, a society which is not informed about itself cannot shape its future. Moreover, societal literacy is also a means to recover, systematize, and transform local or indigenous knowledge. The loose ends (Hirschman, 1958) of potentially productive, technical, and economic information can be linked.

One reason literacy campaigns often have failed is that they have been carried out without proper regard to the language and learning needs of the communities concerned. Literacy programmes advocating the use of one single "official" language in multilingual environments have so far produced little result, often at high cost. Research has consistently shown that learning to read and write in the mother tongue facilitates access to another written language (Goody, this volume; Reh, 1981, p. 544, 545; Geva & Ryan, 1993). Literacy in several languages in a multilingual environment allows for highly profitable forms of transfer: (1) the transfer of elaborate linguistic skills and forms from one language to another; (2) the transfer of writing skills from one language to another; (3) a transfer of local knowledge to wider contexts where it can be profitably applied. Justification of the maintenance of education systems which systematically exclude the use of the majority's vernacular languages, can no longer be ignored by political leaders. The intention to reserve access to the state apparatus and to some sectors of the economy for the "educated classes" (those trained in the school language) seems now to be the most plausible but unacknowledged explanation of much current educational policy. If literacy has neither a societal impact on the rule of law, nor the transformation of previous "local" knowledge, nor the making of markets, that is sufficient reason for most people to ignore literacy campaigns and to give up writing and reading. Maintaining literacy on the political agenda is, however, important for the image of governments and donors in order to show concern for development. But in such contexts, it is merely a symbol or an ornament. Given the high dropout rates and the limited societal impact, such functional, individualistic, or restricted literacy is both costly and ornamental.

Conclusion

One reason why adult literacy projects so often fail is that new literates find nothing relevant to read. Neither laws nor market prices nor health information can be obtained in one's own language. There is no literate environment (Elwert,

1997). Societal literacy implies the promotion of the written language, and this in turn requires the cultivation and development of language. This can be a long-term process. It takes time and institutional support. It also calls for continued provision of written material through markets. This literate environment cannot be created by simple decision. Without markets which give a positive feedback of relevant and reliable information it cannot stand. In addition, to make these texts meaningful a specific institutional setting providing feedback and control is required.

Literacy is self-reproducing only if it is tied into social and economic development. Such social processes are built upon the specific strengths of written communication and of written (elaborated) language which include specificity of address, low costs for storage and transport, and usefulness for the linguistic encoding of nonverbal knowledge. But those linguistic resources must be used within established social and institutional structures, the most important of which are the creation and defense of the rule of law, the normative and informational embedding of a market economy, and the growth of an autonomous system for advancing knowledge. The working of these structures reinforces the demand for literacy. It increases demands for the differentiation of communities of communication and for the specialization and elaboration of language. Thus societal literacy and basic literacy are mutually reinforcing. That type of development which combines technological advance with economic growth has never been triggered by literacy alone. Literacy does not even necessarily produce better persons. Social development requires, in addition to literacy, the concomitant development of a new type of language, and a new set of institutions for using literacy in the fields of knowledge, economics, law, and politics.

References

Ahohounkpanzon, M. and Elwert, G., et al. (1998). Evaluation de la Cellule 3A de la Coopération Suisse au Bénin. Unpublished Manuscript. Cotonou: Bureau de la Coopération de l'Ambassade Suisse.

Bernstein, B. (1964). Elaborations and restricted codes. In J. J. Gumperz and D. H. Hymes (eds.), *The Ethnography of Communication*. Menasha, Wis.: American Anthropological Association.

Box, L. (1986). *The Social Organization of Crop Reproduction* (Working Paper). Paper presented at the 13th Congress of the European Society for Rural Sociology, Braga.

Brice-Heath, S. (1980). The functions and uses of literacy. *Journal of Communication* 30(1): 123–33.

Bruner, J. and Olson, D. (1974). Learning through experience and learning through media. In D. R. Olson (ed.), *Media and Symbols*. Chicago: University of Chicago Press.

Coler, J. (1665). *Economia ruralis et domestica*. Mainz: Nicolaus Heyll.

Doronila, M. L. (1999). Instamation d'une tradition de culture écrite: Correlations entre d'alphabétisation, d'éducation et d'évolution sociale. *Développement et Coopération* 1(99): 22–5.

Elwert, G. (1986). Die Verschriftlichung von Kulturen. *Sociologus* 36: 65–78.

Elwert, G. (1987a). Die gesellschaftliche Einbettung von Schriftgebrauch. In D. Baecker et al. (eds.), *Theorie als Passion*. Frankfurt: Suhrkamp.

Elwert, G. (1987b). Ausdehnung der Käuflichkeit und Einbettung der Wirtschaft. Markt und Moralökonomie. In K. Heinemann (ed.), *Soziologie wirtschaftlichen handelns*. Special issue 28 of the *Kölner Zeitschrift für Soziologie und Sozialpsychologie*, pp. 300–21.

Elwert G. (1988). The social and institutional context of literacy. *Adult Education and Development* 31 (Sept.): 355–407.

Elwert, G. (1997). Pas de développement sans culture écrite. *Développement et coopération* 1: 11–13.

Elwert, G. (1999). Long-term consequences of foreign aid: Insights from anthropological analysis. *Developmental Anthropologist* 17: 98–107.

Elwert, G. and Giesecke, M. (1983). Literacy and emancipation – Conditions of the literacy process and two cultural revolutionary movements (16th century Germany and 20th century Benin). *Development and Change* 15: 225–76.

Elwert, G. and Giesecke, M. (1987). Technologische Entwicklung, Schriftkultur und Schriftsprache als technologisches System. In B. Lutz (ed.), *Technik und sozialer Wandel*. Frankfurt a.M.: Campus.

Elwert, G. and Séhouéto, L. (1999). Local knowledge and the improvement of food production. In U. Kracht and M. Schulz (eds.), *Food, Security and Nutrition*. New York and Münster: St. Martin's and Lit.

Estienne, C. (1567). *L'agriculture et maison rustique*. Paris: Du Puys.

Geva, E. and Ryan, E. B. (1993). Linguistic and memory correlates of academic skills in first and second languages. *Language Learning* 43: 5–42.

Giesecke, M. (1992). *Sinnenwandel, Sprachwandel, Kulturwandel – Studien zur Vorgeschichte der Informationsgesellschaft*. Frankfurt a.M.: Suhrkamp.

Giesecke, M. (1994). *Der Buchdruck in der frühen Neuzeit*. Frankfurt a.M.: Suhrkamp.

Glück, H. (1987). *Schrift und Schriftlichkeit*. Stuttgart: Metzler.

Goody, J. (1986). *The Logic of Writing and the Organization of Society*. Cambridge: Cambridge University Press.

Goody, J. (1968). Restricted literacy in northern Ghana. In J. Goody (ed.), *Literacy in Traditional Societies*. Cambridge: Cambridge University Press.

Havelock, E. (1963). *Preface to Plato*. Cambridge, Mass.: Belknap Press.

Hinzen, H. (1988). Western schooling, traditional education and alternative developments in Sierra Leone. *Adult Education and Development* 30: 379–91.

Hirschman, A. (1958). *The Strategy of Economic Development*. New Haven: Yale University Press.

Horowitz, R. (in preparation). *Talking about Text*.

Humbert, C. (ed.) (1975). *Conscientisation – Expériences, positions dialectiques et perspectives*. Paris: Harmattan.

Johns, A. (1998). *The Nature of the Book: Print and knowledge in the making*. Chicago: University of Chicago Press.

Jung, I. (1998). Qu'est-ce qui en reste de l'alphabétisation sans activité éditoriale? *Développement et Coopération* 6: 9–11.

Lambek, M. (1996). Choking the Quran: and other consuming parables from the western Indian Ocean front. In W. James (ed.), *The Pursuit of Certainty: Religious and cultural formulations*. London: Routledge.

Luhmann, N. (1984). The differentiation of advances in knowledge: The genesis of Science. In N. Stehr and V. Meja (eds.), *Society and Knowledge*. London: Transaction Books.

Maddox, B. (1997). *Decentering Development: Literate use in context*. Manuscript, London, Kings College.

Malinowski, B. (1923). The problem of meaning in primitive languages. In C. K. Ogden and I. A. Richards (eds.), *The Meaning of Meaning: A study of the influence of language upon thought and of the science of symbolism*. London: K. Paul, Trench, Trubner & Co./New York: Harcourt, Brace & Co.

Olson, D. R. (1994). *The World on Paper: The conceptual and cognitive implications of writing and reading*. Cambridge: Cambridge University Press.

Ong, W. (1980). Literacy and orality in our times. *Journal of Communication* 30: 197–204.

Prinsloo, M. and Breier, M. (eds.) (1996). *The Social Uses of Literacy*. Amsterdam: John Benjamins.

Powdermaker, H. (1933). *Life in Lesu: The study of a Melanesian society in New Ireland, by Hortense Powdermaker*. New York: W. W. Norton.

Probst, P. (1990). *Text im Kontext. Eine Untersuchung zum politischen Verhältnis von Schrift und Gesellschaft bei den Wimbun im Grasland von Kamerun*. Ph.D. dissertation, Berlin, Freie Universität.

Reh, M. (1981). Sprache und Gesellschaft. In B. Heine, T. Schadeberg, and E. Wolf (eds.), *Die Sprachen Afrikas*. Hamburg: Buske.

Rennell of Rodd, Lord F. (1926). *People of the Veil*. London: Macmillan.

Scribner, S. and Cole, M. (1981). *The Psychology of Literacy*. Cambridge Mass.: Harvard University Press.

Stock, B. (1983). *The Implications of Literacy*. Princeton: Princeton University Press.

Street, B. (1995). *Social Literacies: Critical perspectives on literacy in development, ethnography and education*. London: Longman.

Thaer, Albrecht von (1812). Grundsätze der rationellen Landintschaft. Berlin.

Triebel, A. (1997). *Cognitive and Societal Development and Literacy*. Bonn: DSE.

UNESCO (1973). *Practical Guide for Functional Literacy*. Paris: UNESCO.

Wagner, D. (1995). Literacy and development: Rationales, myths, innovations and future directions. *International Journal of Educational Development* 15(4): 341–62.

Weber, M. (1922). *Wirtschaft und Gesellschaft*. Tübingen: Mohr.

Chapter 4

Literacy in Ancient Greece: Functional Literacy, Oral Education, and the Development of a Literate Environment

Rosalind Thomas

How many Greeks could read? Large numbers of people in the Greek world in the archaic and classical, and even Hellenistic periods could not read and write at all, or could merely read.[1] Yet equally certainly, we can trace a gradual increase over these centuries in the use of the written word both by individuals, private citizens, and noncitizens, and by the state, for a widening range of purposes. There is great diversity within the Greek city-states and over different periods, and the evidence is fullest and most illuminating for Athens (we will therefore concentrate here mainly upon classical Athens). It was in the fifth century that the radical democracy was initiated (460s BC) and the Athenian empire was at its height in the 450s–440s, yet it is not entirely clear that Athens then was a "literate environment." On the other hand we can characterize classical Athens in the fourth century BC in very general terms as a "literate environment." We may call Athens in the fourth century a "literate environment," or a "literacy using society," even though not everyone could read, in the sense that the political process of the radical democracy kept written records of its decrees, published many of them literally in public in the open on stone, and in many respects was dependent upon the written word as backup for its central processes of administration and policing.[2] We see a development of what has been called a "document mentality," and an "archive mentality," in which there is a feeling that documents should be made and then kept in archives, and for the first time the Athenian use of documents begins to look somewhat familiar to the historian of more modern times.[3] Neither were so obvious in the earlier fifth century.

It is also true that in the fourth century, the century of professionalism and consolidation, of Plato and Aristotle, we can trace a growing respect for the past achievements of the Greeks. These achievements were mainly fifth-century Athenian achievements, mainly political – success in empire and war – and literary, and they were embedded and preserved in written texts. To take one example, it was in the time of Lycurgus of Athens, in the late fourth century, that it was ruled that the texts of the three great writers of tragedy of the previous century, Aeschylus, Sophocles, and Euripides, should be deposited in the central city archive of Athens. He added the astonishing requirement, very difficult to enforce, that actors should have to go and check these authoritative texts before they performed one of these plays: the archive clerk would read out the text to them.[4] Many would see this as symbolizing the end of live creative drama of the classical period. It is shortly afterwards in the Hellenistic period (from 323 BC onwards) that the great Alexandrian Library was created in Egypt, the first institutional and public library, and the first attempt to collect together systematically all the works of literature in Greek. Earlier libraries were the collections of individuals: this institutionalized library was made at the behest of the Ptolemaic king, a product therefore of Greek monarchy (and Greeks) ruling over non-Greeks in a foreign land. Literary scholars thrived in the atmosphere of the Library; so did antiquarianism. In the Greek cities of the Hellenistic world, spread over much of the ancient Near and Middle East, a system of education developed which laid immense stress on the great Greek poets and writers of the classical age – and these were embodied in texts. It is in the Hellenistic period that we first see attempts, usually through private benefactions, to provide schooling to all the citizen children of the city (boys and sometimes girls). For the citizen body, which is itself a kind of broad and non-aristocratic elite, their shared Hellenism is indeed in this period bound to a literate environment, to written records in politics, and in a shared body of literature, preserved in texts, which embodied the Hellenic tradition. This is long past the high period of radical Greek democracy. Yet in many ways the Hellenistic period, where numerous Greek cities and non-Greeks were ruled by kings, seems more similar in its attitude to written literature to the habits of twenty-first century Western nations, than does the earlier world of classical Greece.

The challenge that the UNESCO workshop, from which this chapter arises, set us was to try and analyze in our separate areas what it is that makes a literate environment: what are the factors, social, economic, political, educational, which may help to contribute to a sustained and self-sustaining, literate environment? What other factors, on the contrary, inhibit the use of writing from becoming permanent? Why and how is it that the use of writing may increase? What is the role of writing in the development of society? What is the relation between the organization of a society and the development of literate bureaucracies? How does literacy develop in multilingual settings?

Ancient Greece has played a prominent role in many discussions of the role and effect of literacy, the so-called "philosophical model" discussed in Triebel's chapter above. I do not wish to go over ground that has already been covered elsewhere, and will try to concentrate upon questions that impinge directly on our main questions here. But it will be helpful to make some general remarks first, in order to indicate where or to what extent we may be able to extrapolate from the case of Greece. Then I move on to the precise issue of the creation of a literate environment. The reasons for the developing literate environment are difficult to determine and have had much less attention in the literature than the questions, (a) how many were literate; (b) the relation of literacy to rationality; (c) the increasing use of writing; (d) the interaction of literate and oral practices.

First, it may be noted that when the alphabet was adopted in ancient Greece in the eighth century BC, literacy was not being imposed upon it from outside, from another dominant culture; it was taken up by Greeks for their own uses as they felt moved, and it therefore developed *within* Greek society. On the other hand, the alphabet was borrowed from the Phoenicians, a semitic people who lived on the edge of the bureaucratic kingdoms of the Near East, and who may have transmitted some ideas about how the new system of communication might be used. Nor was it arriving onto a blank slate in Greece itself, but was adopted, obviously, by a living society which was itself complex and developing for many reasons, not all connected with literacy. Thus to take Greece as an experiment for the effects of literacy on a society may be tempting, but involves a model and a process which is much oversimplified, if not methodologically unsound.[5]

Secondly, it can be demonstrated that the use of writing percolated some areas of life and not others, and Athenian society developed only gradually to the "document-minded" Athens of the fourth century BC. Some groups were therefore affected far more than others. Thus the analysis by Maria Doronila (chapter 13 below) of the various groups in the Philippines seems most reminiscent of the various levels of participation in a literate environment that we find in Greece.[6] Even this development cannot be traced all over Greece. Athens was the city-state most dominated by the written word, at least in the political arena, and this was probably connected with the presence of empire and democracy (see below). The prime counterexample is Sparta, set in its fertile river valley deep in the Peloponnese, and holding sway over large numbers of helots by force and over several other major city-states by alliance and League. Famous for its militaristic system, intense cohesion, and wide power, Sparta had very little use for the written word at all. Archaeologists excavating in Sparta have found none of the large stone public inscriptions that are so plentiful at Athens, few of the informal pieces of "graffiti" or written dedications so familiar in other parts of Greece. They prided themselves on not needing written law, since their mythical lawgiver – so they said – thought education was a better way of enforcing obedience. They had some written records kept by the state, including records of oracles, but simply eschewed the public inscription so characteristic of Greek city life.[7] But Sparta is an example which suggests rather strongly that social and political cohesion and wide power can be achieved without much (or any) written communication, if the social and political system can maintain cohesion by other means.

Greece also gives us an instance where literacy is apparently totally forgotten, and this is often neglected: the Mycenaean palaces used Linear B, a syllabic form of writing used for bureaucratic records (and there is no evidence of its use for anything else). Scholars are often puzzled that so useful a skill should have been forgotten in the Dark Ages, but the answer may be simple. Once the palaces and palace systems which needed the records were destroyed, there seemed little use for the cumbersome writing system which they had supported. Such writing was used for bureaucratic lists of payments in the palace economy. It is hard to imagine how such a cumbersome syllabary, so unsuited to Greek, could have been much help in recording poetry, had anyone even thought to do so. Such a writing system belonged to an enclosed enclave, and could be supported only by that enclave. The groups left after the collapse of the palace system may be like those groups in the modern world on whom literacy simply does not impinge.[8]

Greece would strongly support the idea that literacy is not simply an independent skill, a technology whose progress can be charted and predicted. Recent discussions of literacy in the ancient Greco-Roman world would confirm the view that literacy is indeed socially embedded, its effects and manifestations very much a product of the society it is locked into, even if there are indeed certain elements of writing that seem to have possibilities that could be universal, for example, the ability to preserve, or communicate over long distances. Thus while writing may make certain activities possible or easier, the presence of writing in any given society does not, I think, automatically cause or promote that activity; whether or not one potential of writing rather than another is taken up by a given group, seems to depend to a large extent on the habits and aspirations of that society. Many of the ways in which writing is exploited are more easily explained as growing out of the habits and preoccupations of that society. Even once literacy is present in some form, there seem innumerable degrees to which the written word can be utilized. For instance, there is an example of an archive in Athens that was made but never actually used: archaeologists found numerous lead rolls containing information about the cavalry which had never, apparently, been unrolled. While someone thought to make records of details of horses in the cavalry in this case, the structures, or bureaucracy, or "document mentality," do not seem to have been sufficiently present to require anyone to open them ever again.[9] There is plentiful evidence for written curses, and many were intended to impinge upon the democratic processes or judicial trials. The tendencies of an increased use of writing here obviously do not all point in the same direction – writing could be thought to intensify a curse as well as preserve the records of the decisions of the assembly. It may be dangerous to concentrate on the achievements of "high culture" here at the expense of these other manifestations of literacy which may have been very much more widespread, whether we call this "popular literacy" or "insular literacy" or anything else. The development of philosophy is probably more closely linked, as G. E. R. Lloyd suggested, to the atmosphere of competitive and open debate in classical Greece, than to writing alone.[10] The written word helped to preserve, crystallize and enhance this process, but it did so within an environment of debate that was itself crucial.

Finally, it seems also to be highly relevant that ancient Greece was a society (or series of societies) which placed very great value upon orality – oral presentation and performance were highly valued and central to the transmission and experiencing of literature, even when that literature was written down – for example Greek tragedy, or the political satire of Athenian comedy. It can be shown that oral methods of procedure, that is procedures using no writing at all, and oral transmission, continue to be important not only when the alphabet arrives in the eighth century BC but on through the classical period and beyond.[11] Written texts still tend to be heard, for instance, rather than read silently: reading a text in the ancient world usually involved voicing it aloud. The main political process of the Athenian radical democracy lies in the debate in the assembly in front of a large body of citizens. In this direct democracy, the politicians, who were not paid professionals but essentially prominent members of the city, had to persuade the people there *en masse*, in person, and in live debate. So this is not just to repeat the obvious truth that even after the invention of writing, speech continues to be important; or what seems now to be generally accepted, that literacy and orality coexist together.[12] In the case of Greek culture one can go further, I think, and look more carefully at where, precisely, the written word takes over, and where it does not; or at the complex interrelation of written and oral techniques of proof and written and oral transmission. In legal contracts, for instance, witnesses are trusted more than the bare written record. In particular, it is fascinating how in this rather intellectual culture, much educational time and effort is devoted to the development of specific oral skills – to rhetoric, for example, and the skill of speaking, to improvisation, to music and the singing of poetry from memory. Children learned written texts of poetry by heart, and much of the educational process was devoted to massive feats of memorization.[13] Writing is sometimes used simply to reinforce practices which have been carried out orally, as an aide-mémoire, or memorial of what is really meant to be spoken and heard. In other words, while literacy is socially embedded, so is orality, and Greece exhibits manifestations of oral culture which are particularly embedded in her own culture and which, far from dying out with the coming of writing, are in many cases developed to an even higher degree at the same time as a literate environment develops (I return to this below). This developed orality is presumably enhanced in some areas, at least, by writing which builds up the tradition and may perhaps be said to create a different kind of orality.[14] Yet we should not lose sight of the sheer presence of activities which do not use writing, and of functional equivalents to literacy. These continuing, or traditional, oral practices, may suggest some explanation for societies in our time where literacy has not taken, or once imparted, has not progressed.[15]

The Development of a Literate Environment

Let us turn, then, to what we may be able to extrapolate about the development of a literate environment, concentrating on classical Athens where the evidence is richest. To repeat the earlier definition, by "literate environment," I mean a society in which writing is present not just on the margin, in secret societies, religious rites, etc., or amongst a tiny educated elite, or a scribal caste, but in the political center and in the heart of education.

One area where writing is used increasingly, and where we can trace a conscious and deliberate exploitation of writing in Athens, is in the realm of the finances of empire. Athens' maritime alliance of city-states over the Aegean and the north and east coast of the Aegean (478–404 BC) drew much of its strength and stability from the tribute which individual city-states paid (initially in lieu of ships for the common fleet). While it is fairly clear that administration and bureaucracy in general are minimal at this time, the one area where written records were used in a fairly sophisticated way was in the records of imperial finances and debtors to the imperial tribute collection. Extensive and elaborate lists were kept, defaulters and embezzlers tracked down. Less sophisticated, stone decrees which imposed settlements on recalcitrant allies who had revolted, were set up in prominent places in the allied cities, and must have formed a constant reminder of Athenian control. There are several decrees where the assembly decides on increasing written record in order to prevent fraud – to ensure that the proper sums of tribute are both being collected and returned to the treasury at Athens.[16] Written records of defaulters and of debts to the state involve and require increasing written record. We can probably presume, in fact, that it is to the realm of finance in general that much of the record-keeping is directed in Athens, and that written records become more and more prominent in the period of the Athenian empire precisely because the impetus is to control finances and embezzlers. It is intriguing to note that the gods' interest in these finances are also considered: a tithe of the tribute was dedicated to the goddess Athena, and this tithe, one-sixtieth of the total, was deemed important enough to be inscribed in public on huge stone slabs which went up on the Acropolis, surely as public proof the Athenian people were fulfilling their duties to the goddess. Here again, the elaborate and hugely expensive publicly inscribed records are concerned with money. So increasing use of writing goes hand in hand with the growth, and growing complexity, of empire.

In a similar realm, that of trust and proof, it is also interesting that in Athens it is relatively late that written records are accepted as proof in law courts for the personal testimony of witnesses, and nonwritten proof through oaths are much preferred. The common modern assumption is perhaps more often that if you "have it in writing," that will be proof enough (in English law even now the oral contract is in theory legally binding, but it is virtually impossible to enforce it). So we may be surprised that written documents (contracts) seem to gain acceptability in Athenian courts only in the fourth century BC, more than 60 or 70 years after the popular democratic law courts were established in the 460s. More specifically, we do not encounter a written contract made without witnesses until the 320s: the first written contract we hear of in Athens dates to the 390s (though that does not mean it is *absolutely* the first), and thereafter written contracts are used in conjunction with witnesses, witnesses undoubtedly being the older method. Similarly, it is not until the early fourth century that testimonies have to be presented in court in the form of written documents and read out – that is, presumably, to prevent the evidence from being changed. What we may be seeing here is that Athenian courts have recourse to written documents in a period when the society is becoming increasingly complex, the courts and techniques of dealing with the courts are developing, many more non-Athenians are living in Athens or trading there, and the small community with modes of trust dependent upon personal knowledge and contacts, is giving way.[17] The most old-fashioned type of contract is that involving the mortgaging of land, where a stone slab with very rudimentary inscription is literally placed upon the land which has a debt on it, and this stone is the proof of debt, placed there in the presence of witnesses but not accompanied by further written documents: land is obviously unmovable, most literally part of the local community, and could not be owned by foreigners. They did not need to deposit documentary evidence with a remote bureaucratic official or archive and it is interesting that this only develops much later. This would suggest that writing is appealed to increasingly as a society becomes more complex, less stable in its composition, and when commercial interests make the nonpersonal system of confirmation, proof, or contract, seem more reliable.[18] The acceptance of writing as proof seems not to have been an obvious foregone conclusion but developed gradually and according to the perceived advantages of a written text as the society changed. Again, the development of the society seems to go hand in hand with greater use of written record in certain specific areas – but for some reason written contracts become regular long after the increase in public documents we discussed above.

The relation between the political system and the presence or use of literacy seems to be extremely complex. In Goody's original formulation (see note 5), the Athenian democracy was in some sense a consequence of literacy. Certainly literacy and the extensive use of writing seem to be related in some way to democracy, but it may, rather, be the case that democracy itself enhanced and stimulated literacy and did much to make Athens a literate environment.[19] The evidence shows that in Greece cities gave greater prominence to writing, written laws, written documents, when their constitution was democratic: Athens is the extreme example. Yet when we look more closely, it would appear that written law in Greece appears first as an attempt to curb and control the power of officials and give public sanction to such laws: these laws were not in democracies (which did not yet exist) but in city-states developing some kind of constitutional government freed from the traditional and undefined prerogatives of the aristocracy. Such written laws were few in number and still backed up by customary law, tradition, and by the general archaic preoccupation with justice. Greeks believed written law brought justice for all. The habit so developed in democratic Athens (fifth to fourth centuries), of recording the decisions of the assembly and erecting numerous inscriptions of democratic business, had as its aim that the citizens should have public access to these decisions (even, perhaps, if they could not read them), and that the bodies making them should be publicly accountable – just as we saw the tithes of the "tribute lists" are inscribed on stone for Athena. Such habits made Athens a city of inscriptions – public stone writings – whether or not any citizen ever bothered to go to the archives. But these habits may originally have grown out of a use of writing, and particularly stone writing for the public spaces, to create a memorial, an imperishable record of a tomb, or else of an enactment or law which the whole city hoped would be reinforced if it were written up in public.

The role of written record in the democracy, then, has much to do with accountability, the perception that written law was more fair, and also with publicity (in a world before newspapers, it had little to do with the dissemination of news, political propaganda, radical ideas). Writing may have helped to quicken change, to enhance perceptions of the political process, but perceptions of writing and general underlying mentalities are important; perhaps the dynamics of the democratic development in Athens – which was obsessed with accountability and the participation of all citizens – did much to create perceptions of the role of writing. It is still not clear that every citizen in classical Athens could, or did, read and write: but in any case the crucial proceedings of the democracy (*direct* democracy, not representative) were carried out by word of mouth, in the debates and speeches in the assembly, in the law courts which were manned by mass juries drawn from the citizen body. You were not excluded from participating in the democracy by being unable to read and write or having only poor writing skills, nor did voting systems need writing. The one occasional exception here was the system of ostracism (from ca. 508 BC), in which all citizens put the name of the politician they most wanted expelled from the city on a piece of broken pottery, and the unfortunate man who received the most votes had to leave the city for 10 years. However, not only was this an occasional event, but there is an anecdote about an illiterate getting someone to write their ostrakon, and a large group of pottery sherds naming one particular politician have actually been found clearly written out by a small group of writers. But in a system which prided itself on ruling by written law, keeping written records of decrees, and publishing in writing decisions, honors, and traitors, there is every reason to think that the Athenian citizen, surrounded by examples of public writing, would have more opportunity and more reason to learn, than, say, the citizen of Sparta, whose life could be conducted adequately without the written word altogether. However, the truly ambitious politician had to be able not only to read but acquire certain other crucial skills, most especially the art of persuasion. One extreme opponent of democracy, Critias, wished to ban the teaching of rhetoric, as an answer, presumably, to what he saw as the excesses of the radical democracy.[20] The implications are that writing, and therefore literacy, does infiltrate Athenian society and politics increasingly, that it does indeed help, strengthen, and confirm certain social activities: but also that the presence of writing is one factor amongst a very complex range of other processes, priorities, and movements in the development of the Athenian democracy.

Probably very many Greeks had some kind of "functional literacy"; but the nature of "functional" literacy, a slippery concept, must vary from society to society depending on the "functions" which might be relevant. Traders, for instance, kept rudimentary lists and wrote letters from distant parts of the Mediterranean (we have some written on lead, ca. 500 BC); potters added messages to the scenes on their pottery; numerous pieces of "graffiti" in the technical sense, that is, informal pieces of writing, have been found in the Athenian Agora written on pieces of pottery (the ancient equivalent of scrap paper), with lists, simple messages, scribbles, attempts at alphabets – not, one must admit, very impressive. Writing here is obviously grasped because it can take messages over a distance, it can record lists and numbers. It can also give a voice to an inanimate object. From the very earliest examples of alphabetic writing in the Greek world in the eighth century BC, innumerable objects have written messages on them – markers to say that a cup or other object belongs to someone, markers on tombs, curses written out to prevent anyone stealing the object, dedications to the gods with the dedicator's name marked, in writing, and we note the frequent use of a written message in the first person, as if the object itself was speaking (e.g. "I am the cup of Tatie").

Yet if this was the level of "literacy" most frequently encountered in Greece, we may well ask how large a gulf lay between such simple messages and the sophisticated literary products of Greek society. There is no evidence in any Greek writer of an idea that literacy in its most basic sense, that is, the simple ability to read and write in its most basic form, would enable someone to rise in the world (we may disagree with this, but what I am emphasizing here is Greek perception). It is not that there is no discussion of education, of skills and training necessary to have influence in political life, of the virtues and skills necessary for the good citizen: on the contrary, much of Greek political thought (especially Plato, *Republic* and *Laws*, and Aristotle, *Politics*) discusses how best to educate the citizen. But the focus of their preoccupations lies elsewhere than literacy. Indeed, by contrast to some modern discussions of education, they rather take for granted that basic reading is taught early, and go on to concentrate on the more elaborated skills that the ambitious citizen might well wish to acquire: the skills of persuasion or rhetoric, the art of politics and political virtue, the art of argument, and also the arts of music and poetry (any educated gentleman was expected to be able to compose improvisatory poetry). As is well known, Socrates was a master of dialectic yet wrote nothing down, and his pupil Plato thought the written word was not a trustworthy means of true education since true understanding could not reside merely on the written page (see the *Phaedrus* especially) – though it has to be said that Plato was fighting a rearguard action here. The "New education" of the late fifth century BC concentrated on teaching ambitious young men how to win arguments and debates in the assembly. Written manuals were a feature of this, but the ultimate test was the oral performance and the ability to improvise spontaneously in front of an audience. Thus while written texts were undoubtedly used to preserve poetry, speeches from the late fifth century, drama, and other forms of prose, the education for the elite and ambitious shows how orality, the skills of oral performance, were developed to a very high level. As the society made more use of the written word and Athens set up ever more stone inscriptions of its decrees, elite education also developed further refinements in oral skills of rhetoric and declamation – though it should be admitted that these skills were enhanced also by being codified in written texts, always maintaining superiority just when one might expect that there might be some leveling in the radical democracy (where every citizen in theory could speak in the assembly) and with the increasing availability of written literature.

One point which comes across very strongly from the Greek world, is that a vibrant, creative society can exist with very low levels of literacy within the population: since the products of literature are invariably heard and seen in performance, those who are either illiterate or can only read with difficulty are not excluded – their illiteracy would not be "pathological," to use Maria Doronila's phrase for illiteracy which is perceived as socially crippling. And in any case it was so hard to acquire a text, that few Greeks probably possessed their literature in books.

Secondly, orality is as variable in its manifestations as literacy, and as embedded in society as literacy. Ancient Greece elaborated its oral skills in a peculiarly Greek way, towards rhetoric and performance especially. Should we perhaps give more explicit attention to the nonliterate practices in those societies today where literacy projects have been unsuccessful: could it sometimes be the case that an oral culture is sufficiently vibrant and culturally important for literacy (or at least Western literacy) to have no obvious place? Or are there areas where the written word could be adapted in ways more compatible with the habits of the society already there than those functions being introduced along with that literacy?

The presence of bureaucracy may be something of a red herring in the pursuit of literacy and enhanced literacy levels, at least if we go from the ancient experience. Bureaucracy only needs literate officials: unless it really reaches down into every part of life and requires people to participate in it, it seems to be able to continue happily on a quite different level from the rest of the population. In the immensely bureaucratic system in Egypt under Greek Ptolemaic rule (from late fourth century BC), and then later Roman rule, the taxation system and bureaucratic rules did indeed impinge upon the lives of ordinary people, with numerous requests for receipts, numerous official letters. So in that respect it is very probable that the rate of basic literacy in Egypt, at least among Greeks, was higher than that elsewhere, since they lived in a society dominated by bureaucratic documents. Nevertheless, it is clear that there were many who needed to have documents made, such as contracts, documents for selling property, wills, who could not even sign their own name. And these documents invariably had to be made out by the literate and official scribes, whether or not the parties to the transaction were literate. So a huge scribal machinery was in place to create and service these documents: and the ordinary man or woman, whether Greek or Egyptian, was still in the power of the scribal official, and had to pay him a fee. The literate benefited only in that they could read and check the letters or documents afterwards.[21] Here as in some modern examples, the power structures and social structures, not to mention gender relations, meant that literacy could not be a source of empowerment by itself.[22]

The main impetus towards greater and more extensive use of the written word in the ancient Greek world seems, then, to revolve around the following elements: exhibition and publicity – for writing is often public writing, intended to inform, to shame or to advertise; memorials which fight against oblivion and preserve the name of the deceased or the name of the person who erected the tomb; commercial needs, contracts, records of debts, agreements, accounts, particularly in the rather fluid world of traders who did not possess a stable place in the community where their honesty, oaths, and promises could be reinforced and upheld by their family and friends; financial accountability and control (as in the Athenian empire; or the intense stress on accountability in the democracy); and democratic purposes, since it eventually does become a democratic ideal that the business of the democracy must be recorded for the sake of publicity, accountability, and fairness for all. Religious cult and practice do not in this society provide particular incentives for increased use of writing and, with the exception of some marginal cults, there are no sacred texts which are central to the religious experience, and therefore become venerated, carefully guarded, or zealously read.

The presence of bureaucratic procedures may be seen from different angles: in one respect, the esteem in Athens in which written law was held, and the presence of public writing, seem to be connected with a somewhat greater level of literacy than in other city-states. On the other hand, the extreme bureaucratic procedures in Greco-Roman Egypt served to control the population, whether they were Greek or Egyptian, literate or illiterate.

Finally, in a volume which has so much to say about the connections between writing and identity, I should stress the importance in Greek identity and Greek tradition in the later, postclassical period, of sharing in the common Greek literary heritage. In the postclassical world (from the late fourth century), to be truly Greek, it was essential to have knowledge of Homer, Greek tragedy, the classics of the canon (this was the case even if someone was not strictly ethnically Greek). Thus there was in the later period a body of written texts which embodied a tradition, and much later Greek education was aimed at instilling knowledge of that. It may in the end have been this idea, above all, in which cultural identity was tied to the great classical texts, which did most to foster a "textual community" and a literate environment. But we may stress that this occurs, and is even enhanced, in the later period during which Greek cities had lost their political independence either to monarchs or to Rome. For the classical period, I would prefer to emphasize the vitality of oral as well as written culture. From this latter example I would argue that one cannot understand how and why the use of writing increases (or decreases) in a given society without a minute analysis of the cultural and political value placed upon the products of literacy, and also upon the elements of that culture which rested upon performance, communication, and transmission without need for the written word.

Notes

I would like to thank the organizers of the original colloquium most warmly for the opportunity to participate in a very stimulating and productive discussion; also the other participants and the editors for their comments on this paper.

1   That is, the period of the development of the city-state ca. 750–500 BC; the high classical period, 500–323 BC; and post-Alexander the Great, 323–31 BC. The fullest collection of evidence is Harris, 1989: he argues firmly against any optimistic levels of literacy – that is, seldom more than 20% literacy of any level – in the ancient Greco-Roman world, though the evidence does not allow us to provide firm statistics. Our written evidence inevitably tends to give us most evidence about the literate, and most of all, the cultured and educated elite.

2   The difficulties arising from the term "literate society" – how many literates make a literate society, what actually constitutes "literacy"? – seem to be largely avoided by the phrase "literate environment."

3   For this development and further detail, see especially Thomas, 1989, ch. 1; and more generally, Thomas, 1992, which looks at the meaning of literacy and orality in Greece and the changing relationship between the two. I borrow the terms "document minded" and "archive mentality" from M. Clanchy's fascinating book on the Middle Ages (1979).

4   It also shows, incidentally, that while these accurate texts are being authorized and by the state, there is still not so close an adherence to the written text that the actors are handed an authorized written text – there still seems to be an oral element. This is an important example of the need to define rather closely the use of writing, the uses of oral communication, rather than speak vaguely of "literacy," which can mean many things. For details, see Thomas, 1989, pp. 48–9.

5   Goody & Watt, 1968; Thomas, 1992, chs. 1–2: which makes use of the formulation of B. Street, 1984. It should be added, however, that manifestations of "orality" are also culturally variable and culturally influenced, like those of literacy. There are later modifications by Goody in *The Logic of Writing and the Organization of Society* (1986); and *The Interface between the Written and the Oral* (1987). Cf. also the recent study of the influence of writing on our ways of "reading" the world by Olson, 1994.

6   See the chapter by Maria Doronila, this volume.

7   Cartledge, 1978, pp. 25–37; Boring, 1979.

8   Cf. Maria Doronila's chapter in this volume.

9   For details on cavalry archives see Thomas, 1989, pp. 82–3, and further references there.

10   See especially Lloyd, 1979 and 1987.

11   See especially Herington, 1985 on poetry as performance; also Gentili, 1988; and Edmonds & Wallace, 1997. There is a general survey in my *Literacy and Orality*, ch. 6.

12   See e.g. Goody, 1987; Finnegan, 1977.

13   On memory and memorization in the ancient world, see Small, 1997, with my review in *Classical Philology*, forthcoming, 2001.

14   A point stressed by Georg Elwert in discussion.

15   There are of course many possible relevant factors; I find particularly interesting the case of Niger, raised by Hassana Alidou-Ngame in discussion, where the indigenous

writing systems were ignored against the dominance of Western literacy and colonization – thereby factoring out a writing system that already had cultural meaning in favor of one that had none, and "infantilizing" the adults now being taught a new system of writing. A similar point may perhaps be made about the effect of ignoring engrained habits of orality. Note also a point raised by Kwesi Prah in discussion, that "minorities" (in language, modes of literacy) are not necessarily real minorities if boundaries are drawn differently.

16   Further details in Thomas, 1994, pp. 33ff. The whole volume investigates the relationship between writing and power.
17   For distrust of writing and the literate, cf. Georg Elwert's point (in discussion) that in west Africa, written documents are often not trusted because they come from the government; and Chandar Daswani's example (again in discussion) of the play in Hindi on the word for "literate" and the word for "demon."
18   For contracts, further details in Thomas, 1989, pp. 41ff., 55ff.
19   Cf. the chapter above by Georg Elwert on the importance of the "legal state" and on foreseeability. Maria Doronila's chapter, below, makes the important point about the need for communities to develop an *internal* capacity to occupy a place in the democratic process, for the democratizing process to work.
20   For Critias' attempt to ban the teaching of rhetoric, see Xenophon, *Memorabilia*, 1.2.31.
21   For the bureaucracy of Roman Egypt, see the general study Bowman, 1986; cf. Hopkins, 1991, pp. 133–58; and Hanson, 1991, pp. 159–98, which concentrates on the unusually rich evidence from Greco-Roman Egypt.
22   Cf. in particular the illuminating chapter by Malini Ghose in this volume, on the problems for low-caste and illiterate women in Uttar Pradesh.

References

Boring, T. A. (1979). *Literacy in Ancient Sparta*. Leiden: E. J. Brill.
Bowman, A. (1986). *Egypt after the Pharaohs 332 B.C.–A.D. 642: from Alexander to the Arab conquest*. Berkeley: University of California Press.
Cartledge, P. (1978). Literacy in the Spartan oligarchy. *Journal of Hellenic Studies*, 98: 25–37.
Clanchy, M. (1979). *From Memory to Written Record: England, 1066–1307*, 2nd edn. 1993. Cambridge, Mass.: Harvard University Press.
Edmonds, L. and Wallace, R. W. (eds.), *Poet, Public and Performance in Ancient Greece*. Baltimore: Johns Hopkins University Press.
Finnegan, R. (1977). *Oral Poetry: Its nature, significance and social context*. Cambridge: Cambridge University Press.
Gentili, B. (1988). *Poetry and its Public in Ancient Greece from Homer to the Fifth Century*. Baltimore: Johns Hopkins University Press. Trans. from the Italian edn. of 1985.
Goody, J. (1986). *The Logic of Writing and the Organization of Society*. Cambridge: Cambridge University Press.
Goody, J. (1987). *The Interface between the Written and the Oral*. Cambridge: Cambridge University Press.

Goody, J. and Watt, I. (1968). The consequences of literacy. In J. Goody (ed.), *Literacy in Traditional Societies*. Cambridge: Cambridge University Press.

Hanson, Ann Ellis. (1991). Ancient illiteracy. In Mary Beard et al. (eds.), *Literacy in the Roman World. Journal of Roman Archaeology*, Supplementary Series 3: 159–98.

Harris, W. V. (1989). *Ancient Literacy*. Cambridge, Mass.: Harvard University Press.

Herington, J. (1985). *Poetry into Drama: Early tragedy and the Greek poetic tradition*. Berkeley: University of California Press.

Hopkins, Keith. (1991). Conquest by book. In Mary Beard et al. (eds.), *Literacy in the Roman World. Journal of Roman Archaeology*, Supplementary Series 3: 133–58.

Lloyd, G. E. R. (1979). *Magic, Reason and Experience: Studies in the origin* and *development of Greek science*. Cambridge: Cambridge University Press.

Lloyd, G. E. R. (1987). *Revolutions of Wisdom*. Berkeley: University of California Press.

Olson, D. (1994). *The World on Paper: The conceptual and cognitive implications of writing and reading*. Cambridge: Cambridge University Press.

Small, Penny. (1997). *The Wax Tablets of the Mind*. London/New York: Routledge.

Street, B. (1984). *Literacy in Theory and Practice*. Cambridge: Cambridge University Press.

Thomas, R. (1989). *Oral Tradition and Written Record in Classical Athens*. Cambridge/New York: Cambridge University Press.

Thomas, R. (1992). *Literacy and Orality in Ancient Greece*. Cambridge: Cambridge University Press.

Thomas, R. (1994). Literacy and the city-state in archaic and classical Greece. In A. K. Bowman and G. Woolf (eds.), *Literacy and Power in the Ancient World*. Cambridge/New York: Cambridge University Press.

Chapter 5

Literacy in Germany

Utz Maas

Introductory Remarks

Germany is one of those countries that has provided a model for the ongoing debate about literacy, or, perhaps more precisely, has tried to impose its model of literacy, and its perspective, onto the world.[1] In fact, in terms of this established view on literacy, Germany provides a successful model for achieving universal literacy in a population. Thus, within the comparative perspective of this volume, it may be instructive to trace the conditions of Germany's success.

Remarks on Contemporary Literacy

As is the case in all developed countries, the high level of literacy is to be seen in relation to the number of dropouts, to be calculated as a function of the criteria deployed: rates of illiteracy of between 1 and 10 percent are usually given for Germany. The most recent figures in the OECD report of 1995, evaluating literacy in a more comprehensive way, for example, as the capacity for making sense of figures, charts, and graphic illustrations, reported for all evaluated countries that 20 percent of people had difficulty. Germany here fares better than most of the other developed countries in the survey, at 14.5 percent, a lower level of illiteracy than in Canada, the USA, and Switzerland.

Of course in any country with high immigration, estimating the number of illiterates is rather difficult. Quite high rates are to be expected among the immigrant population in Germany, officially about 9 percent of the population, coming in large part from areas with quite low literacy rates. But the public is often shocked by the publication in the press of biographies of "normal Germans" who cannot read, either having never learned or having forgotten how through lack of use.

Since the 1970s many public institutions for adult education have been offering courses in literacy, usually separating students with a German linguistic background from those with a non-German background. Current sources indicate that some 15,000 adults are enrolled in these courses, a figure which represents the tip of the iceberg: adult educators working with this group evaluate the number of people in Germany with real difficulties in literacy at half a million, corresponding to about 10 percent of the population, apparently a realistic evaluation as it fits the rate of illiteracy in those groups where exact counts can be made (army conscripts, prison inmates, and so on; see Hubertus, 1995).

As this corresponds to what is reported from comparable countries, it may represent the threshold for literacy under current social conditions in developed countries. The fact that levels of literacy are much higher in Germany than in third world countries can be explained by the special social conditions prevailing in a country like Germany. I will present an overview of the evolution of literacy in Germany which offers an explanation of the relative success of literacy here as well as the mentioned obstacle to literacy for approximately 10 percent of the population.

An Historical Overview of the Socialization of Literary Craftsmanship in Germany

To retrace the history of literacy in Germany, we have to go back to the medieval period. At the end of the fifth century, after the fall of the Roman Empire, the redistribution of power gave way to a system of new (feudal) states that prefigured the modern world in Europe. But the culturally dominant form in this world tried to inherit the vanished Roman world, with Christianization serving as transmission, and Latin as the only form of sophisticated communication in religion, literature, justice, administration, and so on. Latin remained dominant for an astonishingly long time: even in the seventeenth century, long after the arrival of the modern printing press, the majority of printing was still done in Latin; only in the eighteenth century did university teaching start being done in German – and at the beginning of this century doctoral dissertations were still frequently written in Latin.[2]

The advent of non-Latin culture proceeded rather painfully. Bilingualism must have been a problem for a tiny societal layer – German having only a very distant parental relationship to Latin, unlike the closely related French, Italian, and other Romance languages. Of course, the managers of society, including the nobility and land-owners, were in large part people without Latin culture, especially the powerful. For them, Latin texts had to be translated; oral contracts, for instance, had to be written down in a linguistic form that allowed them to be authenticated after being read aloud to the parties concerned. So a professional group with Latin literacy established itself: clerks, and as the name shows, their associates in the church, the clerics, who monopolized schools and did their teaching in Latin. From the end of the seventh century we have documents not only in Latin, but also in several of the different regional languages spoken in Germany.

Here a note on the linguistic situation in Germany is in order. German territory was not and is still not linguistically homogenous. Besides non-Germanic languages, especially Slavonic languages such as Sorabian which is still spoken in the Lausitz area in the eastern part of the river Elbe region, there were other Germanic varieties, especially Frisian in the northern coast area, and Low German in the northern part, in many regards closer to English than to High German. Even with regard to the so-called High German dialects, mutual communication must have been rather difficult between people from distant regions.

Linguistic unification went through phases of bilingualism, the vernacular competing with the more universal Latin of bidialectalism based on varieties of German associated with the most mobile parts of the population, especially tradesmen. In the northern part of the country it was centered on a form of Low German, bound to the economically as well as politically powerful Hanse towns, and serving as a lingua franca not only in northern Germany but in the Scandinavian and Baltic area and the Netherlands as well. From the sixteenth century on a High German variety gradually imposed itself, following the shift of the economic centers to the south. Only in the second half of the nineteenth century, with the massive redistribution of the population as a consequence of industrialization and the growth of mass urbanization, did a universally spoken variety of High German with strong regional accents come into use: the electronic mass media, radio, and later television, finally accelerated this dynamic in the last century.

The great cultural revolution encountered at the end of mediaeval times, say between the thirteenth and fifteenth centuries, came with the establishment of modern towns, with a production system for the market, and especially with groups of tradesmen no longer traveling with their merchandise but settling in these towns and controlling exchange from their offices. At the same time these towns, with their dense habitation, created new problems of communality, not the least being problems of hygiene which demanded new forms of collective regulation. The first generations in these towns gave form to these regulations, written still in the Latin tradition, as in the town constitutions and in the book-keeping of the great merchants. Soon, however, this gave way to a more communal form, permitting greater participation of the population. Quite soon supralocal forms of German were also established in writing, Low German in the north, different forms of Upper German in the south. Most important, writing and reading in these languages were taught in town schools, explicitly called *German schools* (*dudesche scholen* in the north), which existed in parallel with the church's Latin schools. Noteworthy was the high percentage of women in this new culture who were by definition excluded from the clerical education system. Even if we don't have statistical information giving exact figures, we know of the circulation of reading material, copied by these women. The invention and commercialization of spectacles gave the older generation the opportunity to read, and women even entered the merchants' offices as professional clerks. It is impossible to evaluate the literacy rate of the time in a precise way. In the country, literacy was still an exception; even the lower nobility were generally not literate. But in the towns, everybody who felt the necessity to learn to read and write could do so. Their demand was answered by a profusion of sometimes rather dubious school establishments, where occasionally a passing cleric made his living, but often a craftsman or his wife transmitted what they had learned. All town governments had to cope with the struggles between these establishments in the fourteenth and fifteenth centuries, with files of these trials representing our main source of information. So a rather high percentage of the town population had access to literacy, in all likelihood virtually all those working in trade or in a craft, and along with them most individuals in their homes. Assuming that a third to a quarter of the population were living in towns by the end of the Middle Ages, the literate population might have approached some 20 percent of the entire population.

This dynamic process accelerated in the sixteenth century, where the great upheavals of that century, the Reformation struggles, the peasants' wars, and so on, are only the culmination of this development. For the development of literacy, two factors are of great significance. The first was the *nationalization* of culture. In fact the religious question split the population, tending to become a personal question, even dividing families while at the same time overcoming traditional regional forms. An exploding market for printing products was created, as people wanted to inform themselves about questions of personal concern. In the first phase of the Reformation, printing was still done in regional languages, and even Luther's Bible translation was printed in the northern part of Germany in Low German. But in the last third of the century High German was established everywhere in Germany as the official language of administration, as the language of education beyond elementary teaching, and in addition to Latin, of course, as the language of the church and of literature.

The second factor was the form of *public control* of literacy. The church and in close relation to it the state played an ambiguous role in this process. The Protestant church imposed its doctrines on its school system by teaching the catechism. *Katchismus Schule* is the official term for elementary school in this context.[3] These schools had two roles:

1) Recruiting and educating in an elementary way future clerical staff, which was consequently oriented to Latin in a kind of bilingual teaching system. In fact the humanist emphasis on pure Latin in distinction from the "mother tongue," and the so-called "barbarian" medieval mixing of the two in pragmatic use, paved the way for the beginning of a serious occupation with the German language, as was happening at the same time with the other European languages.

2) Giving access and, at the same time, restricting the majority of the population to the *reading* of the authorized texts. Elementary teaching in the catechism school had been the teaching of reading – learning to write was in general not part of the curriculum, and was eventually offered as a supplementary subject

for advanced pupils for supplementary fees. For the countryside, this meant the universalization of some form of literacy; for the towns it was a retrogressive step, a dissociation of reading and writing unknown in the traditional form of teaching reading by teaching writing and vice versa. Parents and sometimes town governments protested against this kind of pious devaluation of education and eventually succeeded in imposing the continuation of the traditional pragmatic school system. Even in the countryside, where production for the market was increasing and where supplementary jobs like linen-weaving grew more and more important, parents often succeeded in getting the imposed sexton school-teacher replaced by a person, sometimes a local craftsman, who could teach writing to their children.

Once again it is difficult to evaluate the literacy rate of the time. With the ongoing spread of market conditions and the rapid replacement of the barter or exchange system of merchandise by money transactions, more and more people needed access to this kind of written management. From the end of the seventeenth century on, we find that bookkeeping had spread to even the poor day-laborer, who noted his work in a booklet, often the same one used in his elementary learning. So it seems there was a continuous progression of literacy, not homogeneously but rather varying with regional conditions, and even with the devastating consequences of the Thirty Years' War, which nearly depopulated some regions, returning them to conditions comparable to those found a hundred years before. But the dynamic persisted. I estimate that from the sixteenth to the eighteenth centuries the literacy movement reached almost half of the population.

This statement contradicts what you find in most of the handbooks about literacy, including Triebel (see his chapter above). The starting-point for the calculation of literacy used to be the beginning of the nineteenth century, when statistical material, especially signatures on official documents, becomes available. The literacy rate in the population is calculated from the number of those who could sign and those who only signed by crosses. As more and more statistical information becomes available, such as information about the literacy rate among conscripts, a kind of curve of literacy growth is extrapolated that can be continued backwards to an imaginary zero point. In this way, the literacy rate must decrease continually from the beginning of the nineteenth century through the eighteenth, seventeenth, sixteenth, and so on.

This picture is apparently confirmed by the endemic complaints of contemporary intellectuals, clerics, and especially grammar school teachers as to the state of literacy before the nineteenth century. Especially eloquent in this regard were the men of the Enlightenment in the eighteenth and early nineteenth centuries writing for the common people. Historians of literacy have tended to take their complaints at face value, but some criticism is in order. As these intellectuals were frustrated that their writing sold so badly, it is understandable that they found an explanation in the so-called uncivilized state of their potential clients, mostly the uncouth landsmen. There is a strong literary bias in much literacy research, for example, in the standard references of Engelsing, Schenda, and others; such bias has to be overcome by empirical research using the extant sources (see, for example, Peters, 1994 or Maas, 1994).

It has become quite evident over the last few years that this conspiracy of official statistics and intellectuals' attitude is part of the "literacy myth" (Graff, 1979). There is increasing documentation on the real literacy practices of the population, for the most part yet to be explored. Especially in the countryside, in the farmhouses where people used to preserve everything and had the place to store it, rich "archives" of written materials going as far back as the sixteenth century can be discovered: bookkeeping records, letters, diaries, and all kinds of notes (see, for example, the bibliographies and inventories in Hopf-Droste, 1989; Lorenzen-Schmidt & Poulsen, 1992). Analysis of these materials indicates the extended writing practices of all sections of the population that came into contact with literacy and tried to master it.

Economic necessity was the entry to a fuller literacy. Where people kept records of expenses and income, they soon extended this to render accounts of their way of life in general, especially where a rigid Protestant consciousness, which held that success in life on earth prefigures success in life after death, urged them to do so.

From the beginning of "secular literacy," for example, in the records of medieval tradesmen, whether written in Latin or in some kind of German, financial bookkeeping is interspersed with remarks on the general conditions of life. With the change from an exchange system of products to a monetary system, where prices were established in the marketplace, the relation between work and income became opaque. Bookkeeping of all aspects of life was an effort to capture these relations, to make them a subject of ongoing affairs. It became usual by the end of the seventeenth or the beginning of the eighteenth centuries for farmers to write an annual report, reviewing what had happened throughout the year. At the end of their lives, when handing their land to their heirs, they wrote an account to preserve their experience for future generations. As early as the sixteenth century we have peasants' diaries with observations of events inexplicable at the time of their writing, that could be read later with an explanation eventually found and noted that was not available at the time of the experience.[4] Literacy thus became a means of cultural reproduction, worth the pains of acquiring it. It was not unusual for people to preserve all their writing materials when acquiring literacy, and thus we can trace their efforts in detail. Often people practiced writing for its own sake, copying all kind of texts, and engaging in an extended exchange of more or less formalized letters even among neighbors within walking distance.

We don't have enough evidence to definitely establish the literacy figures for these times, but from the documentation available for regions where agricultural historians have started to collect the personal archives of people living in the countryside, farmers, their wives, agricultural workers, and so on, we have enough evidence to falsify the negative picture given in all handbooks on the state of literacy. Where people experienced the urge to acquire literacy they did so in the full sense of reading and writing, not letting themselves be restricted to a simple clerical reproductive practice of becoming familiar with sacred texts, where reading mostly meant reproducing a text learned from memory.

Of course, enormous differences between different regions and different parts of society must have existed. Thus, where serfdom was maintained in rural areas, as in the eastern part of Germany (Prussia) until the end of the eighteenth century, literacy simply was no issue for the lower strata of the population. But where market conditions of production and exchange prevailed, as in the western part of Germany from the end of the seventeenth century on, literacy became accessible[5] – thus the increase in the estimate for literacy to half of the population.

What makes historians of education reluctant to follow the gist of this argument is the evident contradiction with the state of contemporary schools. Compulsory schooling started only in some of the politically and economically advanced regional states in Germany (e.g. Sachsen-Anhalt) in the late seventeenth century, and was extended to a larger proportion only in the nineteenth century. So when you presuppose that literacy can only be acquired by schooling, the negative extrapolation of literacy before the nineteenth century mentioned above makes sense. But I have already mentioned the endemic conflicts between official schools, before the eighteenth century the church's catechism schools, and those growing parts of the population that experienced a need to have access to literacy in its full form. Investigating the preserved rural documentation on literacy practice shows that people eventually found independent ways to become literate when the official institution was not available or not efficient. A helpful neighbor could teach the children, a skillful linen-weaver or even a day-laborer or his wife could earn some money by dispensing literacy skills to children, and especially, the elderly no longer participating in the hardships of farm work could tutor those engaged in self-teaching. All must have been important channels for access to literacy. The mass of preserved exercises in writing in these private archives is rather impressive, for it often simply copies whatever was available as a model, testimony to this grassroots struggle for literacy.

This avenue of early modern access to literacy closed with the advent of capitalist production in the nineteenth century, which had a new kind of urbanization as its sequel. The quickly expanding new kind of towns were instrumental in this development. Until then most towns had a population far below 1,000 inhabitants; in Germany there were some 3,000 towns at the time, only about 20 of them having more than 10,000 inhabitants before the middle of the eighteenth century. These older towns were centers of trade and administration, the larger ones being places of residence of the clerical and political hierarchy, but still dependent on the agricultural production of their inhabitants.

The new towns founded on an industrial basis absorbed the masses of the growing rural population and pressed them into a new system of life-regulation, dictated by the rhythm of machine production that knows no seasons nor even the differences between day and night. The frequently described, deplorable cultural situation of the lower classes in the towns did not continue an earlier, even more deplorable state, but was something new, as was the destruction of the cultural capital of the masses dragged into these towns, often the most flexible parts of the rural population. This is especially true of children. In the country-side children quite normally participated in work as far as they could do so. This meant a strong urge for child labor in summer for herding and so on, and in autumn for participating in the harvest, but not so much in winter. Thus winter was the natural period for formal education in the countryside and hence the appearance of the so-called "winter school" common in the eighteenth century.

This natural regulation of the rhythm of production and reproduction, includ-ing cultural reproduction, had no place in the new towns. The new machines could be manipulated by children as well as adults, in winter as well as in summer, at night as well as during the day. Thus there was no time left for formal education. The deplorable situation of children, so eloquently described in the official "Blue Books" of English parliamentary investigations in the nine-teenth century, used by Karl Marx, had its equivalent in all early capitalist states including Germany. This explains why the cultural situation in these modern nineteenth-century towns cannot be used to extrapolate the situation of earlier times. The new system of compulsory schooling, established in the second part of the nineteenth century, was a reaction to this new situation, with all the problems that ensued, including the resistant block of illiterates that still exists today, after more than 100 years of compulsory schooling.

One might speculate about the future of literacy in the traditional mold if capitalist production had not caused this rupture. In any case, it may be instruct-ive to look at Iceland, which made its way to modern times while maintaining a traditional peasant culture. Iceland is probably the only country in the world where universal literacy has been achieved.[6]

The Establishment of a Writing System (German Orthography) Adapted to the Socialization of Literacy

German orthography is normally seen as an impediment to progress in literacy, perhaps not as "irrational" as English orthography but almost so. So in the pedagogical context every discussion about literacy turns into a debate about a necessary reform of orthography.[7] This is not the place to analyze in detail the structure of German orthography, but I will highlight the very close relationship between orthographic development and the development of literacy.

As previously noted, during the first centuries Latin was the only writing system used and the only one taught in schools. When it was used for writing down German texts, several obstacles had to be surmounted, especially in the phonographic domain (sound-to-letter relation). The basis for the adaptation of the Latin system was of course the pronunciation of Latin in German schools, pronunciation with a dynamic accent lacking in classical Latin, later on without consonantal length which was replaced by syllable, cut prosodies in German as in English. Some of the discrepancies between Latin and the German phonology were less harmful: superfluous distinctions in Latin could be left out in writing

German or be used for semantic and/or grammatical disambiguation. In those cases where Latin orthography lacked the desired distinctions, some daring writers of the first epoch tried to introduce non-Latin signs which could, for example, be invented or derived from runic origins. This, however, was severely frowned upon; even if in German, the aesthetic aspect of a written page had to resemble Latin, so the combination of graphic signs from Latin had to be made use of, a practice which still continues: <ng> for [ŋ]; <sch> for [ʃ], and so on.

One of the greatest problems in German, as in all Germanic languages, was the representation of vowel length. The problem was inherited from Latin, whose "official" orthography does not distinguish vowel length despite efforts to do so from ancient times to the present. Several supplementary markings had been invented and used, for example, as annotations in texts to be read aloud: doubling of vowel signs <aa> for [a:], "apex"; notation <á> for [a:], and so on. These marks were of course known to the educated writers in medieval times and were used experimentally in all early European orthographies.

In Germany, after a long period of experimental writing, which varied according to regional and personal preferences, book printing for the larger public in the late sixteenth and early seventeenth centuries brought about a certain unification with an innovative digraphic notation for <h>, which had lost its value [h] in postvocal position: <Huhn> "fowl", pronounced [hu:n]. Again this notation met strong opposition from orthodox grammarians and teachers, as it is unknown in Latin. This resistance still exists: from the beginning of state regulations on orthographic matters, that is, from the middle of the nineteenth century, there has been a continuous fight against this "Dehnungs-h," "stretching [of vowels]," with each round of orthographic reform biting off some of them. Dutch orthography has had a better chance: here the doubling of vowel signs has been generalized for marking vowel length. As this form is known in Latin, the orthographic authority being Quintilian, there is and has been no similar resistance to it in the Netherlands. On the contrary, it was appreciated as a means for marking here as elsewhere a symbolic distinction from German. In fact, in medieval times differences between Dutch and German did not exist either along political or linguistic boundaries; demarcation between the two had to be created with the advent of national states in early modern times.

Thus there is a continuous process of adaptation of the Latin writing system to the needs of German literacy. If it was not only to be used by professional clerks, who could cope with all kinds of complications including using a foreign language for writing, the borrowed system had to be modified so that it became optimally learnable. That required that it should be possible to base the control of its structures upon the linguistic knowledge acquired with the spoken mother tongue. But the practical tasks define only one side of the process of cultural reproduction.

Another side is the continuous struggle between innovators, who explored the possibilities of an optimally adapted writing system for the newly nationalized literacy in Germany, and the fierce resistance of the guardians of the Latin tradition. It was mostly the printers who introduced orthographic innovations in their books in an effort to win the public in a rapidly expanding market from the early sixteenth century on; when they were successful, they were immediately copied by contemporaries. As printed works were not only read but for a long time frequently copied by hand, both because of the expense of printed material and as a way of undergoing an apprenticeship in writing, these were the models of the new orthography.

Adaptation of the borrowed orthographic system to the structure of spoken German was but one dimension of the creation of the new orthography. Orthography also serves to make even complex texts without immediate models in spoken language readable. This was the reason that Latin was maintained for such a long time in scientific and administrative uses. In medieval times it was often the case that a Latin translation accompanied a German document (juridical instrument) because of the need for it to be authenticated by people not knowing Latin while at the same time to be disambiguated for professional administrators, a task which could only be done in the more flexible Latin language. The development of literacy is congruent with the elaboration of the German standard language which could only replace Latin when it became flexible enough to cope with all tasks facing written practice. Parallel to elaborating the potentials of the German language for these new domains, ways had to be found to represent them graphically in writing – not to be restricted to a simple mapping of the structures of spoken language.

The use of capital letters to mark syntactic functions of nominal groups in the sentence is a good example of this dimension of orthography: capitals orient the reader in the complex pattern of long sentences in printing. Today only German orthography maintains it, but from the middle of the sixteenth century on, this practice expanded to all orthographies in western Europe. Yet all but the German innovators surrendered later to the defenders of the Latin tradition. Still, there might be a structural point in the isolated position of German orthography. In fact, of all languages where this kind of grammatically defined capitalization was used, German shows the most complex sentence structure, which becomes rapidly opaque in proportion to sentence length. German has not only a relatively free word order, but eventually splits up the predicate in a finite part, placed as a second constituent in the sentence, and an infinite part, placed at the end and followed by certain complex and/or peripheral constituents. Thus it makes sense that a special orthographic marking was maintained as an instruction to the reader for parsing sentences. Even today the reform faction fights against this component of German orthography, no longer in the name of Latin as their predecessors did, but rather in the name of an international practice, where English is quoted as a favorite example.

This is a very clear case of cultural heteronomy. What dominates in these debates is an abstract discussion and valorization of prestigious models instead of an analysis of the practice and difficulties of learners. In fact it is quite impressive to follow learners with a different linguistic and writing background making their way to the German language and its orthography, as for example the children of migrant parents. They come to grips quite rapidly with the principles of grammatical capitalization in contrast to the numerous problems they face in the phonographic domain. We can only speculate about the harm caused by this ideologically biased debate, especially in the pedagogical field. Teachers for the most part are simply against this part of the orthography, thus often neglecting it, especially in the context of a communicatively oriented curriculum from the late 1960s, this to the detriment particularly of those learners who have difficulties and need teacher support. Certainly this kind of ideologically biased view of orthographic problems in pedagogy is one of the factors that explains the relatively high rate of literacy failures.

These heteronomous orientations overwrite all domains of discussion of German orthography. We find them with phonographic distinctions, for example, the representation of [s] by <ß> and [z] by <s>, with punctuation on syntactical principles, in distinction to the more prosodically founded punctuation systems of English, for example. (For a comprehensive picture see Maas, 1992; for a succinct exposition see Maas, 1994.) The case of <ß> can serve as a last example, as it figures prominently in the reform debate as well. The sign <ß> goes back to the effort to note the difference between /s/ and /z/ which is unknown in Latin orthography. The details of the balance of the notations for [z] verses [s] in German are in fact peculiar, but the ammunition in the fight against it is not primarily linguistic. The first government to suppress the <ß>, to replace it by <ss>, was the Swiss, formally as a consequence of introducing into the administration in 1880 French typewriters which were not equipped with <ß>. In the 1970s prestigious IBM typewriters pushed offices in all the capitalist areas of German-speaking countries in the same direction. Today computer fonts are more flexible but the pressure still exists. In the present round of reform the domain of <ß> has been reduced.

A closer investigation shows the establishment of modern orthography as a societal process, a product of the market whose forces operate without the knowledge of its subjects; it was less the work of those intellectuals who made a profession of it.[8] When German orthography started to be codified by the end of the eighteenth century, this closed a period of cultural autocentering, emancipating German culture from foreign supremacy, although the Latin tradition as well as new foreign prestige norms, especially French, were very popular amongst the upper classes of the time. Even today intellectuals are at pains to accept this societal matrix; they prefer principled stands that save them the pain of verifying the practical consequences of their proposals, many of which are pedagogically harmful.

If something is to be learned from analyzing foreign models, analyzing literacy in Germany should focus this struggle for an orthography adapted to the need of a democratized literacy, which has been growing in Germany for more than 1,000 years.

The Relation of Orality to Literacy: Preconditions for Access to Literacy Today

The prevailing view of literacy sees it as secondary to speech. This is of course a trivial point when understood in the sense that the acquisition of literacy presupposes, in the statistically normal case, linguistic knowledge acquired with speech, just as riding a bicycle presupposes motor and balance "knowledge" acquired when walking. I have mentioned already the importance of *basing* a certain knowledge upon knowledge already acquired. But in the pedagogical context established with the compulsory school system and its institutions of teacher training, there is a much more restrictive interpretation of this view; oral speech is seen as the real thing, writing but a poor copy of it. In this way the dictum of the priority of orality has been consecrated, especially in the religious tradition of the Reformation, praising the living word of preaching (claiming the imitation of Christ in the New Testament). So the first maxim of all mother-tongue teaching from the seventeenth century on has been: "Write as you speak!"

Of course, even at face value, this maxim is plain nonsense. The development of the national written language in Germany is identical with the movement of decentering from the dialectal, spoken "mother tongues," a development maintained well into the twentieth century. Today new varieties of spoken German appear as older dialectal varieties, bound to sedentary segments of society, are dying out. More importantly, the written language, established in the process of secularization and the democratization of literacy which began in late medieval towns, was modeled on the long-established forms of the effective Latin writing system. As a consequence, the syntax of German is flexible and adapted to the tasks of presenting the reader with the necessary instructions for interpreting even difficult written content. In this way there are parallel traditions of writing in German and Latin.

Acquiring this skill of writing is difficult, going far beyond the simple acquisition of an alphabet and far beyond making a transcription, that is, "reducing speech to writing." This is of course a common denominator for all recent specialized work in this domain (see, for example, Olson, 1994), but in a more generalized discourse, especially in the pedagogical domain, the confusion still prevails. It is necessary to distinguish the structure of the linguistic form in literate discourse from communicative forms in face-to-face interaction. Thus literate vs. oral forms of discourse must be distinguished.

Taken at its face value, the pedagogical maxim "Write as you speak" denies the oral/literate distinction. For intellectuals, assured of their monopolized cultural capital, promoting this maxim is plainly cynical from the perspective of those people who struggle with the difficulties of literacy.

This maxim articulates a reductionist view of language that simplifies the matter far beyond the problems of literacy. Linguistic structures connote the practice for which they were made. Thus even spoken language is learned as a family of different *keys*, *styles*, or *registers* adapted to different contexts. One dimension of these style differences is explicitness or formality. At one extreme it is a strictly context-bound structure of utterances under control of face-to-face interaction, leaving most of what is said implicit. At the other extreme it is context-free articulation of an utterance, submitted to the formal demand of completeness with every piece to be articulated as a grammatical sentence, and permitting the reproduction of identical utterances in different contexts. Oral and literate denote the extremes of this scale; it is not merely chance that in a literate culture a demand for formal reproduction of an utterance is a demand to repeat an utterance *literally*.[9]

Children acquire linguistic structures as *keys* adapted to different social contexts and they make use of this knowledge when confronted with the task of learning to write. In our literate culture, where children grow up in an environment imprinted by literacy, they can make use of this competence to distinguish oral vs. literate structures by the time they start school; our school system can presuppose this competence. Evidently children acquire it in rather diffuse ways in their own home environments.

Until now very little work has been done in this domain, so this acquisition process is not fully understood. For some time now my students and I have been investigating this competence in first-grade children. We ask our subjects to write down something they have recounted themselves in a more or less spontaneous way and which has been tape-recorded. The instruction they are given is to write their utterances down precisely as they spoke them by listening to the recording, that is, to transcribe. As most children nowadays are used to manipulating recording machines, they can do the task by themselves, choosing the span of the record to listen to, repeating the listening, and writing it down at the pace they want. For defendants of the primacy of the spoken word, who promote beginning with the spoken word as the "natural way" to learn writing, this should seem an easy task for children but quite the contrary is true.[10]

Some examples may illustrate what we get in this kind of task. I contrast the transcription of a piece of the oral narrative, in square brackets [ ], with the corresponding writing by the children in < >, with a more or less literal translation into English added in italics:

A: (9–year-old boy from Freiburg [in the South of Germany], presenting a description of a picture)[11]:

['ʔalzo 'z̥o:n: 'man ba:dət 'ta un d̥ɐ 'hun d̥ɛ 'ʃlɛft]
then such-a man bathes there and the dog he sleeps
<son man Badet und der Hund schleft>
such-a man bathes and the dog sleeps
"a certain man is bathing and the dog is sleeping"

B: (a 10-year-old Turkish girl from Osnabrück, reporting on a feast in her family):

[Un ḏa maɪnə 'mutɐ unt maɪnə 'ʃveste di: va:n 'glaʊb ɪç̥ bis um tsvœlf unt maɪnə
fa:tə di: va: bis tsvaɪ]
and then my mother and my sister they were – think I – until twelve and my
father he was until two
<und dann ist Meine Mutter und meine Schwester bis 12.00 geblieben und main
Vater war bis 2.00 Uhr>
and then is my mother and my sister until 12.00 stayed and my father was until
2.00
"and then my mother and my sister stayed until 12.00 and my father was there
until 2.00 o'clock"

The editing of the oral text should be evident. Elliptical passages are completed
(*waren...geblieben* , *2.00 Uhr*), elements of the oral production which serve in
camouflaging thinking, planning utterances, directing the attention of the listener, attenuating comments and the like are omitted ([ˈʔalzo] <also> "now", A;
[ta] <da> "there"A; [ˈglaʊb ɪç̥] <glaube ich> "I think"). But editing goes much
further. Oral syntax optimizes the linguistic means to orient the hearer in a face-
to-face situation, in combination with "nonsegmental" prosodic signals such as
intonation, timing, and intensity distribution, and nonverbal contextual elements such as deictics and gestures. There are many elements that can be used
to direct the listener's attention to what is being talked about, "topicalization,"
what is said about the topic, "focusing," and the like, that are absent from
literate syntax which is designed to function context-free without interference
from nonverbal nonsegmental signals. An almost compulsory means of oral
German syntax is a topicalization marker: The topic is placed in front of the
sentence and marked by a suffix that resembles the form of the article, for
example, [dɐ 'hʊn dɛ], A; [maɪnə 'mutɐ unt maɪnə 'ʃvɛstɐ di:], B; [maɪnə fa:tɐ
di:][12], B). This topicalization marker is quite regularly edited in the children's
texts, often with a complete change in the word order of the sentence, quite
dramatically so in the example B, where the Turkish girl introduces the split
predicate <ist... geblieben> with all the ensuing reordering the literate syntax
asks for, filling the preceding slot of the finite verb <ist> by only one sentence
constituent (adverbial <then>), thus moving the subject <Meine Mutter> after
the verb.

The extensive material we have collected so far is conclusive. This kind of
editing is quite obvious to the children. They need no time to think about it, and
generally they don't comment on it. But often they don't like the task. They say
they would prefer to write the recounted story without listening to the tape.
They manifest signs of irritation when confronted with very oral passages, with
an accumulation of discourse directing particles, extraposition of sentence constituents, anacoluthic passages, and the like. There are few children who try to
fulfill the task of *transcribing*, of putting down all this. These are mostly very
efficient writers, manifesting a rather advanced knowledge of orthography,
presenting the image of very well-behaved children, and accepting even the

absurd task of transcribing an oral text that is imposed on them by an adult authority.

Even if we have not done large-scale research, validated by statistical means, these findings show very clearly how efficiently the system of the acquisition of literacy works in a country like Germany. Those who master it approach the task with a well-defined conception of what literacy is as opposed to orality. As the school curriculum is for the most part insensitive to the problem, "progressive" teachers who maintain the ideology of the primacy of orality by focusing on communicative tasks, fail to provide the necessary support for those children who need it most, the children who are not equipped with this conception and the corresponding motivations to acquire literacy. The result is the high number of illiterate dropouts in German schools. Fortunately most of the children will acquire the skill, in the worst cases despite rather than because of the teaching dispensed to them.

Finally, the example of B, a Turkish girl with manifest difficulties with the German language, highlights another point often overlooked in the debate about mother-tongue teaching. This kind of categorical attitude to literacy, grasping the *oral/literate* difference, is relatively independent of the specific language. The Turkish girl showed a high degree of literate sophistication without really mastering the German language, while other pupils who may be at home with the German language never master literacy, because of a lack of access. This is not to underrate the factor of the mother tongue. Mastering a written language has to be founded upon the knowledge of the structure acquired with the spoken language. Our investigation presents too many examples of immigrant pupils making promising steps into the realm of literacy, as does this Turkish girl, but never making it in the higher grades of school, where tasks, especially in writing, get more complex. The argument here should lead one not to overlook this dimension of literacy: it is directed against the prevailing reduction of literacy to spoken language, not against basing literacy education on the spoken language *per se*.

In fact, the success story of literacy in Germany has at least two facets: Writing finally was based in an optimized way on the knowledge of the national language and its spoken varieties (the epic of the establishment of German orthography), and on an acquisition which proceeded from an established, highly differentiated scale of language *keys*, with the more formal of these providing access to literate structures. When these two facets are in place, the institutions for transmitting literacy in Germany are successful; when they are not, the result is a large number of dropouts and school failures.

Summary

A summary of the argument is shown in tabulated form in table 5.1.

Table 5.1 Tabulated summary

Time	Written language a) non-German(ic)	Written language b) German(ic)	Spoken language	Literacy
9th–11th century	Latin	– some German texts, writing modeled on Latin	– varieties of the German languages (Low and High German) – other Germanic languages – non-Germanic languages – pidginized Latin	Tiny layer of clerics only
12th–15th century	Latin	– supraregional varieties of Low and High German – regularization of the orthographies successively freed from the Latin model	– varieties of German languages (Low and High German) – other Germanic languages – non-Germanic languages – pidginized Latin	– growing literacy in towns: tradesmen, crafts – participation of women in literacy – by the 15th century some 20–25% of the population were literate
16th–18th century	Latin diminishing	– High German, monopolized, especially in school – experimental orthographies in printing, in part independent from the Latin model – German orthography established by the end of the eighteenth century	– varieties of German now as dialects (Low and High German) – other Germanic languages – non-Germanic languages	– growing literacy in towns, – literacy in the countryside in consequence of monetarization – some 40–50% of the population were literate in the eighteenth century

Table 5.1 (cont.)

Time	Written language a) non-German(ic)	Written language b) German(ic)	Spoken language	Literacy
19th century	Latin diminishing	– High German exclusively – Orthography officially regulated (in the federal states, from 1871 on centralized)	– an urban supraregional variety of High German established – dialects (Low and High German) still largely spoken – other Germanic languages – non-Germanic languages	*First half:* – roll-back of literacy in the industrial towns – precarious situation in the countryside – some 30–40% of the population were literate *Second half:* – compulsory schooling enforced, thus literacy mounting to 90%
20th century	–	High German standardized	– propagation of High German by the mass media (broadcasting) – dialects diminishing as well as non-German varieties – regional varieties of High German maintained – from the 1960s on: immigrant languages	Literacy stabilized at 90–95% of the population

Notes

1   This chapter has gained by the debate at the Berlin conference which gave rise to it; I thank especially David Olson and Nancy Torrance for their very helpful criticism of a preliminary version, as well as Neil Johnston for correcting my English.

2   When I got my own doctoral diploma from the University of Freiburg i.B. in 1968, it was written in Latin.

3   Institutions of the old faith soon followed the Protestant model. So in the seventeenth century differences between them decreased.

4   An eloquent example is the diary of the farmer Hartig Sierck from the middle of the seventeenth century, which I have analyzed (Maas, 1995a).

5   Generalizing remarks are of little help here. For example, serfdom could mean different things under different economic conditions. Thus even in Westphalia the peasants were in legal terms mostly serfs, but as monitarization was very advanced here, they produced for the market and paid their debts in money. Even if bound to staying on the farm they could be economically better off than their feudal owner.

6   As industrialization as well as urbanization are a rather recent phenomenon in Iceland, it might be interesting to have a closer look at the situation of the youngest generation there. Along the same line, Sweden, the most agricultural country in the OECD sampling, are at the top of the OECD ranking in the report of 1995.

7   Actually we are once again experiencing a new attempt at reform, to be implemented in 1998. But it is receiving massive resistance from all areas of the public so that it has to be reworked. In Germany we are far from the English situation, where almost everybody has accepted that anyone who wants to acquire literacy has to cope with the given orthography. Debate about orthography distracts a lot of pedagogical energy from the task of helping children with their difficulties in becoming literate – another example in the confusing picture of partial failure of the German educational system in creating "universal literacy."

8   An amusing testimony is reported by the Swiss Grammarian Sattler in the beginning of the seventeenth century, himself a fierce defendant of the tradition, thus opposing sentence internal capitalization. As his admonitions as well as those of his colleagues produced no results, he asked the stubborn local printers why they followed this practice. The only explanation he got was that it is of some advantage for the simple readers, an answer he simply did not understand.

9   There are fascinating insights into these key differences in language and the use made of them in nonliterate societies in Silverstein and Urban, 1996.

10   This kind of experiment is a current technique I use in teacher training, especially those for primary schools undermining the consecrated view of literacy. For many years I have collected ample documentation of children from different regional and social backgrounds as well as immigrant children coping with this task (see for example Maas, 1986).

11   [°] denotes devoicing of (lenizized) consonants.

12   As Turkish does not have grammaticalized gender, Turkish immigrants in Germany often neutralize gender oppositions in German by making exclusive use of the most frequent form: [di:] corresponding in "regular" German to the feminine as well as to the plural form of the article.

100   Utz Maas

References

Graff, H. J. (1979). *The Literacy Myth*. New York: Academic.

Günther, H. and Ludwig, O. (eds.) (1994–6). *Schrift und Schriftlichkeit*, 2 vols. Berlin: de Gruyter.

Hopf-Droste, M.-L. (1989). *Katalog ländlicher Anschreibebücher aus Nordwestdeutschland*. Münster: Nodus.

Hubertus, P. (1995). Wo steht die Alphabetisierungsarbeit heute? In H.Brügelmann et al. (eds.), *Am Rande der Schrift*. Lengwil: Libelle.

Lorenzen-Schmidt, K. and Poulsen, B. (eds.) (1992). *Bäuerliche Anschreibebücher als Quellen zur Wirtschaftsgeschichte*. Neumünster: Wachholtz.

Maas, U. (1986). Zur Aneignung der deutschen Schriftsprache durch ausländische Schüler. *Deutsch lernen*, 11: 23–31.

Maas, U. (1992). *Grundzüge der deutschen Orthographie*. Tübingen: Niemeyer.

Maas, U. (1994). Rechtschreibung und Rechtschreibreform. *Zeitschrift für germanistische Linguistik*, 22: 152–89.

Maas, U. (1995a). Bäuerliches Schreiben in der Frühen Neuzeit. Die Chronik des Hartich Sierk aus den Dithmarschen in der ersten Hälfte des 17.Jahrhunderts. In W. Raible (ed.), *Kulturelle Perspektiven auf Schrift und Schreibprozesse*. Tübingen: Narr.

Maas, U. (1995b). Ländliche Schriftkultur in der Frühen Neuzeit. In A.Gardt et al. (eds.), *Sprachgeschichte des Neuhochdeutschen*. Tübingen: Niemeyer.

OECD (1995). *Literacy, Economy and Society*. Paris: OECD.

Olson, D. R. (1994). *The World on Paper: The conceptual and cognitive implications of writing and reading*. Cambridge: Cambridge University Press.

Peters, J. (1994). Wegweiser zum Innenleben? Möglichkeiten und Grenzen popularer Selbstzeugnisse der Frühen Neuzeit. *Historische Anthropologie* 1: 235–50.

Silverstein, M. and Urban, G. (eds.) (1996). *Natural Histories of Discourse*. Chicago: University of Chicago Press.

Chapter 6

Literacy in Japan: *Kanji, Kana, Rōmaji,* and Bits

Florian Coulmas

Introduction

This chapter is divided into four parts. As indicated in the title, it deals with *kanji* or Chinese characters, *kana*, the *kanji*-derived Japanese syllabaries, *rōmaji*, alphabetic letters for Japanese, and bits, the basic units of computer literacy. While this is a systematic division, in dealing with these elements of Japanese literacy, this chapter also offers a historical perspective on how literacy evolved and what the exigencies of becoming literate in Japan were in the past and are at the present time. For the four units of Japanese literacy mentioned in the title represent both the elements that have to be mastered in order to be functionally literate in present-day Japan and a historical sequence.

The art of writing first came to Japan in the form of written Chinese. *Kana* subsequently evolved from Chinese characters as a means of representing meaningless sounds. In the course of several centuries they were turned into two isomorphic phonographic systems which in spite of their graphical origin in Chinese characters function quite differently, as they map onto the sound structure of Japanese disregarding meaning relations. Chinese characters and *kana* came to be used in combination with each other. By the time the Japanese first learned of alphabetic letters, in the sixteenth century, a mixed character–*kana* orthography was firmly in place. Much as Chinese characters were first associated with the Chinese language, the alphabet was seen by the Japanese as the proper means of writing Western languages. Yet, they quickly recognized the potential of representing Japanese with alphabetic letters, although the first Japanese students of "horizontal writing" experienced considerable conceptual difficulties in trying to understand how the alphabet works.

The alleged simplicity of the alphabet has never convinced large parts of the Japanese speech community. Deliberate interventions for standardizing and simplifying written Japanese were numerous, especially after contacts with the

West intensified in the nineteenth century. They have never resulted in adopting the alphabet for Japanese. Nevertheless, alphabetic letters must now be considered an indispensable part of Japanese literacy. Word-processing technology and other uses of electronic communication play an increasingly important role in this connection. The electronic media exercise two opposing influences on Japanese letters – on one hand they promote the alphabet, and on the other hand they reinforce the traditional writing system.

Kanji

The Japanese word *kanji* means 'Chinese character.' From early historical accounts in the *Nihon shoki* (Chronicles of Japan, 720 AD) and *Kojiki* (Record of Ancient Matters, 712 AD) it is clear that the Japanese were introduced to the art of Chinese writing by scholars from Paekche (Korea) around the beginning of the fifth century. Inscribed artefacts such as mirrors, swords, and coins had been brought to Japan earlier, but to the Japanese these inscriptions had an ornamental rather than a communicative function. The earliest development of writing in Japan was Chinese writing (Seeley, 1991). The writing system and the written language were not at first differentiated. Learning to read and write was tantamount to mastering literary Chinese. However, once Japanese scribes began their own writing rather than confining themselves to copying Chinese texts, their writings exhibit the interference of Japanese grammatical constructions. Hence a hybrid style came into existence which for a long time was typical of scribes not completely versed in Classical Chinese. Until the mid-seventh century, writing in Japan meant composing, more or less completely, in Chinese.

In this early period of Japan's literary tradition, literacy was restricted to a thin educated elite associated with the imperial court and Buddhist clergy. Buddhism was introduced into Japan from Korea early in the sixth century. The Buddhist doctrine became known through Chinese translations of the sutras. Since the religion spread rapidly, a considerable demand for Buddhist texts arose, making large-scale copying of sacred texts one of the most important literary activities. Writing thus continued to be in Chinese and the only writing system known in Japan was the Chinese.

It was not before the eighth century that Japanese writing proper began to take shape. *Kanji* were now more frequently used as phonograms, that is, for their sound values irrespective of their Chinese meaning. In the evolution of scripts, this form of borrowing, which is also known as 'rebus writing,' was quite common. Within the context of writing one language it led to full phonetization, as in Egyptian, where characters of meaningful words were transferred to others which were semantically unrelated but similar in sound. When a given writing system was adopted for another language, meaningful signs were commonly borrowed in a similar fashion and reduced to meaningless, sound-indicating signs – as in the case of Akkadian cuneiform, which used many Sumerian logograms for their sound values only (Coulmas, 1989, pp. 80 ff.). The complexity of the system that evolved from this borrowing strategy was to a large extent a result of the fact that the two functionally different kinds of signs were graphically indistinguishable. In the case of Japanese, too, the Chinese characters that were used for their sound value only were not formally distinguished from Chinese characters in proper Chinese usage. The resulting style of writing which mixed both kinds of characters made for extremely difficult reading. Complex notational forms were often a matter of deliberate choice, a clear indication that writing was a rather elitist skill at the time. The difficulties of mastering the Chinese script together with the Chinese language gave rise to an attitude of revering the written word, its spiritual and aesthetic qualities. Both this attitude and the tendency of literati to prefer idiosyncratic characters continue to be a part of Japan's literary culture today, where knowledge of unusual *kanji* is still recognized as a sign of erudition.

Another aspect of *kanji* usage which has been handed down through the centuries has to do with the twofold employment of *kanji* as sound-indicating characters and meaning-indicating characters. While the phonogram principle was known in early China, where it was used, for example, to indicate Sanskrit names, it was never more than an auxiliary device. In Japan, by contrast, it became a systematic feature of *kanji* usage. As a result, *kanji* have multiple readings originating in sound-based and meaning-based adaptation strategies. These readings are known as *on*, or 'sound,' and *kun*, or 'meaning.' *On* readings refer to Sinojapanese morphemes, while *kun* readings represent Japanese morphemes.

The number of Chinese characters that could be used in Japan was for a long time unrestricted. Potentially every Chinese character was a Japanese *kanji*. Thousands of characters were in use at any one time. In modern times, however, various attempts have been made to restrict the number of characters and thus reduce the complexity of the Japanese writing system. Many reform attempts were thwarted because the traditional script has often been portrayed, successfully, as a repository of national values. After Japan's defeat in the Pacific War, when the force of such arguments was weakened, the first significant reform of *kanji* usage was carried out. While before the war between 6,000 and 7,000 characters were commonly used by Japan's newspapers and publishers, the postwar reform resulted in the 1948 List of Kanji for General Use (*Tōyō kanji jitaihyō*) which comprised just 1,850 characters. These were associated with 2,006 *on* readings and 1,116 *kun* readings. The correct reading of every character in a given piece of writing is determined by context. For example, compound Chinese character words are usually read as *on*, whereas in inflected verb forms the *kanji* is most likely to be given a *kun* reading. In 1981, this list was amended. The Council on National Language drafted a new list under the title *Jōyō kanji hyō*, List of Characters for Common Use, which increased the number of characters by 95. The 1,945 *kanji* of the new list have 2,187 *on* readings and 1,900 *kun* readings. More important than this addition, however, was a change in language policy brought about by the promulgation of the new list. While the *Tōyō kanji jitaihyō* was understood as restricting the use, the *Jōyō kanji hyō* was described in its preamble merely as "a guideline." It presents a standard for the use of Chinese characters in daily life, but the necessity of additional characters in specialized areas is recognized. Thus, the 1981 list can be seen as a backlash against the 1948 reform, as it reaffirms the crucial importance of Chinese characters to written Japanese and Japanese literacy.

As many scholars (e.g., Neustupný, 1984; Rubinger, 1990; Gottlieb, 1995; Taylor & Taylor, 1995; Unger, 1996) have pointed out, a meaningful discussion of literacy in Japan depends on a proper understanding of the complexities of the Japanese writing system. For its structural peculiarities, especially the great number of *kanji* and their manifold readings, make it even more difficult than in other speech communities to unequivocally define a standard of functional literacy. It is due to the Japanese writing system that there is a wider gap between minimal literacy skills and full literacy as an instrument of free participation in all domains of society.

Japanese literacy rates are high and were high early, mainly thanks to social changes which, under the absolutist regime of Tokugawa Japan between the seventeenth and the nineteenth centuries, led to a large part of the Samurai elite losing power and wealth. Thus sociologist S. N. Eisenstadt (1996, p. 200) marvels: the schools, "most of them manned by dispossessed Samurai and not controlled by the *bakufu* [the military government of the Tokugawa], were part of a great educational expansion that made Japan under the Tokugawa probably the most literate pre-modern society." In view of the indisputable complexity of the Japanese writing system, this is a remarkable fact. However, it is the same complexity which must be kept in mind when discussing the nature of Japanese literacy. A gradient rather than a threshold must be assumed which is steeper than that of differences in literacy skills under the condition of less involved writing systems. The large number of *kanji* and the open-ended nature of the standard for common use set in 1981 make it easy to use literacy as a means of social control. Technically Japanese can be written without Chinese characters, but to do so is highly stigmatized. Nonetheless, the possibility is exploited almost exclusively in educational contexts. That it is an option at all is because of the second kind of characters employed in written Japanese, *kana*.

Kana

The word *kana* derives from *kari*, 'temporary, nonregular,' plus *na*, 'name' or 'writing' (Coulmas,1996, p. 252). *Kana* evolved from Chinese characters used as reading aids in annotating Buddhist texts. *Manyōgana*, the *kana* used in the eighth-century *Manyōshō* anthology of Japanese poetry, still look like standard Chinese characters, although they function as phonograms. The system of almost 1,000 characters, if a system it can be called, was highly complex and redundant. But gradually the number of characters was reduced and their form stylized. Each *kana* came to represent one and only one Japanese syllable. Two graphically distinct sets of *kana* signs developed, *katakana* and *hiragana*. *Kata-*

kana were truncated Chinese characters, whereas *hiragana* evolved from a cursive writing style. Originally known as 'women's hand' (*onnade*), *hiragana* was first used primarily by women, while men used standard Chinese characters. However, already by the early tenth century this gender-based distinction in use had broken down and *hiragana* had become generally accepted. By the fourteenth century a near one-to-one correspondence between *kana* and Japanese syllables had been achieved, an extremely simple and elegant system for writing Japanese. The two sets of *kana* characters came to be ordered in a list known as the 'fifty-sounds table.' Some of the most treasured works of Japanese literature, such as *The Tale of Genji* by Murasaki Shikibu, a female novelist of the early eleventh century, were redacted entirely in *kana*. Yet, *kana* never came close to replacing *kanji*; the high prestige of Classical Chinese and the writing associated with it was too great an obstacle.

The great convenience of a simple phonographic script was not lost on the Japanese. *Kana* thus continued to be used in its original function as a reading aid and, in addition, evolved into a supplementary system which came to be used in combination with *kanji* (figure 6.1). In the so-called mixed style (*kanji-kana*

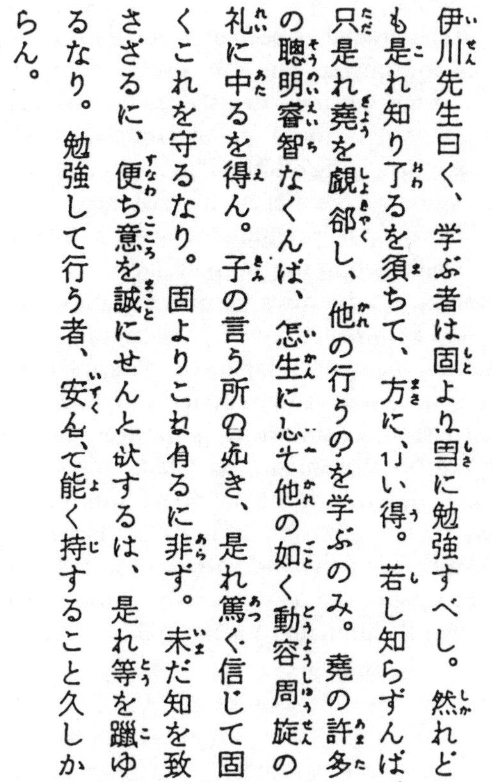

Figure 6.1 Hiragana as a metascript used to indicate the proper reading of Chinese characters, printed in small type next to them

majiribun) content words were written in *kanji* and grammatical morphemes, inflections, and other morphemes hard to represent by means of *kanji* were written in *kana*. Basically this is how Japanese continues to be written today. The present orthography of the two sets of 48 *kana* was officially codified in a Cabinet order of 1946 with minor amendments made in 1973 and 1981. As a representation of the Japanese language, *kana* is so simple that virtually every child has mastered both *hiragana* and *katakana* before entering elementary school.

Not surprisingly, the simplicity of *kana* has often been cited in connection with script reform proposals. During Japan's first modernization period in the final decades of the nineteenth century, pressure groups of concerned intellectuals such as 'Kana no tomo,' 'Irohakai,' and other lesser groups came into existence. They advocated *kana* as the script of Japanese, many of them being motivated by the belief that such a script reform would help improve the lot of the common people. These societies attracted a considerable membership of more than 10,000 (Twine, 1991, p. 233). Hence there was a clear awareness of possible links between writing system, literacy, and social success. However, the conservative defenders of Chinese characters retained the upper hand, the *kana* advocates accomplished nothing.

As in many countries, literacy has been associated in Japan from early on with educational privileges and power. This has always been an obstacle to writing reforms. For such reforms must be devised and implemented by those least interested in bringing about changes in the established ways. From the tenth century on, which saw a flowering all-*kana* literature, all attempts at simplifying the Japanese writing system have met with resistance on the part of the established cultural elites. It would be premature to assume that their grip on Japan's language regime has weakened in our present age.

A key argument the *kana* advocates tried to exploit during the reform-prone Meiji period (1868–1911) in order to the gain support of anti-Chinese nationalists was that *kana* was genuinely Japanese, a script not used for any other language, whereas *kanji* was a borrowed system. Such appeals to alleged authenticity couched in nativist and primordial terms were not available to another faction of the script reform movement, the *rōmaji* advocates. Their proposal to adopt an alphabetic orthography for Japanese was driven by an appeal to universality and easy transferability (Kitta, 1992). However, their efforts were no more effective than those of the *kana* advocates. It is of some interest in this connection that by the time of the first serious proposals to adopt roman letters, the Japanese had known the alphabet for some 300 years.

Rōmaji

Rōmaji means Roman letters. Their career in Japan will be traced here in some detail because, in contradistinction to *kanji* and *kana*, they have not attracted much scholarly attention.

Rōmaji were first introduced to Japan by Portuguese missionaries who came to Japan in the sixteenth century. The first Japanese book in alphabetic letters is a history of saints by Alessandro Valignano (1539–1606), a Jesuit priest. This text of 1591 is entitled *Sanctos no gosagveo vchi nvqigaqi*, 'Extracts of the works of the saints.' According to present conventions it would be spelt thus: *Sankutos no gosagyō no uchi nukigaki*. To Japanese readers this text (figure 6.2) presented considerable difficulties for at least three reasons. They were unfamiliar with the alphabet, no convention for writing Japanese in alphabetic letters was established, and the Portuguese were inconsistent and uncertain about such issues as segmentation. On the very first page we find rival spellings (*tamaite* vs. *tamayeba*) and two different segmentations of the same expression (*to xite xixi tamayeba* vs. *toxite xixitamayeba*) (figure 6.2). The principles underlying Portuguese usage of their letters were quite opaque. They needed several letters to represent a single word, often even more than one for a simple syllable. And, what was even more surprising, they did not consistently represent the same syllable with the same letters: both <e> and <ye> were used for /e/, <cu> and <qu> for /ku/, etc. (figure 6.3). This, in any event, must have been the perception of a literate Japanese trying to understand the alphabetic principle on the basis of Portuguese writing. Clearly, in comparison to *kana* this was a highly complex system. For the benefit of those unfamiliar with it a version of the *Sanctos* in regular Japanese was produced (figure 6.4).   Next, an Italian merchant, Francesco Carletti from Florence, landed on Japanese shores in 1597 and tried to make sense of what he called "Japanese hieroglyphs." In his travelogue *Ragionamenti del mio viaggio intorno al mondo* we find various transcriptions of Japanese verse which he recorded without any knowledge of Japanese. He used the alphabet as he knew it. For our purposes this is of interest because Carletti seems to be the first to apply the alphabet according to Italian, or rather Florentine, conventions to Japanese. Some characteristic differences between his representation of Japanese syllables and what we find in the Portuguese *Sanctos* are summarized in the following table:

Sanctos	qi	qu	qe	xi	ua	tçu
Carletti	chi	cu	che	sci	va	zu

A systematic analysis could have revealed to the Japanese that correspondences such as <x> and <s>; <k>, <c>, and <q>, as well as between such digraphs as <ch>, <sc>, and <tç> were not random. But were they entirely unjustified to conclude that the alphabet was rather unstable and unreliable? Their difficulties were further compounded whenever European travelers of other linguistic backgrounds arrived. A comparison of, for example, French and German representations of the Japanese syllables with initial /k-/ and /g-/ reveals baffling differences:

Kana k-, g-	か	き	く	こ	が	ぎ	ぐ	げ	ご
French	ca	ki	cou	co	ga	ghi	gou	ghe	go
German	ka	ki	ku	ko	ga	gi	gu	ge	go

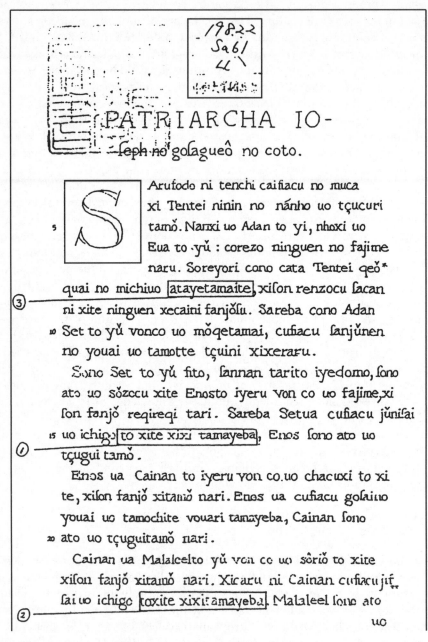

Figure 6.2   *Sanctos no gosagveo no vchi nvqigaqi* (1591)

That was not the end of it. The Dutch who arrived in Japan in 1600 added further confusion, spelling, for example, <tsoe> where the Sanctos wrote <tçu>. Clearly, *the* alphabet was not one system. It was not self-evident either, but rather required a supplementary system for explanation. In this regard the

受け	vqe	uke
せしむる	xeximuru	seshimuru
時	toqi	toki
若き	vacaqi	wakaki
記録	qirocv	kiroku
教え	voxiye	oshie

Figure 6.3   Some words in Japanese spelling, Sanctos spelling, and current *rōmaji*

Japanese were quite experienced, having first developed and then used *kana* as a supplementary or metascript to help them cope with *kanji*. In order to come to terms with the alphabet, they adopted the same approach.

Among the most illuminating documents of how the Japanese viewed the alphabet is Aoki Konyō's essay *Oranda moji ryakkō*, 'Remarks on Dutch Letters,' of 1746. It is one of the earliest systematic studies of the Dutch alphabet by a Japanese scholar. His investigation begins with listing the inventory of the signs (figure 6.5). Three kinds of letters are introduced known in Dutch, respectively, as *trekletter, merkletter,* and *drukletter*. The list is supplemented with certain explanations regarding, for example, the direction of reading, as well as with reading aids with *katakana* serving as the metascript. Since Aoki was unable to discover the principles determining the various pronunciations of the letters, he compiled long word lists. The entry of the Japanese word *fuyu*, 'winter,' has been magnified for illustration (figure 6.6). The Dutch equivalent *winter* is spelled out, each letter being provided with metascriptual explanations in *katakana*. The upper line indicates pronunciations, whereas the lower line provides the letter names in Dutch. Using the syllabic segmentation given in the upper line as a guide, one would arrive at the pronunciation (*uintoru*) which at least approximated the Dutch word. This was a rather cumbersome procedure, especially because words are so numerous. Aoki, therefore, compiled lists of possible Dutch syllables, systematically combining all vowel letters with all consonant letters first, and then all consonant letters with all vowel letters. He disregarded syllables containing consonant clusters, perhaps because of the great number of letter combinations that would be necessary for an exhaustive list.

Aoki's lists evince a characteristic method. He relies on his own script as a matrix and uses its units as the basic units of segmentation. The object of his description, the Dutch alphabet, is thus subjected to the categories of his reference system, *kana*, which functions as a metascript. This is a common procedure of which we find another example in Maeno Ryōtaku's treatise *Oranda Yakubun ryaku*, 'Outline of Dutch Translation,' of 1771 (figures 6.7 and 6.8). Maeno listed the Dutch letters in groups that match sets of same-onset *kana*. Like Aoki, he also compiled a list of syllables of simple VC and CV combinations. He then

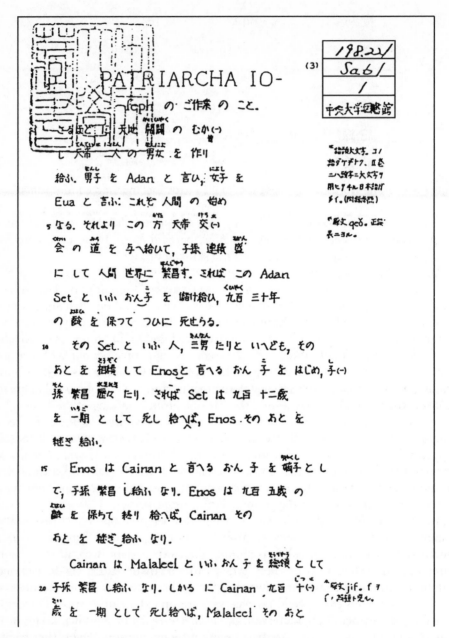

Figure 6.4 *Sanctos no gosagveo* in regular Japanese script

went a step further by providing his readers with an illustration that it was indeed possible to write Japanese in alphabetic letters. His sample is the *Yamato uta*, a mnemonic verse for memorizing *kana* (figure 6.9). In writing the letters as syllable groups he once again applied to the system he examined the segmentation

Figure 6.5 The Dutch alphabet explained by Aoki Konyō in his essay *Oranda moji ryakkō*, 'Remarks on Dutch letters'

principle of his own script. Clearly, these letters could be used to write Japanese. However, the advantages of doing so were far from compelling to Japanese literati. As a matter of fact, it was not before Japan's forced opening to the West in the mid-nineteenth century that any serious proposals for the romanization of Japanese were made.

During the 1870s and 1880s the possibility of abandoning both Chinese characters and *kana* in favor of an alphabetic script for Japanese was discussed by influential intellectuals such as Nanbu Yoshikazu, Nishi Amane, and Ōtsuki Fumihiko. In 1885, some of them formed the 'Rōmaji kai,' an association for the promotion of the Latin alphabet. Among the topics of their deliberations was the systematic nature of the alphabet. Experience with European languages had taught them that alphabetic letters varied greatly in their sound values from one language to another. A system suitable for the Japanese language thus had to be devised. As a result, various systems came into existence, three of which continue to be used today, known respectively as the *kunreishiki*, *nippon-shiki*, and *Hepburn* systems. Dedicated romanization proponents published journals such as *Rōmaji* (figure 6.10), but the alphabet remained a foreign script with which students were made familiar using *kana* as the metascript in terms of which it was understood (figure 6.11).

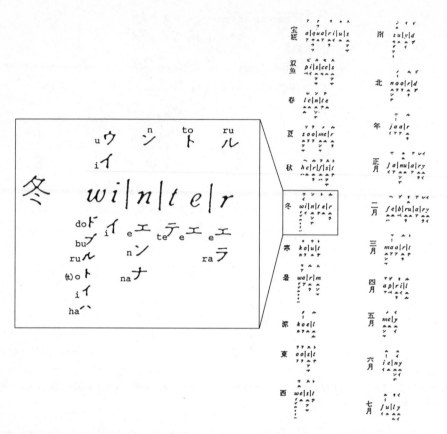

Figure 6.6 The Japanese word *fuyu*, 'winter,' and its Dutch equivalent *winter* with metascriptual explanations in *katakana*: upper line gives pronunciation, lower line letter names in Dutch. Alphabetic letter added by F.C. From the word list of Aoki Konyō's *Oranda moji ryakkō* (1746)

The romanization movement attracted a considerable following in the early Meiji years, and it still commanded some attention in educational circles after the Pacific War which, some argued, had been lost because the allied forces had enjoyed the communicative advantages offered by the alphabet. Yet, realistic chances for the romanization of Japanese have always been slight at best. The predisposition of Japanese intellectuals to regard the Chinese script as an indispensible part of Japan's cultural heritage and the willingness of the Japanese public to accept this view militated against so drastic a departure from the past. However, while a reform that openly indicated a break with the tradition had little chance of success, the alphabet was nevertheless allowed to play an increasingly important role in Japanese letters. Acronyms and brand names make extensive use of alphabetic letters. For example, all Japanese cars have romanized names, even for the domestic market, and virtually all magazines of mass circulation have romanized titles, both in Japanese and other languages, such as

Figure 6.7 The letters of the Dutch alphabet arranged in groups to match groups of same-onset *kana*; from Maeno Ryōtaku, *Oranda yakubun ryaky*, 'Outline of Dutch translation' (1771)

Asahi Journal, Arbeit, Baccus, City Road, Friday, Muffin, Olive, Quark, Viva Rock, etc. Today alphabetic letters are widely associated with the English language, to the extent that these letters which in earlier periods were known as *oranda moji* and then *rōmaji* are now often called *eiji* or English letters. Alphabetic letters are also widely used in commercial advertisements, though the general public is not necessarily expected to know how to read them. *Kana* is still used as the metascript for indicating pronunciation (figure 6.12).

At the present time, romanization for the sake of promoting literacy is less of an issue than ever, if only because most people concerned are unaware of the fact that there is an underclass of Japanese with restricted literacy (Buraku kaihō kenkyūsho, 1991; Coulmas, 1994; Unger, 1996). Moreover, Japan is affluent enough to solve whatever illiteracy or semiliteracy problems remain without changing its writing system. Indeed, the problems a script reform would inevitably engender seem much more arduous than those one has learned to live with through the centuries. There are, nevertheless, developments which strengthen the position of the alphabet in Japan, developments having to do with the fact that in the course of the past two decades the qwerty keyboard has become a household appliance.

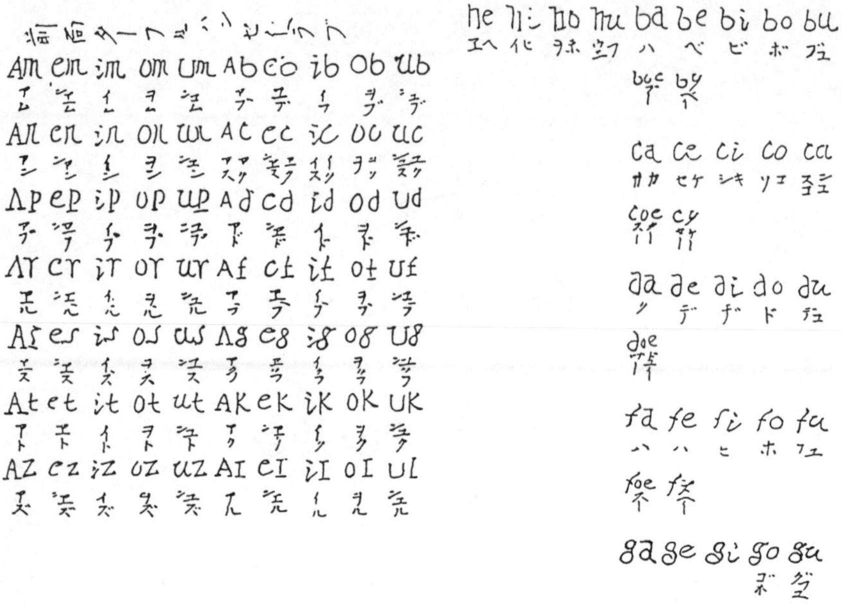

Figure 6.8 Maeno Ryōtaku's list of syllables, from *Oranda yakubun ryaky*, 'Outline of Dutch translation' (1771)

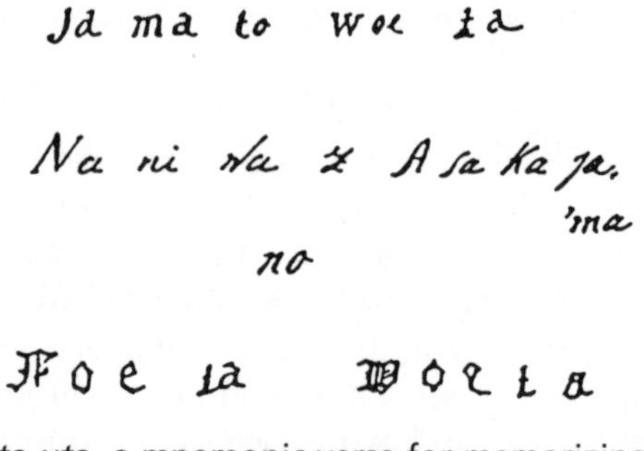

Figure 6.9 The *Yamato uta*, a mnemonic verse for memorizing *kana*. The alphabetic letters are grouped to form syllables. Maeno Ryōtaku, *Oranda yakubun ryaky*, 'Outline of Dutch translation' (1771)

Bits

As in other advanced countries, computer communications technology has an enormous impact on Japanese society and penetrates both work and domestic life in accelerating cycles. Japan is quickly transforming itself into a knowledge-value society where access to and skillful management of information are vital qualifications for ever-wider sectors of the populace. Computerized banking, shopping, ticket reservation, and leisure activities have become commonplace

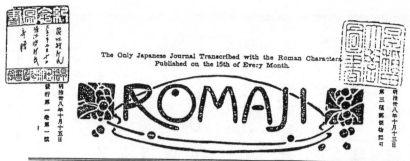

Figure 6.10   The first issue of *Rōmaji*, a Japanese journal in roman letters, October 1905

within a very short time. The impacts upon Japanese society of computer communications technology are manifold and far too complex to be examined here. For our present discussion of contemporary literacy, however, one aspect is of special significance. This is that the computer revolution relies by and large on the alphabetic code.

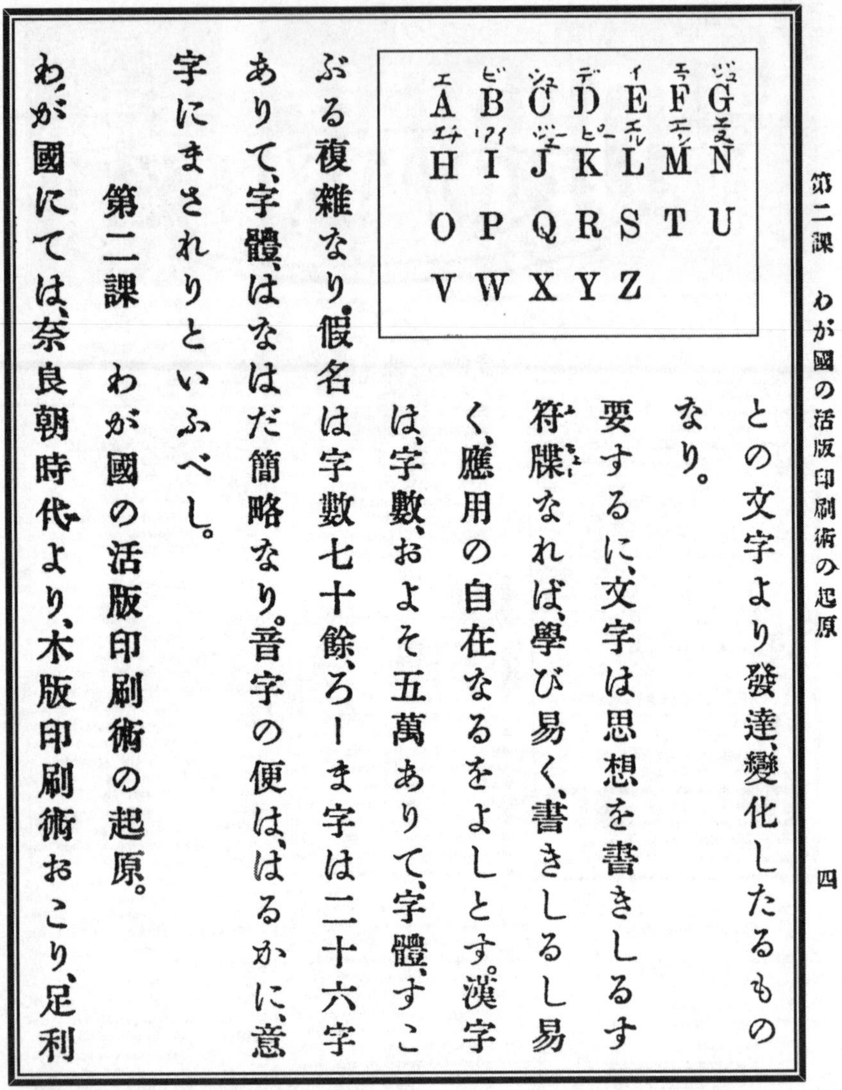
第二課　わが國の活版印刷術の起原　四

A B C D E F G
H I J K L M N
O P Q R S T U
V W X Y Z

との文字より發達、變化したるもの
なり。
要するに、文字は思想を書きしるす
符牒なれば、學び易く、書きしるし易
く、應用の自在なるをよしとす。漢字
は、字數、およそ五萬ありて、字體、すこ
ぶる複雑なり。假名は字數七十餘、ろーま字は二十六字
ありて、字體はなはだ簡略なり。音字の便は、はるかに、意
字にまされりといふべし。
第二課　わが國の活版印刷術の起原。
わが國にては、奈良朝時代より、木版印刷術おこり、足利

Figure 6.11 A paragraph from a Japanese textbook for high school students of 1905. The alphabet is introduced as a phonographic system. Annotations by the student who owned it indicate letter names in English. The student made a mistake, however, giving [pi:] as the name of <K>

Japanese computer manufacturers and software makers have worked hard to make Japanese written language manageable for word processing and other modes of computing. They have been very successful in that Japanese texts can now be written easily and in every conceivable form. The graphics programs of Japanese software as well as printer technology are very advanced, which can be attributed, perhaps, to some extent to the graphic complexity of the Japanese

Figure 6.12 Advertisements and brand names in alphabetic writing with *kana* as reading aids

writing system. However, although input by voice and pen is possible now, the keyboard is and will be for some time the most common means of inputting information. Japanese keyboards are designed for inputting linguistic data using the alphabet or *kana* (figure 6.13). The user can choose the input mode according to his or her preference. The output of Japanese word-processing programs is in regular Japanese writing, that is, *kanji* and *kana*. Since *kana* are not much more numerous than the letters of the alphabet, they can easily be accommodated on an alphabetic keyboard. Yet, it turns out that the vast majority of Japanese computer users prefer an alphabetic input. As already pointed out by Unger (1984), this has significant implications for the cognitive processing of Japanese written language. For, in order to use the alphabetic code for input, one must have a phonographic model of the target word which is then matched by the machine with the suitable *kanji*. As a mental object the word no longer exists primarily as a character which can be written down even if the writer is unsure

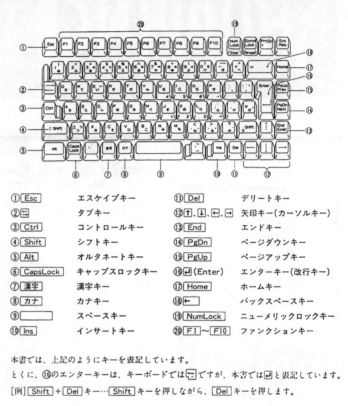

Figure 6.13 A Japanese keyboard designed for input by alphabet or *kana*

about its phonetic form. If we assume that the alphabetic code somehow maps onto the phonetic representation of Japanese words rather than functioning solely as a transliteration, then alphabetic input implies that, mentally, the phonetic representation comes first. Hence, the alphabet creeps into the computer users' internal language model. It is here, then, that for the first time in Japanese literary history the alphabet assumes a function that goes beyond the ornamental and does no longer depend on *kana* as a metascript and reading aid. In this sense knowledge of the alphabetic code has become a crucial component of Japanese literacy.

Conclusion

Written Japanese probably represents the most involved writing system fully implemented for electronic communication today. The long history of Japanese literacy of more than one and a half millennia evolved in several steps of adapting imported letters. The idea that writing is to depict vernacular speech took a long time to become part of Japan's cultural background assumptions and is still not a strong conviction. This is so because, notwithstanding the simplifying tendencies, such as the derivation of *kana* from Chinese characters, which have marked the evolution of Japanese writing, the system repeatedly regained its complexity. Japan's high literacy rates have been achieved in spite of the writing system which its users on more than one occasion kept from developing into a simple phonetic script whose mastery would be less indicative of gradations in cultivation of scholarship. The integration of the roman alphabet into Japanese letters once again testifies to the tendency of adding new components to the system without discarding old ones. Thus, although both *kana* and alphabetic letters are much simpler than *kanji*, their adoption for writing Japanese has failed to reduce the overall complexity of the writing system. This suggests two things: one is that in addition to being adjusted to the instrumental requirements of a practical medium of recording and retrieving information, writing systems evolve in response to other requirements, such as social control and conceptual organization of the universe of letters. The second is that literacy is not just knowing a script. In Japan, several scripts are involved, each in its proper place. And although there is a great deal of spontaneity and playfulness in the world of Japanese letters, the system continues to be too complex for universal literacy to be sustained in the absence of intensive schooling. Japan is a highly literate society because it is a schooled society.

References

Buraku kaihō kenkyūsho (Research Center for the Liberation of the Burak People) (1991). *Shikiji no jinken. Kokusai sikijinen to nihon no dadai (Literacy and human rights)*. The international literacy year and Japan's task. Tokyo: Editor.

Coulmas, F. (1989). *The Writing Systems of the World*. Oxford: Blackwell.

Coulmas, F. (1994). Writing systems and literacy. In L. Verhoeven (ed.), *Functional Literacy: Theoretical issue and educational implications*. Amsterdam: John Benjamins.

Coulmas, F. (1996). *The Blackwell Encyclopedia of Writing Systems*. Oxford: Blackwell.

Eisenstadt, S. N. (1996). *Japanese Civilization: A comparative view*. Chicago: University of Chicago Press.

Gottlieb, N. (1995). *Kanji Politics: Language policy and Japanese script*. New York: Kegan Paul International.

Kitta, H. (1992). *Nippon no Rōmazi-undō (Japan's romanization movement)*. Tokyo: Nippon Rōmazi Kyōiku Kenkyūkai.

Neustupný, J. V. (1984). Literacy and minorities: Divergent perceptions. In F. Coulmas (ed.), *Linguistic Minorities and Literacy: Language policy issues in developing countries*. New York: Mouton.

Rubinger, R. (1990). Shikiji nōryoku no tōzai (Literacy in East and West). In U. Tadao and R. Ogawa, (eds.), *Kotoba no hikaku bunmeigaku*. Tokyo: Fukutake shoten.

Seeley, C. (1991). *A History of Writing in Japan*. Leiden, Köln: E. J. Brill.

Taylor, I. and Taylor, M. M. (1995). *Writing and Literacy in Chinese, Korean and Japanese*. Amsterdam: John Benjamins.

Twine, N. (1991). *Language and the Modern State: The reform of written Japanese*. New York: Routledge.

Unger, J. M. (1984). Japanese orthography in the computer age. *Visible Language*, 18(3): 238–53.

Unger, J. M. (1996). *Literacy and Script Reform in Occupation Japan*. New York: Oxford University Press.

Part II

On Becoming a Literate Society: Literacy in Developing Societies

a) African Case Studies

Chapter 7

Language, Literacy, the Production and Reproduction of Knowledge, and the Challenge of African Development

Kwesi K. Prah

Introduction: The Myth of Development

Over the past 30 to 40 years of postcolonialism in Africa, the single most persistent ideological construct in the articulation of the *raison d'être* of African states has been the notion of development. This idea has been utilized by practically all regimes as the ultimate goal of governance. It is a term descriptive of an experience whose desirability, in all its vagueness, enjoys the blessing of all social groups and classes. In its looseness, it promises all to all men and women. It means different things to different groups, while all agree that it is the single most significant justification for the existence of the state. Many will suggest that it means the improvement of the quality of life of increasing sections of the population, but again this translates differently to people according to their station in the economic and social order. Since the hierarchy of people's requirements and needs differ at both the individual and collective levels of social life, what is perceived by governments as priorities are ultimately advised by the interests of dominant groups within the society. "Development" becomes a slogan which means a better life, to all men.

In his essay *Democracy and Development in Africa* (1996), Ake made the point that the development idea, however nebulous the attempts that have been pursued by African ruling groups appear to be, cannot be abandoned because it is an ideology of survival and an instrument for the reproduction of domination.

Indeed, the concept of development has acquired oracular sanctity in the political language of African dominant elites.

Development Theory and Practice

While African politicians, governmental planners, and civil servants have sought to find the meanings and praxis of the development ideal as their interests dictate and circumstances permit, scholars and social theoreticians have also copiously elaborated on the objects, processes, and prerequisites of development. From W. W. Rostow's *The Stages of Economic Growth* (1960) leading to the "takeoff," to the *Brundtland Report*'s (1987) "sustainable development" as "development that meets the needs of the present without compromising the ability of future generations to meet their own needs," as Dei rightly suggests, "the impulse for 'development' is informed by western hegemonic understandings of what developing societies lack and what they are expected to become" (Dei, 1993, p. 98). African scholarship has tended to follow in train, either in reaction or intention, and has hardly produced autonomous paradigms, inspired by the need to produce homegrown answers to the problems of development in Africa.

In the post-Second World War period, theories of development have ranged in variety from the Soviet-sourced views of the noncapitalist road to socialism, which advised state capitalist and bureaucratic formulae for growth, to structural adjustment as an answer to the challenge of African development. If these two examples stand at the opposite extremities, many others fall in between.

Remarkably, postcolonial Asia, which had only a decade's lead into the era of independence, has produced a visibly successful economic transformation which has assured the entrance of the "Asian tigers" into the next century, virtually in the economic leadership of world growth cycles, in spite of recent setbacks. Over the same period, growth in Africa has declined, stagnated, or retrogressed. Social and economic growth in Africa has been particularly elusive. Western, largely liberal development theorists and their African counterparts have tended to emphasize development as indices of gross domestic product and gross national product. The point has been made that often the statistics used are largely unreliable, the abstract isolation of selected variables and the bald undifferentiated computation of per capita figures, which mask the existential realities of mass society in Africa (Bernstein, 1973). While positive growth figures may be registered in a specific case, the socioeconomic distribution of the growth process may consolidate inequities in the political economy, the sort of scenario that has been described as "a process of forced income transfer, not of shared economic progress" (Johnson, 1971, p. 10). It is therefore important to conceptually separate "economic growth" from "development." They are related, but one does not mean or directly imply the other. Forty years ago, Gunnar Myrdal made this point (Bernstein, 1973).

No sociologically accountable understanding of development can escape the appreciation of the investiture of cultural heritage as the matrix of the development process. Some observers have suggested that "cultural blockages," which imply developmentally inhibitory cultural institutions within underdeveloped societies, hinder and block developmental transformations in these societies. While in some specific instances this may be very true, by and large the idea of cultural blockages can be seen as a point of departure, which does not recognize the wide variety of growth models which "can with ingenuity be enlarged" (Hahn & Mathews, 1967; see also Bernstein, 1973). Cultural blockages exist only insofar as people do not perceive how specific institutions inhibit their ability to augment their production and quality of life; how specific institutions inhabit the area of social practice and everyday life, and serve as fetters on the achievement and establishment of other socially productive institutions. Peter Ekeh has also identified this misconception, which he describes as the tendency to see African culture as antimodern (Ekeh, 1986). Where an understanding and recognition of inhibitory practices preventing social and economic development exist, there is no evidence that people remain attached to such institutions. Perceptible social and economic rewards are the best antidote to "cultural blockages."

But even when that has been said, we would argue that economic and social development needs to be premised on the cultural usages and background of a given society. One of the key differences in the development experience of Asia in contrast to Africa is precisely this point. None of the "Asia economic tigers" is advancing forward on the basis of colonial languages. Capitalist development in Asia has been sufficiently adapted to the cultural baggage of Asia. The cultural dressing of Asian development is more Asian than western. Asia has indigenized westernism. An important facilitatory factor which partially accounts for Asian success in utilizing its culture as a basis for social and economic advancement in our times is the literate base of a good part of Asian cultures. Jack Goody has drawn attention to this point.

> Indeed part of the phenomenon called neo-colonialism has to be seen in terms of this very openness which is associated with the absence of a strong, written tradition that can stand up against the written cultures of the world system. There are important distinctions to be made between different socio-cultural regions of the Third World, of the world system, not simply in terms of their relationship with the metropolis but in terms of their own indigenous, socio-cultural organization, in terms of communications as well as the economy. While the major societies of the Asian continent were strongly affected by the expansion of Europeans, they were more rarely "colonies" in the African, American and Oceanic sense; nor are they today neo-colonial from the cultural standpoint. Their written traditions have provided them with a more solid basis for cultural resistance than is the case with most oral cultures (Goody, 1986).

The validity of this observation is incontrovertible. It is a point which must have implications for future development planning in Africa. However, an additional point which must be made is that while a written culture has made the resistance against cultural neocolonialism of parts of Asia more successful, what has perhaps been most central in this cultural resilience has been the standing of the world religions of the Near East and Asia proper. Western cultural penetration of the non-western world never successfully undermined the status of the major religions of Asia the way they successfully did in Africa. African religious practices were "heathenized" and treated as religious practices of savages. In Asia, although the westerner never in theory doubted the superiority of Christianity to all else, Islam, Buddhism, Hinduism, or Shintoism were never seriously regarded as religious confessions to be replaced as part of the "white man's burden." Crucial in this regard was the fact that they were written religious cultures with verifiable histories. As cultural bases, they provided Asia with a confidence which was not significantly dented by the colonial experience.

Culture, Language, and Literacy in Africa: Leading Issues

If Asia has in its postcolonial experience retreated from the linguistic legacy of colonialism, Africa has remained "trapped" in this legacy. This chapter argues that it is this cultural denationalization of the development endeavor in Africa which largely accounts for the inability of Africa to move forward. We would take the argument further with the suggestion that, until such time as Africans recenter their cultural heritage at the heart of attempts at social and economic development, no headway can be made. Indigenous language usage lies at the core of the solution. In other words, literacy for development in Africa must be based on African languages (Prah, 1995; 1993).

Another way of making the same point is that, until such time as the age-long historical and cultural inheritance is accepted as the cultural base of development in Africa, the productive capacity of the masses to produce and consume cannot be optimized. The use of colonial languages silences the broader social classes. It underlines the inferiority of the culture of the majorities in African society. It disenables the development of a democratic culture by denying the viability of the languages of the overwhelming majority of the people, as languages with no future.

In its "Closing Report," the African Inter- Ministerial Council Meeting on the Use of National Languages in the African Educational System (ADEA, 1996) testified to what was frequently described at the meeting as "the lack of political will" within African ruling groups, with regard to the fuller usage of African languages in education and development. In the context of the discussions which were held during the meeting, this phrase "lack of political will" was a catch-all expression for the social inertia which prevents African authorities from putting into practice language policies which they have in principle for years accepted as the most strategically judicious course of action if education and development efforts are to bear fruit. This is a point which Ayo Bamgbose, Ben Elugbe, Sammy Beban Chumbow, and others have been making for years. It is the inertia of an elite which has reproduced itself in the 30 to 40 years of postcolonialism – an elite which has multiplied considerably but remains unable to transform

African society into modern cultures in social production. The high culture of the postcolonial elite has shifted away from the narrow single colonial cultural power base, to a wider one. While the younger generation may be broader in its points of affinity to a variety of western language communities and western reference groups (so that today, elite Ugandans, Zimbabweans, Zambians, Nigerians, for example, would have representation from elements who have been exposed in their professional formation to western countries or East European ones, as diverse as England, France, the Netherlands, Russia, Poland, Germany, etc.), this elite remains inordinately beholden to the economic and cultural "magic" of western society. The cultural overkill of this "fatal attraction" of the west has paralyzed the creativity of the African elite. There is an unspoken loss of confidence in its own cultural belongings, and it operates as if it is desperate to integrate itself as completely as possible into the western cultural world. Colonial language-use is a hallmark of the social practice of this elite.

Pidgins, Native Tongues and the Languages of Power

Generally the more languages you speak, the wider your cultural world. Obviously, the better you know your languages the deeper the appreciation of the cultural worlds they open up to you. Languages open doors into other minds and cultures; knowledge which strengthens our understanding of humanity. But within the global structure of power differentials, languages have a hierarchy. Some languages are more important than others. While some are growing, equally others are dying.

If present trends in language policy and practice continue, most African languages will be extinct in another century. Those who speak universal or widely used languages also represent political influence in the international order.

Under colonialism, language policy throughout the colonial world had meant the imposition of the language of conquest on the conquered. The overlords required that by plan and purpose the natives should speak the master's tongue. Most natives who aspired towards social mobility and elevation learned French, English, Portuguese, and Spanish. Within the native population (mainly urban, but also some rural people), those who used the language of the new masters employed it in different contexts, while for some it was a "fanagaloor," a pidgin or creole which enabled social interaction at the workplace where not only master and servant met, but also natives from different language groups. For these people, the colonial language was only a useful social tool. It made it possible for people to operate in the new colonial economy and attempt to make a livelihood.

These have been very dynamic language forms which also draw on all other languages they socially relate to. Words or expressions which at any point enjoy sufficient consensual understanding within the creolizing culture are incorporated. Pidgins retain the colonial language at their core. But they evolve so rapidly that with time they dissolve the core and increasingly acquire peculiarities of their own. During the 1950s the pidgin which existed during the late colonial period in English-speaking west Africa was mutually intelligible among Africans in the British west African areas. A Nigerian factory or urban worker would be understood by other pidgin-speakers in the British Cameroons, Ghana, Sierra Leone, or Gambia. This has been particularly true for urbanites. In the rural areas only mining towns and the cash-crop producing areas created conditions for pidgin development and speech. Even then, in the rural areas such elements were relatively limited in numbers. In postcolonial urban Africa pidgin is also popular among some elements of the urban youth from all social strata. Among the more privileged of these youth it is a subversive language, the basis for the cultivation of the counterculture against their seniors in age and the social order. For most, however, pidgins are invaluable tools for communication in multilingual colonial situations.

But pidgins were and are still regarded by all as poor substitutes for the language/s of power. From the early years of the colonial experience, those who attempted to speak in linguistic structures which were close to usage in the metropolis of the colonial powers thrived in schools modeled on western experiences. They were mainly secondary school products. Such types were also in many instances exposed to Racine, Molière, Hugo, Shakespeare, Dickens, or Milton. It is these types who dominated the elite, and gave leadership to the cultural life of African countries before and after colonial freedom. They generally despised the pidgins and were oriented towards greater and increasing cultural affinity to the westerner instead of their roots. If they particularly scorned the pidgins, their attitude to their mother tongue and other indigenous languages was divided. There were no economic and social benefits attached to the use of indigenous languages.

From the early stages of the colonial experience, the westernized elite has had an ambivalent and schizophrenic attitude towards the usage of colonial languages. The colonial language, in the colonial state, was a language of upward social mobility; a language of ascendancy and power. Those who wished to socially advance in the colonial order had to linguistically acculturate. Colonial languages did not principally adapt to Africans, it was Africans who adapted to colonial languages.

In the early eighteenth century, the Gold Coast pastor of the Dutch Reformed Church based in Elmina, Johannes Eliza Jacobus Capitein, faced with the task of translating passages of the Protestant confession into the Fanti variety of Akan, was initially of the opinion that these ideas may not be renderable in his native tongue (Prah, 1965). During the nineteenth century, Alexander Crummell, in his *English Language in Liberia* (1861), dismissed African languages thus: "Let us speak of the African dialects ... there are ... definite marks of inferiority connected with them all, which place them at a distance from civilized languages" (Langley, 1979, p. 357).

Pursuing his contention further, and basing himself on the "authority" of Leighton Wilson, Crummell continued with the assertion that African languages are harsh, abrupt, energetic, indistinct in enunciation, meagre in point of words, abound with inarticulate nasal and guttural sounds, possess but few inflections and grammatical forms. . . . These languages, moreover, are characterized by low-ness of ideas. As the speech of rude barbarians, . . . they are marked by brutal and vindictive sentiments.

These views would not have been as dramatic in impact if it were not for the fact that, as Ayo Langley suggests, Crummell is, "regarded as the leading African intellectual of the nineteenth century" (Langley, 1979, p. 148).

In the opening paragraphs of his *In My Father's House*, Appiah has ironically asked if a century later with well over half of Africa speaking and conducting official business in English and the rest using Portuguese and French as official languages, "The Reverend Crummell would have been pleased with this news" (Appiah, 1992, p. 1). The core of Crummell's argument runs from the implicit premise that culturally Africa's social and economic advancement required a wholesale revamp along western lines. Basically, this assumption was shared by other nineteenth-century African nationalist minds. James Africanus Horton's approach in his *West African Countries and Peoples* was that Africans should be free and are capable of developing themselves, but for this, "Christianity and British example" were necessary (Davidson, 1992, p. 37). Edward Blyden, while asserting "Africanism," equally reflected this ambivalence towards western cul-ture. Ayo Langley in agreement with L. C. Gwam has pointed out that Horton and Blyden were "Black Victorians," contemporary *assimilados* who "firmly believed in the virtues of Christianity, industry and education" and were "unre-pentant Anglophiles" (Langley, 1979, p. 34).

John Mensah Sarbah, Casely-Hayford, and Attoh-Ahuma, who bridge the nineteenth and early twentieth centuries, fundamentally shared most of the attitudes of the contemporary African westernized leadership. They favored the adaptation of western practices to African cultural foundations. In a good part of their writings, they attempted to explain and argue a case for the protection of African cultural and social rights against materially predatory, excessive, and overriding western influences (Prah, 1976). J. E. Casely-Hayford in a homage to Edward Blyden expressed this idea with the words that Africans must "learn to unlearn all that foreign sophistry has encrusted upon the intelli-gence of the African." S. M. Molema writes in similar vein in his *Bantu, Past and Present* (1920). It is remarkable that, not even the more outspokenly radical thinkers amongst such African minds as Tovalou Houénou, Kobina Sekyi, or Orishatuke Faduma provided precise formulae for the sort of cultural engineer-ing which would practically assure the positioning of African cultural institu-tions at the heart of the "modernization" of African society they all envisioned. Their nativism was in a sense more intuitive than coldly deductive. The use of African languages was never really conceived with unwavering conviction as a prerequisite for the development of African society they all desired. The excep-tion appears to be Casely-Hayford.

In his view, "no people could despise its own language, customs, and institutions and hope to avoid national death" (Casely-Hayford, 1969, p. 17). Casely-Hayford argued that, in an African University, the best part of the teaching must be done in the languages of the people. Professorships in African languages were central to his conception of an African university. Sharing A.G. Fraser's approaches to Indian and Ceylonese education, which placed local languages at the heart of the approach, Casely-Hayford endorsed education "on Japanese lines, i.e., thorough teaching of English as a subject and literature, but the teaching of science, engineering, medicine, etc., through the medium of the vernacular, and not of English – with a complete connection between the village school and central college" (1969, pp. 195–6). Direct heir to the intellectual and nationalist tradition of Edward Blyden, Casely-Hayford by available records understood the problem of the cultural prerequisites of African development better than most of his contemporaries.

In contrast to Casely-Hayford and nearer our times, Leopold Senghor echoed, if only partially, the sentiments of Crummell. In his words,

> to educate signifies, in the etymological sense of the word, "to lead outside oneself," outside one's background, to transplant. The significance of education is to assimilate foreign values so that one absorbs new blood. These values nourish us precisely because they are at first foreign to us. Latin, French and Cartesian values are exactly the opposite of Black African values. (Senghor, 1964, p. 229)

While Senghor justified his leaning towards French and French culture on aesthetic and scientific educational grounds, Milton Obote in language riddled with emotion and dilemma justified the use of English on purely political grounds. It is reasoning which most of the postcolonial elite would probably identify with.

> We know that English, before Independence, was the language of the administrator. It was the language of the people who were rulers and by which Uganda was ruled. . . . many of our people learned English in order to serve in the Administration, at least to serve our former masters. . . . we are doing exactly the same; our policy to teach more English could in the long run just develop more power in the hands of those who speak English, and better economic status for those who know English. We say this because we do not see any possibility of our being able to get English known by half the population of Uganda within the next fifteen years. English, therefore, remains the national language in Uganda when at the same time it is a language that the minority of our people can use for political purposes to improve their own political positions. Some of our people can use it in order to improve their economic status. . . . we find no alternative to English in Uganda's present position. We have, therefore, adopted English as our national language . . . it is the political language. No Member of Parliament, . . . is unable to speak English . . . it is a qualification for membership to Parliament. . . . The Uganda National Assembly should be a place where Uganda problems are discussed by those best able to discuss them, and in our situation it would appear that those best

able to discuss our problems are those who speak English. This is a reasoning which cannot be defended anywhere; there is no alternative at the present moment. ...those amongst us in Uganda who speak English and have obtained important positions because of the power of the English language, are liable to be regarded by a section of our society as perpetrators of colonialism and imperialism; or at least as potential imperialists. This, fortunately, has not yet become a public issue in Uganda. ...there is a real possibility that as long as English is maintained as the official language, spoken by a minority, a charge against its use could be made...that it is the language of the privileged group. (Obote, 1968, pp. 3–6; see also Langley, 1979, p. 386)

This piece was written some 30 years ago, at the beginning of the era of independence. With candor and frankness not always available in the rhetoric of politicians, Obote set the record and its rationale out. With the advantage of hindsight we note that the option Uganda selected then in his own words was based on a "reasoning which cannot be defended anywhere." The scenario has persisted and become increasingly entrenched. We would argue that indeed with years a more rational long-term solution becomes even more problematic. Yet still, in our view, without the popular empowerment of mass society which comes with the use of African languages, a durable developmentally sound solution cannot come to Africa. With the passing of years the challenge becomes more daunting and societally more formidable.

A point in Obote's thinking which is noteworthy is the fact that the placement of the colonial language above the local is seen most significantly in political terms. The developmentally antithetical nature of the abandonment of the use of local languages, as total vehicles for social and economic advancement, is missed or underestimated. This syndrome, i.e., the underestimation of the centrality of African languages to development, stretches beyond African politicians, and African and interested western scholarship. The "philosopher king," Busia, arrived at a conclusion similar to Obote. In his *Africa in Search of Democracy*, he wrote that:

> For administration, language is necessary, and since African States are divided by many languages, the legacy of French or English which brings different tribes into conversation with one another within their common State, and brings Africans into conversation with the world outside, must be reckoned one of the contributions to democratic rule. (Busia, 1971, p. 52)

Busia's conclusion appears rational if one departs from the assumption that the postcolonial or neocolonial state in Africa is a heritage we have to live with, but even more crucially, the argument that it is a viable basis for the growth of democracy, emancipation, and development. Within the framework of the post-colonial entity, western language-use has a logical and self- fulfilling inevitability about its hegemonic status. However, if one looks beyond it, to wider or pan-Africanist solutions to African development, the argument falls flat on its face. The view I have over some years now been inclined to and which is variously recorded in *Beyond the Colour Line*, is that developmentally the neocolonial state in Africa is a dead end (Prah, 1998).

Language, Literacy, and the Invention of Africa

The foundations of the postcolonial state in Africa were laid a hundred years ago during the period of the scramble for Africa. African states and territories created by the Berlin Conference (1885) were established without consideration for African history or cultures. Like the languages which were introduced by the colonial powers, these states broke with the precolonial economic, political, and social structures that had hitherto existed. With independence, the ascendant elites were for various reasons (some of their own making, others imposed) unable to break structurally from the colonial heritage, and have since then attempted with increasing failure to construct advancing democratic societies. I share Basil Davidson's opinion on this matter:

> Africa's crisis of society derives from many upsets and conflicts, but the root of the problem is different from these... The more one ponders this matter the more clearly is it seen to arise from the social and political institutions within which decolonized Africans have lived and tried to survive. Primarily, this is a crisis of institutions. Which institutions?... We have to be concerned here with the nationalism which produced the nation-states of newly independent Africa after the colonial period: with the nationalism that became nation-statism. This nation-statism looked like a liberation, and really began as one. But it did not continue as a liberation. In practice, it was not a restoration of Africa to Africa's own history, but the onset of a new period of indirect subjection to the history of Europe. The fifty or so states of the colonial era possessed no history of their own, became fifty or so nation-states formed and governed on European models, chiefly the models of Britain and France. Liberation thus produced its own denial. Liberation led to alienation. (Davidson, 1992, p. 10)

A recent good example of what I describe as "the cultural and linguistic dis-embodiment" of the development problematic is provided by Mark Hobart et al. (Hobart, 1993). In an informationally well-resourced text which attempts to question the view popular in some circles that "western knowledge is uniquely successful in its application to economic and social development," the contributors, "all well-known European professional anthropologists with experience with development," tiptoe around the question of the use of local languages and their centrality in any potentially viable approach to development. The disembodiment process (inadequate cognizance of cultural/linguistic factors) produces a formalistic discussion of development in which the logic and reality of development, or underdevelopment, is obscured and masked by the surface structure of the language and discourse (of course in western languages) about development. In this scheme of analysis, the contradiction between appearance and reality, surface and deep structure of the development problematic is lost. Development involves people and takes place in cultures.

In Jack Goody's enlightening texts on the social organization of societies with and without writing, he reveals a number of issues which are pertinent to our discussion in this chapter (Goody, 1987; 1989). Writing enhances capacities both at the collective societal and individual cognitive levels, "the formalization of discourse, the extension of some forms of abstraction, of logic (e.g. the syllogism) and of rationality, not in the sense that common usage usually espouses but in a more restricted fashion that refers to the analysis of formal propositions in ways that seem to depend upon visual inspection and material manipulation" (Goody, 1989, pp. 290–1). What needs emphasis however is the fact that in the transition from orality to writing, the richness and continuity of the cultural base is only substantially assured if the same language is moved from an oral culture to a written culture. There is sound reason in the argument that it is a mistake "to divide 'cultures' into the oral and the written; it is rather the oral and the oral plus the written, printed . . . for the individual there is always the problem of the interaction between the registers and the uses, between the so-called oral and written traditions" (Goody, 1989, p. xii). However, it is useful to emphasize the peculiar social specifics in which much of contemporary Africa currently finds itself; a situation in which orality and the written are not partially interrupted sources for cognitive references but more or less separate and disjointed codes. It is with regard to this point that the contemporary African situation differs radically from the difficulty of English-speakers of nonstandard English (Goody, 1989, p. 271).

Latter-day literacy in Africa (post-*Ajami*), as a formal structure, has come largely as a blessing of western imperialism. Its garb and trappings are, however, more a bane than a blessing. Literacy was introduced in the languages of the imperialists, dispensed initially almost exclusively in the service of Christian proselytism, while producing social elements amenable to the service of the colonial enterprise. In impact, therefore, literacy in the way it was introduced facilitated the alienation of an emergent elite from its historical and cultural constituency.

The industrial revolution in Europe made it possible for printed matter to become more easily accessible to the masses. In the empires of the western powers they reached a growing social class increasingly influenced by western ideas. In the west African littoral the roots of this group goes back to the late mercantilist period. But it was in the nineteenth century that this social element acquired a distinct and recognizable character. By the second decade of the twentieth century, newspaper production was fairly common in a great part of the African colonial empire, although their circulation remained relatively limited. The expansion of western education consolidated the readership base of African society. The brutality and trauma of colonial society were matched by the orderliness and rationality of its organizational methods and economic regime. The superiority of western technique and production made literacy particularly desirable, since it was clearly on such a basis that this had become possible.

It was the emergent elite of literates in western languages who from the late nineteenth century onwards developed the language of anticolonialism. By the middle of the twentieth century this elite had eclipsed and replaced the old traditional leadership as the representative voice of Africans in African political affairs. One important contrasting feature between them and the traditional rulers was that the linguistic basis of the elite was non-African while the illiterate traditional rulers were the custodians of indigenous languages.

Iliffe, in a study of colonial Tanganyika, writes that during the last decade of German colonial rule, primary education expanded greatly in all parts of the country where missionaries were at work. This expansion was accompanied by the social incorporation of these educated elements into the colonial economy. Education was encouraged, sometimes by compulsion, by the "increasingly confident government." Iliffe notes that the appeal of education for the young was primarily material. The first Nyakyusa pupils left school when they were refused pay by the missionaries. We are informed that literacy had for some "an almost magical quality." A young catechist, Nicholas Mugongo, psychologically divided by engagement with *kubandwa* mediums of the Bahaya, claimed he was taught to read by Christ in a vision. Literacy vested Christianity with authority and apparent rationality. It offered an explanatory capacity which unwritten indigenous religions lacked (Iliffe, 1989, pp. 224–5). Notable in all this was the way in which education, literacy, and Christianity in sum affected the cultural moorings of Africans. Iliffe writes:

> A powerful strand in the converts' thinking was a Manichean view of the world as a struggle between light and darkness. They often condemned non-Christian customs more rigorously than did the missionaries. When a conference of African Christians met at Magila in 1895, members who advocated "greater laxity then could possibly be allowed" were sternly restrained by the African clergy. This and two later conferences, attended only by Africans, outlawed Bondei initiation, marriage, and burial rites, abortion, medicines, agricultural charms, observance of clan taboos, and Sunday markets. Bondei leaders later rejected a proposal to invent a Christian substitute for initiation. In 1913 church leaders in Masasi advised Bishop Weston to ban all initiation rites. (Iliffe, 1989, p. 227)

If literacy and education in colonial languages advanced the denationalization process among Africans, the entrenchment of colonial culture and the effacement of African cultural belongings that went hand in hand with it involved in many parts of Africa a replacement of designations of objects and features of nature and the environment. A new reality with new names was created in the image of the westerner. Animals, mountains, plants, rivers, and streams were given new names. This experience was particularly remarkable in settler-colonial areas. In these areas, colonialists attempted to reproduce Europe in Africa. Father Christmas, Guy Fawkes, and Halloween became features of the calendar of the colonies. Africans needed Christian names to ensure their salvation and a place in the westerners' heaven. Tribes were written into existence by colonial administrators and missionaries in order, respectively, to create administrative boundaries and evangelical spheres of influence. Thompson gazelles, wildebeeste, duikers, boomslangs, Lake Victoria, Lake Rudolf, the Gold Coast, the Ivory Coast, Nigeria, Rhodesia, Salisbury, Brazzaville, Leopoldville, Johannesburg, and Cape Town ("the Mother City") were all part of a "discovered" and conquered world where in the case of the Congo Free State, the land, the natives, and all therein became the private property of the Belgian King, Leopold. In effect, the African was symbolically removed from his/her *heimat* and became part of the invention of the westerner. Literacy in western languages was part of the new order. The legacy of this order still largely remains with us. Today, the continued use of western languages in Africa is both an affirmation of the neocolonial cultural status of Africa as well as a means to this affirmation.

Caliban's Production and Reproduction of Knowledge

Historically and culturally, knowledge production and reproduction in Africa has two sources. First, there is the knowledge which is indigenous to African culture, knowledge which has been produced directly out of the African experience and which is embedded in the social and cultural practice of Africans. Such knowledge is frequently immediately tied to the ecological and environmental conditions of its producers and generationally transferred either by specialists, such as linguists, shamans, or chiefs, or by elders and the general citizenry in the regular processes of socialization. Today, indigenous knowledge of this kind is invariably caught in a time warp, increasingly restricted to social elements whose mode of livelihood and existential conditions reflect "traditional" characteristics relatively less disturbed by the social transformations triggered by the penetration of the colonial and postcolonial political economy. Part of such knowledge has in many cases acquired antiquarian status and is steadily retreating into the realms of folklore.

Secondly, there is the received knowledge which has come with western presence and the *pax Europa*. This is knowledge whose introduction was originally initiated by missionaries, and which originally drew no borders (at least in the minds of the receivers, and sometimes also in the minds of the imparters) between theological factualization and empirically grounded facts. Christian beliefs were as "true" as the fact that the sun rises in the east and sets in the west. In the new society created under western tutelage, access to this knowledge and its acquisition ensured privilege and material benefits. It meant a white-collar job, better housing rigged out with the material objects of modernity, greater social status, removal from the poverty and backwardness of rural life, but also consequentially alienation from historical and cultural roots. For most Africans education and the acquisition of knowledge in both the colonial and postcolonial eras was never an end in itself. Rather, it has been viewed as an agency for social elevation according to the rules of the game established by the colonial order.

This knowledge was dispensed without reference to what people already knew from their indigenous knowledge base. For all intents and purposes indigenous knowledge was like all else which predated western presence, "primitive," "heathen," "barbaric," "savage," and part of the impenetrable darkness of darkest Africa. The new knowledge was tendered as a different rendering, reading, and practical intervention in nature. It was introduced as a product which in structure and intent bore no resemblance or relationship with anything that had historically preceded it in Africa. Indigenous knowledge and culture, which is the basis of not only all collective endeavor but also the reference point for individual action of a rational kind for the overwhelming rural mass of Africa, was brought into question. The new knowledge, which was also a source of power in the new order, was printed matter. When the Yoruba say *omo iwe*, the Ga say *ele wolo*, or the Akan say *onim ngoma*, they literally mean he or she "knows books." It denoted a quality which has been much esteemed in both colonial and postcolonial Africa. However, noticeably in many parts of the continent, since the late fifties and the early sixties, with the emergence of a new urban working class and a growing small-holder or petty bourgeois element, derisive criticism of "jaw-breakers" and "book-long" types who no longer enjoy the comfort and prestige of the late colonial and early postcolonial periods has appeared.

Knowledge production in Africa, at its cutting edge, is primarily located in institutions of higher learning, research stations, and laboratories. In contemporary Africa such establishments are frequently devoid of crucial resources. Furthermore, too often such institutions, in agenda and methodology, set themselves up, in effect, in feeble competition with comparative work in the richly endowed metropolitan centers of the world. Methodologies and concerns which have been learned in the metropolis are either inadequately adapted or reproduced in contexts which bear little resemblance to African conditions. There is more "imitation than emulation" (Azikiwe, 1961, p. 24). The consequence is that where some cognitive gold is gleaned, it is paltry and irrelevant to the immediate needs of mass society in the countries in which these institutions are based. African countries have established universities with faculties of arts, humanities, social sciences, natural sciences, and technology.

A good number of teachers in such institutions have training and qualifications which will rival any, anywhere in the world. Many, indeed, have been trained in metropolitan universities. Students may be required to cover study material, and submit to examinations similar, for example, to comparable University of London examinations. Indeed, in many instances, African universities like Ibadan in Nigeria or Legon in Ghana started as London University degree-awarding institutions. While a Ghanaian or Nigerian graduating student may cope handsomely with University of London examination requirements, what they learn is unable to make a difference in the construction of roads, sewerage systems, or the manufacture of even needles, in the societies in which they live, in which such products are vital necessities.

African scholarship because of the conditions of its birth has operated as a marginal element in the production and reproduction of knowledge based in the western world. As such there is a lack of originality and societal specificity in its product. Strikingly, the same is not true for Asia in even those countries which experienced western colonialism, and which achieved political independence in the late forties and fifties. In Asia, knowledge production and the allied techno-logical output has acquired relative autonomy from its western origins. This is true of late arrivals like Indonesia, Malaysia, Korea, or Thailand, as well as the older experiences of China and Japan. Thus the study of society in China or Japan for Chinese or Japanese scholars is not "otherized" as Chinese or Japanese studies the way Africans continue in African universities to conceptualize and delimit "African studies." When European students and scholars study society, it is per definition a study of western/European society. The reason why for African scholars the study of their own societies is "otherized" is because the academy in Africa looks at African realities from the viewpoint of westerners. The question of audiences complicates this matter further.

Speakers and Listeners

Many western scholars writing on Africa do so primarily for western audiences. For various reasons this point is not in most instances explicitly stated, but it is never far below the surface, and can frequently be read between the lines. I shall provide two examples of this. In Ritchie Calder's introduction to *The New West Africa: Problems of Independence*, he writes that:

> it is strange how blind some people can be to the facts of history, ... we have got to get into such people's heads that the world has shrunk so that Africa and Asia are only a few hours' flying distance away; that the coloured peoples are now our near neighbours; and that we have, perforce, to contrive to get on neighbourly terms ... (Calder, 1953, p. 9)

Another example of this is provided by Hodder, who writes that

> there is nothing about Africa or about Africans that makes backwardness, chaos, instability or disorder either necessary or inevitable. The natural and human potential of Africa is immense; but only Africans themselves can realize this potential. If they fail in this, then the peoples of Africa will lose many of the qualities and values of life which they still retain ... (Hodder, 1978, pp. 153–4)

Both examples are of course well-meaning. Needless to say, western scholarship has bequeathed Africa an enormous corpus of literature without which it would be impossible today to understand and share where we are historically and societally coming from, or where we are going to. But one need not be either a Weberian, sensitive to the implications of the value-laden character of social analysis, or a mind inclined towards *wissensoziologie*, to appreciate the fact that one cannot simply reproduce knowledge focused towards a western audience and expect it to be identical to African views informed from "inside." Such epistemology as is borrowed from either the Chinese tradition of African studies, the French tradition of African studies, or the British tradition, needs to be revamped or rehashed to reflect the perspectives of Africans about Africa. Apropos of this, Hodder has interesting observations.

> One's perspective of African affairs is also suspect to the extent that it is a European, or at least a non-African, perspective; and this is a point worth making if only because the patronizing tone of so many commentators makes it clear that there is no general recognition of what should be a truism. It is, to put it bluntly, impossible for any non-African ever to be sure he fully understands the African's viewpoint, however varied or variable this may be. It is arrogant to pretend otherwise. There is always a certain gap, and no "introduction" to African affairs can ever take one more than part of the way along the path of understanding. (Hodder, 1978, p. 150)

Hodder's view may rub many up the wrong way. But it is a point which needs to be made if African scholarship is to make relevant headway. Edward Said with respect to this issue has made noteworthy commentary, but arguably he has been overoptimistic in his presentation of the case. He writes that

> only recently have Westerners become aware that what they have to say about the history and the cultures of "subordinate" people is challengeable by the people themselves, people who a few years back were simply incorporated, culture, land, history, and all, into the great Western empires and their disciplinary discourses. (This is not to denigrate the accomplishments of many Western scholars, historians, artists, philosophers, musicians and missionaries, whose corporate and individual efforts in making known the world beyond Europe are a stunning achievement.) (Said, 1994, p. 195)

I am not sure how widespread this awareness is. Indeed, as an African voice, it is possible to argue that the idea that somehow knowledge production about Africa and Africans can be based and primarily generated in the metropolitan areas of the world outside and beyond Africa (in the context of a developing Africa) is at least misguided and possibly mischievous. The persistence of that sort of scenario reinforces the entrenchment of cultural or scientific neocolonialism.

A frequently made argument is that knowledge is universal and has no boundaries. Of course at a certain level this is correct. But knowledge does not emerge initially as common universal property. It is invariably sourced in specific countries and within specific traditions of production. At source it maintains continuity with other debates and developments within its traditional base. It is only universalized when it is incorporated cross-culturally by other similar discussions.

African scholarship continues to address debates founded in other, mostly western traditions. Francophone Africans relate primarily to traditions in France and the French-speaking metropolis, anglophone Africans do the same. There is not yet emergent an African tradition to which and from which African scholarship speaks. This is not because of a dearth of material to which African scholarship can speak. Rather I would argue that this condition is part of the result of neocolonial cultural thraldom to the west. The emergence of a consciously constructed African school or schools of scholarship is crucial to development on this continent.

Concluding Remarks

In colonial and neocolonial Africa, there is an often unspoken but deeply entrenched view that scientific and technical knowledge is and needs to be naturally constructed in western languages. Extending from this view is the attitude that African languages for reasons of structural incapacity cannot incorporate knowledge and modern science. This popular and ubiquitously accepted attitude needs to be exposed and discarded, if African development is to be realized. Within the elite, there is enough understanding and awareness of the need to base education on African languages, but the lack of political will and inertia has to be overcome. What needs, however, to be pointed out in this respect is that African authorities need to move beyond platitudes and statements of intent to praxis. Educational policy and practice would need to be urgently undertaken with the view to placing African languages at the center of all educational activity. Furthermore, development needs to be premised on African cultural usages with a selective approach to inputs from abroad. The new must build on the old, and must take into fuller cognizance the material and social conditions in which the people live, produce, and reproduce themselves.

The predicament we are confronted with is no less than the fact that centuries of western dominance has bred in the African an inferiority complex. This is often easily denied, brushed aside, or wished away, but the social practice of Africans displays this syndrome better than the denials.

Dialectically, westerners assume in relation to Africans and things African postures of superiority. The political, economic, and cultural power of the west serves as the basis of western superiority. The language question and the continued impotent dependency on colonial languages is a living attestation of this quandary. I would also add that the tendency for African scholarship to seek legitimacy and paradigm selection through indiscriminate and philosophically inept eclecticism bears testimony to this malaise. If in the late 1950s and early 1960s existentialism was in fashion and many felt a need to "be with it," in the present day numerous African scholars reproduce and mimic postmodernism in neocolonial Africa – in societies which have hardly entered the industrial era. The fact that these various western philosophical schools are direct products of the changing circumstances of western society is not appreciated. The fact that

Sartre, Foucault, or Baudrillard are as French as camembert, and Russell or Ayer as British as cheddar, is not appreciated by many of us. The realities of present-day Africa are as different from contemporary western realities as cheese is from chalk. Ideas always bear the indelible marks of the language, history, culture, and societies in which they are produced.

It is in this sense that we can say that the continued use of European languages in postcolonial Africa attests to the neocolonial status of African societies in relation to the metropolitan powers of the world. The African intellectual enterprise should be Africa-centred in the sense that it should deal with African realities informed by African history, language, and culture. Only then can we make a meaningful and worthwhile contribution to a truly universal fund of culture; otherwise we remain mere scholastic appendages of the west.

References

ADEA (Association for the Development of Education in Africa) (1996). Pan-African Seminar on the Problems and Prospects of the Use of African Languages in Education, Accra, Ghana. *ADEA Newsletter* 8(4), 1 (address: ADEA, 7–9 rue Eugène-Delacroix, 75116 Paris, France).

Ake, C. (1996). *Democracy and Development in Africa*. Washington, DC: Brookings Institution.

Appiah, K. A. (1992). *In My Father's House: Africa in the philosophy of culture*. London: Methuen.

Azikiwe, N. (1961). *Zik: A selection from the speeches of Nnamdi Azikiwe*. Cambridge: Cambridge University Press.

Bernstein, H. (ed.) (1973). *Underdevelopment and Development: The Third World today*. Harmondsworth: Penguin.

Busia, K. A. (1971). *Africa in Search of Democracy*. London: Routledge. First published 1967.

Calder, R. (1953). Introduction. In B. Davidson and A. Ademola (eds.), *The New West Africa: Problems of independence*. London: Allen & Unwin.

Casely-Hayford, J. E. (1969). *Ethiopia Unbound*. London: Cass. First published 1911.

Davidson, B. (1992). *The Black Man's Burden: Africa and the curse of the nation-state*. New York: Times Books.

Dei, G. (1993). Sustainable development in the African context: Revisiting some theoretical and methodological issues. *Africa Development*, 18(2): 98.

Ekeh, P. (1986). Development theory and the African predicament. *Africa Development*, 11(4): 25.

Goody, J. (1987). *The Interface between the Written and the Oral*. Cambridge/New York: Cambridge University Press.

Goody, J. (1989). *The Logic of Writing and the Organisation of Society*. Cambridge/New York: Cambridge University Press. First published 1986.

Hahn, F. H. and Mathews, R. C. O. (1967). The theory of economic growth: A survey. In *Surveys of Economic Theory*, vol. 2, *Growth and Development*. London: Macmillan; New York: St. Martin's.

Hobart, M. (ed.) (1993). *An Anthropological Critique of Development*. London/New York: Routledge.

Hodder, B. W. (1978). *Africa Today: A short introduction to African affairs*. London: Methuen.

Iliffe, J. (1989). *A Modern History of Tanganyika*. Cambridge/New York: Cambridge University Press. First published 1979.

Johnson, H. G. (1971). A word to the third world. *Encounter*, Oct.

Langley, J. A. (1979). *Ideologies of Liberation in Black Africa*. London: R. Collings.

Obote, M. (1968). Opening address delivered at a seminar on "Mass Media and Linguistic Communications in East Africa," held in Kampala, 31 March to 3 April. Published in *East African Journal of Rural Development* l: 3–6.

Prah, K. K. (1965). *J. E. J. Capitein: A critical study of an 18th century African*. Trenton, NJ: Africa World Press.

Prah, K. K. (1976). Some colonized attitudes in the gold coast before the Russo-Japanese war. In *Essays on African Society and History*. Accra: Ghana University Press.

Prah, K. K. (1993). *Mother Tongue for Scientific and Technological Development in Africa*. Bonn: DSE (German Foundation for International Development).

Prah, K. K. (1995). *African Languages for the Mass Education of Africans*. Bonn: DSE/ZED (German Foundation for International Development/Education and Documentation Center).

Prah, K. K. (1998). *Beyond the Color Line: Pan-Africanist disputations*. Trenton, NJ: Africa World Press.

Said, E. (1994). *Culture and Imperialism*. New York: Knopf/Random House.

Senghor, L. S. (1964). *Liberté 1: Négritude et humanisme*. Paris: Seuil.

Chapter 8

Literacy and Literature in Indigenous Languages in Benin and Burkina-Faso

Joseph Akoha

The issue of literacy and cultural production in the form of literature or orature in Africa is inextricably intertwined with that of language policy, both in colonial times and after independence up until now. Given that close relationship between literacy and language policy, this chapter on literacy and literature in indigenous languages first briefly sketches out language policies in colonial and postindependent contemporary French-speaking west Africa. Next, the chapter describes the state of literacy and literature in indigenous languages in two of them, Benin and Burkina-Faso, based on the study done by Séhouéto (1995), followed by a discussion of the role that literacy is playing in these countries. The chapter ends with suggestions on policies likely to promote a literate environment in both official wider-communication languages and local languages in relation to societal development and the democratization process under way in these countries.

Language Policy and Literacy

Language policy in colonial times in French-speaking west Africa

Language policy is a broad term for decisions on rights and access to languages and on the roles and functions of particular languages and varieties of language in a given polity (Phillipson & Skutnabb-Kangas, 1996). It includes language planning, involving political and economic choices closely linked with overall policy matters, such as appropriate educational policy or the facilitation of democratic citizenship. Language policy also establishes hierarchies among languages and has a strong influence, as Phillipson and Skutnabb-Kangas (1996,

p. 432) put it, on "social reproduction and in intercultural communication in a world characterized by the contradictory pressures of vigorous ethnolinguistic identities and strong global homogenizing tendencies."

These homogenizing tendencies of the French colonial language policy took two forms: status planning, the planning of changes in the standing of a language and its societal functions in a community, and corpus planning, concerned with codification, language structures, vocabulary, spelling, and script (Fergusson, 1985).

The aim was to assimilate indigenous peoples through a process of "civilization" whose main vehicle was the French language. Mastery of that language and assimilation to the culture it sustains were the main goal of the whole educational enterprise. Very little was done to encourage a study of indigenous languages, which were depreciated and considered as simple underdeveloped vernaculars. As such they were ruthlessly repressed by the colonial administration.

But despite such a policy only a privileged minority of the population could speak French in Benin (about 20 percent), while the majority continued to use their mother tongues as ethnic monolinguals, and more commonly other languages as well, as internal or external bilinguals.

This policy of promotion of foreign languages at the expense of indigenous languages did not significantly change the pattern of language use by the populations at large. The problem, however, remains, as far as literacy is concerned, that no systematic corpus planning work in terms of codification, elaboration, cultivation from the triple angle of graphization, standardization, and modernization (Fergusson, 1985) of the indigenous language was undertaken. There was also no clear policy of promotion of the various national languages in line with UNESCO national language promotion policy (Sow, 1977).

In these conditions, where most indigenous languages had no standardized written forms, and where apart from a few cases of attempts by priests and pastors at translating the Bible in some indigenous languages using the French alphabet, there were few written cultural productions, one could hardly speak of literacy, at least for the vast majority of French-speaking west Africans. True, one could speak of literacy for the privileged few who had access to French. But to understand literacy more broadly, it is necessary to go beyond a mechanistic view of literacy. Thus recently scholars have moved to a far more complex characterization, which acknowledges that the significance of written language varies enormously from one community to another, depending, among other things, on how it is related to the language that the people speak, what social functions written texts are expected to serve, and how knowledge of the writing system is transmitted from one generation to the next (Parris, 1996; Doronila, this volume).

So the language policy of the colonial administration did not help in the promotion of literacy. Literacy failed to take hold because it failed to reach the majority of people.

Language policy in postindependence French-speaking west Africa

One could expect a change for the better after independence. But not much was achieved in the first decade of independence, as there was no political will to promote African languages. As Mateene ruefully points out, "The foreign colonial languages are more favored now than they were before independence. The idea of linguistic independence is in practice not followed by the very large majority of African leaders and elite. Linguistic unification by means of an African language within one country, and among neighboring countries is not one of the preoccupations of the African leaders either. Whereas linguistic independence is a rejected idea, it is believed that African linguistic unity will be better achieved through foreign European Languages" (Mateene, 1980, in Akoha, 1990, pp. 33–4).

This view was clearly stated at the 1965 session of the OAU Educational and Cultural Commission held in Lagos, where the teaching of English and French in every country with a view to achieving bilingualism in these European languages was strongly recommended. But this did not significantly alter the spread of these languages among the populations. However, it reinforces the neglecting of local languages discussed earlier.

It was in the 1970s and 1980s, in favor of radical revolutionary movements in some west African countries, namely Benin and Burkina-Faso, that the need to rehabilitate indigenous languages and indigenous cultures was strongly felt, unambiguously expressed, and followed by some positive actions, unfortunately short lived. In this period, the timid movement for literacy and postliteracy activities, initially carried out as evening classes, mainly in French, but also as adult education geared toward initiation to reading and writing in local languages, sustained by religions groups, youth movements, individuals, and institutions involved in development sectors and so-called modernization activities, was intensified. As noted by Séhouéto (1995), for a few years' interval, Benin and Burkina-Faso had revolutionary regimes that supported the militant movement in favor of literacy and publication in indigenous languages. They hijacked this movement in favor of literacy as a revolutionary project and succeeded at least partially in bringing it under state control. The program statement of November 30, 1972 in Benin and the political orientation statement of October 2, 1983 in Burkina offered, at least at the rhetorical level, a new framework within which mass literacy was officially and politically endorsed (Séhouéto, 1995).

This irreversible movement, although declining in the postrevolutionary era of the 1990s, has favored the birth of a sizable volume of literature in national languages in these countries, a survey of which was carried out by Séhouéto (1995). The next section presents the results of this survey.

Publications and readership in indigenous languages with special reference to Benin and Burkina-Faso

The excellent study carried out by Séhouéto (1995) on publications in indigenous languages resulted in a 47-page report whose main findings will be extensively drawn on in this section.

Séhouéto (1995) rightly argued that the revolutionary movements in the two countries created favorable conditions for literacy in indigenous languages. In addition he identified six other factors to account for the relative progress in literacy activities over the last 25 years. The first one is the militant advocacy for national languages within or outside state institutions, which can be noted among minority groups defending their identities, and also in cultural and religious movements. The second factor is the external interventions in favor of functional literacy related to development projects or recommendations from organizations such as UNESCO UNICEF, UNDP, WHO, etc. The third factor is the existence of a whole army of civil servants working in official literacy offices whose survival depends on the maintenance of literacy and postliteracy in indigenous languages.

The fourth factor is related to the creation of a whole group of NGOs, giving a new lease of life to literacy activities and to communication activities in general. The fifth factor is the massive injection of financial and material resources by foreign agencies in this sector to support private institutions, such as NGOs working in the field of women, the environment, AIDS, peasant organizations, all of which include a communication–education–information dimension involving literacy. The sixth factor is the existence in both countries of a pocket of supporters of indigenous languages having intellectual, political, or religious motivations.

Thanks to these factors literacy in indigenous languages boomed in the 1980s in both countries. Institutions such as the INA (National Institute for Literacy), with its publishing house in Burkina-Faso, and CEMA (the Manual Production Center) in Benin were set up to promote publications in indigenous languages. These publications were also encouraged and sponsored by development projects in other areas having a training chapter such as the Programme de Formation Technique Continue (PFTC or Continuous Technical Training Programme) in Burkina-Faso and the Cattle Raising Development project in east Borgou in Benin.

Such development projects need to include a literacy program as an empowerment process for the beneficiaries, who are mostly illiterate but need to understand and put to use new technologies and new ways of managing their business in the process of taking control of the project and of their lives.

This self-educational process is what Fagerberg-Diallo (this volume) refers to as "constructive interdependence," the ability to integrate new skills and information into a culturally grounded worldview.

Publications were on issues such as management of associations, animal health, cattle foods, conservation of water, how to make soaps, family planning, sexually transmitted diseases, AIDS. Organizations such as UNICEF, UNDP, WHO, and state institutions dealing with health matters, the environment, and population policies also encourage and finance publications in indigenous languages. So do religious groups and some NGOs. In Burkina-Faso such NGOs include the TINTUA association and the National Institute for Social and Economic Development (INADES). In Benin we have ABEL (the Beninese Association of writers in Indigenous Languages).

In principle the readership of such publications is constituted first and foremost by targeted grassroots development organizations whose members benefit from various projects, and the wider rural community that needs access to information on small business management, primary healthcare, the environment and new technologies.

But in practice few members of these targeted groups read because of poor postliteracy follow-up, lack of sustainable publication policy, and the poor surrender value of literacy in indigenous languages as French continues to be the only language serving as a key to upward social mobility and "juicy" political administrative economic and social positions. As argued by Goody (this volume) with reference to Ghana, "There is a deeper problem for effective L1 adult literacy in Ghana. It can never provide the access offered by L2 literacy to key resources: jobs, status, ability to operate effectively within the myriad manifestations of government bureaucracy, and the skills necessary for higher educational and technical qualifications. It is access to these resources that nonliterate adults desperately want. They correctly see that without it they will remain marginal to modern Ghanaian society. L1 literacy alone can never bridge this gap."

It really cannot bridge that gap if there is no radical change in mentality and active reorientation of language policy including relationship, economic, and political power. It should also be noted that the nonharmonization of orthographic and grammatical rules does not help the expansion of the readership nor facilitate large-scale publication of documents intended for a cross-section of ethnic groups. In addition, the moralizing tone and politically biased orientation of the few existing publications do not favor wide and enthusiastic readership. Most writers and translators are not well trained; in both countries there are no truly operational publishing houses. Although they have printing plants, there is also a total lack of strategic reflection and coherent action for the promotion of a literate environment. Given these circumstances, even before the end of the revolutionary era in both countries literacy and publication were running out of steam. They could not achieve or rather have not achieved enough momentum to be self-sustaining. This state of affairs is worsened in the current era of democratic renewal by the rehabilitation of the French language. As Séhouéto (1995) remarks: "The French language is causing the serious threat – particularly acute in Benin since the beginning of the democratization process, in the opinion of various interviewees – to indigenous languages. The social, political and administrative environment does not favor the use of indigenous languages.

No concrete steps have been taken so far in either of the two countries to promote the official use of written indigenous languages in the administration and in the public arena in general" (p. 6). On the contrary, French has been rehabilitated as the only way to progress, although political cant pays lip-service to the promotion of indigenous language. By way of illustration, it may be pointed out that in Benin, the "centers for the awakening and stimulation of infancy" (CESEs), where indigenous languages were the media of instruction, are being starved out of existence in favor of French-language private nurseries for the chosen few who can afford them. But can democracy succeed without a rethinking of the role of indigenous languages in the African countries' development process?

The Role of Literacy in Developing Countries and the Need for Coordinated Action in Adult and in Formal Education

It is widely held that literacy, as the ability to read and write, facilitates and enables more elaborated discourse and a more reliable transmission of culture from one generation to another, and the more effective sharing of scientific, technical, and other kinds of information across time and space. This chapter argues that literacy in indigenous languages in developing countries may be instrumental too in nation-building, democracy development, and the struggle against poverty.

The role of literacy in nation-building, democracy development, and the struggle against poverty

It is an open secret that most of the modern states of Africa have been carved out of a kaleidoscope of ethnic and linguistic groups with different historical, cultural, and economic backgrounds and uneven development levels, cut off from their communities, and patched together in artificially drawn territories. So we have many states but virtually no nation in the classic sense of a community sharing the same history, culture, language, and economy, and generally (but not always) located in a given territory. The challenge of the governments of these artificial states after independence was to build a cohesive and coherent nation out of this melting pot. This can be achieved only by involving all the various socioeconomic and cultural groups in the development of a common neoculture generated by the contribution of each cultural group, their full participation in meeting the challenge of development; and by the reappropriation of the unavoidable Euro-American cultural globalization power permeating every nook and corner of the world through the information highway. Taking up this challenge is what is referred to here as nation-building.

Nation-building thus understood cannot successfully be achieved in such societies by repressing the cultures and languages of some groups in favor of a foreign language or culture, nor even in favor of a locally dominant group. On the contrary it is in the free interplay of the juxtaposed cultures mediated by literacy and literature in local languages that a nation may emerge, where every component feels involved and concerned. This leads to the issue of democracy and literacy.

A democratization process is underway, not only in Benin and Burkina-Faso but in other areas in Africa, whose essence is the opportunity for individuals and social groups to freely express their interests and make them matter in decision-making and decision implementation, through an active, direct, and indirect participation in the management of their country's affairs. This presupposes a clear understanding of the issues at stake so as to express well-informed interests and opinions and take decisions in full awareness. Literacy in national languages is essential in order to make accessible the main sociopolitical literature in the people's own languages.

So one may wonder if it is possible to achieve the current developmental goals embraced by the new leaders in this period of democratic renewal to reduce poverty and encourage development when indigenous languages are neglected.

Indeed if we define development as the constant effort of an individual or whole societies to ensure ever-increasing satisfaction of the basic needs for shelter, clothes, food, health and moral, psychological, and spiritual growth and happiness, it becomes clear that development must in large part come from within. No one can develop someone else; no one knows where the shoe pinches better than the wearer. Can one achieve development without promoting the indigenous languages and written production in those languages, so as to make the bulk of scientific, technical, philosophical, and spiritual ideas available and accessible to the populations who are the true makers of history, but so far live in utter poverty?

Poverty here is not only lack of shelter, food, health, and other material resources, it also includes, as pointed out in the report of the world summit for social development, lack of access to education and other basic services as well as unsafe environment, social discrimination and exclusion, lack of participation in decision-making, and civil, social, and cultural life (United Nations, 1995). Literacy has an important role to play in addressing these issues. How can we have true control over skills and knowledge, combat social discrimination and exclusion, and ensure full participation in social and cultural life without the literacy in our own languages that enables us to fully access information and participate?

So in nation-building and democratization as well as in the struggle for development and against poverty, literacy may be a basic instrument. But for this literacy in indigenous languages to fully play its role there are some political conditions that must be fulfilled.

First and foremost and in the interest of democracy and the smooth functioning of democratic institutions, the ruling elite in our countries whom Capo (1990) calls Afrosaxons and Afro-Romanic ruling minorities must change mentality or be forced to do so. Indeed, so far they have used Euro-American languages as gatekeeping devices and means for exclusion of the vast majority of the people. They retain or obscure vital information and issues through the sophisticated use of English, French, or Portuguese which they have managed to keep as the sole official languages of administration, law, education, science and technology, diplomacy and the official business and politics. They only pay lip-service to the promotion of national languages and to written cultural production in them, while perpetuating the use of the foreign languages with which they have identified themselves. Many countries, smaller in size, population, and resources than many African countries, use their national languages in all official business, including international gatherings such as the United Nations General Assembly. If we are to make progress in Africa south of the Sahara, we need, as suggested by Ngugi Wa Thiongo, to decolonize our minds (Ngugi, 1986). Apparently a lot is done in the framework of the so-called Francophony movements to translate some of our cultural productions such as proverbs and wisdom into French. An example of this is the excellent book by Boubou Hama, *L'Essence du verbe* (1990). But very little is done to encourage translation of the masterpieces of European literature and philosophy in national languages; it is a one-way process whereby we enrich the western civilization without receiving much in return.

To reverse the trend it is necessary that African governments show a more active political will to adopt both an indigenous language policy and official literacy policy embracing adult education and formal school education through a joint feedback and feed-forward action as well as allocating a conspicuous functional role to such literacy. Such a policy should lead to the choice of a few languages at national and regional levels in west Africa. These languages would be officially used in government, education, and law courts, and in international business. For such a policy to be operational, governments, NGOs, development project managers, publishers, editors, and readers should join their efforts to promote indigenous language and functional literacy as an instrument of social mobility alongside the European language.

Indigenous language literacy in adult education and formal education: The way forward

So far literacy has been discussed without reference to the different categories of people it is intended for. But the survey presented earlier indicated that literacy is mainly seen as the concern of adults in active life mainly in rural areas. Yet the materials do not take enough account of the fact that they are intended for adults, who have their own priorities and constraints. This explains why materials are written with a highly moralist overtone and teaching is carried out mostly on the transmission model (Séhouéto, 1995).

Literacy work in adult education should be a true empowering process in the sense discussed by Freire and Shor (1987). It should be organized on the basis of truly voluntary participation. This means that learners are engaged because of "some innate desire for developing new skills, acquiring new knowledge, or improving already assimilated competencies or sharpening powers of insight"

(Brookfield, 1986, p.15). It also implies that teachers act as facilitators and make participants feel that they are valued as unique individuals deserving respect. They create a climate for learning in which adults feel free to challenge one another and can feel comfortable with being challenged in the process of what Freire has called praxis, that is, "alternating and continuous engagements" by teachers and learners in exploration, action, and reflection (Brookfield, 1986, p. 15) so as to critically evaluate their actions. In other words facilitators of adult literacy should promote self-directed learning based on autonomy and empowerment and, above all, on participants' needs. When learners feel that what they are learning has no practical immediate surrender value they withdraw their participation. Given the overall context of language policy prevailing in Benin and Burkina-Faso and in most of "French-speaking" west Africa, it is not surprising that literacy in indigenous languages is running out of steam. If it is to regain momentum, it must be more directly tied to political, administrative, economic, cultural, and educational structures. In addition, literacy must serve the local functions which make it and production of literature in indigenous languages a worthwhile enterprise, a contributing factor to personal, social, and economic development. In such a view, as discussed at length by Doronila (this volume) with reference to the Philippine case, literacy does not just lead to development, it is itself a process of development.

One of these measures is the introduction of the teaching of indigenous languages in the formal education system at all levels, from higher education down to elementary schools. Such an approach will accelerate work in corpus planning and research work in local languages, which will help resolution of the present confusion about the orthography and syntax of some languages in the region. Making the ability to read and write one or two national languages a requirement for academic success and employment in some sectors of activity will boost the worth of literacy in national languages and create an environment where the production of literature in local languages can be a worthwhile and even a profitable activity.

Conclusion

This chapter on literacy and literature in indigenous languages in Benin and Burkina-Faso, although it draws on many writers and many materials, should not hide the reality that the contexts of both countries are not at all favorable to a true development of a national languages literate community in which the production of literature can thrive. There is a need for political will to take bold and daring decisions about the status of those languages in the official running of the two countries. At present more than 80 percent of the populations in both countries are taken hostage by a minority westernized elite, using their knowledge of French to lord it over the majority. This has to be changed. Foreign languages still have a role to play as windows on the outer world of science, technology, international relations, and business of each country, but their linguistic monopoly is detrimental to true development. It is indeed easier to help people learn and use their own languages to address modern issues than embarking on a campaign of literacy in French aimed at those populations who have never been to school. This is in tune with the characteristics of adult learners discussed in this chapter. Of course we should not underestimate the challenges of the policy advocated here in multilingual societies. But most of the arguments against the promotion of local languages and in favor of the maintenance of French cannot stand objective and scientific criticism (see Capo, 1990). What we most lack is political will. Where there is a will there is a way. Literacy activities and literacy classes can be transformed into true experiential learning, geared toward learners' autonomy and empowerment.

References

Akoha, J. (1990). *Action Research Based In Service Education and Training of Teachers (INSET) and English Language Teaching (ELT) Curriculum Innovation in Benin: An experimental study.* Doctoral thesis completed at the University of London Institute of Education, Oct. 1990.

Brookfield, S. D. (1986). *Understanding and Facilitating Adult Learning.* Milton Keynes: Open University Press.

Capo, H. B. C. (1990). Comparative linguistics and language engineering in Africa. In E. N. Emenanjo (ed.), *Multilingualism, Minority Languages and Language Policy in Nigeria.* Agbor: Central Books Limited and the Linguistic Association of Nigeria.

Fergusson, (1985). *Language Planning and Educational Change.* London: Center for African Studies.

Freire, P. and Shor, I. I. (1987). *A Pedagogy for Liberation: Dialogues on transforming education.* Boston: Bergin and Garvey Publishers.

Goody, J. and Watt, I. (1968). The consequences of literacy. In J. Goody and I. Watt (eds.), *Contemporary Studies in Society and History.* Cambridge: Cambridge University Press.

Mateene, K. (1980). Failure in the obligatory use of European languages in Africa and the advantages of a policy of linguistic independence. In *Reconsideration of African Linguistic Policy,* OAU/BIL 1973–80, Publication 25–6. Kampala: OAU (Organization of African Unity) Bureau of Languages.

Ngugi wa Thiong'o. (1986). *Decolonising the Mind: The politics of language in African literature.* London: J. Currey/Portsmouth, NH: Heinemann.

Olson, D. R. (1977). From utterance to text: The bias of language in speech and writing. *Harvard Education Review,* 47: 257–81.

Ong, W. (1982). *Orality and Literacy: The technologizing of the word.* London: Methuen.

Oyelaran, O. O. (1990). Language marginalisation and national development in Nigeria. In E. N. Emenanjo (ed.), *Multilingualism, Minority Languages and Language Policy in Nigeria.* Agbor: Central Books Limited and the Linguistic Association of Nigeria.

Parris, K. (1996). Culture, literacy and L2 reading. *Tesol Quarterly,* 30(4): 665–92.

Phillipson, R. and Skutnabb-Kangas, T. (1996). English only world wide or language ecology? *Tesol Quarterly,* 30(3).

Séhouéto, L. (1995). *Les Publications en langues nationales au Bénin et au Burkina-Faso.* Monograph.

Sow, A. I. (1977). *Langues et politiques de langues en Afrique Noire: l'experience de l'UNESCO.* Nubia: UNESCO.

United Nations. (1995). *The World Summit for Social Development.* Stockholm: The United Nations.

Chapter 9

Constructive Interdependence: The Response of a Senegalese Community to the Question of Why Become Literate

Sonja Fagerberg-Diallo

Defining "Education" within a Grassroots Literacy Movement

The questions of why and how to develop so-called "literacy programs," which usually focus on adults and are often in a language without a long written tradition, is part of an ongoing international debate. This article gives a voice to a group of new literates in a Senegalese language, Pulaar, who are sandwiched between the national debate over continuing to use an international language in the local school system, and the public policy debate over allocating funds for nonformal education.[1]

The official language of Senegal, both in the administration and in education, is French. There are 22 "national languages," 8 of which have been officially recognized but which are not used in the educational system. Approximately 58 percent of school-age children enter the public French-language school system; but of these, roughly 80 percent fail to finish primary school.[2] The pyramid of Senegal's educational system looks like a sharp needle standing upright on a flat surface, and getting ever narrower as the educational years go by. As a result, Senegal's official illiteracy rate is 67 percent by the latest World Bank statistics.

In the face of such dismal statistics, individuals motivated to learn are turning, as adults, to a nonformal, community-based form of education in Senegalese languages. The most dramatic and dynamic of these grassroots movements is unquestionably that of the Pulaar (Fula, Fulani) language. Pulaar is a language used by roughly one-third of Senegal's 9 million citizens, but it is spoken by some 25 million people speaking mutually intelligible dialects across the Sahel to the borders of eastern Sudan.

Educators and policymakers can learn some important lessons from this language community. This chapter highlights the salient points of this grassroots movement, from exploring the motivations of individual learners to reviewing the sociohistorical events which have contributed to converting a literacy program into a "cause." Few elements of this literacy movement are more important than the link which has been established between cultural identity and literacy. In an interview with a group of voluntary literacy teachers living on the outskirts of the Senegalese capital, the person conducting the interview was told, "we must try to revitalize our culture, and literacy in the Pulaar language is one instrument for reaching that goal" (Madden, 1990, p. 18).[3]

Because education in Pulaar belongs to the community in a way that French and Arabic language education never did, the experience with it is one of self-discovery and liberation; not of striving to catch on, catch up, or remodel the self to fit the educational experience.

A comparison of Koranic school and French education provides the setting for the well-known novel *Ambiguous Adventure*, by the Senegalese author Cheikh Hamidou Kane.[4] Written just 30 years ago, Kane, himself a Pulaar speaker, could not have conceived of a third educational option. His novel unfolds around the struggle of one young man to confront the conflicting claims of these two educational and cultural systems. Jane Hale, African literature specialist, writes:

> In this novel of initiation, young Samba Diallo's voyage to manhood thus began in the ancient, idealized world of his Toucouleur [Pulaar speakers from northern Senegal] and Muslim ancestors, where the object of education was to reproduce the circular path traveled by one's predecessors, to learn the same lessons as they, and their own ancestors, did, to follow these footsteps, walking right alongside one's age group, around the circle of eternal wisdom inscribed by God at the beginning of time and of the world, to rejoin that place and that moment that exist outside of this world in the infinity described at the end of the *Ambiguous Adventure* as the "end of exile," "where there is no ambiguity," . . . Samba Diallo, however, stepped out of this spiritual communal circle that was incarnated in the "noisy circle" – formed by the Koranic disciples chanting together to their master in the center – to try the linear, progressive, non-repetitive, individualized, cumulative, path of the "foreign school" – first in his village school where pupils sat aligned on benches facing their master and rose individually to answer their teacher's questions in their competition to stand out from the group. (Hale, 1994, p. 4)

Since these are the two educational models which all Pulaar speakers have some experience with, either personally or through friends and family, is Pulaar education also primarily based on one of these two models? That is, is it primarily circular, or linear? Continuing to use this geometric metaphor, I would describe Pulaar education as neither. It is rather a back-and-forth movement which combines both – more of a spiral. One goes back to one's roots, in order to make the next step forward. Madden found this to be true when she described literacy in Pulaar – which can be seen as opening up new horizons – as being rooted in a process of cultural embedding;[5] that is, of what she called an *enracinement culturelle* (Madden, 1990).[6]

For the first time, education can be based on the culture's own internal measure, which is what makes it so compelling for the participants. This is not to say that this model is new or original in the world. But it is a new educational experience for Pulaar learners, and it ignites their imagination and loyalty in a profound manner. In the words of a recent evaluation of literacy programs in Pulaar by Kuenzi,[7] literacy in Pulaar succeeds in diminishing the chasm between the "modern and western" on the one hand, and the "traditional or African" on the other. Participation in this educational process is not chosen for individual advancement but for cultural and psychological integration. As she points out:

> involvement in these [Pulaar literacy] programs increases not only participants' feelings of individual efficacy, but also their cultural pride. Moreover, the type of cultural pride it instills is a healthy one as those trained in literacy appear to not only have an enhanced sense of their cultural identity, but also an increased openness to those from the exterior and new ways of doing things. (Kuenzi, 1996, p.25)

This becomes the essence of what she eventually calls "constructive interdependence," that is, the ability to integrate new skills and information into a culturally grounded worldview, both contributing to a dynamic and creative process marked by dialogue.

The Sociocultural Context of this Literacy Movement

New readers in Pulaar are well aware of the context in which they are learning since that context provides part of their motivation for learning to read. Part of the context is *imposed by the outside*, created by an international or national development project which has, for example, installed a new technology, created international marketing ties, etc., and then suddenly turned the operation and management of these systems over to nonliterate and untrained local populations. Just one example are the groups of highly mobile Fulbe[8] pastoralists who need to learn how to manage the 250–meter deep water-pumping stations which were initially installed, financed, and managed by the government, first colonial and then independant, in the 1950s and 1960s. But since the late 1980s, the operation, maintenance, and amortization of these stations[9] has been turned over to local management committees, usually comprised of 12 herders who are rarely literate, and who certainly have not received any specialized training for this task. Their very survival – continued access to water – depends upon being able to quickly learn a whole series of management skills, all of which depend upon a sophisticated degree of literacy.

Furthermore, part of the context is being *created by new Pulaar readers themselves*, those "literacy militants" on a crusade to see that each community sets up and participates in local Pulaar literacy classes. Internal social pressures have transformed being literate in Pulaar into a prerequisite for participating in the active local associations which are involved in everything from environmental protection to women's health issues. Becoming literate serves as a type of training in leadership, and these emerging community leaders and activists are creating their own context for needing and using literacy locally.

Finally, part of that context is being *promoted* through the development of good books and the adequate training of teachers. Very simply, the more books there are, the more that people read; and the more they read, the more they want to continue to learn. Programs which train literacy teachers and set up classes have made it possible for local groups to improve their skill levels, thereby increasing the number of participants and classes. The availability of funding to locally constituted groups has also increased the number of participants and the level of performance in classes.

This convergence of contexts – imposed, internal, and promoted – has had an impact on both the individual learner and on the community. The community itself is defining the reasons to become literate, identifying the type of literacy and education it needs, and generating its own internal motivations amongst individual participants.

In this section, I will present an overview of the historical events, the socio-cultural realities, and the financial resources which are part of the context for this grassroots movement. This complex and original process cannot be seen as a model which can be easily or automatically replicated elsewhere. It is a case study to learn from rather than a methodology to apply.

The sociohistorical context: The events which contributed to the development of a literate environment in Pulaar

Writing in Pulaar has more than a 200-year-old history. Publishing for Pulaar readers, on the other hand, is less than 20 years old. Here I examine ten important chronological periods or events which each built on what had preceded, constituting the continuum which goes from simple writing to publishing in Pulaar. In various ways, each event contributed to the creation of an environment in which literacy in Pulaar was valued and used. Starting with this historical perspective has the further advantage of putting the development of a literate environment into a long-term context, in contrast to the average literacy campaign which hopes to see measurable results within three to five years.

Writing in ajami

There has long been a small elite who could write in Pulaar using Arabic script (known as *ajami*). It was used in personal letters, for accounting records and commercial transactions, in religious poetry, etc. Some documents in *ajami* were destined for the other cultural elites who also mastered reading and writing in both Arabic and *ajami*. Others, however, such as the lengthy poem about an important religious figure, El-Hadj Omar Tall,[10] were written in *ajami* and then memorized by students (*talibe*) who kept the texts alive as much by their capacity to recite from memory as by their capacity to read and write. The impact of *ajami* on the writing of Pulaar has been more to demonstrate the prestige and uses of writing than any practical use, due to the lack of a standardized orthography and to its limited use in contemporary publishing.[11]

Missionaries and colonial administrators (1830–1960)

Colonial administrators and missionary groups have long had a special interest in the Fulbe for a variety of reasons. Due to this interest, the first grammars, lexicons, and transcriptions of oral traditions in Pulaar were published as early as the late nineteenth century. These scholarly bilingual publications were primarily designed for a foreign market, and they continued to be published until the independence of Senegal in 1960.[12] These materials were meant for a university trained audience, whether African or European, not new readers who were speakers of the language. Nevertheless, these publications helped to codify the writing conventions of Pulaar, so that when newly independent Senegal first considered the possibility of publishing and teaching in African languages in the 1960s, Pulaar was comparatively well studied, having both expatriate and national linguists who were specialized in writing the language.

An internationally recognized orthography (1966)

In 1966, UNESCO sponsored a meeting in neighboring Mali to promote the standardization of the orthographies for major west African languages spoken across national boundaries. The orthography suggested for Pulaar[13] was subsequently adopted on an international scale, by African countries as well as by Europe, the (then) Soviet Union, the United States, and Japan, all of which published in Pulaar.[14] Senegal officially adopted this alphabet in 1971 (décret no. 71–566), and in 1980 passed the first legal decree on writing in national languages (décret no. 80–1049). Having an internationally recognized orthography has helped to create a context where texts and publications can be shared between countries, writers, and publishers, in spite of minor differences in writing conventions and the more important differences in dialect.

Literacy classes open in Cairo and Paris (1965–84)

The first 20 years of popular, grassroots literacy activities which were eventually to have an impact *on* Senegal did not take place *in* Senegal. Instead, the community of Pulaar speakers living in Arabic-speaking countries were the first to set up classes, write a primer, and start to publish Pulaar books. The earliest efforts date back to the mid-1960s in Cairo, and continued throughout the 1970s.

The people involved in these activities in the Middle East later attended a meeting held in Bordeaux (France) in 1981 and again in 1984, expanding what had become the "literacy movement" in Arabic-speaking countries to Pulaar-speaking students and workers in France.[15]

Government and parastatal literacy classes (1970s–1980s)
In 1971, the government created the Direction Nationale de l'Alphabétisation (DA) which would later become the Direction de l'Alphabétisation et de l'Education de Base (DAEB).[16] The philosophy from the beginning was to invite "ministry personnel and regional governors to integrate literacy into every development project submitted for outside funding" (DAEB, 1995, p. 6). During these years the government employees of the DA, and then DAEB, contributed in the training of future literacy teachers and to the development of basic primers in the six officially recognized languages of Senegal.[17]

They were also instrumental in helping the various parastatals with programs for improving agricultural production to add literacy as one of the services the parastatals could offer[18] – in large part because these organizations needed a literate "clientele" to reach their production goals. If ever literacy in Pulaar had a primarily "functional" orientation, it was in these parastatal programs where literacy was geared to production.

Senegal's grassroots literacy activities take off (1982)
In 1982 a national association known as the Association pour la Renaissance du Pulaar (ARP) held a regularly scheduled congress, resulting in the promotion of literacy to the position of their primary activity. Stimulated by the return of several key Senegalese figures who had been in Cairo, the ARP moved in the direction of making literacy the central activity and organizational principle of this association which had its roots in a movement for cultural identity.[19] Today, the ARP is a nationally recognized organization with 133 local sections which organized 1,949 voluntary literacy classes in 1997, with 48,625 participants in class.[20]

Contact with Pulaar dialects from other countries (1980–90)
In a 10-year program called MAPE,[21] linguists of two west African languages, Mandinka and Pulaar, had the rare opportunity to come together in a planned series of workshops in order to exchange the results of their research with the goal of harmonizing the written forms of these two languages which are spoken over several national boundaries. To this end, they carried out various dialect studies, as well as working together to create new lexical items which had no traditional equivalents in these languages.

Literacy classes opened by nongovernmental organizations (NGOs) (1985 to the present)
In 1985, the Programme Integré du Podor, a project of one of the oldest and largest Senegalese nonprofit organizations, the Union pour la Solidarité et l'Entraide, began the first major experiment of nonprofits working in Pulaar literacy. Hiring teachers from the ARP, they opened five classes in northern Senegal, reaching a total, then, of 300 students. From that initial experience, the PIP literacy program has reached over 40,000 participants.[22]

This NGO experience is only one amongst many, many others. For Pulaar, however, it is one of the most important, both by the number of participants as well as because of the duration of their program. This experience has been characterized by linguist Fary Kâ[23] as being the first NGO experiment which contrasted with the "functional" approach then being used by the parastatals. For PIP, literacy was a permanent activity that was supported by village committees, as part of what PIP called their *"approche village"* (village-based approach). Rather than promoting a centralized literacy campaign, PIP responded to requests from villages which were already working with PIP on other development activities. In 1991, a study found that out ot 254 villages in the Department of Podor where PIP is located, 200 had opened village literacy classes, meaning that an important "critical mass" of new literates had been reached.

Publishing in Pulaar (1989 to the present)
Given this context – voluntary ARP literacy classes as well as classes being organized by nonprofits and parastatals – five Pulaar authors and linguists came together in 1989, remarking that what was missing were books for all these classes and new readers. They founded the Groupe d'Initiative pour la Promotion du Livre en Langues Nationales (GIPLLN), thereby beginning the first sustained effort at publishing in Pulaar for a local market of new readers in Senegal.[24] Without offices, personnel, or regular financing, the GIPLLN went on to publish 11 books between 1989 and 1990. Given both the successes and weaknesses of the GIPLLN, Associates in Research and Education for Development (ARED) was founded late in 1990 as a nonprofit publisher,[25] and began to publish books in Pulaar in 1991. The GIPLLN and ARED have combined forces from the beginning so that books in national languages, especially Pulaar, can be published.

A government ministry for literacy and national languages (1991)
The final and most recent date of importance for literacy in Senegal was the creation of the Ministère Délégué Chargé de l'Alphabétisation et de la Promotion des Langues Nationales within the Education Ministry in 1991, which today has become the Ministère Délégué Chargé de l'Education de Base et des Langues Nationales. This ministry, by its very existence, demonstrates a will to promote national languages, literacy, adult education, and nonformal education. It has sanctioned a highly diversified and decentralized approach to literacy which it calls *faire faire* (which could be translated as "enabling"), in order to promote the maximum degree of community participation, be it through village associations, NGOs, editors, school programs, parastatals, industry, etc.

The sociocultural environment: Factors valorizing the utilization of written Pulaar

In the preceding section, we have seen how chronologically ordered events have been able to interact to create the context in which today's Pulaar literacy classes operate. The organizing principle in that section was to demonstrate how Pulaar moved from writing to publishing, as well as showing the institutional diversity of approaches. While this chronological continuum is very informative, it is not a sufficient prism for studying the data. With this dynamic historical context in mind, we can also go on to study some of the sociocultural features which provide the backdrop for developing a literate environment.

There is a tradition of literacy

Over the past 200 years, a subgroup of Pulaar speakers[26] have directly used Arabic literacy as a means to gain and maintain social status. This group has clearly demonstrated the possible social and economic advantages in being literate. In this case, they used knowledge of both literacy and a foreign language (Arabic) to create and define their own socioeconomic niche.

Pulaar is regional

As a language, Pulaar is spoken by roughly 25 million people, crossing national boundaries from Senegal in the west to Sudan in the east. Pulaar speakers therefore believe that their language has the capacity to play a regional role, especially if they are able to communicate in it through writing. As one Pulaar literacy teacher from Kolda (southern Senegal) once told me, he had himself learned to read and write in French. However, if he wanted to communicate in writing with a Pulaar speaker 100 miles to the north, he would have to use English (the official language of the Gambia), and 100 miles to the south it would be Portuguese (the official language of Guinea Bissau). But having a written form of Pulaar made communication possible throughout the zone.

Competition with another Senegalese language

While Pulaar is spoken across national boundaries, within Senegal it is not the largest language group, nor is it ever used as the lingua franca. Those roles are filled by Wolof, the language of the rural and urban areas to the west of Senegal, near towns and ports which historically gained in importance with the arrival of a French administration. As long as Wolof remained a spoken lingua franca which was chosen for practical purposes by the the speakers themselves, using it never posed a problem. But in recent years there have been organized attempts to promote it as *the* official national language, in place of or equal to French. Pulaar speakers, however, have always been the first group to protest any attempts to minimize the use of other Senegalese languages. This perception of a "threat" has given the ethos of a "cause" to Pulaar literacy, in which becoming literate is a way of asserting cultural identity on a national scale.

The impact of politics on national language education

The Pulaar literacy movement in neighboring Mauritania has had a substantial impact on Senegal. During the 1980s, the Pulaar, Wolof, and Soninke languages were successfuly used in the primary school system. Mauritania also had a very active Association pour la Renaissance du Pulaar which shared the same literacy goals as its Senegalese neighbor. However, in Mauritania, literacy in Pulaar became the medium through which the population could express their dissatisfaction with a restrictive and racist political regime; and where that same regime saw education in national languages as a means for undermining the French language and shifting the country's educational policy towards Arabic.

> In Mauritania, teaching in national languages had a particular character. It was the result of a struggle mobilized by a powerful grassroots movement for cultural identity whose origins went back to the 60s [the moment of independence]. Just after independence, the black African population of Mauritania mobilized themselves to fight against the "arabization" of the school system, to the detriment of French, and against the "beydanization" of public services. (Ly, 1997, p. 28)

Acute political problems inspired the development of both writing and literature in Pulaar, perhaps best remembered for the galvanizing poetry which was well known on both sides of the border – "I memorized the poetry written by Mauritanian Haalpulaar who were struggling against the cultural imperialism of the white Maures" (Ly, 1997, p. 15).

One practical result of using these languages in the public school system was the increase of both publications and trained teachers in national languages. Furthermore, when overt political troubles erupted between Mauritania and Senegal in 1989, resulting in the deportation of thousands of people in both countries, there was a resulting influx to Senegal of professionally trained teachers in national languages from Mauritania. This had an important impact on the "professionalization" of teaching in Pulaar in Senegal.

The advent of community-based adult education

Literacy in Pulaar has been able to offer a serious alternative to the formal school system, meeting important educational needs through this nonformal system geared primarily towards adults. Control over whether or not a village will have a class is in the hands (and pocketbooks) of the village itself; not the Ministry of Education. I am not arguing that no money should be allocated from the public sector for nonformal education. Rather, that because there is a sense of local "ownership" over the process, money spent on education in this system is very productive. The choice of whether or not people will attend the classes is in the hands of the adults who are themselves the participants; not the parents who decide which of their children should go to school. The time which this educational process takes can be counted in hours and months;[27] as opposed to years in the formal French school system, at the end of which most participants still don't understand, read, or write French particularily well![28] According to the Kuenzi study:

> Literacy teachers noted the massive efficiency gains which are gleaned by learning in Pulaar as opposed to French. When asked whether, if given a choice, they would have preferred to have been trained in Pulaar or French, not one responded French ... Many participants commented on the fact that the training [in Pulaar

literacy] had allowed them to understand much of what they had been exposed to in formal schooling but had never fully grasped. Some noted that they were learning grammatical rules in Pulaar that they had never learned in French...One teacher notes: *In Pulaar, you can learn to do mathematical computations in six months, but in French you can study for three years and understand nothing...* The multiplier effects associated with learning Pulaar were highlighted in one teacher's story: *After one year* [of Pulaar literacy] *I was able to teach...I could not have done that in French.* (Kuenzi, 1996, p. 9)

This sense of community enterprise and ownership over education is an important motivational factor when compared with the centralized French-language system which remains in the hands of ministry officials and teachers who, being appointed at a central level, often do not speak the language of the community to which they are assigned.[29] Furthermore, having access to adult education has liberated women to become involved in the process. As children, they had no say over whether or not they would go to school. But as adults, they have been able to pioneer a mass movement which has opened educational doors for them. Finally, studying in French always poses the issue of how the family and community will react if the person succeeds, and therefore must move from the village to major cities in order to continue in the next round of studies. French education, by definition, contains the potential of alienating the successful student from his or her community, because they must leave the village to pursue it. (This is an additional reason why many parents are hesitant to send their daughters to school.)

Competition between Pulaar-speaking zones

Pulaar is spoken in almost every region and town in Senegal, but in various dialects and by various socioeconomic groups. Therefore, there is a degree of competition between various Pulaar-speaking zones. In the early 1980s, the literacy movement clearly began in the north, along the Senegal–Mauritania border. But today it has moved throughout Senegal. Often groups in the south, or pastoralist groups in the north who initially were not attracted to literacy, express the desire to see their own dialect developed in writing and publishing. This can be a negative factor when, for example, one dialect group hesitates to buy or read books published in a different dialect. At other times, however, this is extremely positive because it adds to the motivation for each community to both learn and to contribute. Furthermore, as education advances and readers become more fluent, many are now extolling the virtues of having such a "rich" language with so many variants.

Emigration and living away from home

The impact of emigration on literacy has had a varied and fascinating effect on the motivation for learning, as well as upon the organization of classes. It is certainly significant that the movement for Pulaar literacy first began amongst workers and students living in Arabic-speaking countries, then moved to France, before finally becoming an important social movement in Senegal. Living in those highly literate societies provided an impetus to learn to read and write. However, living in societies within which they were marginalized "outsiders" perhaps pushed them to turn to their own language and culture in an attempt to develop psychological coping mechanisms as well as reading skills. Secondly, the early voluntary literacy teachers were largely the students who were studying French in major cities and towns throughout Senegal, far away from their own homes.[30] They built a spirit of camaraderie with their student friends, who then all volunteered to teach when they went to their various villages during vacation months. Organizing around literacy has provided an outlet for the energies of potential community "leaders," who are supporting a social and cultural cause by promoting literacy in their own language. Finally, the need to learn to write letters to their emigrant husbands, "keeping our secrets between us," is constantly cited by women as one of the reasons they initially joined a local literacy class.

The impact of individuals committed to Pulaar literacy

A couple of charismatic and altruistic individuals have had tremendous success in mobilizing communities to organize their own literacy classes. The two men who have most profoundly marked this movement at a national level are Yero Dooro Jallo and Mammadu Sammba Joob (a Mauritanian known as "Murtudo," meaning "the rebel"). They are, indeed, proof that individuals can make a difference. Based on a combination of constant travel across Senegal and possessing the eloquence of poets, these two men have literally spoken to the hearts of thousands of people. Furthermore, both are prolific writers, especially in writing fiction and poetry which have a deep emotional impact on the reader. Being able to recite the poetry and read the books of these two individuals is a wish expressed by the vast majority of new literates.

The role of books

Books in Pulaar destined for an audience of new readers who have become literate in that language, as opposed to scholarly collections of oral traditions using Pulaar with a French or English translation, first started to appear in Cairo in the 1970s. Since the early 1990s, two sister organizations, ARED/GIPLLN, have specialized in the publication of books in the Pulaar language. To date they have published more than 60 books in Pulaar, and sell between 1,500 and 2,000 books per month.

It is interesting to note that their most popular books – apart from the basic literacy series for teaching people how to read in the first place – are novels, histories, and books about indigenous knowledge systems. The following excerpt from an interview with a typical book reseller[31] illustrates this preference:

> ARED STAFF: What guides you in the books you choose to buy?
> BUYER: Since I resell what I buy, I buy what is the most popular. What my buyers want the most are books of literature ... They always buy copies of *Ndikkiri Joom*

Moolo, Nguurndam Neddanke, Silaamaka and Pullooru,[32] as well as anything on Pulaar grammar. (from the ARED archives, 1997)

Many experts in designing literacy programs still wonder if it is a so-called "functional" objective which will inspire people to want to become literate. However, members of ARED/GIPLLN point out that the reason most often given by readers who come to buy the most popular book that they sell, the novel *Ndikkiri Joom Moolo*, is laughter![33] An ARED editor once wrote about his own experience in reading this novel in manuscript form. He reports that he found himself sitting on the sidewalk outside his room at three in the morning so that his roommates could sleep, while he read and laughed his way through his first novel in Pulaar:

> I would sit on the sidewalk reading from *Ndikkiri*. With each page, I could barely keep from laughing out loud as I sat alone in the street. Each time this would happen to me, I would get up and look around to make sure no one had noticed me, fearing that someone would think I was crazy. The next day, I would entertain my friends with stories from *Ndikkiri* while we drank tea together. In the end, all of my friends who were literate in Pulaar could hardly wait for this book to be published. (Ly, 1997, p. 13)

Obviously, it is difficult to be motivated to learn to read when there are no books. And conversely, *good* books provide a motivation in and of themselves.

Using radio as a medium of communication
The fact that Yero Dooro Jallo has had a radio broadcast in Pulaar for more than 20 years, first broadcasting from Cairo beamed towards all of west Africa, and since 1982 from within Senegal, has provided another means for mobilizing the literacy movement. Furthermore, the ARP had a 30–minute program each week which often focused on the topic, "the importance of learning to read in one's own language" (Ly, 1997, p. 16). Using this medium, information has been shared, and communities have been motivated by the sense of belonging to a movement larger than themselves.

An organization (the Association pour la Renaissance du Pulaar)
An extremely important factor, perhaps the key to it all, is the existence of this organization which re-created itself in 1982 around the theme of literacy in Pulaar. The ARP, officially recognized in 1964, had its roots in an informal cultural organization for Pulaar-speaking students and government employees who found themselves living and working in Dakar, but who did not want to loose their cultural heritage. Many were thinking of their children, who were now being born and raised far from their extended families of origin. Their desire to have their children speak Pulaar in spite of growing up in largely Wolof-speaking neighborhoods and attending school in French, provided the first impetus towards language issues for this organization.

At the national ARP congress of 1982, Pulaar literacy teaching took center stage. Opening literacy classes became the primary activity and identity of the entire organization. Furthermore, the existence of this organization has created the context for the development of multiple local literacy initiatives. In 1997, although many villages now have their own association dedicated to Pulaar literacy, language, and culture, the model and inspiration for these comes from the ARP.

Computers
The widespread introduction of personal computers, starting in the mid-1980s, had a tremendous impact on the literacy movement, for two reasons. First, it allowed resolution of the problem of using an orthography which had five characters not found on standard typewriters. But more importantly, computers eliminated the need to have an outside editor or publisher prepare texts for publication. Not only did it become less expensive to go to print, but it put the first and final work in the hands of people who could read the language in which they were working.

In contrast, the early publications which came out of Cairo are practically unreadable because of the number of orthographic errors, the lack of punctuation, and the absence of a meaningful page layout. Editors in Cairo were not able to help new writers write because they didn't understand the language. The editorial role totally disappeared. In its place, texts were simply typeset and printed with no editorial input. Today, all that has changed, in large part due to the technology for desktop publishing. In the past 10 years numerous nonprofit organizations, government agencies, and so forth, have acquired the capacity to produce printer-ready manuscripts in national languages, a major breakthrough which makes publishing books in national languages feasible, less expensive, and of better quality.

The role of economic incentives

One of the features which leads me to call this a literacy *movement* (as opposed to a *program*) is the high degree of voluntarism among teachers, as well as the fact that individual learners have been willing to pay classroom dues, buy books and supplies, and find their own teachers. Access to funding has not been necessary to motivate communities to start up classes. Nevertheless, in recent years two clear economic benefits have helped this movement function more efficiently than in the past.

In the 1990s, most organizations (both governmental and nonprofit) which support adult literacy and nonformal education are taking the tactic of offering financial support and training to existing local initiatives. Neither donors, nor the government, nor NGOs come into a community with the idea of starting up and taking charge of literacy classes. Instead, they try to find ways to improve existing community initiatives. Furthermore, the government policy of *faire faire* has been an important contributing factor, supporting a wide variety of methods and experiences by a multitude of institutions interested in literacy, rather than trying to either dominate the field or unify the variety of approaches.

Access to two types of financial resources has had an important impact on voluntary literacy classes: financing for classes and jobs for literacy teachers. However, it is important to point out that the impact has been more one of improving organization than of motivating participation.

Financing for classes

Since 1996, the Education Ministry in Senegal has been able to offer financing to classes and associations already operating in the field. While the Pulaar literacy movement did not wait for financing in order to get started, now that this type of financing has arrived, they are in a good position to make use of it. These funds can cover everything from buying books, to paying trainers, to covering the costs of setting up a classroom, to paying a small stipend to literacy teachers during the months they teach. It can allow a local group to both improve the quality of the services they provide, and to expand.[34]

Salaried jobs for teachers

At first the literacy movement inspired and channeled by the ARP depended uniquely on voluntary teachers; and to this day, they still provide a major portion of the teaching force. According to the Kuenzi evaluation:

> Many respondents exhibit at least a degree (and some, quite a bit) of altruism. While I in no way want to diminish the competitive nature of economic relations or the strong economic incentives driving many to pursue their education in Pulaar, it is also important to point out that many literacy teachers are not paid. When asked why they teach, several of those interviewed responded that they wanted to help their family members, friends, and/or those in the community reach the same level of knowledge and fulfillment that they had reached through the study of Pulaar. (Kuenzi, 1996, p. 18)

This is testified to in the following letter from a person who had participated in a two-week teacher training program organized by ARED:[35]

> Studying [in Pulaar] has changed a lot in my life, beyond simply being able to read and write and do math. I have gained a tremendous desire to help others who haven't studied so that they can learn to write. Wherever I go, wherever there is a meeting about studying, I am very eager to be a part of it in order to gain more knowledge. Wherever I am, I am always thinking "What can I do to help those who are still illiterate?" My relations with people in my village are very good because I now know how to talk with them. Studying has brought me the respect of others, and everywhere I go, I am welcomed with respect. Even when I'm taking care of my own business, other young voluntary literacy teachers want to talk with me. (From the ARED achives, Pette training, Feb. 1997, Usmaan Basum)

The viewpoint expressed here, which is not at all unique to this person, is that it is a privilege to become a Pulaar literacy teacher, and that being paid for the effort is not the crucial element in motivating people.

Nevertheless, the fact that more and more voluntary teachers are being hired by organizations has opened up new jobs – even careers – to them. Increasingly, one meets individuals whose job history has gone from being a voluntary literacy teacher, to working for a project as a teacher or supervisor, even to becoming a trainer of trainers, or, in the case of many NGO staff, to editing books. For them, the only salary they have ever received has, in their words, "come from Pulaar." In particular, significant numbers of women are beginning to be hired by these projects, creating an opportunity which none of them aspired to when they began in literacy classes themselves, since most rural women of this generation have never seen a woman teacher – neither in the French system, nor in the Koranic system, nor in the Pulaar literacy system.

Literacy as a Grassroots Movement: The Personal Motivations

While the larger social context which we have been looking at can be instructive about what motivates participants in literacy, as well as providing useful insights into the role of literacy, it is in the words of the learners themselves that we find the most compelling arguments. Drawing from letters and evaluations written by new literates during various kinds of training,[36] we can gather a glimpse of how the participants themselves view this process.

Who are the participants?

The voluntary literacy movement has been able to mobilize new literates through the dream of becoming literacy teachers themselves. One of the most striking results of the past 15 years[37] has been the creation of a core of self-proclaimed literacy teachers who are not only willing to carry on the basic work in the classroom, but who have also become leaders in their communities and who are defining new uses for this skill, depending as they do on Pulaar literacy in and for their own livelihoods.

I call these teacher-learners "self-proclaimed" because their initial skill level would never lead them to be recruited for the job they are taking on. Looking at the profile of the average person who comes to an ARED training session, roughly half of these participants have had only 3 to 5 years of French schooling well over 10 years previously, and most failed in that system, which is why they did not continue. The other half have never been to formal school, and their entire experience with education has come through Pulaar literacy classes in which they have rarely seen a book or had a trained teacher. But since volunteering to teach is the best way they have of learning themselves, they do so.

When they arrive for training, most of these prospective teachers can write words more or less correctly, and perhaps short sentences, in most cases without punctuation because, never having owned a book, they have never seen periods or commas in use. Most do not read for meaning since they deliberately break words into syllables, in the style of reciting a text from the Koran. The first part of any teacher training program is to work on developing fluent reading skills. Roughly three-quarters of the participants cannot do the four basic math operations. By the end of one month of intensive study, however, these participants have vastly improved their reading and writing skills and learned all four math operations. Furthermore, many have learned how to pass on these skills to others, and a remarkably large number go on to do a very credible job as voluntary literacy teachers in their communities.

The voluntary literacy movement has been able to create a context for developing and utilizing the talents of this remarkable group of people. In her comparative study of voluntary ARP literacy teachers and the participants in a UNICEF literacy program which would eventually pay the teachers, Madden makes the remark that "voluntary ARP literacy teachers wanted to use literacy to save the traditional knowledge of their culture [*sauver le savoir*]. In contrast, the participants in a neighboring UNICEF project expressed the need to be saved by literacy [*être sauvé par le savoir*]" (Madden, 1990, p. 42).

This connection between culture and literacy is a crucial one. Literacy in Pulaar has arrived as a tool to reaffirm Pulaar culture and knowledge, not to replace them with something new. Pulaar literacy and the uses to which it can be put are seen as ways of preserving, promoting, and developing a culture as expressed in its language, echoing the Ngugi position that "Writing in African languages becomes ...an act of decolonizing the mind and a means to 're-connect'" (quoted in Sougou, 1993, p. 65).

The bundle of motivations for becoming literate in Pulaar in the first place, and how the potential role of becoming a literacy teacher attracts people to volunteer, is clearly demonstrated in the following reflections which were written by a staff member of ARED about his initial experiences with Pulaar literacy. In 1987 he failed a French exam in mechanical engineering at the level of the first year at university, leaving him without prospects for either further education or work. As was common, he turned to his local ARP chapter simply as a way of passing time, enjoying the company of friends, and learning more about Pulaar culture. Somehow to him it seemed perfectly natural to have turned to these cultural activities, starting out in a neighborhood theater troop, and ending up teaching literacy:

> When my studies were abrubtly ended in 1987, I went to live with a friend who lived in a lively Dakar neighborhood, Pikine. In this neighborhood, there were lots of young Haalpulaar [Pulaar speakers] who were not studying any more, or who had never been to school. Since we got together everyday for tea after meals, we hit upon the idea to create our own association for all the young people in the neighborhood, inspired by what members of the Association pour la Renaissance du Pulaar were doing elsewhere. Our activities were as follows: literacy classes, debating, performing theater pieces, and doing Haalpulaar dances and songs. Our

objective was to create an environment where young men and women, whether or not they had studied, could get together and exchange ideas, providing animation for the neighborhood. I was very active in the theater troop of this association. But after several invitations, I finally also accepted to take on a literacy class to teach the children from ages 9 to 15 in Pulaar. Some of them had been to French school, others had never studied. (Ly, 1997, p. 15)

The genius of the ARP has been its capacity to inspire this group of teacher-learners. As Madden reports, the people she interviewed told her "A language without volunteers is a dead language!" (Madden, 1990, p. 13). She muses about these teachers:

Someone who decides to voluntarily take on the responsibility of a literacy class must be highly motivated. This group of teachers for the ARP are above all motivated by the desire to preserve and promote their language, and through that, to develop their country. At the heart of the matter, it is their own sense of self-preservation which motivates them. (Madden, 1990, p. 18)

In this context, it is not possible to separate motivations from impact, nor learning from teaching. Given the absence of any other type of context for learning in Pulaar, many turn towards literacy teaching as a way of learning themselves. Since the difference in level between teachers and participants is minimal, the distinction in roles is very quickly blurred. But this very fact encourages thousands of people to believe that they, although minimally literate, can become literacy teachers.

The impact of literacy

Their participation in the activities of literacy has had different types of impact on the lives of the participants. All explain how their studies have given them analytical skills, a new social role, cultural pride, awareness, and, oddly enough, courage! We present here a sample of the responses in letters from one recent training session, hopefully with some of the vigor of expression still intact.

The personal impact: "studying Pulaar woke me up"
It is difficult to present a neat definition of the cognitive skills which people feel they gain by becoming literate. They speak more in terms of generally being more aware. When new literates write, very few of them talk about their efforts in terms of "literacy" or "illiteracy" (known as *humambinnaagal* in Pulaar). To describe their experience with learning to read and write, almost all consistently use the term *jande* (whose meaning is much closer to "studies"). As one woman said, "Studying made me literate," *not* "Because I'm literate I can now start to study." This phrase captures the sense of participating in a learning process which is perceived as a wake-up call. All new literates claim that becoming literate brought them *pinal*, from the verbal root *fin-*, meaning "to wake up."

The noun *pinal* is used to mean "culture, values, awareness" – that is, "being awake." Kuenzi reports this same metaphor in her evaluation report:

> Many respondents expressed the idea that literacy training had allowed them to explore and get to know themselves. They also spoke of being generally more aware and conscious than they had been previous to their literacy training. Interestingly, the metaphor of sleeping was frequently used by many when asked about the impact of literacy. In describing the effects of literacy on villagers, one respondent commented, *They are now more awake. They are able to document things, they are aware of everything that is happening in the world. The others are sleeping.* (Kuenzi, 1996, p. 14)

Amongst the things which people say about the personal aspects, both cognitive and empowering, of becoming literate and studying are:

- Studying opened up my intelligence.
- Now I can take notes of all my thoughts.
- I can now listen to things and make a choice.
- It is only through studying that a person can change.
- At first, I didn't even know how to write my name. Now I know what I should do with my life.
- I now know my own mind, and refuse to be tricked.
- From now on, everything that I do, I will stop first to think about it, to get information about whether it is a good or bad action.
- Studying woke me up, gave me knowledge, and improved my behavior and patience.
- What has changed in my life is that now I have become a more humble and forgiving person.

Oxenham presents these same thoughts in a more elegant form:

> The technology of literacy has served not simply the intended practical purposes of storing and communicating information. Vastly more important, it seems to have enabled the growth and development of the human reason and its power to combine different sources of information to produce even more understanding and inspiration. It has been potent, too, in the growth of self-consciousness and self-understanding. (Oxenham, 1980, p. 43)

One particularily articulate respondent with only one year of Pulaar literacy training and no formal schooling in French shared the following reflection in the Kuenzi evaluation:

> The fact that I have pursued literacy has helped me in my work. It has given me courage to go all the way with things, to be more rigorous and curious. I used to do things by routine. Before, I couldn't give the dates of your visit. I didn't have

memory, precision or observation. Writing has been the most important thing because I can fix firmly on something. (Kuenzi, 1996, p. 15)

Kuenzi views the often repeated theme of writing letters and keeping secrets not as a trivial use of literacy, but as a sign of the increased empowerment of those who are able to do so:

Overall, the respondents seemed to feel empowered by their experience with literacy... Many of the respondent's replies pertained to issues of personal efficacy and independence. Numerous respondents note that, after literacy training, they were able to read and write their own letters. Many respondents stressed that being able to do so allowed them to keep their secrets. While some might dismiss these often heard remarks as trivial in light of the magnitude of the problems facing villagers and their communities, one would be in error to do so. The sheer frequency with which respondents recounted this new-found ability indicates that it represents something important to people. Indeed, being able to read and write one's own letters appears to be associated with the ideas of being able to protect one's interests, keep one's personal business to oneself and thereby maintain control over self. Throughout all of the topics discussed with respondents who participated in a literacy program, the theme of no longer needing an intermediary was emphasized. (Kuenzi, 1996, p. 13)

In other words, individuals are fully aware of the numerous ways in which literacy has affected them. This is largely expressed in terms of personal capacities to think and plan.

The social impact: "I now dare work in a group"
Because of the issue of empowerment, it is difficult to separate most comments into those which show *either* a personal *or* a social impact. The juncture between the two is perhaps best expressed by the use of the verb "to dare," which appears in the vast majority of letters. Daring starts from a sense of personal empowerment, but implies a social action as well. Ong captures the dialectic between the heightened sense of self generated by participation in a literacy program, and the heightened sense of sociability, when he writes, "Writing... intensified the sense of self and fosters more conscious interaction between persons" (Ong, 1991, p. 179). Doronila points out that the participation in literacy classes increases an awareness of how to act in a group through learning the communication skills of "discussion, facilitation, synthesizing, public speaking, bargaining, negotiation" (Doronila, 1996, p. 125). As Kuenzi reports:

At the same time that the idea of getting to know oneself was stressed, respondents also strongly emphasized that they had become more social as a result of the training. Many of the same themes regarding changes in demeanor and an openness to the outside emerged in these interviews. (Kuenzi, 1996, p. 14)

The issue of change in public behavior is well expressed in the following excerpts from letters:

- Studying gave me the courage to stand in the middle of people and speak the truth.
- Now when I enter a group, first I listen to what the others have to say, I try to understand, and then I respectfully add whatever I can, based on the technique of good listening.
- What has changed in my life is that now I dare sit with the elders, something which I couldn't do before.
- Whether the person be old or young, a man or a woman, I now know how we can be together as equals.
- Studying taught me a lot about people.
- Studying improved my social relationships.
- What we've seen in studying is that men and women are equal in work.

This group of voluntary teachers see themselves as actors in the social process of creating and sharing knowledge, not as the passive recipients of it, as expressed in the following letter by a young woman:[38]

> After giving thanks to God and his Prophet, I thank our teachers who have taught me since the time when I didn't even know one letter. When my husband enrolled me [in class] and advised me to start Pulaar, it was because he really loved studying Pulaar. At that time, I was totally illiterate, and I answered that even if I studied, I wouldn't be able to learn. But from then until today I've been studying and, God be blessed, I am no longer illiterate, and I am beginning to know a few things. Since the time when I didn't even know one letter, I now know how to formulate words, I know the entire alphabet. I have read the first and second reading books, I have read the Pulaar grammar book. I now can do calculations, I have read the first and second math books. I am no longer ignorant of any of the things in these books. In the trainings, I was shown the contents of these books, and also how to behave [as a teacher]. First the trainers helped us formulate our objectives; they taught us about group dynamics, leading a group, techniques for teaching, techniques for evaluating our progress, how to take notes, how to talk with others. We were shown JOHARI's window, and what use that has in our lives. All I can say is that this is all useful in every part of my life. (From the ARED achives, Pette training, Feb. 1997, Faatimata Sileymaan Aan, 20 years old)

One woman felt that a combination of being illiterate and being shy had kept her from fully participating in her community. She managed to triumph over both "weaknesses" through participation in literacy classes:

> Studying has changed many things in my life. In the first place, I'm no longer lost. I truly know the value of knowing how to read and write in my own language. And I am enormously "energized" by this. I dare to take my place in society. I now know the value of working in a group, and what comportment I should have to do this work. I have the skills to stand up in front of people, be patient with them, teach

them what they don't know...Today in my village, everyone, even children, address me, and I never imagined that I could be so well known because I am so quiet and shy...I am now entrusted with work both in the village and outside of the village...I hope to become a writer in my language. Studying Pulaar has been very useful to me. (From the ARED archives, Pette training, Feb. 1997, Aysata Aliwu Ndemaan, 23 years old)

Clearly, personal empowerment and new skills have led these participants into the social arena, where they can act as both leaders and resource persons to the larger community to which they are attached.

Conclusion: What Can We Learn from the Pulaar Experience?

A good deal has been written about the relative merits of the autonomous and idealogical models for supporting literacy.[39] The Pulaar model demonstrates an integration of the two. New literates can very clearly identify both the cognitive and the social gains they have made through becoming literate. Furthermore, these gains are realized both on a personal level and on the level of the entire community. But the Pulaar model also emphasizes the importance of a cultural dimension in which becoming literate becomes a medium both for knowing one's own culture better, as well as for supporting that culture in a time of rapid social change. While some of the gains of literacy are thought to be having access to what is "new" and from the "outside," somehow new literates have also transformed literacy in Pulaar into a tool to discover and transmit the "soul" or core of their own culture.

Notes

1 By definition, African language education must be nonformal.
2 According to the Le Soleil, Senegal's official newspaper, the Ministry of Education released the following statistics in September 1997 concerning the number of students who would be admitted into seventh grade after taking a national exam: "In contrast to an exam where it is sufficient to have the average, the 7th grade entry exam only allows a limited number of students to pass, based on the number which can be handled by the school system...For public school classes, 107,452 students took the exam, while the number of places was fixed at 25,500, or 23.76 percent. Some 71,952 students have therefore been eliminated this year" (Le Soleil, Sept. 17, 1997, p. 6).
3 All translations from French or Pulaar in this article are mine.
4 L'aventure ambiguë, 1961, Paris: UGE-10/18.
5 See Triebel, this volume.
6 See also Fagerberg-Diallo, 1995b which explores the themes of the first novels being written in Pulaar, demonstrating this preoccupation with the meaning of being Fulbe.

7   Nora Madden and Michelle Kuenzi both specifically analyzed the motivations of participants in various Pulaar literacy programs in Senegal, and the impact of these programs in their lives and communities. Therefore, their work is quoted extensively in this article.

8   Speakers of Pulaar call themselves Fulbe in the plural, Pullo in the singular. French and English authors have generally used the terms Fula, Fulani, and Peul in referring to the Fulbe. In Senegal there is a second important group of Pulaar speakers, the Haalpulaar, who are incorrectly referred to as Toucouleur or Tukulor in many documents.

9   Averaging up to $20,000 per year.

10 See *La Vie d'El Hadj Omar: Qacida en Poular*, by Henri Gaden, published by the Paris Institut d'Ethnologie in 1935, for an example of a text originally written in *ajami*.

11 A survey in 1990 found that, of those people literate in a national language, 75 percent used the script based on Latin characters, and 8 percent used Arabic characters. (It is not clear what script was used by the rest.) See Diop et al., 1990, pp. 36–7.

12 After independence, national institutions such as the Institut Fondamental d'Afrique Noire continued to publish similar materials.

13 Using a latin script and five special characters.

14 These publications are usually bilingual texts destined primarily for nonspeakers of the language, not new literates.

15 Since that time, this movement has also spread to other European countries, such as Italy, Germany, and Switzerland, and to the United States. Senegalese Pulaar speakers are also organized in literacy classes in other African countries such as Gabon, Cameroon, Ivory Coast, Angola, etc.

16 It is interesting to note that initially the DA was part of the Secrétariat d'Etat à la Jeunesse at aux Sports. Between 1971 and 1993 this unit was moved and/or changed its status seven times before what had become the DAEB was finally made part of the Education Ministry.

17 Official national languages include Wolof, Pulaar, Mandinka, Seereer, Soninke, Joola, and more recently, Hassaniyya and Balante.

18 Amongst the most important parastatals which extensively supported Pulaar literacy at the time were: PDESO for raising cattle in Tambacounda, SODEFITEX for cotton growing in Tambacounda, SAED involved in irrigated rice in the region of Saint-Louis, SODESP for commercializing cattle in the northern sylvopastoral zones, and SODEVA for peanut growing in the regions of Thies, Louga, and Sine-Saloum.

19 The roots of the ARP go back to 1958, when a Dakar-based association called Groupe d'Etudes Poular was formed, later to become the Association des Jeunes Poularophones. This association was officially recognized as the Association pour la Renaissance du Poular in 1964.

20 These statistics were presented at the April 1997 ARP Congress held in Dakar. (Personal communication from the president of the ARP.)

21 MAPE was a program created by the francophone organization Agence de Coopération Culturelle et Technique (ACCT).

22 Ninety-six percent of their literacy centers are in Pulaar, the remaining being in Wolof and Soninke.

23 Personal communication, Sept. 1997.

24 There are other individuals and organizations which print books. The importance of the GIPLLN, and later ARED, however, is that they have both sustained the effort, and are primarily a publisher rather than a development organization. According to ministry statistics, in 1997 ARED/GIPLLN was the only organization to have more than 10 books in any one national language to offer. They are also the only organization to publish materials for anyone who wishes to buy them, not primarily or exclusively for the groups with whom they work. Other active organizations include the Union de Solidarité et l'Entraide and Groupe d'Action pour le Développement Communautaire, which both incorporate literacy as one activity among many others; Aide et Action, Société Africaine d'Education et de Formation pour le Développement, Tostan, and the Centre d'Expansion et Formation Pratique, which print specialized books in Pulaar for their own programs, while also printing in other Senegalese languages and in opening their own literacy classes.

25 Being a nonprofit organization, ARED depends upon donors to cover the cost of developing books. Books are sold, but the prices only take into account the costs of printing plus distribution.

26 The Haalpulaar in general, and the Toorodbe, a clerical class, in particular.

27 Due to the highly consistent orthography, it takes no more than 100 to 200 hours to become an independent reader in Pulaar.

28 Kuenzi makes the following observation about the level of French of many of her informants: "Perhaps another indicator of the insufficiency of the French language as a medium of education and communication is the fact that a significant number of the female respondents with six or more years of formal education insisted on having an interpreter when speaking with me. One respondent who had ten years of education claimed that she could speak French 'only a little'" (Kuenzi, 1996, p. 9).

29 This is a common feature of all branches of the civil service, which tends to use a limited form of French or Wolof with those community members who understand one of those languages, or to depend upon translation.

30 In the 1980s, many village literacy classes depended on the return of their students to hold classes. However, in the 1990s that dynamic has changed because many villages now have a resident local group of potential teachers who have never been to French school, but who have been persuing an education in Pulaar for the past three, five, even ten years. More and more, literacy teachers are coming from a group which has never been through the formal school system. Moreover, in the 1980s all teachers were men. But in the 1990s women can constitute up to 60 percent of this core of teachers in a given community.

31 There is no distribution system in place for national language books, so that these books can reach rural areas where the potential market largely lives. Given the lack of any bookstores in rural areas, ARED/GIPLLN partially depend upon a type of individual who, on his own initiaitve, comes to ARED to buy roughly 20 books at a time and then resells them door-to-door in his hometown. To favor the development of this initiative, ARED/GIPLLN offer a 25 percent discount any time 10 copies or more of one book are purchased. However, books always must be paid for immediately since there is no system in place for collecting money at a later date.

32 These three works of fiction are all by Yero Dooro Jallo, and published by ARED/GIPLLN.

33   Not only does this novel *not* have any redeeming "functional" value, but it is long (196 pages), the most expensive book at ARED (selling for $4), with small print and no graphics. That is, it conforms to none of the norms usually suggested for postliteracy materials. Nevertheless, new readers do not hesitate to buy it as soon as they have completed their primer.

34   As an example of the impact of the availability of funding to local groups, in the three months from January to March 1997, ARED/GIPLLN sold 37,215 copies of basic literacy materials in Pulaar. This figure can be compared with the previous trimester in which only 3,331 basic literacy books were sold. Although part of this can be attributed to the time of year – most classes starting up in January, and most groups waiting to buy books after classes have begun – nevertheless, the extraordinary number of basic literacy books sold in the first trimester of 1997 is largely due to the availability of funds through the Education Ministry for classes which are locally organized.

35   ARED is not only an editor, but also provides trainings to local groups who want to be better prepared to teach from ARED books. As a training organization, ARED has an archive of letters and evaluations written by the people who have participated in these training programs. All translations from Pulaar are mine.

36   These lettters are all drawn from various teacher training programs carried out by ARED. Since 1990, ARED has trained 2,500 literacy teachers in 150 programs for roughly 75 different organizations.

37   I am using the 1982 ARP Congress as a date marking the "popularization" of literacy.

38   In a teacher training session, ARED addresses issues pertaining to the teaching adults, teaching by objective, experiential learning, group dynamics, feedback, listening to others, and evaluation. This participant makes reference to these topics in her letter.

39   For a clear summary of these models, see Fiedrich, 1996, pp. 3–4.

References

Abadzi, H. (1994). *What We Know About Acquisition of Adult Literacy: Is there hope?* World Bank Discussion Papers, no. 245. Washington, DC: World Bank.

Archer, D. and Cottingham, S. (1996). *The Reflect Mother Manual: A new approach to literacy.* London: ACTIONAID.

Ballara, M. (1992). *Women and Literacy.* London/Atlantic Highlands, NJ: Zed Books.

Bhola, H. S. (1994). *A Source Book for Literacy Work: Perspectives from the grassroots.* Paris: UNESCO.

Boeren, A. J. J. M. and Epskamp, K. P. (1990). *Education, Culture and Productive Life.* CESO Paperback no. 13. The Hague: CESO.

Chambers, R. (1997). *Whose Reality Counts? Putting the first last.* London: Intermediate Technology Publications.

Coombs, P. (1989). *La Crise Mondiale de l'Education.* Brussells: DeBoeck-Wesmael Université.

Diop, B., Faye, A., Sylla, Y., and Gueye, A. (1990). *L'impact des journaux en langues nationales sur les populations sénégalaises.* Dakar: Association des Chercheurs Sénégalais.

Diop, C. A. (1971). *Nations nègres et culture*. Paris: Présence africaine.

Direction de l'Alphabétisation et de l'Education de Base (DAEB) (1995). *La Direction de l'Alphabétisation et de l'Education de Base: 25 ans d'expérience*. Report from the DAEB, Dakar, Senegal.

Direction de l'Alphabétisation et de l'Education de Base (DAEB) (1997). *Bilan, 1996: L'Alphabétisation en chiffres*. Report from the DAEB, Dakar, Senegal.

Dixon, J. and Sumon, T. (1996). *Whole Language Action-learning Manual: A guide for literacy practitioners*. Amherst, Mass.: Center for International Education.

Doronila, M. L. (1996). *Landscapes of Literacy: An ethnographic study of functional literacy in marginal Philippine communities*. Hamburg: UNESCO Institute for Education.

Elwert, G. (1997). Pas de développement sans culture écrite: Réflexions sur la persistance de la pauvreté dans les pays moins avancés d'Afrique. *Développement et Coopération*, 1/97 (Germany).

Fagerberg-Diallo, S. (1995a). *L'education et la lecture en langue pulaar: Le cas de Sénégal*. Unpublished manuscript.

Fagerberg-Diallo, S. (1995b). Milk and honey: Developing written literature in Pulaar. *Yearbook of Comparative and General Literature*, 43. Indianapolis: Indiana University Press.

Fagerberg-Diallo, S. (1997). Création d'un milieu lettré en langues nationales: L'exemple du pulaar au Sénégal. *Développement et Coopération*. 1/97 (Germany).

Fiedrich, M. (1996). Literacy in circles? Working paper no. 2. London: ACTIONAID.

Hale, J. (1994). Reading, writing, and schooling. In Cheikh Hamidou Kane, *Ambiguous Adventure*. Unpublished paper, Brandeis University.

Hutchison, J. and Nguessan, M. (eds.) (1995). *The Language Question in Francophone Africa*. West Newbury, Mass.: Mother Tongue Editions.

Kuenzi, M. (1996). Evaluation of project no. 1653, ARED Adult Literacy (Phase 2). Unpublished evaluation, ARED, Dakar, Senegal.

Ly, M. A. (1997). La diffusion du livre en langue pulaar: Le cas de l'ARED au Sénégal. Unpublished monograph for the Collège Coopérative, Paris.

Madden, N. (1990). La motivation dans l'alphabétisation en Pulaar au Sénégal. Unpublished study for ENDA–MSID.

Ngugi wa Thiong'o. (1986). *Decolonizing the Mind: The politics of language in African literature*. Nairobi: Heinemann.

Ong, W. (1991). *Orality and Literacy: The technologizing of the world*. London: Routledge.

Oxenham, J. (1980). *Literacy: Writing, reading and social organization*. London: Routledge.

Rogers, A. and Pemagbi, J. (1995). *Guidebook for the Production and Use of Real and Learner-generated Materials*. London: British Council West Africa Regional Project.

Sougou, O. (1993). The issue of literatures in African languages: A survey. *Université, Recherche et Dévéloppement*, no. 1, Saint-Louis, Senegal.

Street, B. (1984). *Literacy in Theory and Practice*. Cambridge: Cambridge University Press.

Sylla, Y. (1988). *Des Etats Généraux aux Classes Pilotes: Comment faciliter l'introduction des langues africaines au Sénégal*. Paris: UNESCO.

World Bank (1996). *World Development Report*. Oxford: Oxford University Press.

Chapter 10

Literacy for Gonja and Birifor Children in Northern Ghana

Esther Goody and JoAnne Bennett

This paper seeks to pose several questions:[1]

How can education policy effectively support truly open access to L2 literacy?
If initial L1 literacy is recognized as markedly improving subsequent L2 literacy, why is initial L1 literacy not central to educational policy in Ghana?
How can existing local-level resources, especially adult vernacular literacy programs, be utilized to improve teaching and learning of L1 and L2 literacies?

There are understandably many critics (both local educators and international experts) of the achievements of developing countries in attaining universal literacy. They should remember that the colonial legacy was excellent schools for the select few. At independence new governments willingly embraced the demand for universal education but lacked both trained personnel and financial resources to make this massive change. To effectively educate all children is something that even western countries with long traditions of literacy have not yet succeeded in doing.

Background

Modern Ghana encompasses a number of partly overlapping subcultures of literacy associated with the educated middle classes, Islam, Christianity, bureaucratic structures (banks, courts, hospitals and clinics, government offices, post office, police, etc.), and education. Associated with each subculture is a set of people who use its ways of thinking and acting and have access to its resources. Some people belong to more than a single subculture of literacy. Certain subcultures of literacy tend to reinforce each other (socioeconomic middle class, bureaucracies and higher education). Others like Islam and Christianity are effectively opposed in language and scripts as well as belief.

These subcultures of literacy have powerful implications not only for their members, but for those outside them. (i) In developing countries membership of L2 literate subcultures entails status and power *vis-à-vis* outsiders as individuals trying to negotiate their lives. (ii) Members of L2 literate subcultures control access to and exclusion from key resources at local and higher levels (courts, hospitals and clinics, offices, schools, etc.). (iii) Their children grow up in an L2–literate world. This gives the children an immense head-start in primary school, the effect of which multiplies geometrically as the child moves through successive grades.

The distinction between literacy in the child's own language (L1) and literacy in a second language (L2) has several important implications. Probably everywhere this second language of literacy is the language of government, education, and national identity. In modern Ghana it is only L2 literacy which gives access to subcultures of literacy linked to key resources. Thus truly fair access to effective L2 literacy is a prerequisite for individual mobility within the wider society. Without this fair access ethnic, class, and rural–urban divisions will become increasingly stratified and increasingly encapsulated.

The question then is, "How can education policy effectively support truly open access to L2 literacy?"

Learning to Read and Write in L2 in Two Societies in Northern Ghana Today

Observational accounts: Birifor and Gonja Government Education Service (GES) schools.[2] [Initial literacy in L2.]

Gonja

i) The P1 (Primary 1) teaching in the Local Authority primary school in the District center:

The schools in this town are better staffed and supervised than other schools in the District. This Gonja P1 teacher is habitually drunk and hardly ever comes to class – the crafts teacher sometimes takes the class. After three years of complaints by parents he was moved into the District Education office, only to be replaced by another habitually drunk P1 teacher who had been brought from a village school to the District center so he could be kept under observation. For at least five years the beginning primary class in this school has had virtually no GES teaching.

ii) Helping a P4 girl of 14 to write to her father:

One day a girl attending the Methodist school who lived in the compound where I had an office asked me to help her write a letter to her father. As she was in P4 I thought she wanted help with her spelling. It quickly became clear that she could not put even one word on paper; when I had written the letter she was unable to sign her name.

iii) English reading texts – availability and comprehension:
  I asked this girl to bring home her reading text, as I was curious whether, although she could not write, she could read. She said the teacher would never agree to this. There were 7 or 8 texts for her class of 40–odd, and the teacher kept these in the school cupboard. At that time (1992) it was not possible for pupils to buy textbooks. I finally managed to borrow a P4 English reading book from the Education office, and found the girl could read nothing in it. Then I asked her to take me to some of her friends with the book, to see if they could read. Of five children in P4, two could recite some passages while looking at the page. But they did not really understand what the text meant.

iv) A science lesson in P4 (Mankuma village, Dagaba teacher, class entirely conducted in L2, English):
  The blackboard is covered with English the teacher has copied from the textbook, at least two full pages' worth. The children are set to copy down everything from the blackboard. Since I know the children hardly understand the English in their very simple reading texts, I wonder how they will understand this explanation of how heating water changes its form. It turns out not to matter, as the teacher first reads the English from the blackboard aloud, and then goes around to be sure each pupil has copied it correctly into their exercise book. Most of the rest of the period is spent correcting these exercise books. Perhaps they talked about heating water the next day. But since the teacher does not speak Gonja, and the children understand very little English, it is unlikely many will understand the teacher's explanation. It is even less likely that they will be able to link what they hear to the laboriously copied text in their exercise books.

Birifor

Observations of English classes in Baale village:
  Baale is one of two Birifor villages in my study. A single head teacher/teacher (a Gonja man) is responsible for all six primary classes; he speaks no Birifor and so teaches entirely in English. He has been given a room in the village, and comes fairly regularly to school. The average school week over several months was between two and three days. There is never school on Friday because the head teacher always "has to go" to the town market, held on Fridays. One day a week is devoted to work on the head teacher's farm. If it rains there is no school. In 1994 a second, newly trained government teacher was posted to Baale. However, by December he still had received no pay, and borrowed money to return to home in the south. There, he said, at least he would have food. By March the pay for newly trained teachers had still not come through. The District Education

office was crowded with desperate new teachers and Baale was still back to a single teacher. The head teacher in Baale was sometimes assisted by a Birifor ex-pupil teacher who received no pay.

The Baale school has been under two huge silk cotton trees since it was first founded in 1957. The children sit on poles supported by forked sticks, and lean elbows on another, higher pole which serves as a "table." The lower classes sit in the front row, and the upper classes behind, but a big boy who is in P2 sits on the higher pole with those in P5 and P6. For most of the morning the children in the front are mainly playing, as the teacher is busy helping a P6 boy who is preparing for the final primary school exams. He is sitting on a stool under a different tree. There are no books visible, but this is not surprising since everything has to be carried back to the head teacher's room when school finishes at noon, and brought out again next day. (Some books and the blackboard were burned when the thatched room they were being stored in caught fire. Money for another blackboard has finally been collected from village parents.)

The teacher leads P1 and P2 in reciting the English alphabet, but makes no attempt to sound out the letters with them. He writes "m," "n," "o," "p," "q," and "r" on the blackboard, and tells them to practice these letters. Some write letters in the sand, and a few use pencils in tattered exercise books. The teacher now turns his attention to P3/P4.

It is time for English reading – three copies of the P3 English reader appear from somewhere – for the eight children in this group. But neither teacher nor children look at the reader. The teacher puts three sentences from the reader on the blackboard (is this a new passage, or review?). He reads the first word and the children repeat it after him, then teacher reads the second word, it is repeated, and so on. The teacher asks one of the girls to start reading. She falters after the first few words. He calls on another child who has no more success. The teacher now reads the passage. Next he asks the first girl to read again, and she does better this time. The words on the board seem to help. Each of the children in this group is called on to "read" the same passage. (By now even I can remember it.) Now the teacher calls out one of the words on the board and the children are called on in turn to come up and identify which it is. The child points to the word, repeats it, and the rest repeat it after her. Finally the words are erased from the board and the children write them from dictation in exercise books. Three children do not have exercise books and they write in the sand. The teacher marks each child's work and writes the correct spelling on the board. Mistakes are erased and the word written correctly so that the exercise books contain only correctly spelled words, with no trace of the error or how it was corrected.

There is no discussion of what this reading passage means, nor is the meaning of individual words mentioned. There is only the "naming" of the English words. No child asks a question. There are no exercises which let the children select words with appropriate meanings. The children do not put words together themselves into phrases or sentences. The emphasis is on being able to recognize words and speak them correctly. This is "reading."

By now none of the P1/P2 children is still practicing letters. Some girls have gone to kick a leaf "ball" in a counting game. Boys are tossing a snail shell so that it spins on the point. If you don't get it to flip the right way up it won't spin and you lose your turn.

Effectiveness of L2 literacy teaching in Ghanaian schools

Beginning in 1992 Criterion Referenced Tests of English reading have been annually made on a one-sixth national sample of children in the final year (P6) of state primary schools. In 1995 5 percent of children in the final year of primary school were reading English at or above the expected level; the expected level was set at 60 percent. In 1996 the actual figure had risen to 6 percent. With the present system of teaching over 90 percent of children in primary schools are not learning effective L2 literacy.

Clearly there are many factors involved in this stark situation. Shortage of trained teachers, lack of money to meet teachers' already low salaries, the great reluctance of trained teachers to live and teach in villages are all acknowledged as central. The recent Review of Basic Education in Ghana (Kraft et al., 1995) concluded that overall the main problem was the low number of hours of actual teaching available for school children, and that this situation was the result of low teacher motivation. Some of the reasons for poor teachers' motivation are clear (see above). There is much debate about others. A newly prevalent view is that parents' interest is the key: that the local school communities should set targets for their children's achievement, and that teachers should be held responsible for meeting these targets (DFID – Department for International Development, UK).

However, my conversations with teachers and school observations suggest that an underlying factor is teachers' awareness that despite their best efforts children are not learning much. Perhaps the better teachers are more readily discouraged by what they feel is their own failure. Surely where skilled and difficult work is involved, ultimately the most effective motivation is a feeling of competence, and of pride in one's achievement. In Ghana today, effective L2 literacy is the framework on which all other primary and further education depends. Present methods of teaching patently do not achieve effective L2 literacy, and indeed force children who do remain in school to plod year after year through classes they do not comprehend. Able teachers cannot fail to recognize this no-win situation, and many become discouraged and "switch off." They can see no way their efforts can help to improve matters.

Learning to Read First in the Child's Own Language: L1 Initial Literacy

In a recent research project I examined the relationship between effective learning and the contrasting authority structures of egalitarian and hierarchical societies (Goody, 1996). The first phase looked at children's informal learning of adult skills in the community. Phase II was to follow these children into primary school to look at the role of authority structures in classroom learning. However, when I began to work in primary schools it was impossible to find much effective learning to observe. Village children who had never heard English were being entirely taught in English (L2), and few children seemed able to follow what was going on in the classroom. Since I had seen these same children learning very well outside school it was unlikely that their failure was due to lack of ability; the obvious difference was that for them school was "beyond understanding." The problem for my research was how to have meaningful classroom activities to study. The obvious solution was to provide teaching in their own languages (L1), so it was decided to teach L1 literacy in the early primary grades of nine government schools. This was the Local Languages Initial Literacy pilot project (LLIL), and was my serendipitous introduction to the issues of L1 and L2 literacy.

Because the original research design was based on a replicated comparison of hierarchical and egalitarian societies, the LLIL project works with children/ schools in four northern Ghana societies speaking four different languages. Thus teaching of L1 literacy has had to be truly local, drawing on literates living in the same or nearby communities for each school. Of necessity this has meant training teachers locally and using these teachers to develop teaching materials. I must stress that I have no training in education; teaching/learning of literacy in the LLIL project was not based on any theoretical stance but on rough *ad hoc* solutions to problems as they arose. Further, as the LLIL project had not been part of the original research design there were no funds earmarked for either teachers or materials. The Economic and Social Research Council (UK) which funded the main project has a policy of not augmenting grants to meet additional costs encountered as a project develops. However, ESRC was admirably flexible about reallocation of monies within the grant, and this made it possible for LLIL to proceed, though on a shoestring. It is suggested below that the local base and low cost of LLIL L1 teaching may have useful implications for low-resourced effective teaching of L1 literacy in early primary grades.

Teachers were recruited from local literates who could also read and write in their own languages. Although literate, these teachers do not have higher teaching qualifications; many were pupil teachers who had not completed training under the previous system of A and B levels of certification. Most had themselves attended school during the period (which seems to have ended during the 1970s) when children were first taught to read and write in their own language, before beginning to read in English. (Indeed it is these older literates in Ghana whose excellent command of English is often favorably compared to that of present-day graduates with formal higher qualifications.) Already literate in their own local language, the teaching of initial literacy at the primary school level presents no special problems for them. Indeed, many themselves learned with no formal materials other than what their teachers made – mainly verses and short stories written on the board and flash cards. Other LLIL teachers have learned their vernacular literacy through the Non-Formal Education Program sponsored in

Ghana by the World Bank, USAID, and DFID. The largest category of LLIL teachers probably combines these two features, having originally learned vernacular literacy in school, and perhaps for this reason, having become active in the Non-Formal Education Program as teachers of adult literacy in their local communities ("facilitators" is the term used in NFEd). A series of training sessions, and later workshops, has been held for LLIL teachers in each of the four languages spoken by children in the project schools. Thus for each school we have trained locally resident dual English and vernacular literates to teach early primary children to read and write in their own language. LLIL teachers work for only half the school day, and are paid at half the lowest government rate for pupil teachers.

Simple teaching texts were available for three of the LLIL project languages in material printed by the Ghana Institute for Linguistics and Bible Translation. For the fourth, Gbanyito, it was necessary to write teaching material with the help of the Gonja LLIL teachers. Some reading material for the children has also been prepared with teachers' help in each of the four project languages. These materials were put on mimeograph skins and duplicated for the children's use. LLIL teachers were encouraged to make their own materials from card (in fact few do so). The children's own work was used where possible.

The immediate goal has been to give children a measure of command over reading and writing in their own language – as a personal skill. And to do this in a way that lets the child understand that reading and writing are just other ways of representing what we say and what we think. There is clear if simple evidence from the products of written exercises, end-of-year test results, and videos of class interactions that two or three years of even this very rudimentary teaching in their own language can give many children basic literacy skills. At the end of the second year children finishing P2 wrote short stories in L1, and read these to the class. In some LLIL schools second- and third-year children wrote short essays about personal experiences. In the third year one child chose to write three short paragraphs on how nervous he felt about the approaching end-of-year L1 literacy tests!

Effects of first learning to read in the child's own language on English literacy skills

Vernacular literacy was not the purpose of the LLIL project, but a means for obtaining classrooms in which effective learning was taking place so that patterns of learning could be observed. The widely held view (which I share) is that it is basic skills in reading and writing English that are going to be fundamental for a child's success in basic education. It was therefore very interesting to find a number of GES teachers in the LLIL project schools commenting that they thought the children who had learned to read first in their own language were also doing better in reading English, which is taught only by the GES teachers. Some of the GES teachers encountering the first class of LLIL children to have reached P4 told me with real excitement how much more these children understood and how well lessons with them went. "No trouble from them! No difficulties at all! They just read what is in the [L2–English] book!" (head teacher, Mankuma).

These positive reactions were discussed with Mr. Kumbal, Director of Education for Bole District. On his suggestion a systematic comparison of reading comprehension in English was made in July and August 1996 between pupils in P3 of the LLIL project schools and P3 pupils in matched schools with no teaching of initial literacy in local languages. Matching schools were selected in the three Districts involved in the LLIL project; two comparison schools were taken for each of the four languages (Gbanyito, Birifor, Wali, and Dagari). All children in the P3 comparison classes selected, and all those in the LLIL classes, were asked to read the same two paragraphs from Unit 6 of the English reading text. Children in both LLIL and comparison schools were tested by one of the LLIL teachers speaking their own language (usually not their own teacher) with either Dr. Goody or Dr. Bennett. The child was interviewed entirely in his/her own language, except when actually reading in English. The child chose whether to answer questions about the text in English or vernacular. Scoring was based on indices of reading comprehension drawn from the child's retelling in his/her own language of the gist of the passages read, and answering questions based on these passages.

Reading comprehension scores are given for the LLIL project schools and the comparison schools in table 10.1.

Table 10.1 Comparison of P3 English reading comprehension for children first learning to read in their own language (LLIL schools) and those learning to read only in English (comparison schools*)

	HIGH				LOW			Can't read	
	6	5	4	3	2	1	0	English	Totals
LLIL schools	26	21	31	14	5	7	26	42	172
(no. and %)	15%	12%	18%	8%	3%	4%	15%	24%	99%
Comparison schools	0	0	3	3	2	6	20	58	92
(no. and %)	–	–	3%	3%	2%	7%	22%	63%	100%
Totals	26	21	34	17	7	13	46	100	264

* Scores for one of the comparison schools (an elite private school in the town of Wa) were impossible to compute due to incomplete records. Those comprehension test records for this school which could be scored included several with excellent to good English reading comprehension, as well as many with fair to poor comprehension; as in all comparison schools there were also a great many in the "can't read" category. Had it been possible to include the data from this urban school there would thus have been several Comparison school reading comprehension scores in the good to excellent range, and the overall difference between the two sets of schools less extreme. However, as there were no such high scores in the other comparison schools, the overall pattern of markedly more high comprehension scores in the LLIL project schools would remain the same.

This is not the place to discuss these findings in any detail. However, it is worth noting that initial L1 literacy is clearly associated with greater reading comprehension as well as with many fewer children who fail to read at all. The low scores (2–0) probably reflect rote memory skills rather than comprehension. The findings of this small study agree with earlier research comparing L1 and L2 literacy.[3] In her chapter in this volume Doronila shows that Filipino children did worst on the two subjects taught in a foreign language, English. They did well on those subjects taught in Filipino.

Policy questions

It is said that the importance of first learning to read in the child's own language – L1 initial literacy – for effective L2 literacy is widely recognized among scholars; indeed that further research to demonstrate this would be redundant.[4] Yet although the Ghana Education Service and government officials recognize that the present approach to teaching L2 is not working, the possible role of initial L1 literacy in improving this drastic situation is ignored. (Ghana cannot be the only developing country in which schools are failing in teaching L2 literacy. Is initial L1 literacy central to government policy elsewhere?)

If initial L1 literacy is recognized as markedly improving subsequent L2 literacy, why is initial L1 literacy not central to educational policy in Ghana?

Clearly there are many factors involved. Here I can only pick out a few as I see them operating in Ghana.

1) Among the highly educated elite concerned with effective schooling there is a conviction that school time spent on initial L1 literacy would be wasted. Far better to put more resources into better and earlier teaching of L2 literacy. Such people are likely to comment that in the schools they work with, good teaching of initial L2 literacy gives excellent results. However, these schools tend to be urban schools with good resources. Perhaps more important, the children are mainly middle-class, second-generation literates (if not third generation or more). The children in these schools *hear* English at home and in the community; many *speak* English. For them learning to read in English is L1, or L1½ literacy.

This educated elite preference for teaching literacy only in the L2 language also has an element of apparent egalitarianism. Since it is L2 literacy on which higher education and middle-class status are based, we must make this critical resource available to all children through government-funded schools. To spend the early primary years teaching literacy in local languages would be unfair to the children, since L1 literacy does not contribute to success in the important school subjects (which are all based on L2 texts). And of course initial L1 literacy would reduce the time children can spend on learning L2 literacy.

There is a certain attractive simplicity about this view. Our goal is good L2 literacy, therefore we should concentrate resources directly on L2 literacy. The problem is that added resources are not available for the bulk of the population.

And even if they were, this would not solve the problem of trying to teach reading in a language children cannot speak or understand. It seems that on the national level, initial L2 literacy only works for those who are already members of this literate subculture (for whom it is not really L2 literacy at all).

2) It is government and GES policy that the child's own language be the medium of instruction for the first three years of primary school. However, the GES does not distinguish clearly between L1 as the oral medium of instruction for the first three primary grades, and L1 as the basis of first learning to read. There is fairly wide agreement that children in the first three grades of primary school should be taught in their own language. However, it is recognized that in many parts of Ghana this is often impossible because trained teachers speak a different language; they are forced to teach, indeed to communicate, with the children entirely in English. (Holders of the elite view feel this is probably a good thing since it will improve the children's command of English. They might come to see things differently if they sat in rural early primary classrooms where L2 is the only oral medium of instruction and children patently understand very little of what is going on.)

No teaching of L1 literacy in the early primary grades was found in the schools studied for the Review of Basic Education in Ghana in 1995 (Ministry of Education and USAID; see Kraft et al.). Indeed teachers were surprised to be asked about this. There are no texts available for teaching L1 literacy. Teachers say it would be impossible to have GES L1 texts because there are so many different languages in Ghana. There is no provision in training colleges for teaching how to teach literacy in local languages in early primary grades. Teacher training college curricula are oriented towards proficiency in L2 and in the substantive knowledge required for teaching core subjects (English, maths, science, social studies). All texts for children and teachers are in L2. Until the present year all trainee teachers for Basic Education (primary and junior secondary schools) received the same preparation in training colleges. From next year it is intended that training for primary and junior secondary teaching will be at least partially different.

Ironically, "Ghanaian language and culture" is one of the subjects of the core curriculum in junior secondary schools. Texts here are in one of the 17 designated Ghanaian languages. Children are expected to be able to read these with little help, and through them to learn about Ghanaian history and culture. Teaching materials and examinations are prepared by language specialists trained at the Institute for Ghanaian Languages, formerly at Ajumakwa, now at Winneba. There is considerable emphasis on grammar and spelling in this material, with a rigidity which creates difficulties for the many children having to learn a dialect rather different from their mother tongue. The many children whose mother tongue is not among the designated 17 languages must, of course, learn a new Ghanaian language. There has been general surprise at the disappointingly poor results on Junior Secondary School "Ghanaian language and culture" examinations. It was thought this subject would be both easy and interesting for the pupils. What seems to have happened is that the course is taught as if it were another academic subject, with little or no direct attention to learning to read the language. In Bole one of the best of the Non-Formal Education teachers (i.e. adult vernacular literacy, see below) has been drafted in to get the pupils through their examinations. He starts by teaching them to read L1, and his examination results are good.

3) The structural adjustment in education, on which international funding explicitly has depended, required that all government teachers be trained in teacher training colleges. It was argued that with a high proportion of the national budget committed to teachers' salaries, only highly trained teachers should be employed. This would ensure the best value for the money spent on salaries, and at the same time improve the quality of teaching. Consequently local "pupil teachers" have been abruptly removed from the schools. "Pupil teachers" are those who have not completed formal teacher training; they are often skilled teachers with long experience. Almost without exception pupil teachers are local literates who speak the L1 language. Frequently they also read and write in L1 since this was formerly regularly taught in primary schools.

The rapid removal of pupil teachers is a policy paradox, but I think an instructive one. The official directive from the GES to Regional and District Directors of Education stated that wherever trained teachers were available, they should replace pupil teachers. District Directors of Education are supposed to have one teacher for each class unless class numbers are very small. Official policy is that P1 is never taught in a doubled class. Only one of the northern Ghana schools we studied for the Review of Basic Education had a teacher for each of the six primary grades. The rest had between two and four teachers to cover the six grades. Class sizes ranged from 130 (a P1 class) to 12 (the P6 class in the same school). (This contrast in class sizes eloquently illustrates the close relationship between pupil/teacher ratios and the rate of dropping out in primary schools.) However, there simply are not enough trained teachers to fill available posts. Repeatedly we were told that it had proved impossible to replace a pupil teacher who had been removed. Directors of Education who acted quickly to remove pupil teachers were caught by an unexpected ruling that replacements would only be provided for currently acting pupil teachers. In fact there seems to be an informal competition among District Directors of Education to have the lowest number of pupil teachers still employed.

Why should there have been such alacrity in fulfilling what has proved to be a highly problematic directive? Of course every Director of Education wants his staff to be as highly qualified as possible; and pupil teachers are implicitly identified with the "old fashioned teaching" of the colonial period. But there is another factor involved – what we might term "anxious overcompliance." In the bureaucratic climate created by the combination of international demands for structural adjustment in education, and increasingly centralized government/political control of careers and resources, it is unwise not to be seen as willing to fulfill central directives. Pressures from external funding agencies for specific changes in policy and practice leave the national government with no choice but to comply or lose access to funds. Local administrators are now in the same position *vis-à-vis* the national government: comply or go. Such a situation blocked the feedback from Regional and District levels about how government policy initiatives actually work in practice. The Minister of Education did not want to hear about any problems because he saw his task as getting directives enacted in order to satisfy externally imposed policy – in effect whether they worked well or not.

The more general policy issue – particularly apt for education – is how to combine recommendations for structural change with sufficient flexibility of implementation that the "spirit" of the structural adjustment is achieved effectively. This problem appears clearly with the structural adjustment requiring that all government-paid teachers be highly trained. Unanticipated consequences of this apparently benevolent change are directly relevant to the teaching of literacy in rural schools.

Inevitably there are not enough highly qualified teachers to fill empty teaching posts. Further, trainees come disproportionately from areas of the country with the longest experience of middle-level and higher education: the south. Due in large part initially to colonial policy, the north has been late in receiving its own secondary schools, and its first university started only three years ago (Bening, 1990). Thus the highly trained teachers coming from teacher training colleges are disproportionately from areas where northern languages are unknown. Such teachers are extremely reluctant to accept teaching posts in the north. The best of the newly trained teachers are actively sought out by head masters of the best schools, nearly all in the south. Teachers in the middle range can express a preference for where they will teach. It tends to be the weakest of the newly trained teachers (often having to re-sit one or more of the qualifying exams) who have little choice but to accept posts in remote rural schools in the north.

Teachers from other parts of Ghana who are "persuaded" to take rural posts are unable to communicate with the children except in English. The children's own language is neither the medium of oral instruction nor can it be used as a basis for gaining literacy skills. It must be remembered that in rural areas, particularly in the north, children neither hear English spoken nor see it written on signs, instructions, or in shops. The occasional radio is tuned to a local channel; newspapers are rarely seen. The local literates who used to serve as "pupil teachers" were able to use L1 languages for instruction in the early primary grades. From their own L1 literacy they understand that reading and writing are anchored in spoken language. This may well have made them better teachers of L2 literacy, able to use L1 literacy as a bridge for the children's L2 literacy. In this way they introduced a "culture of literacy" through the child's own language. Many older teachers were educated in this way, and their command of English is often markedly superior to that of recently qualified teachers who have had the benefit of "modern" training methods.

We have an unintended paradox: the structural adjustment policy of replacing pupil teachers by highly trained teachers was intended to improve the standard of teaching throughout Ghana. However, for early primary education in rural areas this has often had the opposite effect by removing the bridge between L1 and L2 literacy on which effective L2 literacy was previously based.

Adult Vernacular Literacy Programs in Ghana: Where do They Fit In?

The Non-Formal Education Program (NFEd) in Ghana has been massively supported by external funds especially from the World Bank. NFEd is aimed at teaching adults to read and write in their own language (L1). Seventeen of the most widely spoken Ghanaian languages were designated for inclusion in the program, and texts were prepared in these languages. The substance of the chapters is the same in all 17 languages: family planning, sanitation, hygiene, safe water, nutrition, local democracy, improved farming practice, etc. The message would seem to vie with the medium for importance. It appears that a nationwide but village-level adult literacy program was seen as a good international investment because it promises universal L1 literacy and uses this as a tool to educate the nonschooled population in key areas of health, population control, agriculture, and political awareness.

A new complex of buildings, Literacy House, was built in central Accra and opened by the head of state, Flight-Lieutenant Rawlings. It is here that the national level NFEd work is carried out. There is a regional coordinator in each of the 10 regions of Ghana; district coordinators, first with motorbikes and now with vehicles, train and supervise teachers/"facilitators" at the town and village level. Local NFEd teachers are not paid, but after three or four years diligent workers are given the choice of receiving a bicycle or a sewing machine.

Program objectives

One initial purpose of teaching L1 literacy to nonliterate adults was to convey information about family planning, hygiene, and local democracy. This material is covered in the NFEd L1 texts. With the new government policy of universal, free, and compulsory child education, future generations will know these things. Thus there should be no need to continue or repeat a national vernacular literacy program for this purpose.

The second major purpose of the national vernacular literacy program was to bring literacy to all, even those adults who did not have the chance to go to school. There appear to be several intertwined sub-agendas here:

1   "Literacy" is good to think with. In learning vernacular literacy through didactic texts people would think more deeply about the message, and discuss this with their nonliterate fellows. Perhaps it was hoped that

vernacular literacy would "help people think more logically" in a general way.

2 Vernacular literacy may well have been seen as a basis for more effective future communication from the center to a dispersed population not literate in English (L2).

3 Vernacular literacy would make it possible for local history and traditions to be preserved in writing at a time when society is changing rapidly and many traditions are disappearing. This would be a way of giving people pride in their past and in their culture.

4 In all these ways adult vernacular literacy promises to provide literacy for all Ghanaians, whether or not they have been to school. Although the languages of vernacular literacy (L1) are many, having learned to read and write would give people access to the subculture of literacy which they share with all Ghanaians. L1 literacy is a way of bringing everyone into the modern world.

Why do adults want to become literate in their own language?

1 Being able to read is seen as a modern skill, which makes you like other literates – who are seen as having ready access to important resources – jobs, government institutions like hospitals and banks, patrons.

2 Many adult literacy pupils join the NFEd classes because they think they will be able to learn to speak and read English. These are people who realize that it is L2 literacy which will give them the opportunities they seek. Probably many of those who drop out do so when they find this is not going to happen. Others do not really understand the difference between L1 and L2 literacy.

3 Pride in their own language and culture and the wish to be able to use this in the modern "literate" way are important for many students, and particularly to those who go on to become NFEd teachers.

4 Several Christian missions have translated the Bible into vernacular languages. Being able to read the Bible is an important incentive for Christians to become L1 literates.

Adult literacy program achievements (an impressionistic view)

A great many adults have learned to read in their own language. There are of course many communities in which there was no NFEd teaching. And a number of languages and many dialects are not included among the 17 designated for teaching, and communities of speakers of these are outside the NFEd program entirely. However, the impact of this program at the local level even in these nonparticipating communities has been impressive. Birifor is not among the designated languages, but in two communities I know well local literates are independently teaching adults to read Birifor. Blackboards and printed texts written for missionary adult literacy classes are used for teaching.

The real resource created by NFEd has been the dedicated local teachers/ facilitators of adult L1 literacy, supported in many cases the effective supervision at the local level. By teaching others to read, these L1 literates have themselves become much more fluently literate, and understand in a new way the dynamics of becoming literate. This taking of the teaching of literacy as an object for practice and active study might be termed "metaliteracy." Perhaps this is what happens with experienced trained teachers that permits them to move actively into the subculture of literacy. Many NFEd local literacy teachers are also literate in English, having had various levels of schooling.

Problems of the Non-Formal Education Program in Ghana

The most evident problems concern sustainability of new adult literacy skills, and of the high level of motivation of NFEd teachers.

i) In northern Ghana new local language literates are proud of their skill, but do not use it much. There appears to be very little letter writing in local vernaculars. It may be that since the teaching emphasizes reading from a single didactic text, pupils get little practice in putting their own words into written form. "Writing" is taken to mean knowledge of the alphabet and the ability to write the letters. Practice takes the form of copying a text or writing from dictation. Perhaps to "own" the skill of writing requires active use of writing in ways that are individually meaningful.

It may be that in northern Ghana vernacular literacy is too local, with too many local languages/dialects to make letter writing useful. Also it may be too recent to have produced a "critical mass" of local vernacular literates who share this skill; there are too few people to write to.

ii) There is almost nothing to read in local languages, and typically the available material has been used in teaching, and is therefore too familiar to constitute "reading material." The NFEd program included the printing and distribution of newspapers in each of the designated languages. These do appear from time to time, but even the NFEd teachers find them difficult to decipher. Very local shifts in oral dialects cannot be represented in publications meant for the whole "language." But in the absence of standardized phonetics/spelling the resulting written material is hardly reader-friendly. Written English seems to have been similarly variable in Chaucer's time.

Recently there has been renewed emphasis on the crude screen printing of local news-sheets. These will be in the local dialect of the designated languages and thus hopefully more easily read. It is hoped that by using local NFEd literates to write on local events for the news-sheet both writing and reading will come into more regular use.

iii) The deep commitment of local NFEd teachers ("facilitators") has been truly impressive; without this the program would simply not have worked at all. These men and women have never been paid. They are trained, given a black-board, chalk, and a lantern for night classes, and the promise of a bicycle or a sewing machine after several years of successful teaching. But those who have mentioned the reward of the bicycle to me have seen it as a recognition of the importance of their work, not simply a form of payment. This system has worked surprisingly well during the first stage of the NFEd program. However, local teachers are beginning to lose this early enthusiasm. Altruism has limits. It has not been clear that a second bicycle or the equivalent will be in prospect. Teachers are feeling taken-for-granted, just at the point when their pupils need continuing motivation and support to keep their new literacy active – or even alive. The sustainability of NFEd teachers' motivation is becoming a real problem, and one that will increase rapidly.

Sustainability is thus a serious problem for both adult L1 literacy itself, and for the motivation of the local teachers on whom continued L1 literacy depends.

There is, however, a deeper problem for effective L1 adult literacy in Ghana. It can never provide the access offered by L2 literacy to key resources: jobs, status, ability to operate effectively within the myriad manifestations of government bureaucracy, and the skills necessary for higher educational and technical qualifications. It is access to these resources that nonliterate adults desperately want. They correctly see that without it they will remain marginal to modern Ghanaian society. L1 literacy alone can never bridge this gap.

Theoretical Issues Underlying Educational Policy Directions

Literacy as an object of thinking

Being an L1 teacher/facilitator can lead to what is almost a new kind of literacy – literacy as the object of thinking about how to make others literate. This can be a kind of "playing with literateness"; this has happened with several of the LLIL project teachers. I never see this sort of control and play in teaching L2 literacy. How is this related to subcultures of literacy? How related to using literacy to question and challenge? This insight certainly does not happen for every teacher. How can training make it more likely to happen? Can gifted NFEd teachers lead workshops for teachers and pupils on thinking about what it is to "do literacy"? How can it be given to learners of L1 literacy? By peer teaching?

Competence and practical learning

A major weakness of the NFEd program is that there is little if any element of "practical learning." Passive reading seems to be the main activity and goal. This is almost inevitable given the highly didactic nature of the teaching texts. Since there is for many of the designated vernaculars no literature to read and little if any being written, there is little read except teaching texts. Writing letters does not seem very common.

If we take a Vygotskian view of learning as occurring in the zone of proximal development where performance precedes competence, there is very little opportunity for using L1 literacy as a tool for improving competence. Nor is there literacy "play" in which skills can be explored and risks enjoyed.

How can practical learning be brought into adult literacy classes? The didactic nature of NFEd texts would seem to make this particularly difficult. Can NFEd classes-and-teachers together prepare reading material for school children's L1 literacy texts?

Rote memory, "reading," and "writing"

There is an overwhelming emphasis in L2 literacy on rote memorizing of texts. Trained teachers see accuracy as their goal, and as a test of successful teaching. Is this because no attention is paid to comprehension? Certainly it is closely linked to children's tiny L2 vocabulary; teachers think that by memorising text children are adding to their vocabulary.

Why isn't writing, not dictation, but written accounts, descriptions, stories, letters – more central to L2 literacy teaching? Almost anything that engages children in productive use of L2 vocabulary would surely improve L2 oral and written competence. If writing were linked to peer games, and to peer-supported producing of material for reading, this would introduce practical learning and the dynamics of facilitating performance before competence.

Rote memorizing of texts deprives children of any framework for assessing how and why their performance is not correct. The only criterion becomes exact identity with text. Mistakes are not used to help children understand the meaning of the text or the reason why one form is wrong and another right. But if children themselves write simple accounts of events, these can be used as texts for looking at meaning and simple grammar. Such material would lack the canonical authority of school texts, and thus invite critical discussion in ways that permit performance/competence development. This use of text material produced by the children themselves would also reduce the power differential between teacher and children. Many of the key elements of scaffolded teaching (Wood, Bruner, and Ross 1976) are less effective in high-authority teaching settings (Goody 1996; 1998).

Utilizing existing local resources: L1 or L2 literacy, or both

How can existing local-level resources, especially adult vernacular literacy programs, be utilized to improve teaching and learning of L1 and L2 literacies?

According to the most recent nationwide Criterion Referenced Tests (1996) only 6 percent of children in the final year of state primary schools (P6) can read English to the expected level. The present methods of teaching L2 literacy in primary schools are not working. Judging by the poor quality of the oral and written English of pupils in secondary schools, teacher training colleges and universities – and of many recently trained teachers – this has been the case for some time.[5]

The teaching of L1 literacy to adults in the NFEd Program has been popular and in some ways quite effective. However, there are very serious doubts as to the sustainability of either this newly acquired adult L1 literacy or the continued motivation of teachers of L1 adult literacy. Nor does L1 literacy alone give adults access to resources necessary for full participation in today's Ghana.

The Local Languages Initial Literacy project has taught early primary school children to read and write in their own languages, before they attempt L2 literacy. Most children learn L1 literacy without much difficulty; they seem to enjoy it, and are proud of their accomplishments.[6] GES teachers are finding that LLIL children do substantially better in the other school subjects than children who have only been taught L2 literacy. In a systematic comparison of reading comprehension for initial L1 and initial L2 literates the former had markedly higher scores. As has been found by other researchers, children more successfully learn to read in a second language if they first learn to read in their mother tongue (L1).

Many of the best teachers of early primary children in the LLIL project have been local literates who were involved in teaching adult L1 literacy in the NFEd program. They already have quite fluent L1 literacy, and know how to teach this. Their motivation is high; teaching school children seems to them a real invest-ment in their culture's future. As their LLIL pupils have proved to also do well in other school subjects, especially in L2 literacy, they have become even more enthusiastic. They have continued to teach adult L1 literacy, but now feel that this is being reinforced by the children's L1 literacy. It no longer seems an isolated, short-term endeavor. In the LLIL school communities children have a new respect for adult L1 literacy, and adults encourage and support the chil-dren's efforts.

These findings support an observation often made by those working with adult L1 literacy – that individuals, especially women, report that having learned to read has made them more able to participate freely, even forcefully, in com-munity discussions and decision-making (see the chapter by Ghose in this volume).[7] But why should learning to read influence an individual's willingness to engage in and effectiveness in public debate? Is this an effect of a general sense of empowerment achieved by becoming literate? Is it a matter of feeling that, as a literate, my participation in public affairs has a new sort of legitimacy? Is it a result of practice in expressing one's self in the safe, but nondomestic, setting of the literacy classes? Or is there some way in which the cognitive effects of learning to read also alter, enhance, the cognitive processes involved in planning an argument and delivering it effectively?

There are echoes here of the fascination of the ancient Greeks with both public oratory and the writing, possession of, and study of books of rules for successful oratory. In her study of functional literacy in ancient Athens, Thomas found that books on oratory were by far the most common written documents actually in use (chapter 4, this volume). Oratory is an eminently verbal performance. Why should orators want to write books about rules for oratory? Why should the citizens of Athens want to read them? Clearly these were literate orators, and just as clearly they used their literacy to improve their debating and oratorical skills. But why should there have been this link between public speaking and written texts? It would seem that for literate Athenians effective public oratory came to be seen as depending on mastery of these written texts. And probably the very process of writing these texts led to making explicit "rules" underlying effective oratory which gave further promise of success. But why should the oral and written modes have so powerfully entailed one another?

If today rural adults find that their new literacy also gives them new skills in public speaking, perhaps there is something about becoming able to read that builds new cognitive processes also available for "oratory." This might be in relation to planning how to represent ideas in spoken form. It might be an ability to objectify thoughts in relation to how others will hear and understand them. It might be on the level of a new awareness that individual words convey meaning in different, specific ways; that speaking is composed of putting "words" together. Perhaps these are all aspects of a single kind of new sensitivity to *words* as vehicles of meaning for the way we are able to influence others. Olson has argued that literacy gives access to new insights about one's spoken language, and more specifically that in the process of moving between oral and written forms the individual comes to parcel out the flow of speech into the units required in their written form – in linguistically based scripts, into words (1994; 1997).

It may be that this new insight into the elements of her language permits the speaker a new control over the *use* of the properties of spoken language. Linguists are coming to see that language can only be well understood by studying language-in-use; the classic formal analysis of grammar and syntax through ideal texts is proving to have been very narrow. And the basic characteristic of language-in-use is the continuous negotiation of shared meaning (Clark, 1996; see also Goody, 1998). In public debate and effective oratory this ceases to be the dyadic negotiation of meaning in conversation. Instead the speaker must express her meaning so as to convey it to many people simultaneously; and in this task she can not rely on the continuous minute exchanges on which conversational meaning depends. Perhaps the active practice in literacy of objectifying speech-as-writing is also a potential tool for objectifying speech-as-oratory. Is this what is reflected in the "literateness" of Greek oratory, and the perceived empowerment of Indian women in public discussions?

Subcultures of literacy, communities of literacy

At the beginning of this chapter it was noted that even within the domain of English literacy (L2 literacy) there are many subcultures of literacy. These are grounded in primary and further formal education, and reinforced by their continuing importance to individuals in their occupations and for negotiating bureaucracies. The editors and several other contributors to this volume raise the basic question of how such subcultures of literacy can emerge and flourish at the local community level, particularly for L1 literacies (see especially the chapters by Fagerberg-Diallo, Lopez, Doronila, and Ghose). The material discussed in this chapter suggests that involving local adult L1 literates in teaching the community's children in local primary schools may contribute to their own community of literacy in several ways: by giving the adults who teach a richer understanding of their own literacy; by giving the children L1 literacy skills which they see to be valued by respected adults; and over time by crossing the gap between generations of literates. The bridging of the literacy generation gap may be particularly important, since it would mean that new adult literacy programs need not be continuously provided. Rather, as the number of local L1 literates increases, and also their proportion of the local community, a "critical mass" may be achieved which permits easy everyday use of literacy within the community. If this happens village children will grow up within a community of literacy and as a matter of course will first learn to read through themselves acquiring these skills. By having already learned to read in L1, learning to read in a second language is a problem of learning the language – but not of having to learn how to read. A person only has to learn how to read once.

L1 or L2 literacy or both

Only time can show whether this sort of dynamic in fact occurs, though thoughtful use of other studies might provide important clues. However, the contradictions and weaknesses of the present insulation of L1 and L2 literacies in northern Ghana discussed above argue the merits of exploring ways of enabling the two literacies to support each other.

Educationists speak of the "transfer" of literacy skills from L1 to L2 literacy. This does seem to be occurring for the LLIL children. It would be interesting to know whether in "experiencing" such a transfer of literacy skills the individual may not gain a new level of insight into the nature of literacy itself.[8] This might help to account for the higher level of LLIL project students' performance in other subjects in the later primary grades that teachers report. Typically they are still poor in the English skills required by all their texts.

For the teachers of L1 literacy there seems to be something else going on as well. Many started by learning L1 literacy themselves, either as school children or with one of the Christian missions. They mainly read the Bible, and perhaps a few folktales crudely published for teaching purposes. However, in becoming L1 teachers they have gained an added facility in their L1 literacy in comparison with L1 literates who are not teachers. Of course there must be an element of selectivity here; less competent L1 literates do not seek to teach. But over the course of the LLIL project I have seen some just adequate teachers become excellent ones. It seems that teaching is itself a learning process.

This appears to be more than a transfer of skills from one domain to another. Rather it is a new level of comprehension of literacy; not just "doing" but "understanding doing." Trained teachers, and many experienced pupil teachers, share such an understanding of "doing literacy"; it must be central to the subculture of literacy of teachers everywhere (shared in Ghana with the many bureaucrats and professionals who started out as teachers). In Ghana today there are thus two subcultures of literacy, that of the English literates and the dispersed one of the many L1 literacies. In each of these subcultures of literacy teachers of literacy share (in varying degree) a more conscious awareness of the understanding of "doing literacy." (See particularly chapter 8 by Fagerberg-Diallo on Fulani literacy, in this volume.)

This awareness seems to be compartmentalized; English literacy teachers share theirs, and L1 literacy teachers may share theirs. If this additional level of "metaliteracy" of those teaching English and those teaching the many L1 literacies could come to be shared, then the national level metaliteracy and the local level metaliteracy could support one another. This would create a bridge between local communities of literacy and the national subculture of L2 literacy.

Notes

1   The research on which this paper is based was first supported by the Economic and Social Research Council, UK, Major Grant Number R000 23 1852 (1990–5) and is currently supported by the Spencer Foundation, Chicago, USA. Their assistance is gratefully acknowledged, though they are, of course, not responsible for the substance of the paper. Dr. JoAnne Bennett, whose Ph.D. research on Islamic schools was conducted in Wa, northwest Ghana, has worked with the Wa and Dagaba schools for the LLIL project. Her research and ideas have been central to this enterprise.
2   The accounts included here are typical of many in the field notes.
3   Unfortunately as this is being written in northern Ghana I do not have access to references for this research. David Olson (personal communication) informs me that: (i) J. Cummins (1984, chs. 5 and 6) found that immigrant children in Canada with some competence in literacy in their first language (L1) do better in learning literacy in L2 than those without; (ii) Ezzaki, Spratt, and Wagner (1987) showed that children who spoke a vernacular form of Arabic learned to read standard Arabic more readily than those children who spoke Berber, a non-Semitic language.
4   Three applications for a grant to continue this research on the effects of initial L1 literacy on subsequent L2 literacy were made when the ESRC grant was about to end. Referees for all these applications commented that this was a well-established finding, and did not need further study.
5   Even university teachers at the prestigious University of Ghana, Legon, complain about the poor oral and written English of their undergraduates. More significant, the level is substantially worse than it used to be.
6   I recently went to one of the project schools to arrange with the LLIL teachers for some tests, and suggested it was better not to warn the children as this might affect attendance. "Oh, no," said one teacher, "if we tell them they will all come. They love taking the tests!" (There has never been any kind of reward given for taking LLIL tests.)
7   This struck me while watching a live, two-way video presentation at the 1997 UNESCO International Conference on Adult Education in Hamburg. This was a discussion between teachers and learners of adult L1 literacy in several current projects in India. One rural woman was quite eloquent about how, after participating for some time in the local L1 literacy class, she was now able to take a leading role in

public discussions in her village. Thinking about it I realized that this theme seems to come up often in quite different national settings. Some authorities (e.g. Triebel, 1997) have noted that the achievements of adult literacy classes were more evident in "the ability to debate about circumstances and to engage in collective activities and mutual self-help" (p.11) than in actively sustained literacy. But he concludes from this that "the development of literacy and self help actions are different things" (ibid.). They are different things, but they may not co-occur by accident. Rather this may be another instance where literacy has an effect on empowerment to act within a group through the mediation of cognitive tools built through literacy.

8   I remember as a high-school student learning Latin grammar that I suddenly thought, "Oh, that's what they meant by 'nouns' and 'verbs' in English." Somehow one's own language is so automatic that it is, as it were, grammatically transparent. Having to sort out grammar in another language renders "grammar in general," the meaning of grammar, more accessible. Is this transfer effect a more general phenomenon in second literacy?

References

Afolayan, A. (1976). The six-year-primary-project in Nigeria. In A. Bamgbose (ed.), *Mother Tongue Education*. London/Paris: Hodder and Stoughton/UNESCO.

Bening, R. B. (1990). *A History of Education in Northern Ghana, 190 –1976*. Accra: Ghana Universities Press.

Clark, H. H. (1996). *Using Language*. Cambridge, New York: Cambridge University Press.

Criterion Referenced Tests (1996). *Report on the Administration of Primary 6 Criterion Referenced Tests*. Accra: Ministry of Education.

Cummins, J. (1984). *Bilingualism and Special Education: Issues in assessment and pedagogy*. Clevedon, UK: Multilingual Matters.

Ezzaki, A., Spratt, J. E., and Wagner, D. A. (1987). Childhood literacy acquisition in rural Morocco: Effects of language difference and Quaranic preschooling. In D. A. Wagner (ed.), *The Future of Literacy in a Changing World*. New York: Pergamon.

Goody, E. N. (1996). Authority and learning in northern Ghana. End of Award Report, Social and Economic Research Council, UK.

Goody, E. N. (1997). Education and development: A Case study in social anthropological research looking towards the 21st Century. Keynote address on the theme – Africa on the Threshhold of the Third Millennium: Anthropological Perspectives. Presented at the 1997 Meetings of the Pan African Association of Anthropologists, Legon, Ghana. To be published with Conference Papers in R. Kraft et al. (eds.), *A Tale of Two Ghanas: The view from the classroom*. Accra: Ministry of Education.

Goody, E. N. (1998). Social intelligence and the emergence of roles and rules. The British Academy Radcliffe-Brown Memorial Lecture, 1997.

Kraft, R. et al. (1995). *A Tale of Two Ghanas: The view from the classroom*. Accra: Ministry of Education.

Lave, J. (1988). *Cognition in Practice*. Cambridge: Cambridge University Press.

Lave, J. (1991). Situated learning in communities of practice. In L. B. Resnick, J. M. Levine, and S. D. Teasley (eds.), *Perspectives on Socially Shared Cognition*. Washington, DC: American Psychological Association.

Olson, D. R. (1994). *The World on Paper: The conceptual and cognitive implications of writing and reading*. Cambridge, New York: Cambridge University Press.

Olson, D. R. (1997). What is a word and why does it matter? Address to the International Reading Association, Atlanta, Ga.

Rogoff, B. (1990). *Apprenticeship in Thinking: Cognitive development in social context*. New York: Oxford University Press.

Triebel, A. (1997). *Cognitive and Societal Development and Literacy*. Bonn: Education, Science and Documentation Center, DSE.

Vygotsky, L. S. (1962). *Thought and Language*. Cambridge, Mass.: MIT Press.

Wood, D., Bruner, J. S., and Ross G. (1976). The role of tutoring in problem-solving. *Journal of Child Psychology and Psychiatry*, 17: 89–100.

b) Central and South American Case Studies

Chapter 11

Literacy and Intercultural Bilingual Education in the Andes

Luis Enrique López

> Los indios del Pirú, antes de venir españoles, ningún género de escritura tuvieron, ni por letras ni por caracteres, o cifras o figurillas, como de la China y los de México; más no por eso conservaron menos la memoria de sus antiguallas, ni tuvieron menos su cuenta para todos los negocios de paz, y guerra y gobierno . . . Los libros pueden decir de historias, y leyes y ceremonias, y cuentas de negocios, todo eso suplen los quipos tan puntualmente, que admira. (José de Acosta, *Historia Natural y Moral de las Indias*, 1590)
>
> [Before the Spaniards came, the Indians of Peru had no type of writing, no letters, nor characters, nor ciphers, nor figures, like those used in China or Mexico; but in spite of this, they conserved no less the memory of their antiquities, nor did they have any less account and memory of all their affairs of peace, war and government . . . Books speak of histories, and laws, and ceremonies, and business accounts, all that can the *kipus* do so punctually, that one is astonished.]

Introduction

The relocation of orality and literacy, both historically and in contemporary educational programs, is critical to the understanding of education in indigenous Latin American contexts.[1] Becoming literate cannot be considered independently of the role of indigenous languages and of bilingualism in an otherwise predominantly functionally oral society in which the hegemonic language – Spanish – is perceived both as the language of writing and of other formal types of communication. Neither can literacy be considered independently of the rediscovery and relocation and understanding of the ancestral and traditional textualities that were historically constructed by Andean civilizations through means other than the alphabet and the book. In this general context, the development of intercultural bilingual education projects is of some relevance for a general discussion of literacy in rural settings.

General Background Information

Latin America has largely been described and referred to as a "Spanish-speaking" and culturally Hispanic part of the world. Governments and dominant classes on both sides of the Atlantic have managed to create an imaginary homogeneous communicative scenario as well as an equally idealized, and to a certain extent, imaginary, longstanding history of a common cultural and linguistic heritage, thus concealing the region's great linguistic and cultural diversity and complexity as well as inhibiting the maintenance and development of that diversity. Indeed, it must be acknowledged that there are over 40 million indigenous inhabitants (cf. Gonzalez, 1994) and more than 450 different languages spoken in the region. Nowhere is this linguistic and cultural complexity more true than in the Andean subregion, from Venezuela to Chile, with more than 200 Amerindian linguistic groups, a few of which (particularly in the Amazonian rain forests) have recently come into contact with the hegemonic westernized ways of life and with other, generally larger groups that were colonized and thus subalternized much earlier.[2]

Such diversity goes well beyond the linguistic sphere. In spite of the long period of both external and internal colonialism that imposed Occidentalism and a western type of civilization, the social and political organization of indigenous communities as well as their cultural paradigms, understandings, and forms of knowledge have generally been unacknowledged by mainstream culture and society. Such is the case, for example, of the official educational models, based on idealized notions of culturally and linguistically homogenous Latin American societies that do not in fact exist. These models until recently determined both the organization and functioning of the educational system as well as of the school curricula and educational materials that everybody, including indigenous children and adults, had to study with.

This cultural and linguistic diversity is perhaps most obvious in Bolivia, the country with the greatest proportion of indigenous language speakers (approximately 60 percent of the total population) in the Andean region.[3] Two other Andean countries profoundly marked by their indigenous roots and ethnic components are Peru and Ecuador. Peru has the highest absolute number of Amerindian language speakers (over 6 million) and in Ecuador a little less than one-third of the total population speaks an indigenous language (approximately 3 million).[4] In the other three Andean countries – Venezuela, Colombia, and Chile – the demographic relevance of indigenous populations is regional rather than national, but their presence is felt nationwide due to the attention that indigenous political and social leaders have managed to attract, even in mainstream culture and society.

The Quechuas and Aymaras comprise the largest Amerindian language groups in the region. Quechua speakers number approximately 10 to 12 million living in 5 of the 6 Andean countries as well as in certain regions and cities of the Argentine. Aymara speakers total roughly 2.5 million between Bolivia, Peru, Chile, and the Argentine. Numerous smaller language groups, particularly in the Amazonian region, account for the remaining indigenous language speakers. However, one must also consider that there is an undetermined number of people who now define themselves as indigenous but who no longer speak their ancestral language. In the same line there are surely a good number of individuals who although indigenous deny their ethnic and linguistic affiliation due to the low social prestige attached to indigenous institutions.

For centuries, beginning with the imposition of Spanish colonial rule in the sixteenth century, the Quechua and Aymara languages were seriously affected by their subordination to Spanish and by social denigration (Albo, 1979; Mannheim, 1984) and hence their process of natural and autonomous development was abruptly interrupted. The prohibition of Quechua and Aymara and the imposition of Spanish around 1780 brought about a radical change in the official colonial language policy, which for the previous 200 years permitted, or at least tolerated, the development and elaboration, both oral and written, of these main indigenous languages so that they could be instrumental in evangelization and in the formal education of the native elite. Linguistic atrophy began to set in as a result of this language policy change and the gradually diminishing social roles and functions for these languages.

In the last quarter of the twentieth century, however, the political and legal conditions under which these languages continue to be used have been changing. Such counterhistorical processes started in 1975 when Quechua was declared an official language of Peru, co-equal with Spanish. Although this policy was later attenuated, Peruvian legislation continues to recognize Quechua and Aymara as official for specified regions and purposes. The new constitutional legislation of 1993, for the first time, grants all Amerindian languages the same status (see Hornberger, 1988; Lopez, 1989; Pozzi-Escot, 1996, for further details).

In the other five countries similar legal shifts have been made for the benefit of indigenous languages and cultures. In Colombia, all of these languages are official under the constitutional amendments of 1991. In Bolivia, while there is no legally recognized official language, the 35 Amerindian languages spoken in that country have – in practice and *de facto* – official status in certain social domains: they are widely used in oral mass media and in the national educational system which, since the Educational Reform Act of 1994, has been declared intercultural and bilingual. Similarly, legislation in Chile, Ecuador, and Venezuela recognizes the right of indigenous adults and children to be educated in their ancestral languages.

Legal shifts such as the ones briefly mentioned have generally gone hand in hand with other social and political changes and with the wider importance that democratic rule has received all throughout the region. In this context, particularly in Bolivia, Colombia, and Ecuador, indigenous organizations have become accepted and officially recognized valid governmental interlocutors. They are frequently consulted about issues regarding their own local interests and are to a certain extent becoming national, since they also offer, whether asked or not, their points of view regarding matters of general national interests. In this regard, it is important to mention that in Ecuador, for example, the management, both pedagogical and institutional, of the educational system when applied in indigenous areas has been transferred by law to indigenous professionals elected by their own ethnic and political organizations but officially appointed by the Ecuadorian government.

Within this general scheme, new practices of political, financial, and administrative decentralization are being implemented. These new practices are contributing to a relocation of the community, the neighborhood, and the local; in particular; they are fostering the reinscription of the local community or the municipality as the main locus of decision-making. This reinscription also contributes to the revitalization of local social, linguistic, and cultural practices. In this new scenario, the Amerindian languages face new challenges and possibilities, and indigenous organizations, from Chile and the Argentine in the south, to Mexico in the north, are amongst the most innovative agents of the new Latin American social movement.

As is to be expected, these political and social changes have been closely related to the implementation of educational innovations in the region. As in most of the world, so too in the Andes, formal education has been seen as a vehicle for the implementation of language policy; thus, the above policies have been accompanied by or sometimes embedded in educational policies. In Bolivia, for example, the decentralization of school curriculum administration forms part of the new educational legislation of the country. In Peru it was also an educational decree that determined that local municipalities assume the responsibility of education, and it is in such contexts and within a social setting closer to the indigenous communities' needs and aspirations that bilingual education has recently reemerged.

Indeed, in the six countries considered here, bilingual education initiatives are now embedded in larger and quite ambitious educational innovations or national educational reform efforts. In all of these cases, the juncture of language policy and educational reform promises new possibilities for the oppressed indigenous languages and their speakers, and particularly for the development of writing and for the linguistic elaboration of these languages. This is certainly the case for Bolivia and Peru. In Peru, the officialization of Quechua took place in 1975; three years after a nationwide reform affected the whole educational system. In Bolivia something similar could soon happen, since not only indigenous organization leaders, but also specialists and politicians are considering the need for a national language policy which could complement the principles and bylaws included in the Educational Reform Act of 1994.[5] In so doing the issues of the officialization of all indigenous languages and of their oral and written use and cultivation are being raised. As one can see, the social, cultural, and political changes we have referred to are closely related to the appropriation of alphabetical writing and to the development of a literate environment, which could no longer be monoliterate as in the past, and thus would have to naturally include the promotion of literacy in the indigenous languages spoken in the country.

Historical Demands and Struggle Regarding the Appropriation of Writing

In the Andes, the relationship of indigenous peoples to the written word has historically been a controversial one. The arrival of the Spanish invaders over 500 years ago coincided with and was in itself the arrival of the written word as we now know it. As is to be expected, the mere fact that the alphabet and gunpowder appeared at the same time in the New World made the relationship between the neocolonized and alphabetic writing a conflictive one.

It is worth remembering that all across the Amerindian and pre-Columbian world there were other forms of textuality and of graphic or even written representation that the Europeans were unable to understand. In the Quechua language, for example, a word exists for "symbol," "sketch," "painted or engraved image," or even letter or writing. The existence of the word *qillqa* and its close meaning to what the European invaders understood as writing made it possible for them to resignify it and extend its use to mean precisely what they were looking for. To this day and in contemporary varieties of the Quechua language such a word is used to mean precisely "letter." Nonetheless, the Europeans never took the real meaning of this word seriously, since they were unable to understand or even conceive of other modes of textual and graphic representation that differed from the alphabetic tradition they belonged to.

It is fair to assume that in the Andes colonialism was also marked by a clash between different modes of representation, which were culturally and historically determined. As Mignolo (1995) clearly states "Writing does not presuppose the book, although during the sixteenth-century celebration of the letter, it was narrowed down to mean just that almost exclusively" (p. 76). Mignolo also reminds us that the image of the book is so strong that those who do not belong to the culture of the book "are not always aware of what a book means" (p. 78; cf. Olson, 1994, on the history of reading and writing).[6]

When Atawallpa, the last Inca ruler, met the Spaniards in the courtyard of his royal palace in Cajamarca, in virtue of the special invitation he had earlier made to his messengers, he was given an object he was told contained the Divine Word. According to the European faith and understanding of writing, such an artifact was a holy book and encoded the teachings of their Lord; that is, the words he had used in teaching his disciples. For the Inca ruler, however, such an artifact to be divine had to be made of gold and precious stones and not simply of leather and of simple and thin layers of a material totally unknown to him. Similarly, if it were to hold words, divine or not, such a device had to contain sounds one could hear or listen to; and as such it should have reproduced the oral messages his visitors had referred to. Obviously, that was not the case. After examining the Bible and after turning it upside down and not being able to make any sense of it, nor hear anything from it, Atawallpa simply dropped it as a useless object. He probably judged this first incident absolutely inexplicable and the foreigners dumb. The invaders, on the other side, could not understand what was going on either, since they could probably not conceive that a king or ruler could not read. Let us not forget that at the time there was only a thin line between royalty and divinity.

This first intercultural conflict and clash of understandings became the perfect excuse for the Spaniards' subsequent brutal and bloody attacks on the unarmed Indians. Thousands were killed in the name of a God and right after the Bible had been dropped.

Since then, numerous legends and historical anecdotes allow us to infer how, from very early and from the very first intercultural contacts, indigenous people came to associate writing with power and alphabetic writing with the unknown, even assigning to it magical powers.

There are indeed numerous historical accounts and anecdotes related to the indigenous people's astonishment at the uses of letters as predictors of future incidents (cf. Glave, 1990; Mignolo, 1995). One of these examples relates to an anecdote (or a legend?) of early colonial times according to which a master sent his two servants with sacks full of melons from his farm to a relative's house in the city of Lima. Together with the sack went a letter in which the master informed his relative of what he was sending. In the middle of the journey, tired and thirsty, the illiterate Indian servants decided to open the sacks and eat a melon from each, thinking nobody would learn what had happened. Upon their arrival, however, they were punished, because after reading the letter the master's relative knew what they had done. While being punished the two Indians commented to each other on the magic of writing: their master had put into writing what he had predicted they were going to do, or else it was the written piece of paper they carried with them that spoke up and told the master's relative what it had seen them do! This conflictive encounter has been widely described in the literature, beginning with the early friars and priests who registered the first accounts of Hispanic colonization. Glave (1990) is an excellent source for further and detailed information on this incident. (His article is titled "Grito de pueblos silenciados. Intermediarios lingüísticos y culturales entre dos mundos: historia y mentalidades" – Silenced peoples' cries: Linguistic and cultural intermediaries between two worlds: history and mentalities.)

As we can see, the clash of mentalities between the Amerindians and the Spaniards during very early colonial period was manyfold and was related not only to differences in languages and modes of communication but also to profoundly different worldviews, beliefs, and ways of knowing, and perhaps even to different ways of reading and understanding textual and graphic representation. In fact, the first American nations were far from illiterate if we abandon the evolutionist understanding of the conquerors. In the clash between

European and Native American cultures, divergent forms of textuality and representation confronted each other: the alphabet, on the one hand, and the complex and abstract iconography, geometrical designs, and drawings found extensively in textiles and ceramics, on the other. Different encoding devices also came into confrontation: the inexplicable book versus other encoding artifacts such as the *kipu*.

The *kipu*, for example, formed part of an apparently complex record-keeping system and it was a device used extensively by the officers of the Inca Empire. It consisted of a bunch of knotted strings of different colors in which a diversity of knots and colors meant different things. Early Spanish accounts of the Inca way of life are filled with references to the *kipu* and the abilities and wisdom of *kipu kamayuqkuna*, the Inca government officers responsible for record-keeping who used the *kipu* to encode and decode detailed information. The kipu was a device not only to be looked at and decoded but also to be felt, touched, manipulated, and interpreted. This fact must be highlighted: if the notions of information encoding and processing and of text were attached to textiles one could phys- ically manipulate, the very idea of decoding and reading must have been totally different and closer perhaps to a more symbolic and conceptual process than to a linguistic or verbal one.

According to the early Spanish chronicles, the *kipu* could be used to encode not only numerical accounts and registers but also long and detailed historical descriptions and day to day accounts. Apparently, there were different types of *kipu* and different uses attached to them as there are now different written registers and different styles of writing and texts. In the quotation dating back to 1590 by Jose de Acosta with which I began this chapter, the Spanish writer marvels at how the *kipu* can replace a book: "Books speak of histories, and laws, and ceremonies, and business accounts, all that can the *kipus* do so punctually, that one is astonished."

Regarding historical and everyday life descriptions, ceramics also became a means to register and thus deliberately record and transmit stories, histories, and knowledge. Complex and detailed Mochica iconography has very recently been decoded and interpreted (cf. Hocquenghem, 1990) and transformed (or perhaps reduced) into what we now regard as writing, so that mainstream Peruvian schoolchildren can have access to this "new" kind of literature. Through alpha- betic writing and Spanish this type of Mochica knowledge is being reinscribed in contemporary Peruvian society, and a few storybooks based on the reinterpret- ation of these late fourteenth- and early fifteenth-century drawings can now be found (cf. Golte, 1994).[7] Whereas in the past such ceramic representations were judged merely artistic, in recent years they have come to be valued for the information they contain, and are now considered one of the most important sources for understanding the structure and functioning of this pre-Columbian society.

All through the Andes, and particularly in the central and southern Andean highlands, textiles appear to be a privileged medium for "written" or rather textual representation. To this very day, for example, in Coroma, Bolivia, textiles which in cases date back to pre-Columbian times are treasured in the communities that have inherited them and are valued for the information they are said to contain and transmit (often referred to *as messages left by the early souls*). These *q'ipinaka* or bundles of textiles are transmitted from one generation to another, and with them, the culture and social history of this particular region (Cristina Bubba, personal communication).

Coroma is neither an exceptional nor an isolated case but rather part of a historic cultural complex in which indigenous groups' organization of space, colors, and geometric and iconic themes and motifs is generally tied into precise meanings. Andean textiles can be "read" as texts that speak of given thoughts of particular understandings of the world (Fundacion ASUR, n.d., p. 3). What is interesting is that this longstanding tradition persists and is being reinforced in certain regions such as in the Jalq'a and Tarabuco regions of Bolivia.

Approximately 1,000 Quechua-speaking female weavers are involved in a project where new means of aesthetic expression and meaning are being sought from a perspective profoundly based on tactile and visual languages used for thousands of years throughout the Andean region (ibid.). These indigenous weavers do not simply reproduce motifs created by their elders but are also immersed in a process which reflects that they are alert to the changes experienced by their societies and communities: nowadays they are "very open to expressing the clashes of indigenous peoples with the modern world" (ibid., p. 4). Such new ideas are expressed in rather abstract terms.

Various researchers are now looking into Andean textiles as a means to understand different styles of meaning-making, signification, and cognition. Margaret Gutmann, a German anthropologist and linguist, has recently discovered a close relationship between the syntactic structures of textile representations and the rhetorical structure of Quechua oral narratives in rural communities of the area of Cuzco. She has even been able to establish close connections between given linguistic markers and the organization of paragraphs with certain stitches and "textual" marks in Quechua textiles (M. Gutmann, personal communication).

The confrontation between ways of knowing and understanding we have referred to might also be related to the contrast between different modes of decoding previously encoded messages, since the new and, so to speak, modern way of uncovering the messages (i.e. reading alphabetic texts) was more obvious and evident – a fact which must have caused confusion in the natives. The new mode simply aimed at recovering previously orally produced messages. It left very little to the decoder's imagination and creativity. The indigenous way of knowing was different, combining aspects of orality and of graphic representation, or shall we say writing. From that perspective, it also relied on the decoder's previous knowledge about the facts he tried to interpret. Similarly, the imported mode of decoding was mainly individual while the traditional one heavily relied on socially transmitted practices, beliefs, and knowledge.

As Mignolo (1995) explains, "In the West, particularly during and after the Renaissance, the purpose of writing was perceived as making the reader hear the spoken word behind it [consequently all reading was reading aloud]. According to this conception, the written word itself contained no information but merely transmitted information that was stored elsewhere. Thus alphabetic writing, together with a conception of what it was, introduced a substantial modification in sending messages across space and time, since it provided a graphic form for replacing the spoken" (p. 172). According to Olson (personal communication), one of the peculiarities of western writing in general, not just as of the Renaissance, was its connection to the linguistic forms of speech, and this is why the Spanish failed to recognize it as "writing." While this was the case in the western world, in America, decoding textile and/or ceramic representations, on the other hand, implies the involvement of capacities that go far beyond merely reproducing the oral; the decoder engages in a process of interpretation or even reinterpretation, rather than simply attaching sounds to written symbols. In a process such as this one, the decoder brings in his previous relevant social and cultural experiences both as encoder and as textile user and thus in the "reading" process puts in part of himself and of his society as a whole.

While that might have been the interpretation of reading from the indigenous point of view, from the western one, and particularly regarding religious texts, written messages were only to be read and believed but not constructed in the reading process. Such messages, however, had so much built-in power that in their name people could be severely punished and even killed. That was precisely what happened to Atawallpa, who was accused of blasphemy simply because he was unable to read alphabetic writing or even make sense of the Bible.

I have tried to explain and interpret what could possibly have happened at the first violent and conflictive intercultural encounters in the Andes, since they could indeed help us understand the relationship indigenous peoples have historically constructed with the written word and particularly with alphabetic writing. From very early on, Andean populations discovered how important it was for them to learn to read and write as the Europeans did. On the one hand, they wanted access to what they considered was one of the tools that supported the power the foreign invaders enjoyed. On the other, they may have become aware very early on that their ancestral means of constructing textuality and of representing and transmitting meaning was considered by the foreigners simply as primitive picture-writing. In fact, it must be considered that even until very recently, non-alphabetic scripts were thought to be only primitive pictographs (Boone & Mignolo, 1994). This European preconception as to what writing was is surely responsible for the historical fascination with alphabetic writing one finds nowadays amongst indigenous peoples. Little attention is now paid to other means of representation and textuality; as occurred in early colonial times, if education is carried out in vernaculars, these are reduced to alphabetic writing. (Such a prerequisite, more often than not, induces endless discussions centered on one sole issue: the alphabet. We must also recognize, however, that such discussions are generally induced by linguists often solely concerned with one of their fundamental objects of study: speech.)

Nonetheless, with the exception of the Inca elite and families, the benefits of the new system of written representation were not made accessible to the common people, since the educational system imposed was exclusive for only a few. This situation was paradoxically perpetrated with the arrival of republican rule, since Spanish-speaking and Creole-literate landowners did not consider it suitable or convenient to their interests that indigenous peasants learn to read and write. Such opposition was expressed through sayings coined at that time such as "*Indio leido, indio perdido*" (An Indian who can read is an Indian which[8] can no longer be used) or "*Indio leido, indio torcido*" (An Indian who can read is a twisted Indian).

It was only at the beginning of the twentieth century that in certain areas of the Andes schools reached some rural settings and that Indian adults and children were taught to read and write. However, the general context was one of permanent struggle whereby vernacular-speaking peasants claimed educational access by their own volition, built schools, and demanded that the State appoint trained teachers to teach them both to read and write and to speak Spanish.

In the Peruvian highlands, around the turn of the century, a whole Aymara- and Quechua-speaking area of Puno was on the verge of a civil confrontation due to the reluctance of the hegemonic sectors of society to accept the indigenous communities' demands for formal education, and particularly for their right to reading and writing (cf. Lopez, 1988). Vernacular- speaking peasants organized evening schools under the guidance of an Aymara peasant educator who had previously learned to read and write. Manuel Z. Camacho had learned the basics of reading and writing from Adventist pastors in the Argentine, and upon returning to his original area of residence took it upon himself to teach his peers. Such insolence awakened the fury of landowners and city landlords accustomed to exploiting Aymara peasants. Appealing to religious differences and potential dangers, they convinced the Catholic bishop of the area to lead a crusade against the unfaithful. The peasant schools were set on fire and the Indian teacher and many of his assistants and followers put into jail (cf. Lopez, 1988).

This terrible incident, however, did not kill or abate the peasants' desire for learning to read and write. Nor did it prevent the Adventists from responding to the call Indians had made. A few years later, there were dozens of rural schools in the area, but Aymara children and adults were still struggling to learn to read and write. This time the reason was different: no use was being made of the language the pupils best understood and spoke – their mother tongue – and thus they were being expected to carry out two tasks simultaneously: learning a foreign language and learning to read and write. This failure of the educational system was interpreted by everybody, including the indigenous peoples themselves, as a sign of incapability on the part of the learners: Indians were incapable of learning as whites or mestizos did since they were unsuited for such difficult intellectual tasks as reading and writing. There was no questioning at the time about the adequacy of the methodology employed nor of the language used as a medium of literacy, since the Quechua and Aymara languages were not considered apt or valid for educational purposes. Furthermore, the ruling ideology of the time was linguistic and cultural homogenization, to promote assimilation into the dominant national culture as well as into the Spanish language.

It was only around the early 1930s that another vernacular-speaking teacher, although this time a mestizo one, set up a bilingual scheme to partially remedy this situation. That was the beginning of bilingual education in the area referred to, and to a certain extent in the Andean subregion in general. A trilingual (Quechua, Aymara, and Spanish) educator, Maria Asuncion Galindo, was among the first to attempt bilingual modes of teaching in the thirties.[9] She designed primers that initially relied on the pupils' mother tongues and which later gradually introduced reading in Spanish on the basis of the knowledge constructed by the learners through their own, although subalternized and stigmatized, languages. As is to be expected, in so doing Galindo relied upon the Spanish written tradition and alphabetic writing and used Quechua and Aymara alphabets designed by linguists and users of these languages.

Nowadays, social demands regarding the appropriation of alphabetic writing persist and are perhaps stronger than ever. Writing and literacy are closely associated with the hegemonic language, in a typical diglossic relationship whereby Spanish is perceived as the language of writing and formal social functions. Thus, learning to read and write is generally understood to mean acquiring Spanish. The representation indigenous people have constructed of learning a foreign or second language and becoming literate is not of two different and separate processes; these latter are rather conceived as subprocesses of a general process related to the acquisition of the dominant language: Spanish. This is perhaps the main reason why it is often difficult to convince Indian parents to rely on the pupils' mother tongue to facilitate the appropriation of reading and writing. The reinscription of the indigenous languages as fully fledged idioms promoted by bilingual education programs is thus confronted with this rather adverse metalinguistic perception grounded in a long history of ethnic and linguistic discrimination and on the results of the almost generalized implementation of rural schooling which to this date relies mainly on the dominant language.

School expansion in indigenous territories has brought about other changes as well, including the advancement of hegemonic cultural industries such as television, which have been detrimental for the self-perception of the indigenous communities, operating together with the school as tools for cultural uniformization and linguistic homogenization. A recent study on the Mexican situation, which indeed could also be generalized to describe the Andean school context and indeed all of Latin American, states that

> the rural Mexican school [is]...seen, first of all, as an agency for acculturation whose end product is to be the configuration of a one and only Mexico, whereby all those born within its borders share only one culture, that of the mestizo population. Such culture is seen as a Creole or hybrid one, because although it is of

European origin, once on indigenous cultural territory, it incorporates numerous
elements from the indigenous tradition. From the mixture of both, a new physiog-
nomy was shaped…[The prestige the rural school acquired] was based on its
supposed capacity as the most expeditious means to "progress," in so far as it
taught Indians to speak, read and write in Spanish; it gave access to a world view of
western tradition and to its modern and efficient civilization; it gave the possibility
of abandoning the language, clothing and other signs of indigenous identity which
the mestizo population judged as primitive, obsolete and even shameful. (Acevedo
et al., 1996, p. 48, my translation)

It is important to bear in mind, however, that in a context of political, social,
and cultural subordination and of linguistic diglossia, hybridity or hybrid cultures are seen only as variations of an otherwise strong underlying mainstream of
hegemonic cultural traits. There is by no means any balance as to how much is
taken from each culture. In all fairness there is very little mix since the mixture
undergoes a permanent process of purification and standardization through the
generations as a result of the strong influence of mainstream social institutions,
among which the school plays a vital role.

Nonetheless, bilingual education programs are carried out in indigenous areas
of the Andes to promote the development of alphabetization and literacy[10]
through the indigenous languages. Such programs are based on the knowledge
and conviction that indigenous languages constitute useful pedagogical
resources for constructing a literate environment, together with the other language the pupils need to know: Spanish. The implementation of bilingual education in the region has been accompanied by empirical research whose results
have been used to convince educational authorities and governments of the
advantages of bilingual intercultural education. All through the region experiments that employ indigenous languages as main languages of the reading and
writing learning process and as media of education in general have been developed with both adults and children. (For a summary of findings and a comparison with those obtained in other regions of the world and particularly in North
America, refer to Lopez, 1997a. See also Dutcher, 1997.) In one of the countries
studied, Ecuador, such programs are of national scope and serve all vernacular-
speaking pupils, and in another one, Bolivia, an ambitious educational reform
program for vernacular literacies is gradually being implemented.

As has been stated here, in the Andes in general, the historical relationship of
the indigenous languages and their speakers to the schools has by and large been
one of oppression and exclusion (cf. Albo, 1979). Formal education – and thus
writing – has been directly linked to social and cultural stratification, with
education and the written word serving as sources of both "structural stability
and individual change" (van den Berghe 1978, p. 293, cited in Hornberger and
Lopez, 1997). "Although in fact only a small percentage of the population
attains social advancement through formal education, education, the written
language and the Spanish language with which they are identified, are nevertheless perceived as the necessary routes to social mobility" (Hornberger &

Lopez, 1997, p. 6). (See also Luykx, 1998, for the role teacher training institutions fulfill in Bolivia regarding indigenous student-teachers' self-steem.)

In this context, to introduce the use of the indigenous languages into formal
education and furthermore to resort to writing and written materials in these
languages for literacy development produce paradoxes. Among the paradoxes
engendered by indigenous language education initiatives "are the tensions and
contradictions inherent in transforming what were conceived as tools for standardization and control – formal education and writing – into vehicles for
diversification and emancipation" (Hornberger & Lopez, 1997, p. 20). As we
have seen, the ideology of the one culture, one language – and hence one literacy
– nation-state took education as its main agency for the implementation of such
uniformization policies. Once the indigenous languages are introduced into
education and the official curriculum is diversified and decentralized, so as to
include diverse ethnic and cultural educational content, all sorts of tensions and
conflicts emerge that affect not only the organization of schooling but also the
way in which the various educational actors involved – from the center to
the periphery – view the role of the school and also of the local communities
in the development of education, as well as the way in which such a role
responds or not to the aims and expectations of the societies involved.

That is why, elsewhere, we concluded that the main paradox arising as a result
of the inclusion of indigenous languages in the official educational system is
ideological, and that "the choices made between conflicting alternatives are
ideological rather than technical ones, reflecting differing conceptions of possible futures, for the country and its peoples" (Hornberger & Lopez, 1997, p.
25). As is to be expected and as a result of both internal and external colonialism, such an ideological paradox very often marks the implementation of cultural and educational policies and projects as well as the development of literacy,
beyond the level of declarations and legal instruments. Furthermore, and as one
can well understand, when literacy was implemented only through Spanish, the
literacy that served as an emancipatory tool for a few became an instrument of
oppression for the many.

The Written Language and Perceived Educational Needs *vis-à-vis* the Functional Use of Writing

After five centuries of the presence of alphabetic writing in the area, alphabetic
writing has become both a desirable and a consumable good, due to the power
attached to or embedded in it. Everybody, whether young or old, expresses the
desire to learn to read and write, and even small children know that it will be
their duty to learn to do so when they attend school. However, the situation
regarding the functional use of writing in rural and indigenous communities has
little to do with the expectations and representations just mentioned.

The fact is that in a good number of rural communities in general,
and particularly in those inhabited by indigenous people, the role of writing is

generally very limited outside school activities and the school building itself. For the most part, the social territory of writing is that of the school, while the inner space of the indigenous community remains largely unwritten, unalphabetical, and a privileged locus of oral reproduction and transmission. Exceptions to this rule are those activities related to social demands and functions originating outside the community and which arise out of the present needs of the indigenous communities to maintain contact with the outer hegemonic world (cf. Hornberger, 1988 on the *ayllu*, non-*ayllu*, and *comunidad* domains of language use, for example). In those instances, however, indigenous communities have developed a specific strategy whereby those who can read and write best – and hence have a relatively fluent oral command of Spanish – are chosen by their peers to represent the community before those foreign organizations and institutions they need to maintain contact with, since these individuals are considered best suited for the kind of intermediation needed.

Nonetheless, certain uses of alphabetical writing have been truly incorporated into communal social life, if only to fulfill ritual purposes. One of these cases is that pertaining to the production of detailed accounts of community meetings and accords. The *actas*, as they are called in Spanish, however, were also introduced by the outside world as a means of controlling what went on inside the community. The *acta*-keeper is generally chosen amongst those community members with more schooling, better command of oral Spanish, and more alphabetical writing experience. Until very recently, it was most often the schoolteacher himself who was asked to play this role. With the expansion of schooling this is no longer the case, except for very remote and isolated communities.[11]

Newspapers and other written media, with the sole exception of school textbooks and perhaps the Bible, very seldom reach rural communities, but when they do they are generally kept as small treasures, read over and over again, and even used to decorate households since they are also a sign of prestige.

However, the traditional linguistic landscape in indigenous communities is being rapidly transformed into a new communicative scenario. On the one hand, more and more people are bilingual, speaking some variety of Spanish as well as the indigenous language. Furthermore, increasing numbers of indigenous people learn to read and write at school, although with very little opportunity to exercise these competencies in everyday life, unless they leave the community, temporarily or permanently, and move into the cities. The fact is that ill-designed school curricula prepare Indian children to live and work in the cities and thus lead them into migration and into valuing the hegemonic urban lifestyle as standard and better than their own.

There is in fact a close relationship between migration and school coverage. In Peru, for example, the number of schools in rural areas has increased significantly over the past five decades and now more than 90 percent of rural school-age children can and do at least begin their formal schooling. Similarly, in this very period the ruralization index (percentage of population living in rural areas) dropped from almost 70 percent in the 1940s to approximately 25 percent in the 1990s. Once again, except for very isolated communities and particularly in the Amazonian lowlands and jungles, the situation is similar in all of the countries considered in this chapter. The only exception to this rule is Bolivia, where there is still a high percentage of rural population (nearly 55 percent).

In Bolivia, where rural settings retain almost half of the population, government policies are being implemented to improve the economic and social conditions in which rural populations – largely indigenous – live. One of these policies is called "popular participation," whereby government income is redistributed on a per capita basis, so municipalities and local communities can make local investments in order to improve conditions and facilities for both health and education. In this new scenario, other uses of writing are arising out of the need to comply with regulations and bylaws regarding the use of public funds. As a result of decentralization, Bolivian schools are confronted with new learning needs regarding reading and writing, and the society itself is facing new challenges concerning literacy. If one also considers that these popular participation measures are being developed concurrently with a new educational reform which promotes both biliteracy and, in general, bilingualism and interculturalism, it will be very illustrative to find out whether or not the combination of new state structures and redistribution of public funds with bilingual and intercultural education successfully contributes to creating a literate environment, and, what is more, the biliterate subjects that such societies seem to require.

The Relocation of Indigenous Languages to Meet New Needs: Bilingual Intercultural Education

As a result of the processes briefly described in this chapter, most indigenous languages are being transformed into written ones, most generally due to the official recognition they enjoy and/or to their gradually increasing acceptance and use as languages of education. A great number of these languages now have officially recognized alphabets and writing systems, in some cases after much orthographic turmoil and endless war-like discussions (cf. Hornberger, 1995, on the Quechua case). Such debates, although to a large extent sterile for the specific purposes involved, have contributed to placing literacy and the indigenous written word as key issues of the social debate, and, by so doing, have indeed contributed to revaluing the oppressed languages and through them to reinscribing indigenous knowledge and cultures in the general national debate, as well as to opening up possibilities for the development of new indigenous textualities.

As I suggested, numerous indigenous languages are now being used in bilingual education programs, in most cases as primary languages of literacy. In many cases, the speakers of these languages are being confronted, perhaps for the first time ever, with written materials in their languages which go beyond Bible translations and other religious materials. Perhaps even more importantly, written materials in the vernaculars now also depict aspects of the ancestral culture and of indigenous contemporary everyday life, as well as other cultural traits embedded in the languages themselves. The written word is being used now to refer to knowledge and values that, up until a few years ago, were exclusively transmitted and recreated through the oral word.

The past two decades have been fruitful in terms of language revitalization and development in nearly all of the Andean countries. These processes which emerged out of specific communicative needs related to the implementation of intercultural bilingual education projects have contributed to the development of writing in general. There is now an increasing number of written materials and of vernacular-speaking writers – indigenous or not – involved in this social and political process of-reinventing a literate tradition in some of the vernaculars widely used in early colonial times.[12] In Puno, Peru, for example, more than 40 different titles in Quechua and Aymara were produced in the 1980s to implement a regional experimental six-year bilingual education primary school program. Similarly and more recently, in Bolivia, in the context of a national educational reform, hundreds of thousands of books and school textbooks are being produced in Quechua, Aymara, and Guarani to supply all primary schools in the rural areas of the country. In this context, for example, in 1997 over a million books, written either only in vernacular languages or in a bilingual format, were distributed in Bolivian rural areas within a new school library scheme. Other examples are those of Peru and Chile. In Peru 270,000 school textbooks in 8 different languages were produced and distributed, and in Chile, for the first time ever, a beautifully illustrated trilingual – Mapuche, Spanish, and English – children's dictionary was produced and distributed both in Mapuche-speaking urban and rural areas of the country as well as in other schools where Mapuche was not used, so as to contribute to the promotion of this indigenous language and to make the society at large aware of the existence of Mapuche people in an area considered one of the "most modern" and most homogeneous of South America.

In this new communicative scenario specialized meetings and congresses have been held to discuss the elaboration of the vernaculars so as to make them apt for formal oral and written communication (cf. for example Lopez & Jung, 1998). In the Andean subregion, such movements have marked the overall situation of languages of wider scope such as Quechua and Aymara as well as real minority languages like Mapuche and Guarani.

The situation of the Bolivian Guarani is perhaps illustrative of these processes and of other uses of ancestral language as a result of the implementation of formal bilingual education. Arising out of the decision of the Guaranis themselves, the indigenous language is now also serving as a means of constructing an alternative political discourse and as a means of building ethnic and cultural cohesion (cf. D'Emilio, 1997; Lopez, 1997b, and more generally, Doronila's chapter in this volume). Here too, one can find new opportunities for the development of a partially written culture. Based on needs and possibilities they foresaw, the Guarani political organization decided to organize an educational campaign by means of which they would use the Amerindian language to alphabetize those who had not had the opportunity to learn to read and write.

Perhaps more important was the Guarani decision to use the ancestral language to generate a process of ethnic revival through the written medium. They took advantage of the wide social prestige writing enjoyed, both within their own communities and outside them, to – as they themselves defined it – guaranize those who spoke their own language but who could only read and write in Spanish (D'Emilio, 1997; Lopez, 1997b).

The Guaranization process was widely accepted, and for over a year more than 10,000 Guarani youngsters and adults were involved in a process of transferring knowledge and competencies, previously acquired through "an alien" language, to reading and writing in the ancestral language: "their own." The facilitators of this process were approximately 500 Guarani youngsters previously trained as popular educators, who themselves could hardly read and write in the vernacular at the beginning of this project. As the process started, a large social movement began to emerge arising from the relocation of a language which for centuries suffered from low prestige, and that according to certain specialists was on the verge of linguistic extinction. At the same time, ancestral knowledge was being reinscribed in a contemporary and clearly defined political strategy (D'Emilio, 1997; Lopez, 1997b; cf. also Fagerberg-Diallo in this volume, on the conditions that determine success in adult literacy programs).

It is important to highlight that such a strategy was not a Messianic one; it rather looked towards the future. But to do so, it postulated the need to look first to the past to recover ancestral knowledge, means, and cultural artifacts, so as to reinscribe them in a new perspective, whereby Guarani knowledge and language are seen as complementary to Spanish and to the hegemonic mainstream culture. Both were regarded as important and necessary for modern everyday life, but different functions and purposes were assigned to each.

Interestingly, this Guaranization campaign was a byproduct of a prior inter-cultural bilingual education project, which had been implemented in about 30 primary schools and in the rural communities themselves. The need to learn to read and write in the ancestral language emerged when the pupils' parents were confronted with a different type of education – bilingual intercultural schooling – whose outcomes were also different: children who could read and write not only in Spanish but also in Guarani; and who furthermore enjoyed going to school and were happy learning and living within their own culture and through written materials that turned out to be very familiar, meaningful, and significant, since they depicted social activities and cultural traits that not only the pupils but all of the participants as well as the parents were familiar with. Perhaps the happiest were the grandparents who had, to an extent, regained the grand-children they had been quietly resigned to losing. The formal educational use of the children's mother tongue helped reinscribe social and family ties and relationships either lost or under threat because youngsters and children had "forgotten" who they were and their ancestral language when they went to school. Once the Guarani political leaders became aware of what was happen-ing, and of the potential their ancestral language had in the redefinition of power within their territory, they began to imagine what their society would be like if everybody knew and used two languages and, more importantly, if everybody could resort to the vernacular to construct a new tradition or, if you like, a Guarani-specific modern project.

Nowadays, the Guarani language is not only used in radio transmissions and programs but also in posters, signs, leaflets, as well as in letters, particularly when messages are exchanged that other people – the *karai* (Christians or the Spanish-speaking) – should not understand. A battery of Guarani school text-books has been produced for both children and adults; groups of Guarani youngsters have put together a dictionary of their language, and student teachers are preparing a grammar of Bolivian Guarani, which they intend to write and publish in the ancestral language itself. The language obviously continues to be used as a primary means of oral communication in domains related to everyday community and family life. Even if they now have access to writing, the Guaranis do not want to do away with the orality that characterizes their culture. They have indeed firmly stated that their new model of literacy is not divorced from the ancestral or traditional orality but rather complements it.

The project has had a big impact not only on the self-perception of the Guaranis, but also on the new image they have projected of themselves before the national global context, in spite of the fact that there are only now about 60,000 to 70,000 Bolivian Guaranis in a country of 8 million inhabitants. Today the Guarani experience is a landmark for other indigenous peoples both in Bolivia and beyond its borders. In Paraguay, for example, one the most cited cases in the literature of bilingualism in the world, the Bolivian Guarani experience was seriously taken into account and analyzed in 1994, when bilingual education had to be reinvented when democratic rule was reinstated and an educational reform program was being designed. Various Guarani- and Spanish-speaking Paraguayan specialists traveled to the Bolivian Guarani area to obtain information on how the Bolivian Guaranis had introduced the ancestral language into the educational system. What is interesting in this particular case is that, on the one hand, Guarani is both a national and a widely spoken language in Paraguay, which although prestigious had until very recently in modern times almost exclusively been used orally; while on the other hand, it might also be worth remembering that Guarani is not only the language of indigenous groups but the language that Paraguayans of all social classes and ancestries say to be proud of.

Concluding Remarks

The historical and contemporary perspectives presented in this paper allow us to conclude that alphabetical literacy should be built on the previous textual representational experiences and traditions of the populations involved, whether these are alphabetical or not. This should be the case with both children and adults who learn to read and write with the alphabetical system, although it is perhaps more important for the latter. In any case, thought should be given to the need to make the indigenous populations aware of the mechanisms and devices that their cultures and civilizations have created to represent aspects of everyday life, and more importantly perhaps to convey meaning and thought. Approaching alphabetical literacy from the indigenous modes of textual and graphic representation might also prove extremely useful for the appropriation and discovery of new ways of producing texts and literatures and hence for the development of a literate environment, since such an environment would be grounded in the local traditions and would include different kinds of textualities.

On the same line, serious consideration should be given to the benefits, cost, effort, and social acceptance of orthographic and writing reforms, aiming at linguistic or scientific accuracy, where the vernacular has already been reduced to alphabetical writing and a given alphabet is in the process of being implemented. Given that the alphabet is a convention – to a large extent arbitrary – to represent oral forms, more emphasis should be placed on the development of a fully fledged written code in the vernacular and on the individuals' appropriation of the necessary tools and mechanisms for textual production, of which the alphabet is only one. The main objectives in this endeavor should be to contribute to the development of a literate society and to the empowerment of the learners; thus, in the elaboration of representational or orthographic systems, linguistic and phonemic representational accuracy should be subordinated to these main social aims.

Similarly, adult literacy should be developed in connection to school life and activities so that what adults learn and do is related to what their children do. Formal education and adult literacy strategies have many aspects in common, particularly in indigenous contexts where intercultural bilingual education programs generate specific adult learning needs related to reading and writing in the vernacular. Combining adult and child literacies in traditional oral contexts, such as the indigenous ones, one also contributes to the development of a new literate environment.

Finally, nowadays in Latin America, the development of a literate environment in an indigenous setting presupposes literacy not only in one but also in two languages, since indigenous peoples are either bilinguals or in a rapid process of acquiring Spanish. That is the case also of real minority indigenous groups in the Amazon jungles and lowlands. In this context, biliteracy can be considered a strong component of a process of empowering minorities. On the one hand, indigenous literacies can and indeed do contribute, as we have seen in the Guarani case, to the reconstruction and reaffirmation of local identities as well as to the relocation of local knowledge and to developing a positive image of one's self. On the other, literacy in the dominant or hegemonic language serves a double purpose: it opens paths and possibilities for connecting with the new and alien as well as contributing to building bridges with other indigenous populations with languages different from one's own. Furthermore, one must also consider that being literate in the dominant language, indigenous peoples are also better armed to defend their right to being different and even to continue speaking their own and ancestral languages.[13]

That is why one must not view mother tongue or primary language literacy only as a bridge to dominant or hegemonic language literacy, but rather as a simultaneous or concurrent process whereby these learners, generally oral bilinguals, develop their interpretative and productive capacities, as well as their creativity in general, in their two languages and not only in one of them. In other words, one should abandon those models of literacy typical of or grounded in the monolingual tradition. This is necessary, not only because the monolingual model no longer matches local communicative oral behavior (both individual and societal), but also because historically, indigenous societies have effectively and efficiently been able to cope with more than one language for everyday communication. Furthermore, one must remember that whatever they do in one language contributes to enriching what they can do in the other, and writing is no exception to this general principle.

Last but not least, literacy development has to be closely connected to the rediscovery, relocation, and reinscription of indigenous knowledge. That is, literacy should be a means whereby indigenous people recover, systematize, and – if they wish – transform local knowledge and, by so doing, also develop cognitive strategies and competencies that will ease the understanding of other logics and other modes of "writing." Along these same lines, one should not look at orality as opposed to literacy, identifying the former with the indigenous language and culture, and the latter with the national language. Rather, as with biliteracy, traditional orality and the "new literacy" outlined in this paper could complement each other, in the same way that traditional knowledge and outside knowledge do, in the struggle for survival that indigenous peoples have been engaged in for at least five hundred years.

Notes

1 Revised version of a presentation made at the International Conference on Literacy, Education, and Social Development. This version has benefited from useful and judicious comments and suggestions made by Nancy Hornberger, Aurolyn Luykx, and Lucia D'Emilio. This article was revised for publication at the end of 1998. After that, I took note of a manuscript published in 2000 in La Paz with an excellent chapter on this same matter by Denise Arnold and Juan de Dios Yapita: Contacto y la lucha de significados: la introducción de la escritura, fase 1. In El rincón de las cabezas, *Luchas textuales, educación y tierras en los Andes*. La Paz: Universidad Mayor de San Andres & ILCA, 67–90.

2 It is not easy to offer exact figures regarding indigenous demographies and languages, and I am fully aware I am assuming a rather conservative figure in this chapter. On the one hand, the most accessible source is the information provided by the national populations censuses which, at best, offer information on languages spoken by inhabitants over age 5 or 6. On the other hand, as far as the language classification issue is concerned, discrepancies in the area of linguistics and language description

can be observed. For example, just for the case of Mexico, while Mexican government agencies speak of 56 different languages, certain specialists would prefer to speak of over 200. In other cases, the situation may be clearer, such as in Colombia, where there seems to be a consensus that there are over 80 different ethnic groups but no more than 64 to 68 different languages (Maria Trillos, personal comunication). And in another case, such as the Guatemalan one, most people, including specialists, would speak of 21 different Mayan languages within the Guatemalan borders, when in fact some of the varieties classified as independent languages are mutually intelligible and hence could be considered as dialects belonging to a given language.

3 Guatemala – whose population is over 65 percent indigenous – is the only other Latin American country where the national majorities are still indigenous and vernacular-speaking; hence terms such as linguistic or ethnic minorities do not really apply in these cases. That is why it is common to read in the specialized literature produced both in Latin America and Spain references to *minoritized* languages and groups, precisely to make evident the political processes that determined their present situation and status.

4 Indigenous languages are defined here as those languages which were already spoken in Indigenous America at the time of the sixteenth-century clash with the Europeans and their languages (primarily Spanish and Portuguese). In this paper we will alternatively use the adjectives Amerindian and vernacular when referring to indigenous languages.

5 In 1994 the House of Representatives (Camara de Diputados) discussed and approved a proposed law which declared the co-officialization of Spanish and all of the indigenous languages spoken in Bolivia. In June 1997, organized jointly by government agencies and by indigenous organizations, a three-day meeting took place to discuss the implications of new language policy. In relation to this it is worth mentioning that unlike most Latin American countries the Bolivian Constitution does not consider Spanish nor any other language as official. More recently, the Ministery of Education, Culture and Sports with the support and technical advice of UNICEF and of PROEIB Andes, is organizing a series of specialized seminars to discuss and analyze proposals for a new and comprehensive national language policy.

6 Mignolo 1995 is an excellent reference for counteranalyzing from a historical perspective the European forms of literacy *vis-à-vis* certain Amerindian forms of graphic representation. The title of one of the sections of chapter 2 of Mignolo's book (1995, p. 76) is in itself revealing: "Writing without Words, without Paper, without Pen."

7 Well-known academicians such as Jurgen Golte and Maria Rostorowsky and an important and prestigious research center (Instituto de Estudios Peruanos), amongst others, have contributed to the reinscription of Mochica knowledge and culture in Peruvian society.

8 The use of the relative pronoun "which" instead of who is intentional. It is meant to portray the landowners' shared view of "their" servants.

9 María Asunción Galindo in Puno, Peru; Dolores Cacuango in Cayambe, Ecuador; and Avelino Siñani and Elizardo Pérez in Warisata, Bolivia, amongst others, were the pioneers in the Andes of bilingual education and of rural education in general at a time when landowners did not show any sympathy whatsoever regarding the education of "their" peasants. More information about M. A. Galindo's experiment can be found in López, 1988; on D. Cacuango's actitivies, in Rodas, 1989; and Claure, 1989, can be consulted on the well-known school nucleus of Warisata.

10   I would rather treat alphabetization and literacy as different, precisely to make explicit that learning to read and write is not necessarily the same as being really literate, since the latter goes far beyond the mere act of learning the basics of writing and calls for other competencies, both cognitive and particularly social, that have to do with the functions and uses of the written language in a given context. Similarly, we argue in this paper that certain indigenous civilizations of the Americas may have been literate although not necessarily alphabetized.

11   An exception to this rule might be the case of the minority languages of the Amazon region where the main literacy agent, and in certain cases an effective one, has been evangelism. In fact most of the alphabets for these languages emerged out of the need to prepare religious translations. In the Amazon region, reducing the indigenous languages to writing and basic education went hand in hand. Since the 1940s in the Andes and earlier in Mexico, the North American Protestant organization Summer Institute of Linguistics assumed (through official agreements with various Latin American governments) direct responsibility for the education of indigenous populations, particularly in the Amazon basin and lowlands. SIL has produced Bible translations and other religious and educational materials in vernaculars.

12   I am referring to languages such as Aymara, Guarani, Nahuatl, and Quechua, reduced to writing by Catholic friars in early Colonial times, after being declared "major or general languages" by the Spanish Crown due to the vast territories in which they were used as forms of lingua franca. In the case of the Quechua language, for instance, the first written text dates back to 1560. From that time on and until the eighteenth-century prohibition from Madrid, various books were written and printed in the indigenous languages, including also certain translations of Greek classics.

13   There is a classical example of biliteracy in colonial Peruvian history when in 1613 Guaman Poma de Ayala, an Indian cacique from the area of Lucanas, took it upon himself to write a 1,200-page letter to the King of Spain. In his *Nueva Coronica y Buen Gobierno* (New Chronicle and Good Government), the biliterate chief informs the King of Spain of Europeans abuses in the New World. In so doing, he uses a variety of means and modes of expression to construct his long text: drawings, detailed illustrations and inconography as well as alphabetical script; although written in Spanish, the text includes passages, sometimes long and detailed, in at least two indigenous languages: Quechua and Aymara.

References

Acevedo, M. L. et al. (1996). *Educación interétnica.* Mexico, D.F.: Instituto Nacional de Antropología e Historia.

Albó, X. (1979). *El futuro de los idiomas oprimidos.* Cuadernos de investigación CIPCA 2. La Paz, Bolivia: CIPCA. 3ra. Edición.

Boone, E. H. and Mignolo, W. D. (1994). *Writing Without Words: Alternative literacies in Mesoamerica and the Andes.* Durham/London: Duke University Press.

Claure, K. (1989). *Las escuelas indigenales: otra forma de resistencia comunitaria.* La Paz, Bolivia: HISBOL.

D'Emilio, L. (1997). Processes of change and indigenous participation. *Cultural Survival Quarterly,* Summer: 43–6.

Dutcher, N. (1997). *The Use of First and Second Languages in Education*. Washington, DC: The World Bank.

Fundación ASUR. (n.d.). *Renacimiento de un arte indígena. Los textiles de Jalq'a y Tarabuco del centro sur de Bolivia*. Sucre: PROINSA.

Glave, L. M. (1990). Grito de pueblos silenciados. Intermediarios lingüísticos y culturales entre dos mundos: historia y mentalidades. *Allpanchis*. 35/36(2): 435–513 (Cuzco, Perú).

Golte, J. (1994). *Los dioses de Sipán. Las aventuras del Dios Quismique y su ayudante Murrup*. Lima: Instituto de Estudios Peruanos.

González, M. L. (1994). How many indigenous people? In G. Psacharopoulos and H. A. Patrinos (eds.), *Indigenous People and Poverty in Latin America: An empirical analysis*. World Bank Regional and Sectorial Studies. Washington, DC: The World Bank.

Hocquenghem, A. M. (1990). *Iconografía Mochica*. Lima: Pontificia Universidad Católica del Perú.

Hornberger, N. (1988). *Bilingual Education and Language Maintenance: A southern Peruvian Quechua case*. Dordrecht/Providence: Foris Publications.

Hornberger, N. (1995). Five vowels or three? Linguistics and politics in Quechua language planning in Peru. In J. W. Tollefson (ed.), *Power and Inequality in Language Education*. New York: Cambridge University Press.

Hornberger, N. and López, L. E. (1997). Policy, possibility, and paradox: Indigenous multilingualism and education in Bolivia and Peru. In F. Genesee and J. Cenoz (eds.), *Beyond Bilingualism: Multilingualism and multilingual education*. Clevendon, UK: Multilingual Matters.

López, L. E. (1988). La escuela en Puno y el problema de la lengua. In L. E. López (ed.), *Pesquisas en lingüística andina*. Lima/Puno: CONCYTEC/UNA- P/GTZ.

López, L. E. (1989). La política lingüística peruana y la educación de la población indígena. In L. E. López and R. Moya (eds.), *Pueblos indios, estados y educación*. Lima: PEB-P/P.EBI/ERA.

López, L. E. (1997a). La eficacia y validez de los obvio: lecciones aprendidas desde la evaluación de procesos educativos bilingües. *Revista Paraguaya de Sociología Año*, 34(99): 27–62 (Asunción, Paraguay). (It also appears in J. Calvo and J. C. Godenzzi (eds.) (1998). *Multilingüismo en España y en América Latina*. Valencia, España; Cuzco, Perú: Universidad de Valencia y Centro Bartolomé de las Casas.)

López, L. E. (1997b). To Guaranize: A verb actively conjugated by the Bolivian Guaranis. In N. Hornberger (ed.), *Indigenous Literacies in the Americas: Language planning from the bottom up. Contributions to the Sociology of Language*, 75: 321–53. Berlin; New York: Mouton de Gruyter.

López, L. E. and I. Jung (eds.) (1998). *Sobre las huellas de la voz. Sociolingüística de la oralidad y la escritura en su relación con la educación*. Madrid: Ediciones Morata.

Luykx, A. (1998). *The Citizen Factory: Schooling and cultural production in Bolivia*. Albany: SUNY University Press.

Mannheim, B. (1984). Una nación acorralada: Southern Peruvian Quechua language planning and politics in historical perspective. *Language in Society*, 13: 291–309.

Mignolo, W. (1995). *The Darker Side of the Renaissance: Literacy, territoriality and colonization*. Ann Arbor: University of Michigan Press.

Olson, D. R. (1994). *The World on Paper: The conceptual and cognitive implications of writing and reading*. New York: Cambridge University Press.

Pozzi-Escot, I. (1996). Reflexiones sobre la política lingüística peruana. In *Políticas lingüísticas. Número temático de Signo&Seña. Revista del Instituto de Lingüística*. No. 4. Facultad Filosofía y Letras, Universidad de Buenos Aires.

Rodas, R. (1989). *Dolores Cahuango: Memorias de un sueño*. Quito: EBI /Abya Yala.

Taylor, G. (1988). La tradición oral andina y la escritura. In L. E. López (ed.), *Pesquisas en Lingüística Andina*. Lima/Puno: CONCYTEC/UNA- P/GTZ.

Chapter 12

The Uses of Orality and Literacy in Rural Mexico: Tales from Xaltipan

Elsie Rockwell

Comparative research on literacy (including Graff, 1981; Tannen, 1982; Goody, 1986; Gee, 1990; Olson & Torrance, 1991; Boyarin, 1992; Fabre, 1993a; Barton, 1994; Street, 1996; Hornberger, 1997) has brought to light multiple histories of reading and writing in different cultural regions, periods, and groups.[1] In examining how writing was appropriated in one village of central Mexico, Xaltipan, and particularly by one individual in that village, I hope to add to this evidence of diversity. In this chapter, I describe literacy as embedded in cultural practices and particular domains, and then focus on the local representation of literacy in oral accounts of situations involving the use of writing. I also propose to show how local perspectives on literacy may challenge theoretical assumptions. My approach has sought to give temporal depth to ethnographic research by combining oral and archival history with fieldwork.

Underlying this research is a conception of literacy that owes its development to several theoretical traditions. Sociocultural research, drawing on the work of Vygotsky, has viewed literacy as one of the fundamental tools or artifacts of culture, and has discussed possible consequences of writing in the cultural formation of human cognition (Scribner & Cole, 1981; Feldman, 1991; Cole, 1996; Bruner, 1996). In a parallel development, researchers working in the tradition of the Annales school (Fabre, 1993a; Chartier, 1995; Chartier & Hébrard, 1994) recovered Lucien Febvre's notion of *outillage mental* (mental utilities) and applied it to literacy. While the notion of a cultural tool is central to each perspective, in neither case is the existence of writing systems and tools seen as a sufficient condition for literacy to evolve.

Leading scholars in these traditions have insisted on viewing literacy as necessarily embedded in social activity (Cole, 1996) or cultural practice (Chartier, 1995), rather than regarding it as a decontextualized technique or mental skill. While the availability of technical means may be seen as an enabling or constraining factor, only the social uses of writing explain the diverse developments of literacy. It is the appropriation of these artifacts, by particular persons, within particular cultural domains and practices, that accounts for the social emergence of literacy. In each of these traditions, current research describes the range of resources available in each cultural horizon, and then focuses on the way these were put to use in precise activities, tasks, and manners. The concept of *appropriation* captures this perspective well, as it implies an active use and transformation of cultural resources (Chartier, 1995, ch. 4; Rockwell, 1996). Thus, as people select and appropriate the tools of literacy from the available stock, they reshape them to fit into cultural practices and to accomplish particular social tasks. It is only then that these resources acquire meaning and are of consequence in a given society, or indeed become part of social history.

Parallel theoretical developments, summarized by Street (1984), Gee (1990), Olson (1994), and Bloch (1998), among others, have called for careful reflection upon relationships between literacy and power, knowledge, and social development. Literacy is not a neutral cultural artifact, rather it has contradictory effects in different social contexts. Therefore, I found it necessary to keep in mind what Natalie Davis (1975) expressed long ago: "social structures and values channel the uses of literacy." The question facing researchers is no longer what writing has done to people, but rather what people have done with writing.

The Appropriation of Literacy in Rural Societies

The process of appropriation, of reshaping the tools of writing to fit particular cultural practices, is particularly evident in peasant and indigenous societies. Literacy entered the rural world through multiple channels, including the processes of religious conversion, the organization of political movements, the growth of nation-states and of their institutions, the process of colonization, and the dissemination of agricultural knowledge. Priests, missionaries, lawyers, doctors, notaries, administrators, scribes, and, finally, teachers, each had a role in producing social literacy. Each of these channels favored a particular set of practices, produced different sorts of texts, and communicated diverse contents. Schooling was not necessarily a prerequisite for the adoption of literate practices in the rural world. When it did arrive, it added yet another set of contexts fostering particular uses, styles and values of writing. The assorted histories of adoption of alphabetic literacy in rural societies show a diversity in the range and sequence of domains and cultural practices that precludes any linear model of development.

Literacy practices adopted in rural societies were not simply elite models imposed from above as some have suggested (Furet & Ozouf, 1982); they were constructed within particular historical contexts. As rural populations took up and used dominant languages and symbol systems, at times they turned them into weapons to be used against those in power (Scott, 1990). Thus, official texts have been used to exact government compliance with prior commitments, or to legitimize opposition movements. This has occurred in places as distant as medieval England (Justice, 1994) and twentieth-century central Mexico (León-Portilla, 1996).

Peasant societies have also developed alternative literacies. Daniel Fabre (1993b) has described the case of European shepherds, during the seventeenth to nineteenth centuries, who used special systems of annotation to control herds and to disseminate heretical beliefs, and to set in writing their own poetic tradition. Similarly, during the early colonial period in New Spain, the Nahua elite, although educated by friars in Spanish, continued to develop prehispanic pictographic writing, using it both to record their own language and to transcribe Spanish words (Gruzinski 1991; Lockhart, 1992; Kartunnen, 1998). They also continued to cultivate the corresponding oral skills required for reading this sort of writing. For over two centuries, this parallel literate tradition survived in some domains, such as cartography, poetics, and legal rhetoric (Pellicer, 1993; Lockhart, 1992). Indeed, despite the disappearance of Nahua writing, it is possible that the indigenous tradition has continued to influence the relationship to the written word that one finds in rural central Mexico to this day.

Of particular interest in the history of indigenous literacy is the relationship between oral and written media. The recent conceptual approach to literacy also underscores the rich interplay between orality and literacy (Goody, 1982; Tannen, 1982; Heath, 1982; Finnegan, 1988; Thomas, 1989; Farr, 1990; Havelock, 1991). We might begin to recognize that these abstract terms – literacy and orality – gloss over specific practices that generally combine, in varying proportions, the use of oral and written language, as well as other modes of representation. An excellent example of these combinations can be found in the scriptoriums of the Middle Ages, where voicing, copying, interpreting, composing, dictating, and illustrating texts were all acts performed by different persons (Saenger, 1997). This sequence slowly gave way to the idea that reading and writing necessarily imply one another, and are regarded as distinct from the use of oral language. Our very notion of literacy is a product of this cultural history. When approaching cultural practices in other societies, we must be sensitive to different relationships between orality and literacy, found for example in the rules governing what should be put into writing, and what is best left to oral transmission. Although the uses of writing may be diminished in such situations, this strategic shift may in fact represent an "active manipulation" of the resources of literacy (Scott, 1990, pp. 30–3), and should not be confused with a "restricted use" of literacy.

As we abandon the radical dichotomy argument (Finnegan, 1988), the intermeshing of oral and literate skills within most cultural practices anywhere again becomes evident. Furthermore, just as writing may have led to a new conceptualization of oral language (Olson, 1994), so too oral representations of cultural practices involving writing may help us rethink literacy. In recounting some of the tales told by Cleofas on the uses of documents in Xaltipan, I propose to regard these oral accounts as means of reflecting upon our own cultural conceptions of literacy.

Narrative Accounts of Literacy

Cleofas Galicia is a literate weaver, adept at telling stories, resident of the town of Xaltipan, in the state of Tlaxcala. Born in 1938, his life has spanned the six decades during which his village became a town. During the early 1980s, he was the town's *agente*, the locally elected officer in charge of all dealings with the municipal government. At that time, he made it possible for me and my colleagues to do fieldwork in the local school. I subsequently visited him often, sometimes as a guest to local celebrations, sometimes to talk over aspects of my research on the history of schools in the region. It was particularly during these visits, rather than in the formal interviews we had initially conducted with him, that Cleofas would talk about events he had witnessed during his lifetime. The narratives interwoven through ongoing conversation often gave information about village life. Cleofas tended to repeat these accounts on different occasions, or with different audiences. These repetitions not only allowed me to listen to them again. They also justify considering these narrative sequences as tales or stories, an oral genre that is widely recognized as part of Mexican rural culture (Briggs, 1988; Farr, 1993; Pellicer, 1995). These tales are created to entertain, when the proper social conditions emerge, rather than to inform.

Although the tales told by Cleofas were not about literacy, they often represented acts of reading or writing, or of dealing with the written word, as embedded in social activities. Writing often appeared within problematic situations, moments when social tasks were to be accomplished, wrongs redressed, projects negotiated, people convinced, authorities held at bay, and such. Rather than treating my field notes[2] as a potential inventory of literate practices, I attempted to recover these accounts as expressions of local knowledge. When treated as narratives, such accounts give access to meaning (Bauman, 1977; Bruner, 1996), and reflect the local significance of literacy. The indirect nature of this window on literacy – I had not directly asked about writing – revealed facets that rarely emerge in formal interviews on the subject. Cleofas's stories conveyed a perspective on the social efficacy of writing as well as on its limitations in this particular context. Indeed, within these tales there was a constant tension between the assertions regarding the written word, and the elaborate oral discourse that enveloped references to written documents. This tension disturbed the academic preconceptions of literate practice that I had brought to bear upon my research. In order to give a sense of what some of these stories convey, consider the following summary.

In response to a question regarding the last school meeting, Cleofas remarked: "Haven't I told you? At that meeting a man even cried." The gist of his long tale was as follows. Cleofas and a number of *vecinos* (local citizens) had accused Don Cristobal, president of the school board, of mismanaging the funds raised by the Pro-feria (town fair) committee, which were supposed to be used for building a town hall. Cleofas reproduced in detail the discussion that ensued at the meeting. At one point, he said, Don Cristobal offered a moving defense of his use of the funds to add a principal's office to the school. Then he actually turned his back to the audience, covered his face with his hands (Cleofas showed us how) and wept, winning the sympathy of the teachers and of many parents. The principal seemed to be interested in having the whole affair forgotten, so that he could get on with a new project. So he drew up an *acta*, and had it signed by most of those who were present, wherein it was agreed to withdraw the charges, though Cristobal and his committee members were to pay a fine. Cleofas did not sign the document, arguing that they had not put in writing the fact that Cristobal had wept [he said this somewhat tongue in cheek]. "Let's see, why should he cry?", he asked us. Cleofas, though at the time town *agente*, was accused on the spot of dividing the assembly, and lost his case. The Pro-feria committee members later conferred with Cleofas; they agreed that Don Cristobal was guilty and promised to add to their own file that he had cried just like Hernán Cortés when he was routed and fled from México-Tenochtitlan.

In recounting this incident, Cleofas implicitly denounced Cristobal's manipulation of the meeting, and questioned the written version drawn up in the official minutes. His motion to include what actually occurred had been considered out of place, as *actas* are a very strict genre, admitting only general reference to oral language, such as: "after a heated debate, it was agreed that..." However, the reference to Cortés's tears gives a clue to his insistence. Hernán Cortés, the Spanish conquistador, had been defeated by the Aztecs on his first incursion into the valley of Mexico, and had been forced to retreat to Tlaxcala, where he camped under a tree, ever since named *el Arbol Triste* (the Sad Tree), and wept. The story of Cortés's tears has been registered in every history book, so why was it not possible to set in writing what actually occurred at the meeting? Furthermore, if Cortés had wept after being routed, recording Cristobal's behavior might have changed Cleofas's defeat into a sort of victory. The mocking tone of Cleofas's account verged on parody, and showed awareness of different rules regarding what could or could not be put into writing in such situations.

This subtle comprehension of the relationship of writing to power raises questions about the more prosaic uses of literacy. In Cleofas's tales, there were few references to writing in domains such as ritual and work, where one would expect "instrumental" or "memory-supportive" uses of literacy (Heath, 1982). Cleofas wove blankets with intricate patterns, on a wooden loom, in the traditional artisan manner. The only document involved in selling his ware was the handwritten receipt for the value of the materials he had received from the local merchant; this amount was deducted from his weekly pay when he delivered the blankets. I once asked Cleofas whether he ever used any printed or hand-drawn designs. The suggestion must have seemed ludicrous; he immediately asked whether I had to look at a book to know how to type, or whether I copied the books I wrote: "This is my work, I have the designs in my mind," he added.

Other stories revealed the significance of orality in certain situations. Some of the most striking were those referring to spatial orientation, and seemed to hark back to the oral skills that prehispanic systems required for reading the elaborate pictographic maps. During one conversation, I mentioned to Cleofas that anyone who could read should have no problem locating places in Mexico City, otherwise it would be difficult to get around. Cleofas countered this remark, arguing that his aunt could find her way anywhere there, though she could not read. Then he went on to relate the verbal instructions that his aunt had given him in order to reach her home in the city. By using her indications, with no notes, Cleofas had been able to reach her house. He described the route, in minute detail, mentioning street names, corners, buildings, signs, metro stations, bus routes, symbols, street stands and stores where he could check directions, even the color of gates. Memory, thus structured through oral narrative, captures graphic detail and spatial orientation, and suffices where those of us who depend on literacy might be at a loss.

The use of these stories as evidence of cultural practices involving literacy poses the issue of the relationship between individual narrative and historical development. I do not claim that Cleofas is representative of his time or generation. Literacy is multiple, and is appropriated in distinct ways, in the course of particular lives. Thus, Cleofas's vision may be familiar to those of his generation who shared his circumstances, yet may seem strange to others, even in Xaltipan. I would suggest, however, that by focusing on the experience of this one individual, ethnographic analysis might gain temporal depth. Cleofas's tales contain recollections reaching back into the history of an Indian community, and convey perceptions of life in a town on the verge of urbanization. They reflect both the deep continuities and the rapid changes that mark this place and time.

The Appropriation of Literacy in One Town

The people of Tlaxcala, a tiny state in central Mexico, have had at least five centuries of dealing with Western alphabetic literacy, plus another millennium interpreting pictographic writing, always within a multilingual context. Therefore, this is not a simple case of contrasting "oral" and "literate" traditions. The hybrid forms of representing the world that emerged after the Conquest continued to influence local perceptions and practices for centuries. During the colonial years (1521–1821), alphabetic writing of both Spanish and Nahuatl developed and was used extensively in this region for recording matters pertaining to governing, civil organization, litigation, and religious conversion. By the time of the Independence from Spanish rule, the parallel writing system was no longer in use, and Nahuatl had ceased to be admitted in official domains. However, rural communities continued to sustain schools for boys, as they had years before, for establishing a school was part of attaining the autonomous status of town. From the mid-nineteenth century on, the ruling Liberal faction fostered the extension of literacy in the indigenous towns of Tlaxcala, and placed schools under state administration. Toward the end of the century, the state government founded girls' schools and established secondary and higher education. Teachers of this period disseminated music, theater, and poetry, together with the related literacy skills. However, the new system abandoned the smaller, more indigenous *barrios* and towns, stressed Spanish language and urbanity, and concentrated educational opportunities in the larger cities.

The inhabitants of the indigenous region of Tlaxcala were small communal landholders, who had become part-time workers in the agricultural haciendas and textile factories established during the nineteenth century. Political and civic life was strongly tied to the community, and offered the organizational basis for the extensive participation in the revolutionary movement that swept Mexico between 1910 and 1920. The centralized federal state that was formed after the revolutionary conflict established its legitimacy in the rural areas by trading off public services, including schooling, for support of the governing party. The post-revolutionary period brought thorough social and economic changes to Tlaxcala. In the following decades, the rural populations of this region slowly entered the urban network, while guarding their basic allegiance to the local townships.

During the first decades of the twentieth century, most rural inhabitants of villages on the foothills of the Malintzi volcano, where Xaltipan is located, spoke Mexicano (Nahuatl). For nearly five centuries, they had preserved their language, while devising strategies for dealing with the Spanish-speaking world. The increasing use of Spanish in the official domains tended to restrict the use of the native language, however Mexicano continued to thrive in local assemblies, letter-writing, rituals and oral poetry, joking and telling tales, and it was consciously adopted and renewed by certain groups (Hill & Hill, 1986). However, through the extension of federal schooling during the twentieth century, Spanish literacy became a universal requisite for earning a living. By mid-century, parents were pressuring their children, including the girls, to attend school and to learn Spanish. By the end of the century, few children were learning Mexicano, and those who did rarely admitted that they understood the language of their grandparents.

Although Spanish is quickly replacing Mexicano, in the rural towns and villages of Tlaxcala, the ongoing organization of domestic life, spatial and temporal orientation, and the fabric of civil society are still strongly tied to orality. Past and distant realities are recovered and future actions anticipated through oral conversation, though references to documentary evidence are constant. However, everyday life takes residents to the larger nearby cities, where they encounter a literacy environment of urban fabrication. An inventory of literacy acts and tools would show that most people of the towns now have the skills to meet the demands they encounter in such domains as commerce, health, and labor.

Local oral history traces the origin of Xaltipan to the end of the nineteenth century. As the story goes, the land was originally an hacienda belonging to a nearby convent, and later to a cattle rancher, who abandoned it when he found that his bulls were systematically disappearing from the watering hole. Sometime before the revolution, a few families from nearby San Pablo moved in, set up a cross, changed their own names and throughout the following century worked to transform Xaltipan into a town. For Xaltipeños, becoming a town meant defending their autonomy and collectively financing and promoting the series of public spaces that identify a pueblo: church and school, streets and a public plaza with a kiosque. They also proceeded to establish clear boundaries with the municipal headtown, San Bernardino Contla, and to build roads and bridges to connect Xaltipan to the state capital.

The delimitation of Xaltipan's territory and its incorporation into the national context are reflected in local conversation. The irregular outline of Xaltipan melds with the outer *barrios* of Contla, and it is difficult for a stranger to discover the limits. Residents identify the boundaries through anecdotes tied to each ravine, crossroad, bridge, tree and shrine, and references to fields that have proper names. Local people also communicate their experiences of the ramified networks of everyday life beyond Xaltipan. They talk about commuting by bus to work or study in nearby cities, undertaking pilgrimages to sanctuaries in other states, selling blankets in various commercial circuits, receiving relatives who return to the annual *fiesta* from distant parts, and resorting to noted healers and doctors within a wide radius. Consequently, Xaltipeños are cognizant of and comment upon the nation's contradictory array of people and diverse languages. Such local knowledge is transmitted through tales and anecdotes and is scarcely dependent on literacy. Radio and television complement the oral network with a variety of reports and images, but they have not yet formed an urban worldview.

Organizing civil and religious life in Xaltipan also involves intensive use of oral language. Both the complex distribution of the patronage of saints' day celebrations through *mayordomías* and the rotating assignment to committees that sponsor public works are determined through private consultation and public discussion in assemblies. When Cleofas was proposed as *agente*, he commented, he selected eight trustworthy men as his *comité de vigilancia*. This committee would meet on weekends and share the work of thinking through courses of action: "What shall we do, we are all here, let's think." The collective use of oral word was essential to this process of deliberation (cf. Thomas, 1989). When this was accomplished, Cleofas explained, it was possible to reach agreements at the assemblies: "When there has been so much thinking, so many headaches, the result cannot be negative . . . you must be able to reach consensus."

Although Xaltipeños consider knowledge, memory and thinking to be related to orality, they too (as any of us) resort to writing when the occasion calls for it. Literacy in this context is not exclusively a product of modernity. Written documents, including maps and books, are referred to in connection with some of the oldest traditions and testimonies of local culture, such as Catholic doctrine, attributes of sorcery, legal claims, and authoritative versions of legends.

Literacy skills and practices in the region have evolved over the years. Most of the founders of Xaltipan could sign, and had received some schooling in San Pablo. Leaders had learned to read and speak Spanish, primarily through participation in the revolutionary movement. For nearly 40 years, Xaltipan did not have its own public school, though a few children attended the state school in Contla or received private classes. The initiative to establish a school went hand in hand with the struggle to become a town. It was the first of a series of steps linking local autonomy with the appropriation of literacy.

In order to exercise their right to address written petitions and complaints to the governor, early residents of Xaltipan would hire scribes, who were noted for their exceptional calligraphy and mastery of the appropriate written models for addressing authorities. As the men would deliberate in Mexicano, the scribes often translated their petitions to Spanish, as well as rendering oral requests into the formulaic genre of official petitions. Some scribes accumulated considerable power, as they controlled the gateways to the state government. This system began to change in the years following the revolution.

The changing forms of literacy are reflected in the archival documents from Xaltipan, which slowly progressed from elaborate handwritten *oficios*, through the curt typed responses, to the increasing use of standardized forms, filled in by government officials, with information provided by local committee members. The town's *Libro de actas* disclosed the continuous minutes of town meetings between 1947 and 1980, in which secretaries recorded by hand the course and outcome of public projects. These *actas* show a wide range of styles, from brief reports set in near-oral terms, to samples of the elaborate rhetoric and handwriting, which are evidence of the various capacities of the men, including some head teachers, who took on the position of town secretary.

The public school established during the late 1930s opened access to literacy, though classroom activities probably gave only rudimentary skills. Cleofas recalled that the large stone schoolroom was dark, as it had no windows. Students of all ages were crowded onto a few benches. They used thin paper notebooks and had a few readers, and no library. They copied their assignments with pens dipped in inkwells which would often spill over. In the one-room school, only a few children qualified as third graders and received special training. Fewer still were chosen to continue. The local teacher urged Cleofas to go to a boarding school, and filled out the application form, but his parents feared he would then "belong to the government," so they refused to sign. Cleofas has retold this story several times, with certain regret, and his daughters have remarked, "he could have been a teacher or a *licenciado*" (university graduate). Yet Cleofas and others his age have insisted that a third grade schooling in those years was equivalent at least to the present-day sixth grade.

During Cleofas's lifetime the significance of schooling has changed radically. When he was young, a fourth-grade certificate could lead to a prestigious teaching position. In the 1980s the town had a full primary school and a small secondary school, and several of those who finished each year went on to university studies. Nevertheless, as Cleofas commented referring to his niece, "now sixteen years of study do not assure one a job." At times, he questioned the whole policy: "Why did the government provide schools if it was not going to hire more teachers?" I countered this argument, remarking that schools might have other values. Cleofas then advised me, using the repetition of phrases and questions that characterizes the rhetorical forms of political discourse (Tannen, 1989): "Certainly it is worthwhile, at least one can defend oneself... schooling enables one to carry out certain *encomiendas* [commissions] of the pueblo... it enables one to sustain a family... to write a letter, to say a few words at an assembly, and many other things. One learns how to sign, how to answer a question, how to scribble a few words. Isn't that so? If you're entrusted with an office, you can help your town... so it benefits the town. Isn't that so?... It helped me, even though I only finished third grade." Although Cleofas had probably used similar arguments to convince skeptical parents to back the Xaltipan school, he was also reflecting on the meaning of schooling in his own life.

Cleofas's Appropriation of Literacy

Cleofas is among the more literate of his generation in Xaltipan, yet his appropriation of literacy was not simply a product of schooling. Rather, the various skills of writing in his present reserve were constructed over the years. Some 20 years after he had left school, the requirements of public life confronted him with new tasks. By then, he knew enough to obtain a document from the state police force, to back his authority as local *comandante* (police officer). As he progressed through the successive elective (unpaid) local offices and committees, he learned ways of speaking and handling administrative documents, often counting on his *asesor*, an acquaintance in the state bureaucracy that offered him free counsel. In the course of his public life, he appropriated ways of handling documents that became tools in his everyday life. However, the uses were not always utilitarian: in private life, Cleofas was not as strict an accountant as he insisted on being in public life. Rather, he became aware of the possibilities of influencing or modifying the course of events, by skillful reference to the written word.

Several innovations mark Cleofas's period as town *agente* (1980–3). The minutes of town meetings were set in script, the new form of writing introduced in schools during the previous decade, and acquired a more colloquial phrasing than had been used by many of his predecessors. Cleofas has also described how he created a filing system, for he had received an old soapbox full of papers, which could not qualify as an archive. In Xaltipan, official papers had never been kept in public places, but rather were safeguarded in private homes. Cleofas carefully kept each pending affair in a separate folder, numbered each document, and registered each one in a notebook: "This way nothing would be lost." However, even after the two-room town hall was built in the late 1980s, the *agentes* continued to keep files at home, for fear of sabotage.

Cleofas expressed a new awareness of the import of documentation in his account of the first confrontation with the local authorities. The municipal president would invariably address correspondence to the Barrio of Xaltipan, as he did to other villages under his jurisdiction. The town elders insisted that Xaltipan was not a *barrio*, but had been decreed a *pueblo* in its own right many years before, but they lacked written proof thereof. Cleofas and his secretary spent several days going through papers at the state archive until they found the decree of 1932, and obtained a copy to back their claims against the municipal authority. After gaining this new independence from local powers, he went on to promote a number of public services, including a health center and a library.

As *agente*, Cleofas probably did little actual writing. He has mentioned taking notes at the meetings, mainly to remember amounts and dates, and has spoken of having to sign people up[3] for services. His task was often getting others to write up petitions, after he and his committee had thought up what to say: "We go before them and tell them what we are lacking, we don't have such and such...there they write the document, free of charge." Requests directed to the municipal president were written by the local secretary, but the first letter addressed to the governor was formulated by the *asesor*, Cleofas explains, as he was able to word it with reference to the constitutional articles requiring officials to respond to petitions. Several government *licenciados*, acting somewhat as modern day scribes, would actually write many of the *oficios* that Cleofas signed, adding to them the proper references to legal points and programs. Within this world, it appeared that Cleofas's ability to deal with the official bureaucracy owed more to his ample stock of oral strategies for using written documents than to writing skills as such.

As forms of written language changed and literacy skills became widespread, the balance between rural villagers and governing authorities shifted. The spread of literacy weakened the power concentrated in the town scribes and secretaries as gatekeepers to the government. The oral mediation of writing reflected this changing position of rural communities in relation to governing powers. In one sense, Cleofas had inherited the ways of relating to authorities characteristic of the scribal tradition. Nevertheless he achieved a more effective use of literacy in official transactions, through his growing knowledge of the way documents are handled – drawn up, signed, stamped, copied, obtained, de-livered, and saved – and his understanding of the subtle effects of written texts in all sorts of situations. The stories told by Cleofas portray different facets of writing, inserted within situations of power and persuasion, where human relationships are altered.

The Oral Mediation of Literacy

In many of the stories embedded in the ongoing conversation with Cleofas, I found references to situations in which the outcome hinged on a strategic use of written documents. A distinctive element of these situations is that the use of these documents seemed to be most effective when mediated by a skillful use of oral discourse. This does not mean that writing was without effect. It does mean, however, that documents were relatively powerless if not presented, supported, enveloped, and amplified by oral discourse, in precise moments of human interaction. I have organized the following examples under four analytic categories of my own making – persuasion, litigation, negotiation and conversation – that suggest some of the ways in which oral strategies afford writing its power to influence situations.

Persuasion

Cleofas told of several situations in which documents were used as means of persuasion, or to back up oral argumentation. In some cases, parts of written documents were read aloud, in the context of ongoing interaction. In other situations, references to written documents were woven into the oral discourse, and served to render it more persuasive, although the documents themselves were not presented. Finally, in a few cases, the documents or books themselves, as objects, were presented and perhaps accompanied by gestures, although the written contents were not read. One particularly striking set of stories related the use of certain books by a variety of local "sorcerers." These people were seen to have special gifts, that enabled them to read such books without being "overpowered" by them, as were ordinary humans. One such person was a *granicero* in charge of turning away hailstorms that threatened the village crops. He used a book in the context of an elaborate ritual, with candles and other symbolic objects, incantations and invocations, and was rewarded by the villagers when successful. When he died, of course, the book was not instrumental in recovering the knowledge of a lost tradition. In a sense, the power attributed to books on sorcery is but an instance of a more general effect of the objects that support or carry the written word.

One such case is found in the story about Genaro, who had been *agente* of Xaltipan some 50 years before. The role of the *agente* was administrative, and in no way carried judicial authority. Nevertheless, Genero was known for his ability to establish order. In doing so, he resorted to a nineteenth-century hardbound copy of the Constitution of Benito Juárez (then no longer in force). The volume was priceless, and had probably been handed down from previous generations. It was stolen some time after Genaro had lost his eyesight as an old man.

Cleofas in turn followed the tradition when elected *agente* during the 1980s. One of his first moves, he explained, was to buy a copy of the current Constitution, as well as copies of civil and criminal statutes. When dealing with young delinquents, he would read to them from these texts, and point out that their misdemeanors were subject to a fine or a jail sentence. With the law in his hands he would then ask whether they would behave, or preferred to be turned over to the judicial authorities in Contla. This, he added, would subdue them (*"sí se sometían"*). Such uses of the printed law were persuasive, rather than instrumental. Cleofas was aware of the limits of his jurisdiction; he reminded me that he was not actually "applying the law." Only a judge, he explained, is capable of discerning who is responsible in such cases and of determining the corresponding punishment. Yet the fact that he could find and read some of the relevant legal precepts and show those involved the actual books that contained these laws, was apparently effective in persuading the youths to change their ways.

As *agente*, Cleofas was in constant contact with the governmental domain of the written language. As intermediary between the inhabitants and the government, he was in charge of taking written petitions to the authorities, and communicating the replies during the local town meetings. Many of these documents involved the continual promotion of public services. In the process of negotiating the necessary agreements for undertaking new public works, Cleofas used references to the documents as part of his persuasive arguments. Thus, he claimed, he was often able to convince either the Xaltipeños or governing officials to take certain steps, by having copies of the proper documents, always with corresponding signatures and seals. Once he insisted: "The project will be carried through, I have all of the documents, so they [the people] will believe me. The papers say everything." It was clear from his reports that often he had not actually read the documents aloud at the meeting, but had only showed them to those who were present. His oral exposition of the content of the documents made the presentation of the written documents effective. At the same time, the fact that he was able to show the documents rendered the oral arguments credible.

Such was also the case when village representatives, including Cleofas, were invited to present written petitions as *ponencias* (papers delivered orally) at a special convention of the official peasant union. These papers requested various services, and were signed by all the heads of households of each village. During the convention, Cleofas recounted, the union secretary read the petitions, with great formality, in presence of both the town delegates and the government officers whose responsibility it was to "resolve" them. The intention was to persuade the government that the requests were justified. Through the collective, oral, presentation, the delegates also learned of each other's petitions and acquired some means of evaluating the eventual results. The fact that the petitions were in writing was crucial, and villagers were discouraged from dealing with government officials in a purely oral manner. According to Cleofas's account, the secretary had added (echoing an age-old phrase): "Here only papers speak, nothing else speaks." He also urged delegates to "speak through writing to Mexico, to the President," if their petitions were not answered. Cleofas noted that to be valid the documents had to refer to the constitutional article that requires government officials to answer written petitions in writing.

However, what is interesting in Cleofas's account is that the binding force was the oral presentation. As the ponencias were read in presence of the village representatives, they had the effect of publicly committing the government representatives to respond in some way. In fact, petitions are not nearly as effective when the villagers simply deliver a written letter to a receptionist at a government office. The power attributed to the written word by those involved in these matters thus seems to result from the oral discourse that surrounds it.

As these examples show, the everyday process of persuading those in power, or even those without power, is often tied into the use of the written word. However, persuasion cannot rely on the power of documents themselves, but rather obtains its force from the ongoing oral reference to documents, by those involved either in enforcing rule or in defending their rights. References to written laws, agreements, and petitions add to the persuasive force of oral discourse. Yet the written documents never actually replace the need for oral discourse.

Negotiation

In the context I have been examining, public life involved active negotiation. Though literacy has often been associated with the exercise of power, this process shows that both governed and governing parties have ways of using written documents to their advantage. The growth of Xaltipan involved continuous dealings with governing officials. The stories Cleofas told of these moments reflect the strategies that villagers employed for either using or not using writing to increase bargaining power and influence outcomes.

Constructing and enlarging the school building involved complicated negotiations among various groups and committees, as well as with the official school construction agencies. In order to obtain government funding for these projects, the *vecinos* were required to contribute a certain percentage of the total cost. School principals would continually attempt to persuade villagers to sign a written agreement (*acta*) to that effect. As Mercado (1987) has shown, villagers would resist, as signing the agreement committed them to fees for a service that was purportedly free. Nevertheless, since they were also interested in access to schooling for their children, they complied whenever they felt that the projects were justified.

An education committee was elected each year to collect and account for the local contribution, yet frequent conflicts would occur when receipts were not requested or preserved. As village agent, Cleofas promoted the practice of giving receipts, rather than just registering the amounts ("funds should not be accepted on one's word, but rather with a receipt"). However, he was also aware that not doing so was sometimes a useful strategy, and not just the result of ignorance. If proper accounts were not kept, then no one could figure out who owed what. In such situations, government authorities often cancelled pending debts, and started new projects from scratch: "after all, they could not put everyone in jail," Cleofas explained. Though theoretically the agreements written down in *actas* could not be altered – Cleofas often claimed that "a written agreement could not be undone" – in practice, they were often modified by successive negotiations. Thus, in the ongoing struggle for free schooling, villagers forced government officials to forget old accounts, as they embarked upon new projects involving federal funding.

Cleofas reported similar strategies for private affairs. For example, he told me how he had managed to get a booth at the Tlaxcala fair, by relying on certain tricks he had acquired as *agente*. He would occasionally seek alternative outlets for his blankets. On this occasion, he rounded up several weavers that he trusted and went through the moves of setting up a Xaltipan section of a national union, linked to the governing party. This was an unofficial requirement for getting ahead in dealings with the government. With the initial documents of this application in hand, he approached the organizers of the fair. When they turned him down, he asked them to put their response in writing, so that he could show it to the other weavers. This request changed matters, as a written rejection could muddle relations with the potential new union members. A booth was soon made available. All the same, Cleofas and his friends barely broke even and soon forgot about the affair with the union.

Sometimes the avoidance of written documents was considered the most effective strategy in negotiating with authorities. When he first took office, Cleofas complained to the central urbanization agency that a certain villager did not want to leave room for the sidewalk on the main street. The authorities asked him to submit a written complaint, signed by at least fifty Xaltipeños. Cleofas studied the situation, with the help of his advisor, and realized that this document would have authorized state intervention in all local affairs, subjecting Xaltipan to urban development and altering the tax basis. So he decided not to comply and overlooked the transgression. After telling me about this, Cleofas pulled from his folder of papers a copy of an official map that showed Xaltipan as scheduled for full-scale urbanization. The authorities had not yet acted upon the written plans, he explained, as perhaps they were aware of potential local resistance.

Not signing documents was also used as an effective way of resisting the commitments and costs associated with "progress." Sometimes services were obtained without having to pay the local counterpart, for state authorities also had a stake in promoting development, and had to spend federal funds within the fiscal year. Cleofas told me of the time that authorities had sent materials for building the local kindergarten, and how he was able to store them, before a contract had been signed with Xaltipan. The authorities went on with plans to build the school. Meanwhile, they kept sending Cleofas requests to sign the agreement, but he disappeared for a while, saving the town a considerable sum in contributions.

In these cases, it again appeared that oral interpretation provided whatever force written proposals and commitments acquired. At certain moments of the negotiation process, agreements were fixed in writing. However, further negotiating could affect actual compliance with these written agreements. Furthermore, the power of writing was limited, and could be effectively countered by action, persuasion, or even passing time. Underlying the power of writing, we find another form of negotiation that rests upon oral strategies and actions. In this sphere, not signing a written agreement was often the means of limiting the force of those in power.

Litigation

One of the principal contexts for the use of writing in the Tlaxcalan region for centuries has been litigation. In this densely populated region, conflicts between individuals, families, or villages were constant, and the parties often resorted to the judicial system for redress of grievances. Many cases involved conflicts over land. Claims were backed by an array of maps and written documents. In different contexts, Cleofas mentioned such things as deeds or land grants dating from various periods, forestry permits, wills, tenancy rights, tax slips, sales contracts, and handwritten receipts. During the late colonial times, fictitious titles (called *títulos primordiales*, see Lockhart, 1992) were drawn up by villagers, in order to back up claims with reference to ancient rights or decrees, and some continued to be used. The written claims were rarely clear-cut, however. In the final judicial outcome, actual possession and usufruct of land were the strongest elements to be considered, and sometimes even took legal priority over documented claims. However, proof of possession also involved producing such written documents as testimonies of continual use of the plot, and written agreements with neighbors regarding boundaries. For any of these documents to be of use, they had to be presented in court.

Cleofas had several stories involving the use of writing in litigation. He was fond of retelling one case in which he was the accused party. When the village assembly appointed him *agente*, it entrusted him with creating a central square, bordered with wide streets, for Xaltipan. This had been planned and disputed for years, as all villages aspiring to become a proper *pueblo*, it was believed, needed a central square. However, the project would affect the interests of several *vecinos*, as it required expropriating several parcels of land that surrounded the church and schoolhouse. As a result, Cleofas had to face legal charges filed by the owners.

His versions of the trial underscored the particular way in which oral argumentation and uses of literacy were involved in his defense. For example, his advisor had counseled him: "Never interrupt or contradict a judge, or you will be considered a novice, wait your turn and listen, so you can figure out how to reply." So, he claims, he would listen until the end and then ask permission to put forward his case; he would then give his own explanations of the legal basis of his actions. For example, he would explain that he had "the right to expropriate land, and the plaintiffs had to donate land to the public good of the town, as the Constitution states." He also produced the minutes of the assembly in which villagers had asked to go ahead with the plan. By following the advisor's indications as to the proper manner of presenting his case in the oral hearing, he was able to convince the judge of his case.

Another case involved a conflict with several persons who presumed to be owners of the lot to be purchased for the secondary school. In retelling it, Cleofas contrasted the actions of two lawyers assigned to the case. The first one never gave him any papers; therefore, Cleofas argues, he sought a second lawyer. A settlement was possible only when this lawyer actually allowed him to see the files and have copies of all the documents involved, at each step of the process. Cleofas clearly saw the possession of these documents as a means of empowerment, and as a way of keeping tabs on the lawyer. This is particularly true in his case, as he was wise in the ways of the bureaucracy, though not versed in legal language. He changed his relationship to the legal process by having the documents, even though he did not engage in specific acts of reading or writing during the trial.

Cleofas told me about other cases, including one involving a kidnapping. A woman of Xaltipan (suspected of being a sorceress) had convinced her *comadre*[4] to let her 10–year-old godchild go work in the city with a couple (Cleofas described the interaction and all actors involved in great detail). As it turned out, the couple took the girl to Austria and trained her to act in pornographic films. When the local police, tipped off by Austrian investigators, came to inquire, Cleofas gave further proof of the evil character of the woman who had taken the girl from her home. To back up his claims, he showed them a news clipping reporting the lawsuit he had brought against the same woman for stealing his animals, some 20 years before. Cleofas urged the dubious investigators to look up her police record: "It would have to be there, and they found it." While telling me of this incident, he asked his daughter to retrieve from the wardrobe another newspaper (yellow, torn, and taped). This local paper had reported the kidnapping and eventual recovery of the girl. Cleofas showed it to me as documentary evidence backing up a story I was finding incredible.

Conversation

The sort of narratives that appear in everyday conversation, *plática*, have an important function in the maintenance of social relationships in Xaltipan. Unlike written stories, their development is co-constructed among speakers and they include a variety of rhetorical means aimed at maintaining interest and achieving credibility. One resource, which Cleofas is inclined to use, is reference to written documents.[5]

When I first showed Cleofas some files on the founding of the Xaltipan school, which I had recovered from the state archives, I asked him about an incident of violence mentioned in one of the inspector's reports from the 1930s. I told him that the documents claimed that a group of bandits had burned the school and stolen the construction funds from the local authority. Cleofas looked over the document, and noted the date. He then commented: "yes, this is true." Then he continued, relaying a long story that his mother had told him in Mexicano, years before. The incident had involved a band of brothers, belonging to a reactionary political movement, who assaulted the school committee president, stole the money, and set fire to the new building. When villagers complained, a soldier was sent to look into the situation. Cleofas described the grim details of how the soldier was killed and carried away by the band. This account had many of the characteristics that make for a good story in the region, such as repetition and detail. At times Cleofas would hesitate, searching his memory for a name, yet he never suspended the narrative flow of the event.

Cleofas's interest in the documents increased as he began to identify signatures, and to comment on the public actions of each person involved. He then asked for copies of the file, explaining that they would be useful for *plática*, whenever he might have occasion to speak of past events: "Because we often tell these histories, but with no grounds." Reference to the written version would allow him to back up the story (*darle fundamentos*), particularly if the documents came from archives. However, Cleofas himself told stories only of situations that he had witnessed, or that had been orally relayed to him by others. He never seemed to take his tales from written sources although he had a small collection of textbooks and history books; he was interested rather in documents that backed up those incidents with which he was already familiar.

In other stories, Cleofas had likewise mentioned books. He referred to them as specific copies that he owned or had located in certain places. Nevertheless, his narratives did not reproduce a "bookish knowledge" of Mexican history, in the way that the local teachers tended to do. He was not one to consult the small local library that he himself had helped establish for the town's students. Thus, the search for *fundamentos* may have indicated a need to legitimize oral accounts in a world that was increasingly questioning their validity.

From this perspective, writing was thus not only embedded in orality, but was also used to produce oral conversation. This passage of contents from literate culture to oral tradition has been documented for other places (Fabre, 1993a) and merits attention in a field where the reverse relationship, the transition for oral to literate, has been favored. The process is consistent with a local meaning of the term *publication*. Several persons in the region mentioned that they had "published" a text or verse they had written, meaning they had read it at a public event, or on a radio program. In this sense, only oral presentation actually makes a text "public," as was true in Europe well into the eighteenth century. This association of the oral with the public domain makes one aware of the relatively "private" nature of much reading and writing. In fact, as I read my notes on some of these conversations, I thought it ironic that I would take information transmitted orally and transform it into the limited genre of the essay, while Cleofas would take writing, often of a restricted sort, and transform it into the elaborate mode of story-telling, conversational narrative, *plática*.

Within this view, *plática* seemed to be valued over reading. Not only was oral mediation necessary to make papers "talk"; it was also the preferred mode of transmission. Likewise, memory was recognized as the greater skill, in both work and conversation. Orality seemed to have other advantages over writing. In many of the tales, documents and books were perishable objects. For example, at least three times, Cleofas mentioned that notable books had been stolen or destroyed (the nineteenth-century Constitution and two books on sorcery). He generally assumed (rightly perhaps) that papers would disappear, unless guarded in an official archive, such as the one at the parochial church at San Bernardino. Even then, documents preserved in archives as such had little social consequence, unless someone actually found them. In the final analysis, in Xaltipan, as elsewhere, people had to rely on memory to recall documents of the past and use oral strategies to bring them out into the light. The permanence associated with writing was valued more as proof of present claims than as preservation of forgotten matters.

Retracing the Argument: From Cleofas to the Academic Debate

I have attempted to convey some of the meanings of literacy as represented in accounts of social practices in Xaltipan, Tlaxcala. My documentation is constructed primarily from my notes on stories embedded in the ongoing conversation with one resident, Cleofas, and reflect his own experience with literacy. My reading of current writings on literacy obviously led me to select certain arguments. Nevertheless, what emerges from this interpretation of a local interpretation is a view of literacy that I believe addresses current academic debates.

Over a span of 40 years, and after finishing third grade, Cleofas had become quite capable of dealing with the bureaucratic world of writing in the ongoing negotiation for obtaining public services on the best possible terms, as well as spotting relevant uses of written documents for many everyday situations. In Cleofas's tales, literacy appears as a resource to be used, or actively not used, for persuasion, negotiation, litigation, or simply for conversation. Written texts acquire persuasive power in situations where an individual must confront natural or human forces, such as a hailstorm or disorderly public behavior. They are deftly used to increase chances for personal and public benefit through negotiation. In litigation, they become a means for proving contending claims and for pressing charges. They corroborate stories told while conversing, particularly with those of us too incredulous to take oral tradition at its face value.

As one listens to these tales, however, it becomes evident that the written documents are always seen as embedded in oral performance. They have no efficacy on their own. The ritual invocation of the hailstorm, and the stern warning to misbehaving youths, add weight to the volumes used to command authority. A written petition plays an important part in dealing with government officials, only if it is presented and used at an opportune moment in the ongoing oral negotiation. In stating one's case or in telling a good tale, mastery of the proper oral genres and the timing of one's intervention render reference to a written precedent credible. We thus face a world in which a dichotomous conception of orality and literacy is of little use. If, following Chartier (1995), we regard the performances described in these tales as cultural practices, and examine the ways in which oral performances mediate the uses of the written word, we might approach the social efficacy of literacy from a different vantage point altogether.

This interpretation recovers the idea that literacy is "a mere upstart" (Havelock, 1991) within a world largely constructed and reproduced through oral practice. In Xaltipan, writing seemed of little use for the everyday tasks of living and working, but it was readily employed for dealing with city life and trade. In the tales I have retold, many cognitive processes seen by proponents of the strong view as "consequences of literacy," seemed quite securely contained in oral language. Knowledge of distant places and of past times, memory of recurrent patterns and processes, and reflective or anticipatory thought were all strongly linked to oral skills, even though the tools of literacy were readily available. On the other hand, a skillful use of the documentary requisites of the bureaucratic world, coupled with oral strategies, had been essential to construct and preserve the town's relative autonomy. It is in these situations that literacy takes on its just proportions.

This representation of literacy contains references that are no doubt specific to the cultural context. Nevertheless, I would argue that it is not as "exotic" as the ethnographic mode might make it out to be. Though as scholars we do not resort to sorcery, nor have we fought for land, the view of literacy I see in Cleofas's stories might allow us to take a second look at our own familiar world. Even some of our academic practices might be closer to those described in Xaltipan, than they are to idealized notions of "essayist literacy." For example, many of us have had the experience of being overpowered by a book, or have used references to documents as an oral strategy, for gain or consent. We too must rely on socially constructed memory to recall documents from the past and use them to back present-day claims. In the academic world as well, it is often oral presentation that renders written discourse persuasive, or even intelligible. Thus, I am suggesting that it is necessary to integrate the analysis of oral performance and the uses of written texts, as cultural practices, when studying any context, even those marked by tradition.

Notes

This chapter is a modified version of a paper which appeared in *Cultural Dynamics* 5(2) (1992): 156–75 (published by E. J. Brill).

1   Substantial parts of this chapter were previously published in my article "Tales from Xaltipan: Documenting orality and literacy in rural Mexico," *Cultural Dynamics* 5(2), 1992. The original version was presented as a paper at the I Sociocultural Research Conference, Madrid, 1992, and published in the conference proceedings (*Explorations in Socio-Cultural Studies*, vol. 3, eds. J. Wertsch and J. D. Ramírez, Fundación Infancia y Aprendizaje, 1994). Research was supported by my institution and Conacyt Grant no. 211–085–5–1377.

2   I do not reproduce his tales verbatim, as only a few were taped. Some of the initial interviews were recorded by myself or by my colleague, Ruth Mercado. The rest of the stories were embedded in ongoing conversations that precluded the use of a recorder. These, I later translated into my own rather restricted (in time and space) written mode, the particular genre of ethnographic field notes, with considerable violence to phrasing and sequence. Thus, I do not pretend to represent Cleofas's versions directly. My own account of this field experience evolved slowly, as comprehension and trust grew over time, and as I reflected upon my own academic concerns. In this paper, I have further condensed my field notes.

3   Significantly, Cleofas used the verb *escribir* (to write) rather than *inscribir* (to sign up), in this context.
4   Being a *comadre* is a relationship formed by the system of ritual kinship, based on becoming a *madrina*, or godparent, of someone's child at his/her baptism, graduation, or wedding. It entails strong reciprocal obligations between parents and godparents.
5   Other elderly informants, including some who were not literate, also used this practice in retelling legends that circulate in central Tlaxcala. They referred to versions found in books as being most accurate, although they do not reproduce them literally.

References

Barton, D. (1994). *Literacy: An introduction to the ecology of written language*. Oxford: Blackwell.
Bauman, R. (1977). *Verbal Art as Performance*. Prospect Heights, Ill.: Waveland.
Bloch, M. (1998). *How We Think They Think*. Boulder, Colo.: Westview.
Boyarin, J. (ed.) (1992). *The Ethnography of Reading*. Berkeley: University of California Press.
Briggs, C. (1988). *Competence in Performance: The creativity of tradition in Mexicano verbal art*. Philadelphia: University of Pennsylvania Press.
Bruner, J. (1996). *The Culture of Education*. Cambridge, Mass.: Harvard University Press.
Chartier, A. and Hébrard, J. (1994). Lire pour écrire là l'école primaire. L'invention de la composition française dans l'école du XIXe siècle. In Y. Reuter (ed.), *Les interactions lecture-écriture*. New York: Peter Lang.
Chartier, R. (1995). *Forms and Meanings: Texts, performances and audiences from codex to computer*. Philadelphia: University of Pennsylvania Press.
Cole, M. (1996). *Cultural Psychology: A once and future discipline*. Cambridge, Mass.: Harvard University Press.
Davis, N. Z. (1975). Printing and the people. In *Society and Culture in Early Modern France*. Stanford: Stanford University Press.
Fabre, D. (dir.) (1993a). *Ecritures ordinaires*. Paris: Editions POL, Bibliothèque Georges Pompidou.
Fabre, D. (1993b). Le Berger des Signes. In D. Fabre (dir.), *Ecritures ordinaires*. Paris: Editions POL, Bibliothèque Georges Pompidou.
Farr, M. (1993). Essayist literacy and other verbal performances. *Written Communication*, 10(1): 4–38.
Feldman, C. F. (1991). Rational thought in oral culture and literate decontextualization. In D. Olson and N. Torrance (eds.), *Literacy and Orality*. Cambridge: Cambridge University Press.
Finnegan, R. (1988). *Literacy and Orality*. Oxford: Blackwell.
Furet, F. and Ozouf, J. (1982). *Reading and Writing: Literacy in France from Calvin to Jules Ferry*. Cambridge: Cambridge University Press.
Gee, J. P. (1990). *Social Linguistics and Literacies: Ideology in discourses*. New York: Falmer Press.
Goody, J. (1982). Alternative paths to knowledges in oral and literate cultures. In D. Tannen (ed.), *Spoken and Written Language: Exploring orality and literacy*. Norwood, NJ: Ablex.

Goody, J. (1986). *The Logic of Writing and the Organization of Society*. Cambridge: Cambridge University Press.

Graff, H. (ed.) (1981). *Literacy and Social Development in the West*. Cambridge: Cambridge University Press.

Gruzinski, S. (1991). *La colonización de lo imaginario. Sociedad indígenas y occidentalización en el México español Siglos XVI–XVIII*. Mexico: Fondo de Cultura Económica.

Havelock, E. (1991). The oral–literate equation: A formula for the modern mind. In D. Olson and N. Torrance (eds.), *Literacy and Orality*. Cambridge: Cambridge University Press.

Heath, S. B. (1982). Protean shapes in literacy events: Evershifting oral and literate traditions. In D. Tannen (ed.), *Spoken and Written Language: Exploring orality and literacy*. Norwood, NJ: Ablex.

Hill, J. H. and Hill, K. C. (1986). *Speaking Mexicano: Dynamics of syncretic language in central Mexico*. Tucson: University of Arizona Press.

Hornberger, N. H. (ed.) (1997). *Indigenous Literacies in the Americas*. New York: Mouton de Gruyter.

Justice, S. (1994). *Writing and Rebellion: England in 1381*. Berkeley: University of California Press.

Kartunnen, F. (1998). Indigenous writing as a vehicle of postconquest continuity and change in Mesoamerica. In E. H. Boone and T. Cummins (eds.), *Native Traditions in the Post-conquest World*. Washington, DC: Dumbarton Oaks Research Library and Collection.

León-Portilla, M. (1996). *Los Manifiestos en Náhuatl de Emiliano Zapata*. Mexico: Universidad Nacional Autónoma de México.

Lockhart, J. (1992). *The Nahuas after the Conquest*. Stanford: Stanford University Press.

Mercado, R. (1987). *La educación primaria gratuita, una lucha popular cotidiana*. Mexico: Departamento de Investigaciones Educativas, Cinvestav.

Olson, D. (1994). *The World on Paper: The conceptual and cognitive implications of writing and reading*. Cambridge: Cambridge University Press.

Olson, D. and Torrance, N. (eds.) (1991). *Literacy and Orality*. Cambridge: Cambridge University Press.

Pellicer, D. (1993). Oralidad y escritura de la literatura indígena: Una aproximación histórica. In C. Montemayor (ed.), *Situación actual y perspectivas de la literatura en lenguas indígenas*. Mexico: Conacult.

Pellicer, D. (1995). Qué crees?, por ahí dicen que… Narración conversacional en español-mazahua y en español lengua materna. In I. Munguía and J. Lema (eds.), *Serie de Investigaciones Linguisticas I*. Mexico: Universidad Autónoma Metropolitana, Ixtapalapa.

Rockwell, E. (1996). Keys to appropriation: Rural schooling in Mexico. In B. Levinson, D. Foley, and D. Holland (eds.), *The Cultural Production of the Educated Person: Critical ethnographies of schooling and local practice*. Albany: State University of New York Press

Saenger, P. (1997). Lire aux derniers siècles du Moyen Age. In G. Cavallo and R. Chartier (eds.), *Histoire de la lecture dans le monde occidental*. Paris: Seuil.

Scott, J. (1990). *Domination and the Arts of Resistance: Hidden transcripts*. New Haven: Yale University Press.

Scribner, S. and Cole, M. (1981). *The Psychology of Literacy*. Cambridge, Mass.: Harvard University Press.

Street, B. (1984). *Literacy in Theory and Practice*. Cambridge: Cambridge University Press.

Street, B. (ed.) (1996). *Cross-cultural Approaches to Literacy*. Cambridge: Cambridge University Press.

Tannen, D. (ed.) (1982). *Spoken and Written Language: Exploring orality and literacy*. Norwood, NJ: Ablex.

Tannen, D. (1989). *Talking Voices*. Cambridge: Cambridge University Press.

Thomas, R. (1989). *Oral Tradition and Written Record in Classical Athens*. Cambridge: Cambridge University Press.

c) Asian Case Studies

Chapter 13

Developing a Literate Tradition in Six Marginal Communities in the Philippines: Interrelations of Literacy, Education, and Social Development

Maria Luisa Canieso Doronila

Introduction

Two major implicit assumptions underlie current mass literacy campaigns and nonformal adult literacy programs. The first is that literacy results in a qualitative change in the thinking processes of individuals and leads to more "literate" practices; thus, the emphasis on literacy measures to determine individual literacy levels in the hope that individual literacy may be generalized to the population. The second is that literacy leads to development, not only in its socioeconomic aspects but also in its cultural aspects, including the development of a literate tradition. In both instances, the relation is assumed to be simple and straightforward.

In this chapter I will first show, on the basis of previous Philippine research (Bernardo et al., 1995), that it is not literacy in individuals which makes a difference in their thinking processes; it is their participation in community activities which have been altered because of the incorporation of literate practices in these activities. We will then describe six marginal Philippine community types at different stages in an ongoing process of social change and development, and analyze how these processes relate to the passage of these communities to a literate tradition.

In these two related discussions, we will attempt to show that there is indeed a close relation between literacy practice and development, but not in the simple formulation that literacy in individuals leads to development. In this relation, many other factors need to be considered of which the most important are: (1) the social organization of the community itself; (2) the processes of social change and development which are ongoing within that community; and (3) the inter-play in sociohistorical context among literacy, property relations, access to education, language choices, and relations between knowledge in the oral trad-ition and knowledge in the written tradition.

The passage of communities to a literate tradition may thus be conceptually defined as a series of interactive relations through time and within a given context between literacy practices and development processes. In this passage, various factors come into play, which factors help to determine the nature of the choices that people make with respect to both literate practice and develop-ment.

Some definitions

Two main concepts, literacy practice and development, used in this paper are briefly defined below.

The concept of *literacy practice* was advanced by Scibner and Cole (1978) as "the carrying out of goal-directed activities, using particular technologies and applying particular systems of knowledge." We operationalize practice into three interrelated elements assumed to operate not only at the level of the individual but, more importantly, at the level of the group or the community: (1) the set of activities; (2) the technology involved (e.g., a mechanical, electrical, electronic, or related equipment such as a weighing scale, or a process such as rice milling); and (3) the knowledge which guides and gives meaning to both, where knowledge is conceived to include facts, norms, skills, and values. In each of these three elements, the application of literate and numerate skills (in the sense of reading, writing, computing and measurement) is a matter of empirical observation, particularly in a situation like the Philippines where a whole range of community types exists: from oral, to mainly oral, with some practices carried out in writing, to communities with a predominantly written tradition. We need to reiterate at this point the salience of the activity itself (e.g., rice milling, vending in the market) in the investigation, and secondarily on how literacy skills enter or do not enter into these activities, to the point where it becomes or does not become part of the practice (Doronila, 1996).

We define *development* in this context as follows:

> Development is here viewed as a process of human development, a process of social transformation in which man/woman is both the subject and the object, and in which s/he participates at all levels of decision-making. Self-reliance is both a means and an end in this process. It is a process which starts with the release of creative energy, assumes equal access to and a rational use of resources by the poor and vulnerable groups, tends to eliminate the difference between mental and

> manual labour and uses the full range of technological choices available from other sources properly adapted. This kind of development is not only more humane but also represents a new man/woman, nature, technology mix. In the participatory process which results in growth, human development and equity are not trade-offs. (Wignaraja, 1991)

This definition of development is preferred because: (1) it places man/woman at the center of development; (2) it assumes his/her creative and powerful potential to participate meaningfully in the entire development process; and (3) it recognizes that social development must start with how people themselves respond to the forces which constrain or encourage social transformation. Given the heterogeneous character of Philippine society, the emphasis in this paper is on the development of a literate tradition in communities in the margins of economic and political life.

Contexts of the Literacy Situation in the Philippines

A brief historical sketch on the relations of property, literacy, language, and knowledge

Before the Spanish colonial period which began in the sixteenth century, Filipinos already had their own native script called *alibata* (alphabet).[1] Writing materials were bamboo, tree barks, leaves, and sometimes smooth stones, a sharp, pointed instrument called *sipol*, and ink from plants. This phonetic alphabet had 3 vowels and 14 consonants. Every consonant is understood to be followed by the vowel *a*. If a consonant has a mark on top, *a* becomes *i*; if the mark is at the bottom, *a* becomes *o* or *u*. A small *x* mark after a consonant means that it is pronounced without the vowel *a*. A big *X* at the end marks the end of a sentence. A vowel is written only if it is the initial letter of a word. A handful of tribal communities still know this script but do not generally use it. Figure 13.1 shows the Philippine *alibata*; a sample sentence written in this script is also given.

Spanish friars branded this alphabet as the "handiwork of the devil," burned a lot of written materials in the process, introduced the roman script and rendered whole populations illiterate in the new script. Various colonial decrees in the sixteenth and seventeenth centuries ordered the teaching of the Spanish language, but the powerful Spanish religious orders, who were in charge of the indoctrination of the Filipinos into Christianity and of what little education was offered, continuously defied these decrees and instead taught the Christian doctrine in the local languages using a romanized script (Corpuz, 1989). It may be argued that the deep roots of Catholicism in the country spring from the fact that Filipinos learned it in their own language, indigenizing it into "folk Catholicism" in the process.

Those who fled to the hills, refusing colonization, remained illiterate in the new script, although it must be said that many among those who remained did not become literate either, owing to the lack of schools and the prevailing pedagogy of the friars, which emphasized rote learning and memorization. Filipino Muslims in the south, earlier Islamized in the fourteenth century, learned Arabic to read the Koran and resisted Spanish colonization. To this day, they resist the writing of their local languages in the roman script. Tribes in the virtually inaccessible Cordillera mountains of the north also resisted Spanish colonization but were much later introduced to the roman script using English, largely taught by American Protestant missionaries.

When the Spaniards introduced the concept of private ownership of land (from a largely communal type of ownership), members of the *principalia* (native nobility who had earlier been co-opted to become collectors of tribute for the Spanish crown) were the first to recognize its value (Ofreneo, 1980). Being literate in both Spanish and in the native roman script was important for the land-titling process. Together with the friars and Spanish administrators, they started to accumulate large tracts of land at the expense of the actual tillers, many of whom were reduced to landless and debt-ridden share croppers (Ofreneo, 1980).

The children of the native elite had a chance to study in schools originally established for the children of the Spanish colonial administrators (*peninsulares*), learning Spanish and Western (European) knowledge in the process.

The arrival of the American colonizers in the late nineteenth century on the eve of the Philippine revolution against Spain, and their subsequent occupation of the Philippines after the Treaty of Paris, did not substantially change the country's agrarian structure. The elite who joined the masses in the revolution against Spain in the late nineteenth century reneged on their agreement to pursue agrarian reforms; instead, they were co-opted by the American colonial administration and were able to retain their landholdings. The agrarian structure continues to be the single most important issue in Philippine society, and the principal motivator of unrest.

The Americans established a more widespread mass education system in which English was used as the medium of instruction, using textbooks essentially derived from those in the United States. But the children of the elite, already proficient in Spanish, continue to study to this day in private sectarian schools of better quality, where they are not only exposed to Spanish (in some schools) but to better-quality English instruction and the knowledge content that goes with it. This is the reason why the elite in the Philippines are much more Westernized than the marginal community folk, much better educated, and generally proficient in English.

When policy-makers say that illiteracy is usually equated with poverty, the relation is essentially correct, but it is important to understand how people became both poor and illiterate in the first place. The relations among property, literacy in the roman script, the languages in which it is learned, the distribution of educational provision, and the knowledge accessible in a given language constitute the proper contexts for the understanding of literacy particularly in marginal Philippine communities.

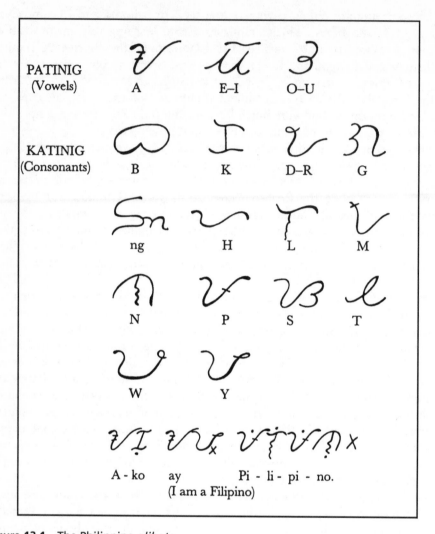

Figure 13.1   The Philippine *alibata*
Source: M. L. Doronila, *Landscapes of Literacy* (Hamburg: UNESCO Institute for Education, 1996); script by Vincent Angelo Doronila.

General description of the literacy, language, and education situation in the Philippines

The Philippine population of 65 million is divided into more than 80 ethnolinguistic groups of which the 8 major ethnolinguistic groups have populations ranging from 159,000 to 2.5 million households (*Philippine Almanac*, 1990). Urban poor groups, on the other hand, are generally multiethnic. The principal characteristics of these ethnolinguistic groups are: (1) a distinct language (however, all belonging to the Malayo-Polynesian linguistic family), and (2) occupancy of a distinct territory, region, or province. In the case of the Muslim

Filipinos in the Southern Philippines, there is a further distinction as between the Christian majority and the Muslim minority. The archipelagic nature of a country composed of 7,100 islands accentuates these distinctions, accounting, in part, for the regionalistic orientation of the population.

However, on account of the mass media, the constitutionally mandated national language, Filipino, generally based on Tagalog, has also become the lingua franca. The use of English in the formal education system since 1903 (American colonial period) has made it the language both of status and privilege, and remains the major language for government, the courts, higher education, business, and most of mass media.

At present, all subjects in public formal basic education are taught in Filipino except for science and mathematics which are taught in English. Not surprisingly, it is in these two subjects where Filipino students rate poorly, ranking in the bottom rungs of some recent international comparative studies in educational performance in science and mathematics.

In the Muslim areas, the local languages are written (in romanized script) and widely used in oral communication, but Arabic is the written language of the *madaris* (traditional Muslim community schools). Filipino tribal groups have their own languages (some not yet written), and those with access to mass media and the market need to understand and speak at least one other language (the dominant regional language) as well as Filipino and a smattering of English.

In the communities, the following printed types of material are generally available, except in Boheh Umos (community of sea nomads): (1) comic books for rent mainly in Filipino but some in English; (2) streamers, calendars, posters, billboards for advertisements, announcements, and political campaigns, in Filipino but some in English; (3) newspapers for sale, in English but some in Filipino or Cebuano in southern Philippines; (4) pocketbooks for rent, mainly in Filipino, some in English; (5) brochures and pamphlets from government agencies (e.g. soap-making, agricultural techniques); (6) the Koran for the Muslim communities in Arabic, more widespread than the Holy Bible (in English and some in Filipino) is in Christian communities; (7) textbooks if children are in school, in English or in Filipino according to the medium of instruction; and (8) magazines for rent especially on movie stars and entertainment, in Filipino and some in English. Other more specialized materials are found in schools, offices and government agencies, mostly in English. No reading centers were reported in any of the research sites. Radio is widespread and the most popular programs reported are on entertainment and news, mainly in Filipino. Television is generally not available except in more affluent homes but the same preference for entertainment and news is reported.

The relations among literacy in the roman script, property, knowledge, and access to formal education are thus historical roots of the prevailing importance attached to formal education as a vehicle for status and social mobility, and the small importance attached to nonformal/non-"voc-tech" adult education. As a result, Philippine education is characterized by a large formal education sector, in which mass public education at the primary level is relatively accessible to all with children attending school on average between 6 and 7 years. This has a direct consequence on the basic literacy rate which in 1994 was 93 percent, one of the highest in the Asia-Pacific region. Thus in the Philippines, basic or simple literacy is a function of elementary school provision, and it is correct to assume that basic nonliterates are to be found mainly in marginal communities without schools.

However, this is only half the total picture; the other half has to do with the general performance of public elementary education, the relatively high drop-out rate, the problem of literacy retention and the much lower functional literacy rates. Functional literacy, as measured by a test may be used as a common reference seen across quite different communities. When we do so, as we shall see, it is as often as misleading as it is useful. A few observations will suffice to indicate the nature and magnitude of our problem on basic education and functional literacy.

First, there is a relatively large gap of 16 percent between basic and functional literacy rates, implying that those who learn the rudimentary skills of reading, writing, counting, and simple computation are not able to expand these skills to a point where they become functional and integral to their daily activities. Another explanation is possible: community activities do not require the use of these skills.

Second, in a comparative international study conducted by Anderson and Bowman (1965), while most countries show a positive correlation between functional literacy and GNP per capita, the Philippines was among the few countries registering a negative relation between the basic literacy rate, which is among the highest in the Asia-Pacific Region, and low economic growth as measured by GNP per capita. This finding not only corroborates the gap between basic and functional literacy rates, but also suggests that the kind of literacy and related skills imparted through adult education programs do not necessarily lead to development. Put in another way, it suggests that the relationship for example between literacy and the eradication of poverty is not simple and straightforward as is commonly supposed. At the very least, it implies (1) the need to teach skills beyond basic literacy, (2) that literacy teaching should be closely tied to poverty alleviation and social development programs, such as livelihood and income-generating activities, and (3) that these activities in order to be sustainable should integrate literacy and education into complete systems of productivity, marketing, and income generation.

A 1992 study (Cortes, 1992) concluded that basic formal education which includes literacy has not been able to impart the skills needed for work and productivity:

> The phenomenal growth and expansion of the Philippine school system appears to have made little change in the life of the large majority of the population 6 or 7 years and older whose highest educational attainment has not gone beyond elementary education. The general observation in the 1960s that the Philippines is a

nation of fifth graders who lack proficiency in the 3Rs and skills for gainful employment, was still true in the 1980s.

Access to educational opportunities and the distribution of effects and benefits derived from formal education are far from equitable. Those who have access to more resources are the more affluent communities or those with strong connections in government. The children who benefit most from formal education are those who belong to the upper-class or who reside in more economically developed regions. The same observation applies to access to quality education and benefits derived from such education.

And what of the drop-outs from this system, the children and adolescents from marginal communities who become adults, the eventual target participants of nonformal literacy and education programs? A composite profile of the drop-outs based on data from my previous study (Doronila, 1996) and on a 1983 study of literacy retention done by the Department of Education on two large national samples (N = 8,009 and 1,420) is given below:

> Four out of every 5 drop-outs left school between grades 3 and 5, with the highest frequency at grade 4, owing to poverty, incomplete elementary schools (up to grade 4 only), distance of the school from the house, and migration. About 16 out of 100 of these drop-outs increased their literacy skills from work or other community experience for an equivalent of 2 to 5 grades higher, while the rest (84) retrogressed in their knowledge and skills by an equivalent of two grade levels. Of the three academic subjects tested (Filipino, English and Mathematics), English had the most losers.
>
> The general probability for a drop-out to retrogress is present whatever grade level s/he drops out from; however, the possibility for retrogression is higher if s/he drops out at grade 3 or below. In my 1996 study, when drop-outs were asked what literacy skills they have retained, their answers ranged from nothing or about nothing, to writing their names, reading, basic addition and subtraction, counting up to 100, some English words, some school poems and songs, some national heroes, some stories.

Those who said they have forgotten skills they learned in school cite the following reasons: (1) lack of opportunity to use skills learned in school in their daily lives or activities, (2) lack of reading materials and opportunities for writing, (3) lack of access and exposure to media especially print, (4) no opportunity to attend nonformal literacy training because of work, a problem particularly true for married women.

On the other hand, drop-outs who did not revert to illiteracy ascribe their retention of literacy skills to: (1) involvement in community activities where literacy skills are practiced and new ones are learned, (2) application of skills learned in school to work and daily activities, and (3) the need to learn new skills because their work and other community activities require these.

The reasons for retention of literacy skills learned in school by drop-outs are reiterated by those who acquired literacy on their own.

In my previous study (Doronila, 1996), efforts were exerted to find individuals who learned to read and write on their own. It is significant that all of them learned these skills originally in the home language or in Filipino, and that none of them have reverted to illiteracy. Some of their stories follow.

Vignette no. 1
A 46–year-old laborer in Alaga, Iloilo, Mang Carding learned basic literacy and numeracy skills on the job. He wanted to go to school but was not allowed to do so because of work. As it was, he found it difficult to learn on his own. He says, "*Mahirap makaintindi agad. Mahirap magkuwenta ng pera pati mga bagay na binibilang at sinusukat*" (It's difficult to comprehend things. It's also difficult to count money and measure things). This difficulty was offset, however, by his strong desire to learn. Now, he is able to apply his acquired skills in carpentry and other household chores, in his buy-and-sell business (banana and firewood), and in doing mechanical repairs. With his children's help, he is able to continue to improve his literacy skills.

Vignette no. 2
Early marriage and child-rearing responsibilities prevented Aling Rita of Magdalena from going to school. But she was able to learn the basic literacy and numeracy skills on her own and to improve these with the help of her children. She explains that at home, she practices reading and writing through comic books. She learned to compute and use these skills in counting her wages as a laundry-woman and determining the amount to be paid for her debts plus interest. The primary advantage she ascribes to being literate and numerate is: "*Matutong makatulong sa sarili at matutong makisama sa kapwa tao at sa lahat ng bagay*" (Ability to help oneself, to adapt to others and to all things).

Vignette no. 3
Ka Ferning from Corona is the present director of the communication program of the multisectoral people's organization in Corona. In his position, he is in charge of research, documentation of seminars, and production of the newsletter. He finished grade 2 but left school without learning to read and write. He had to work for his uncle by tending carabaos (water buffaloes). Sometimes, he would pass by the school and outside the window he would copy some words being taught to the schoolchildren and then practise reading and writing them at home. His mother taught him how to count and compute. When he joined the people's organization, he was forced to learn to read faster and understand more complex material so he could participate in the discussions. His skills greatly increased when he became a contributor to the newsletter and finally director of the communication program.

Yet, beyond the questions of literacy retention and functional literacy, it is apparent that there is a qualitative difference in the development of the literate practice of Ka Ferning in vignette no. 3. In his story we sense a more dynamic and interactive relation between the development of his literacy skills and the increasing demands of the activities in which he participates. This interaction is

what we propose to examine further in this paper. But first we need to understand the relation, if any, between simple literacy in individuals and their thinking processes.

Cognition and Literacy Practice

What happens to individuals who have become literate?

In the quasi-experimental study of the cognitive consequences of literacy in five
Filipino communities, Bernardo et al. (1995) found no reliable differences
between literates and illiterates. They assessed the direct effects of literacy on
thought by comparing performances of illiterate, nonformal literate (those who
learned to read and write in adult nonformal education programs), and formal
literate (those who learned to read and write in formal school) in the five
different communities. There was no systematic difference among the performances of the illiterate, nonformal and formal literate participants in conceptual
understanding, conceptual organization, or deductive reasoning.

In an explanation task, they found that formal literates were more likely to
provide complete or even fragmentary explanations for given events than the
illiterates and nonformal literates. Since the nonformal literates did not demonstrate similar patterns of performance the effect cannot be attributed to simply
learning to read and write but rather learning to use literacy in a particular
academic way associated with schooling.

On the other hand there were several indirect effects of literacy on thought.
These effects were mediated by the degree to which literacy skills have been
integrated into community activities and practices. That is, communities with a
relatively higher degree of literacy integration demonstrated different cognitive
approaches to a variety of tasks but only for those strategies and skills that were
associated with the community practices incorporated in those literacy skills. To
illustrate, it was found that the residents of Cardona incorporated literacy skills
into such activities as community training seminars, discussion groups, and so
on. These activities led to a deeper conceptual analysis of people's experiences, to
recognize the structural similarities, and to identify structurally-relevant differences among concepts. These literacy-based discussions also encouraged logical
reasoning that is sensitive to the contextual realities of the reasoning problem
and the use of more context-sensitive logical reasoning strategies.

The authors noted that these are mediated effects. That is, they are brought
about by participating in the activities of a literate community, here, they affect
even the illiterate members of the community. The importance of these community activities is shown by the fact that differences in thinking were greater across
the five communities than the differences brought about by literacy within a
community.

In a somewhat comparable ethnographic study of literacy practices in
the Philippines, Doronila (1996) found that an important determinant of the

sustainability of nonformal literacy programs and of literacy skills in a community was the extent to which literacy skills have become integrated into other community practices. The study revealed that literacy had an effect on thinking but only in communities that have a relatively higher degree of literacy integration.

Further, the study showed that the cognitive consequences of literacy are specific to particular cognitive skills. Consistent with Scribner and Cole (1983) they regard literacy as a practice which develops only those cognitive skills that relate to that literacy practice. They modify and extend Scribner and Cole's position to accommodate the variable identified as degree of literacy integration into community activities. Like Scribner and Cole they concluded that literacy has no global effect on thought, but rather affects only those thinking skills that are associated with the community practices that have incorporated literacy skills.

In the strictest sense, therefore, the effects were not literacy effects but mediated effects. They were effects of the activities that were altered in character because of the incorporation of literacy skills into a community practice. The incorporation of literacy practices in a community activity changed its very nature. This new approach gave rise to new or modified cognitive skills for engaging in the activities. As a consequence, the changes brought about were not limited to those who were literate. Instead, the effects could be found even among the illiterates who took part in these community activities. These communities bear some relation to the "textual communities" described by Stock (1990) in his analysis of the role of literacy in Medieval Europe.

Thus, the community becomes an important unit in understanding the development of literacy and of the cognitive functions that are affected by literacy skills. It would not be adequate, therefore, merely to speak of literate individuals; rather one must speak of literate communities.

Communities are not to be seen as literate or not on the basis of a head count or a measure of the proportion of the population that can demonstrate literacy skills. Instead, "it would be more appropriate to consider literate communities as those that have incorporated literacy practices into the central community activities" (Bernardo et al., 1995, p. 126). In such literate communities, the literate practices would have transformed the character of the community activities and the manner in which people think about and engage in these activities.

The most literate communities in the world do not only differ from other communities in terms of the number of literate individuals in their population. Instead, in highly literate communities, literate practices are integral to community life. The most basic forms of employment, communication, business and trade, social interactions, religious activities, political exercises, cultural practices, transportation, entertainment, education, scholarship, all involve literacy practices. In such communities, a literate tradition has developed as part of the people's daily lives. How does this tradition develop?

In the next section, we will describe six marginal Philippine community types at different stages of their passage towards a literate tradition. The data are drawn from my previous study on adult and functional literacy (Doronila, 1996).

Developing a Literate Tradition in Six Marginal Community Types

Preliminary typology of marginal Philippine communities

A brief sketch will suffice to suggest the heterogeneity of Philippine life even in marginalized communities, keeping in mind that regardless of other consider-ations, the common characteristic of these communities is the fact of their marginality with average incomes below the poverty threshold. Current statistics based on the 1991 Family Income and Expenditure Survey (FIES Official Survey) show that in all, 8.98 million families (77.12 percent) live below the poverty threshold, out of a total of 10.7 million families in the Philippines. They differ, however, in major livelihood-economic activity whether fishing, farming, or urban poor, ethnolinguistic groupings, majority–minority relations, and general lifestyle or rhythm of life in the community.

A fourth and new category of marginalized communities is the refugee/reset-tlement type, such as those more or less permanently affected by the Pinatubo eruption. Less permanent are evacuation centers for victims of other natural and manmade calamities such as minor volcanic eruptions, floods, typhoons, and hamletting of populations due to military-rebel operations.

In terms of general lifestyle or rhythm of life, marginal Philippine communities would range from traditional or "whole" cultures to organized communities practicing a relatively modern version of participatory democracy. In this chapter, six widely scattered marginal communities which differ in terms of general lifestyle or rhythm of life are described to show how these cultural factors affect the development of a literate tradition. Following, the ethno-graphic convention, all names of communities are fictitious; the names of the provinces are real.

A traditional oral community of sea nomads: the Sama of Boheh Umos

The first community type (here represented by the Sama community of Boheh Umos, a community of sea nomads) is a traditional, mainly oral community characterized by wholeness and integration of traditional knowledge accessible to all, and a form of social organization characterized by equity, communalism, and people's participation in community life.[2] The metaphors for community life all carry the same meaning: the *pehak* or fish gonad, eggs tightly packed together and covered with a protective membrane; the *komkoman* or handgrip, this metaphor also physically expressed in the cluster housing pattern on the strand and called by the same name; the injunction "what I eat is what you eat." The

Boheh Umos metaphors are static, and these too explain in part the continuity of the community social organization from antiquity to the present. A whole village of sea nomads can disappear in the face of an external threat, but the community survives because the members remain together; the sea in their parts is still bountiful; and the *komkoman* or the community cluster on the strand is readily transformed into the social organization of the *munda'an*, a sea-going community organized for escape or a fishing expedition, its rules known to all.

Such a community has its share of difficulties born out of a marginal existence, but with little contradiction between knowledge and practice. As expressed by some of my Sama respondents: "What we know is how we live." Knowledge and practice are one and the same. In due course, the young Sama takes up adult roles under conditions of competence acquired through practice, personal obligation, equity and participation.

The wise man is one whose previous experience, knowledge and meditation have earned him the right to be consulted; the leader of the fishing expedition is elected by consensus based on physical prowess, knowledge of navigation and climatology, good leadership abilities, reputation and conduct. Since everyone knows the requirements of the voyage and the implications of a successful fishing expedition for community survival, the leader is chosen wisely by everyone.

When the catch comes in, everyone gets the same share, and voluntary deductions are decided on, again by consensus, for additional amounts to the leader and to those who contributed the use of a sail or a gas lamp or a boat for the expedition. The whole process of distribution is transparent to all, as well as precise in computation, with recourse to an objective third party, the Chinese *sukih* (partner-capitalist of the expedition) and his abacus, are regarded as the final judge of the arithmetic computations, which have the potential to create divisiveness and tension within the tightly knit community.

Literacy (in the sense of reading and writing) and literate practice are nil or absent, but it is not correct to consider the Sama illiterate, since their lore and their knowledge suffice for the life they live.

Tawi-Tawi where Boheh Umos is located, has a reported 34 percent functional literacy rate (NSO/FLEMMS, 1989), the second lowest in the country. But surely this does not capture the Samas' elaborate knowledge of the sea, encoded in the oral mode, and of the values of loyalty to community, wise choice of leaders, a sense of personal obligation and responsibility for the common good, equity and participation. The Sama of Boheh Umos experience no anxiety over their nonliteracy (in the sense of reading and writing). Significantly, the necessity to read and write comes only when the Sama need to relate to people outside the *komkoman*. Thus, the expressed need for literacy in order not to be taken advantage of by those not belonging to the *pehak*. Letters which occasionally come to Boheh Umos are read and answered by any one who happens to be literate, and no embarrassment accompanies this request since it is everywhere understood that this knowledge is "of the outside," not of the *pehak*.

In this community, oriented to itself and organized for escape from potentially disruptive outside elements, there is virtually no encounter between literate practice and social change or development. Indeed, Sama nomadic communities in their present social organization are similarly described in ancient Chinese historical records (Han, 1997), attesting to the continuity of their oral and communal tradition.

Two transitional communities: the rice-terracing Ifugao of Kala and the Bukidnon of Alaga

The second type of marginal community may be termed transitional, having some relations with the market and with the lowland majority, as well as limited exposure to mass media and formal education. Yet, significant aspects of the traditional culture remain, particularly in the system of production, even as younger generations, exposed to formal education, exhibit some doubt or anxiety about these practices. This community type is here represented by two tribal communities: the Ifugao of Kala and the Bukidnon of Alaga in Iloilo.

The Ifugao of Kala

The Ifugao of Kala have practiced extensive and sophisticated rice-terracing agriculture involving engineering and irrigation technology since precolonial times. Ownership of the *payew* (rice terraces) is with families, but in order to construct and maintain these terraces which form an integrated system, communal work is required. Those who do not wish to join the communal work are left alone, but this does not usually happen precisely because of the integrated system. The communality of their social organization is dictated by this requirement, and relatively ensured by reference to common ancestry, rituals, beliefs, rules on property relations (e.g. the sale of *payew* to non-community members is sanctioned).

The Ifugao and other tribes of the Cordillera successfully resisted Spanish colonial rule for almost three centuries but were finally brought into the national framework by the American colonial administration, mainly through the public school system and the American Protestant missionaries.

There is an incomplete public school (up to grade four) where young Ifugaos learn to read and write, either in English or Filipino, but not in their home language, using content that has generally little or nothing to do with their real lives. Much of these will be about Manila, or the lowlands, or lands abroad. Math and science would be taught in English, further intensifying their separation from Ifugao reality, without reference to the science and technology behind their rice-terracing agriculture or to the algebraic complexity of their music and weaving patterns. Indeed, very little, if at all, of their traditional knowledge has been encoded in the written mode.

If they have converted to Christianity, some Bible reading would be done, especially by Protestants, but Catholics who are usually not Bible readers, would be more interested in reciting prayers and learning catechism. Local government is present in the persons of *barangay* (smallest unit of local government) officials whose secular functions are distinct from those of the tribal leaders and ritualists.

It is reported that Ifugao has a 47 percent functional literacy rate (NSO/ FLEMMS, 1989), one of the lowest in the country. But surely this takes no account of their own capacity to maintain, through community discipline and participation, an elaborate system of rice-terracing agriculture, whose symmetry and technical precision are almost never discussed in Ifugao or other schools.

According to a recent study, the Ifugaos follow at least 24 steps in rice terrace construction, with corresponding agricultural calendar, labor organization, tools, rituals, and explanations of the practices (Cariño et al., 1994). The Cordillera rice-terracing agricultural system has been identified by UNESCO as a great cultural achievement and a world heritage. The people's communality and participation, commonality of interest, and complete understanding of the technology transmitted in the home language regulate discipline and cooperative work.

It is nevertheless true that population growth has severely limited the capacity of this agricultural production system to feed its tillers, and therefore some of my respondents have expressed interest in new improvements in rice technology. Information on these are not generally available, however, and if so, are accessible only in English. This development presents an opportunity for the integration of traditional and literate knowledge, but the problem of "fit" remains. As Bonifacio (1994) has pointed out:

> If the interest is really to find the "fit" between innovation and farmers' practice, the conceptual framework will have to be different. Basically, a program of technology transfer must depart from the premise that the technology to be transferred is necessarily superior to the old method and that the tradition of farmers will have to be transformed. Instead, the approach must deliberately and judiciously map out all the technologies being used in the production systems. Once this is done, the question to be addressed is how the technical resources of the production systems can be improved, with emphasis on improvement and not on change.

Some young people growing up in Kala experience a conflict in values and beliefs precisely because traditional and literate knowledge have not been integrated (with the former being consistently undervalued, particularly in school texts) and because of contact with people from urbanized and more affluent areas. Still, it seems that the Ifugao are able to hold on to their traditional knowledge encoded in the oral mode particularly because it encompasses a significant portion of their productive life and activities.

Some changes have been introduced in Kala, and it will be noted that the direction of the accommodation, such as in the establishment of cooperatives, is towards the traditional values of communality, participation, and organization for work.

Literacy practice in Kala corresponds to the general line of development in the area. Their rice-terracing system of production, transmitted to the young in the oral tradition, remains intact except in a few places where the introduction of vegetable production of the temperate varieties (cash crops such as cabbage, carrots, broccoli) has required literate practice.

With the penetration of the national political system, the main lines of change have been through participation in elections and in the courts. However, it should be noted that the lines of "expertise" between the local government officials (barangay captain) and the *mumbaki* (wise men/ritualists) are clearly drawn. The *mumbaki's* expertise is in conflict resolution and rituals related to sickness and death, rice production, ritual feasts, marriage, and house building (note that the seasons for marriage and house building are part of the agricultural calendar). All of these are encoded in the oral mode.

On the other hand, the barangay captain's expertise is on matters related to government (taxes, local courts) and during national disasters such as earthquakes during which he relates to provincial government relief agencies. These transactions are encoded in the written mode.

In general, it is fair to say that: (1) traditional knowledge centered on the practice of rice-terracing agriculture which is very important to their economic and social life remains relatively whole and oral; (2) literate knowledge learned in school has almost no function in these activities, although literate knowledge associated with the courts is slowly being integrated with traditional knowledge; (3) literate practice remains very limited; and 4) mutual enrichment of traditional and literate knowledge is very slow on account of the discontinuity of literate practice.

Thus, Kala generally holds on to its traditional knowledge, especially of rice-terracing agriculture, in the oral mode, whose survival is relatively well ensured because it is part of a whole sociocultural system where social organization, rituals, beliefs, and rules on property relations form a structure of support, even as the literate knowledge is limited and confined to elements peripheral to its agricultural system.

The Bukidnon of Alaga

In Alaga, the Bukidnon practice shifting *kaingin* (swidden) agriculture in a very marginal subsistence economy involving production of rice, corn, coffee, and banana, the latter two being raised as cash crops.

Apart from some common reference to local heroes and traditions, there appears to be no singular basis for community. Activities are not communal primarily because houses and swidden farms are dispersed and cultivated by single households. Part of the loss of identity is due to the change of names sometime in 1960 from archaic (*ligbok*, which carry their own commonly understood meanings) to Christianized (following Spanish colonial practice of having surnames whose first letter corresponds to that of the town). Continuity cannot be ensured by the precariousness of their lives as swidden farmers, while the absence of a strong basis for community explains the lack of capacity to start a process of change from within. Thus, all the change elements appear to be externally generated: development projects, some of which were abandoned in the Marcos–Aquino transition, the presence of the military and the rebels both of whom they fear, the recent establishment of a school. Development projects in the area have had no significant impact on literate knowledge because people have little or no participation in planning, implementing, and evaluating these projects.

Thus, aside from the difficulties of marginality, life in Alaga is fraught with problems, particularly: loss of identity as mentioned earlier, serious doubts about traditional knowledge, and a strong sense of dependence on external help.

It is usually argued that the mass education system enables otherwise diverse Philippine ethnolinguistic groups to develop a "national culture." But an examination of the elementary school textbooks will reveal the cultural and intellectual poverty of the content. With 25 percent of students dropping out at grade four (Congressional Commission on Education, vol. 1, 1993), it is difficult to be enthusiastic about the nature of this "national culture" that is being transmitted through the textbooks at the elementary level, especially when it makes people like the Bukidnon feel inferior about their own traditional knowledge, with only trivial poems like "Jack and Jill" to replace it.

The simple-mindedness of textbook content derives from the unexamined assumptions (a throwback to the low opinion of Filipinos by American colonial policy-makers (May, 1975)) of most curriculum writers (1) that when students enter school they know nothing; (2) that knowledge is that which is purveyed by the formal school; (3) that traditional knowledge in the oral mode is not knowledge, simply because it has not been translated to print; and (4) conversely, that whatever comes in print *is* knowledge, only to be received without the need for critical analysis. Indeed, all over the country, when we ask parents why they send their children to school, the answer is "to gain knowledge"; while those who have not gone to school are called *mangmang* (ignorant), a definition that the poor and illiterate themselves have unfortunately accepted.

The functional literacy rate for Iloilo (NSO/FLEMMS, 1989) is 64 percent, but this is not reflected in Alaga where reading and writing are not widespread for lack of materials as well as demands and opportunities for writing. However, numeracy skills particularly oral computation, are relatively high, given the community folks' participation, if limited, in the market economy. Where modern concepts of measurement are understood but no actual measurement tool is available, the Bukidnon resort to approximations (e.g. *dangaw-dangaw* or a thumb–middle finger length is 6 inches, one *kaltik* or Caltex can is one liter).

Traditional knowledge among the Bukidnon may be classified into three types: (1) a wide body of songs, stories, magic words and riddles, with some *babaylan* (shaman), keeper of the traditional lore, able to recite whole epics; (2) herbal lore and practical advice, and (3) animistic beliefs and practices meant to propitiate environmental and ancestral spirits. Some of the latter are mixed with Christian signs and symbols.

The folklore comes in many forms: *sugilanon* (oral epics), chants and songs, *dilot* (love songs), *talida* (repartees), *bisuyan*, and *composos* (ballads) which are forms of contemporary oral history narrating important events such as the Second World War and an encounter between the military and the New People's Army. If one examines the folklore mentioned across age groups, it will be noted that it is the older folk who mention most of these, with the younger ones mentioning more modern titles of songs and stories learned from schoolbooks (e.g., *Jack and Jill, The Three Billy Goats*).

The recourse to ancestral and environmental spirits with corresponding explanations is more marked in the above-40 age group. Good spirits are given offerings; evil ones need to be repelled or propitiated. Sometimes the Christian Cross or similar symbols are used as signs or objects that would repel evil spirits or ensure good harvest. With younger respondents the recourse to environmental and ancestral spirits decreases but practical advice on the weather, the agricultural cycle, hunting and fishing remain, as does herbal lore which is very extensive. The popularity of the *arbularyo* (herbalist) over the doctor, if available, is explained by a respondent in this way: "Doctors heal physical illness; the *arbularyo* knows if the illness is caused by spirits."

Literate knowledge, on the other hand, appears to be limited to barangay notices and those associated with the market: computation, lists of debts, calculation of board feet for lumber, use of weighing scales, liquid measures for cooking oil, and kerosene. Many have memorized the addresses of relatives and Christian prayers while some reported having memorized the multiplication tables. As in the case of Kala, there appears to be little interaction between traditional and literate knowledge, especially since the incomplete elementary school has just been established in the area. Government development projects generally do not increase literate practice because of lack of participation of the people in the planning and decision-making prior to implementation.

In the Bukidnon of Alaga, we can imagine the beginnings of a loss of identity in colonial times, a loss of confidence in their own traditional knowledge, and a growing dependence on external factors to generate change.

A Muslim Filipino community: the Maranao of Taka

In Taka, Lanao del Sur, the basis of community is Islam and its practices, and this defines the way the group views its relations with the dominant Christian majority, whose presence in mass media, education, and the very definition of literacy (in the roman script but not in Arabic) impinges itself on community life. As a result Muslim Filipinos have an ambivalent attitude towards education and literacy.

Community knowledge in Taka is also defined by Islam, not only as a religion but as a way of life. Islamic beliefs and practices are proverbial boundaries between pre-Islamic beliefs and practices, on the one hand, practices and beliefs perceived as Christian on the other. Regarding the latter, an additional complication is that literate knowledge purveyed both by the Western and Christian-oriented school system is carried out in English and Filipino, while the *madaris* (sing. *madrasah*, Islamic community schools) provide instruction in the Koran in Arabic.

Boys and girls must attend the *madrasah* to read the Koran (in Arabic), as well as understand the concept of *umma* (community), separate from the rest of the (Christian) country and part of an international *umma* (Majul, 1973). Boys learn to do their brasswork because Maranaos are master brass craftsmen; girls sit at their mother's side to memorize and weave the intricate designs of their cloth. The literacy rate in Lanao del Sur is 62 percent, but this does not take account of their literacy in Arabic.

In the public schools, meanwhile, there is ambivalence about the literate knowledge encoded in English or Filipino. On one hand, both are perceived as the language of the Christian majority; on the other, these languages, especially English, are perceived to be good passports to a job here or abroad, and to politics. Their textbooks mention nothing of their brasswork, their weaves, or other traditional crafts in which they excel. The local language (Maranaw) could be written in roman script but there is resistance to this, even as there is no resistance in using roman script to write in English for utilitarian purposes (such as for work abroad).

Thus in the Muslim community of Taka, the relation between traditional and literate knowledge, compounded by the language and education situation, is characterized by multiple discontinuities in which literate practice in all the available languages suffers, and the sense of separateness from the national community is heightened.

Taka therefore pursues its separate history, not only because of its organized and successful resistance against both Spanish and American colonization, but also because of its special situation involving pre-Islamic, Islamic, and Western literate knowledge under conditions of being a minority in a predominantly Christian country, and having two sets of formal education systems with different literate traditions (Western and Islamic). However, Islamic practice, not only in religious matters but as a way of life, provides a focus for meanings and integration as well as mechanisms for boundary maintenance.

Maranaos are integrated into the national framework by territory, population count, participation in local government (led by fellow Muslims), and voting in national elections; also perhaps by education in the public school system, which they resist but attend nonetheless with some ambivalence, if not hostility. But there is an absence of loyalty to a national government "of the others," that discriminates against them, that does not offer equal benefits and fair distribution of what they consider to be their ancestral land, and that wants to assimilate them through an educational system that conflicts with their religious principles and cultural identity (Majul, 1973).

The most recent development in the Muslim Filipino regions was the signing of the peace agreement in September 1996 between the MNLF (led by Nur Misuari) and the national government. Accompanying this is the establishment of the Southern Philippines Council for Peace and Development (SPCPD) which gives Muslims substantial control of the resources of certain provinces in Mindanao but not police powers. Misuari is now the Chair of SPCPD as well as the governor of the Administrative Region for Muslim Mindanao (ARMM).

Without glossing over the numerous problems of political and economic integration attendant on these developments, the possibilities for expansion of literacy practice may be gleaned from policy decisions related to the integration of the *madrasah* (Muslim community school) into the public school system, the teaching of Arabic in schools, and the increased participation of Muslim Filipinos in governance, and in political and economic life.

However, the main cultural problem for literate practice continues to be language choice and the script to use for encoding the three major local languages in the Muslim areas (Maranao, tausug, and Maguindanao), given that Arabic limited to the Koran is read by many, but there are very few secular materials in Arabic. Writing in Arabic (except to copy the Koran) is not widespread, but the resistance to writing the local languge in roman script continues.

At present, scholars are divided on which script is to be encouraged, having recognized both the emotional attachment to Arabic and the practical and integrative implications of writing the local languages in the roman script.

Four marginal communities of the Christian majority

The rural groups belonging to the lowland Christian majority are represented by four communities whose major activities are: agricultural monocrop (Magdalena, Negros Occidental), and farming-fishing communities (Magayon, Sorsogon; Calamansi-Lapulapu, Mindoro Oriental; and Palihan, Bulacan). The ethnic groups represented in these communities are: the Ilonggo of Magdalena, the Bikolano of Magayon, and the Tagalogs of Calamansi and Palihan.

In the process of social change and segmentation, the main bases of community life have evolved into three: the family, the practice of Christianity, and elections. Thus, most community activities are of a religious (e.g., fiestas observed to honor local patron saints, Holy Week) or of a political nature (i.e., elections), while the family, both nuclear and extended, remains the main economic unit and a solid and principal basis of self-identification and loyalty.

Participation in religious celebrations in the modality of *fiestas* is the principal mode of traditional practice in Catholicism, together with rote learning of Christian doctrine and prayers with a heavy underlayer of folk beliefs and practices from an earlier animist tradition. Bible studies and reading of the liturgy for Sunday Mass are of relatively recent origin, started by progressive Church elements after Vatican II. However, the people's piety and religiosity are very apparent, as well as a general submission to what is perceived as the will of God, and an optimism born of Christian hope.

Since the mid-1960s a shift has been occurring in Church orientation, influenced partly by the more radical liberation theology from Latin America. This trend has sought to change the emphasis of Christian practice from interest in rituals towards a more theology-based practice with political undertones aimed at the promotion of peace and justice in the world, and towards a new understanding of "the will of God."

Except in the more highly educated and the emergent politically progressive sectors, elections in the Philippines continue to be defined by fleeting relationships between politicians and voters during the elections, and by clan loyalties, rather than by issues or political platforms. Nonetheless, much interest in elections remains, since elections are still major community activities where everybody who is literate can participate. Its major meaning to voters is the sense of momentary power to decide local or national outcomes. In all these communities, the major and sometimes only venue for the exercise of participative political practice is elections.

Since the EDSA revolt in 1986, a second venue for participative political practice has been "people power," which has been used for issues as disparate as: the increase in oil prices, the value-added tax, and the case against Singapore for the unjust hanging of a Filipina domestic helper. The often emotional nature of people's participation in these events cannot be explained adequately by allusions to our "inherently emotional" character or temperament as a people, but perhaps by the combination of two conditions: first, the venues for political participation are so limited that when an opportunity presents itself in which people can find a common interest, the response is immediate and spontaneous; second, a deeper or less superficial understanding of the issues is not developed either in the schools or by the mass media, which are mainly in English and generally lack concern for a systematic education of the public on issues of common interest (most serious talk shows are in English). Without an understanding of issues and without a general political framework, or a common national vision, personalistic criteria are used, which soon degenerate to emotional reactions without a clear conception of the political issue that needs to be resolved.

Familistic-individualistic orientations

In many communities, the main trend has been intensified family-based activities, as well as increasingly high levels of formal education for the children. This explains in part not only the great desire for education of whatever type at all levels but also the sometimes extreme family-orientedness of Philippine society. Many social analyses focus on this *family-orientedness* and sometimes mistake it for *high communality*, but this is not exactly true. For one thing, "conflict mediators" (*taga-areglo*) have been important in many communities; what this suggests is not commonality but the closed family coming in conflict with other families of the same orientation. Studies on national identification (Doronila, 1989) trace the problem of developing national unity partly to the inability to transcend family and self-interest in favor of those of the local and national community.

The emergence of the family as the most important basis for self-identification, as the focus of loyalty, and the core of economic activities may be clearly seen in the passage from a largely communal social organization such as that in Boheh Umos; to the family-owned but communally cultivated rice-terracing agriculture of Kala; to the dispersed swidden farms of Alaga operated by households; and finally to the lowland Christian communities.

My data from a previous study on national identification (Doronila, 1989) show that even before self, the family comes first. In the absence of social services, the family functions as a safety net, explaining its capacity for survival but at the same time placing a severe burden on its working members who are far fewer than the dependent household members (Gregorio, 1980).

Processes of continuity and change
Across these rural Christian groups, differences in processes of continuity or change can be observed, with resulting effects on knowledge, values and literate practice. Exploitative working conditions in the sugar plantations of Magdalena have developed, on one hand, a paternalistic feudal orientation and, on the other, reason to support rebel groups. Heightened awareness of these conditions has also encouraged efforts to gain greater numeracy practice to avoid underpayment. In Calamansi and Lapu-lapu, community life remains stagnant (no development projects, little capacity for generating change) and literate practice is inactive and restricted, even though individual literacy levels are adequate. In Magayon, with the plans for development projects as well as the organization of sectoral groups requiring more people's participation, literate practice becomes more extensive even as the continued dominance of a few families in both business and politics may be constraining elements. In Palihan, family-based agribusiness development as well as efforts to educate the children well beyond basic elementary level, have resulted in more extensive literacy practice.

In such communities, there seems to be no conflict in adopting modern modes of life, primarily because the transition has been taking place over a much longer period, from Spanish colonial times to the present. But a closer analysis suggests that this transition is labored and fraught with contradictions. On the one hand, there is a marked adherence to urbanized values and institutions; on the other, there are beliefs and practices harking back to the oral tradition. In a situation where the small elite groups with their Westernized practices, language and world-views are dominant in all aspects of life, their kind of knowledge is privileged over community knowledge whether oral or literate. As a consequence, the knowledge of the marginal communities is itself marginalized, and their own traditional and literate knowledge assumes relatively fractured and diffuse forms, resulting in a loss of confidence over their own knowledge and reliance on ill-understood Westernized forms of knowledge. The result is what is more popularly called a "colonial mentality," and an emphasis on form, rhetoric, and emotionalism, owing to difficulties in self-analysis and reflection where thinking is carried out in the local language but knowledge encoded in English is valorized but inadequately understood. Thus, traditional knowledge and literate knowledge, which are of relatively equivalent "size," exist side by side as different and unintegrated knowledge systems.

Practical advice based on experience and received knowledge is most often associated with health, childbearing, economic activities, and the weather. The maintenance of these practices is usually based on demonstrating their efficacy, shared with others by word of mouth. Since these practices do not usually enter into the school discussions or are not tested in scientific research, the usefulness of this knowledge cannot be demonstrated formally and included in the literate tradition. Respondents give various answers to the questions on belief or practice: "You don't lose anything by doing this"; "We don't practice some of these anymore"; "I am afraid not to follow because it might be true"; "I was born into this knowledge."

Functional literacy levels in these communities are: 43 percent for Sorsogon; 59 percent for Oriental Mindoro; 60 percent for Negros Occidental; and 80 percent for Bulacan. Higher educational levels in Bulacan account for the people's high literacy rate, which allows them to independently select and avail themselves of new knowledge in the literate tradition. In all others, however, literate knowledge as measured by FLEMMS is marginal to the main production activity of community life, which is agriculture. Thus, only limited integration occurs if at all between literate and oral traditional knowledge. To quote Bonifacio (1994) again:

> It is crucial to recognize that while technology is basic to agriculture, it is in reality a human activity with its own organization. In the Philippines, the research community has generally been biased against the farmers' traditional mode of production as reflected in the taken-for-granted premise that the technology scientists are developing must be superior to the farmers' practice. What is often not understood is that the displacement of the farmers' tradition undermines the substance of their lives.
>
> The extension workers' lack of appreciation of the farmers' system of production has prevented them from feeding back the farmers' own innovations and technologies to researchers...A less recognized consequence is the marginalization of the farmers who could otherwise have been encouraged to participate in the process of developing and transferring technology.

The absence of this integration is due not only to the biases and present framework of agricultural extension but also to the fact that oral traditional knowledge does not enter the literate tradition, while the literate tradition of new agricultural technology, remains inaccessible to marginal farmers and other community folk.

Development projects, which are quite numerous in these areas, consistently ignore the community folk's traditional knowledge, wishing to trade it for new or modern knowledge which then becomes difficult to integrate into the existing system, as pointed out by Bonifacio (1994), resulting in the failure of the development project and the continued inaccessibility of new knowledge and technology to marginal community folk.

Meanwhile, the inequity in the distribution of resources and social services develops increasing reliance on family as the principal source of security, without expanding loyalties to include the national community. As one respondent put it to us, "It is not easy to say 'This is our land' when one has no land." The capacity to dissemble, to pretend compliance in form but not in substance, perhaps springs from the "otherness" of government and separation from the elite. No doubt it is exacerbated by absence of services and inequitable distribution which we have also seen earlier among the Muslims of Taka.

A multiethnic urban poor community in Manila

The central reality of life in the urban poor communities (represented here by two communities in Manila: Labasan and Martires) is its precariousness and the daily struggle for survival under threat of demolition, loss of employment usually on daily-wage basis, and general urban blight in the form of drug addiction, prostitution, overcrowding, absence of the most basic sanitation facilities. These conditions are heightened by juxtaposition with the affluence of the elite and middle-class sectors for whom the urban poor work, and amenities of urban life seen at close quarters but often inaccessible to them.

Traditional knowledge in the urban poor research sites includes some of the beliefs, practices, and sayings from various rural communities earlier reported, but these are decidedly fewer in view of their removal from sites of practice such as farming and fishing. Instead, respondents mention rules and sayings which are norms of good conduct, to be expected in communities living at very close quarters, and statements about poverty which alternate between toughness and cynicism on one hand and resignation on the other.

These are contradictory values and attitudes, which schools do little to help resolve. While literate knowledge is quite extensive because of the presence of more schools and more written materials, these do not appear to be integrated, nor are their odd jobs and shifting lives. The fragments of traditional knowledge are expected to dwindle further while literate knowledge will be replaced as new types of odd jobs become available with new technology. In this situation, both the literate knowledge and its practice will continue to lack focus and integration, remaining limited but diverse, marginal, and precarious.

The absence or weakness of a basis of community life is occasioned by their shifting existence, characterized by odd jobs, impermanent addresses, very substandard living conditions, and the ever-present threat of demolition of their very community. One community (Labasan) has organized itself in an effort to establish community among the dwellers and obtain from government a modicum of amenities. They have been able to secure the opening of a service road in order to avail themselves of municipal services (electricity, garbage disposal).

They have also obtained title to their home lots through organized representations to the National Housing Authority. The other community, lacking in organization, has chosen to remain "invisible" behinds the walls constructed during the Marcos years to hide their unsightly community. The reason they give for this "invisibility" is to avoid demolition. Thus, processes of change, always on the fast track in a metropolitan setting, remain externally generated even as urban folk attempt to accommodate to these changes in shifting, diffused, and unfocused ways.

Two developmental communities: the Tagalogs of Inipon and Corona

Developmental communities, here represented by Inipon in Quezon and Corona in Rizal, while still poor and marginalized, are markedly different from the other groups earlier described. Here, the processes of change are more internally generated (with the initial help of catalysts), and people participate more fully in community life: in Inipon through the community radio station which has done much to generate literate practice as well as issue-oriented mass actions, and in Corona through the politicization of community members towards the solution of common problems. In these two communities, the capacity for people to take control of their lives and participate in concerted action has engendered a practice of literacy and education that appears to be sustainable and, in the end, developmental. How did this come about?

In Inipon (Functional literacy rate: 66 percent), the local Catholic church headed by a progressive-minded bishop remains one of the most powerful institutions. There are a number of NGOs and federated sectoral organizations in the community (e.g., fisherfolk, women, vendors, farmers), against such problems as dynamite fishing, illegal logging, human rights violations, and military operations occasioned by the presence of rebels in the Sierra Madre. For local issues, the community has a church-owned radio station which has become a catalyst for social mobilization and community development by pioneering in participatory or community-based broadcasting. The station is committed to the propagation of the *bayanihan* (helping each other and working together) spirit among the people of Inipon. Its stated mission is to contribute to nation-building through community-building.

The station is likewise concerned with conscientization and people empowerment by making the people more knowledgeable about certain issues. It encourages volunteerism on the part of the community and strengthens democratic principles and institutions through its participatory process in program planning and production. By serving as a communication center, it links the far-flung barangays to the town center of Inipon and to the rest of the country. As a mobilizer of people for mass action, it has helped to organize fisherfolk to lobby against illegal fishing, illegal logging, and human rights violations. The people's support of this radio station is best illustrated by the fact that despite their poverty, their contributions helped finance the repair of the station's facilities when it was damaged by typhoons on several occasions.

Six types of broadcasts, all done in Filipino (which is mainly Tagalog-based), are shown: (1) news and information (on farm technology, weather forecasts, sports, legal matters, commodity prices, home tips, local and foreign news); (2) commentaries, discussions and people's feedback on news and issues, radio forums, and calls for mobilization; (3) cultural-historical programs (Philippine history, music, riddles and stories for children, radio drama on a specific theme or focus performed by the local people, talent shows featuring poems and songs composed by local people; (4) post-office-on-the-air (to announce letters, love notes and essays, requested songs for and by individuals; (5) religious programs (Bible reading and discussion, prayers, Mass on the air); and (6) radio school-on-the-air which has been in existence since 1977.

Aside from the decidedly local-community orientation of most of the programs and their attempt to cater to all ages and sectors, several observations can be made about the nature of the programming. First is the use of Filipino in programs, making these accessible to everyone in the community. Second, the popularity of letters, notes, music, local dramas, riddles, and talent shows by local people themselves is recognized and encouraged. Third, forums on the air and local feedback reveal not only people's views, values, and beliefs but are also mechanisms for developing consensus, correcting misinformation or misconceptions. Fourth, programs related to the improvement of economic and home activities, prices, and legal matters recognize that most people have no access to newspapers and other printed sources of information, and these are therefore provided on the air. All these programs encourage and demand literate knowledge from participants even in the relative unreliance on reading.

In this context, the possibilities of integrating traditional and literate knowledge could exist at several levels. First, by airing all programs in Filipino, traditional and literate knowledge achieve equal status and become available for comment, comparison, criticism, and closer analysis by everyone, including those not literate in either or both languages. Power and prestige relations are thus altered: between literates and nonliterates; between those articulate in Filipino and those articulate in English; between Filipino and English which is viewed as more prestigious; between the statuses of traditional and literate knowledge.

Second, by encouraging literate practice (e.g., through letters on the air, written feedback from listening groups participating in the school-on-the-air program, writing of poems, dramas, riddles, folk songs, etc.), traditional knowledge has the possibility of entering the written tradition, and therefore entering into history, skepticism, and the intellectual tradition (Goody & Watt, 1963; Olson, 1994). At the same time, when people write their hitherto oral knowledge, the possibility of "holding on" to their own knowledge becomes greater, to use, modify, transmit, expand, or even discard as they see fit.

Corona

Corona, in the province of Rizal, is near Laguna Lake, the largest fresh-water lake in southeast Asia. Once noted for its natural beauty and bounty, Laguna Lake today is an ecological disaster because of unsustainable fishing practices and toxic waste from the numerous industrial factories around the lake. Among the coastal towns, it is Corona that is most heavily dependent on the lake for its main source of income. An estimated 60 percent of its population of 33,967 is directly involved in fresh-water fishing.

Barangay Lagda, located in this town, is the center of operations of the biggest people's organization (PO) in the region. Originally it was just a confederation of small fishermen which an NGO helped to organize and develop. To respond to the major problem of lake degradation, the local organization expanded its membership to multisectoral groups – fisherfolk, women, youth, tricycle drivers, even children. The leadership saw the necessity of enlisting the help of all sectors to achieve the common goal of improving the situation of the lake, which is their main source of livelihood. From tackling the issue of the lake's destruction, the organization's concerns now include current national issues such as the regulation of the fishing industry in the Philippines and protests against the transformation of agricultural areas into industrial zones.

"Towards a just and humane society" is the vision, mission, and goal of this people's organizations, to be achieved through a process which empowers people to take greater control of their lives, determine priorities, and take the necessary action by working together. According to the leaders, all its organized learning experiences are linked to this vision. It focuses on total human development to achieve equitable social development. They believe that real participation can only occur when people are in a position to develop their own alternatives and make decisions.

Limited formal education among the members has not been a hindrance to active participation in the various undertakings of the organization. The present head of the organization's communication program is an elementary school drop-out at grade 2 who taught himself to read and write in the course of his participation in the organization's activities. Continuing education including functional literacy is integral to the organization's activities, although there is no separate education program. In their experience, the function of education is real, its indispensability confronting them along the road to development and their participation in achieving it.

Organized groups are venues for training from which individuals can derive experiences which help them deal better with their own lives. Activities of the organization provide learning experiences to community leaders and members in community organizing, problem-solving, advocacy, and social mobilization. Aside from these, there is also a scholarship program for deserving students who would like to pursue further studies. The organization has been able to establish linkages with some schools and universities in Metro Manila for this purpose. Linkages have also been set up with other organizations in other fishing communities.

The organization regularly conducts seminars and training for its members and officers on leadership, organization, ecology/environment, art classes for youth, livelihood, accounting and bookkeeping. Learning modules have already been developed by leaders and members. The use of group media offers ample opportunities for learning as well.

Data from Corona that were used for this analysis may be sequenced by level of complexity of content and presentation as follows: (1) photographs and explanations of symbolic compositions of fisherfolk using available materials (e.g., leaves, stones, sticks) done at a workshop, (2) leaflets announcing calls for mass mobilization and participation, (3) the script for a slide presentation on Laguna Lake, (4) several issues of their community newsletter, (5) sample guides for running seminars on various topics, and (6) a primer (with slides) on the fishing industry of the Philippines. All the materials are in Filipino, and except for the poems and short stories, all are without authors as a sign of the collective and evolved nature of the written product, just as all material in the oral tradition goes without authors.

Some general observations could be made on the nature of these instructional materials: first, the attempt to integrate traditional and literate knowledge is very apparent. Traditional knowledge is found in the choice of symbols, folk metaphors, local information, riddles/sayings, locally produced poems and stories; literate knowledge is found in the technical and historical information and legal matters. Traditional knowledge is translated to written form first through drawings and illustrations, then through folk metaphors and short riddles, then through longer writing such as poetry and stories.

The nonliterate organization members have an opportunity to be gradually introduced to literate practice through this sequential presentation, aided by slides and oral narration in the more complex presentations. This is the context in which it is reported that even limited formal education among some members seems never to have dramatically hindered any undertaking of the organization. In fact, leaders do not consider illiteracy or low educational attainment as a problem. Becoming literate perhaps only happened to be a requirement in order to get things done. (The functional literacy rate for Rizal is 72 percent.)

Second, the extensive use of folk metaphors and word combinations to form new words with new meanings is noted. For example, for the relatively modern concept of *subsistence*, the usual method of translation would be again to use the English term (usually written in italics) or the Filipino respelling (*subsistens*), both of which do not convey the meaning of the concept to those not familiar with the definition of the term subsistence in the first place. Their new word, *tawid-buhay* (literally cross-life), conveys the exact and essential meaning of the concept, while preserving the metaphor, "a bridge to maintain life," which is embedded in the concept of subsistence. This metaphor is not new to Tagalog speakers because there is already a similar and generally used word, *pantawid-gutom* (literally, cross-hunger, to refer to small amounts of food to take the place of a larger or regular meal where this is not available).

In fact, what seems to be operating in these examples is a kind of double "translation" in which the characteristics of the oral language are preserved in its written form by not losing the metaphorical mode of oral expression, and by combining words into new ones to express the exact and precise meaning of the new concept. In these few examples (which need to be subjected to more rigorous semantic analysis) we can see a more subtle form of integrating traditional and literate knowledge in the process of transforming them into the written mode.

A third general observation is the explicitly political nature of the materials whose objectives of conscienticizing, informing, educating, calling to mass action are geared towards the principal social projects of making the lake their own again and finding common cause with other fisherfolk in the country to address the problems of the fishing industry in the Philippines.

A fourth general observation is that the whole set of materials (in sequence) has a pedagogical objective of raising the levels of literacy skills and information, expanding the worldviews of the membership through history and geography (e.g., the information that Laguna Lake links provinces perhaps not even visited by some members; Philippine seas, rivers, and lakes are important to every Filipino, especially fisherfolk), to develop a comprehensive and multidimensional understanding of the organization's social projects without losing their roots in the personal lives and future of the members themselves.

Inipon, and especially Corona, provide us a contrary instance of a people's organization attempting to enter the literate tradition without losing their traditional knowledge, firmly holding their knowledge in their own hands for their own uses and purposes, and for explicitly common social projects: to build a community in Inipon; to take control of their lake again in Corona and to find common cause with other small fisherfolk in the country.

In general, six main modes of integration have been identified: (1) the use of their own language (Filipino), (2) consistently encouraging literate practice, (3) combining both traditional and literate knowledge in new forms, (4) coining new word combinations to express new concepts, (5) attempting to incorporate the characteristics of their oral expression into the written mode, and (6) seeing to it that even the mode of producing their own texts is under their control by using only whatever technology is available to them.

The integrating principles which run through all these modes are: (1) that everybody participates in the whole process, even as the various materials follow a pedagogical sequence which enables nonliterates to initially participate but in which are encouraged to learn to read and write; (2) thus, passage into a literate tradition will include everybody; and (3) all these activities are for the explicit purpose of realizing their social projects.

The two developmental communities, while still poor and marginalized, are markedly different from the other groups in their attempt to recover some control of the change processes. In a manner of speaking, both are building new communities: in the case of Inipon, still through the auspices of the local Church, which itself has moved in its own orientation from sociocultural to include the political as well. In the case of Corona, the fisherfolk themselves have consciously made a change in their community life by enlarging the basis of their social organization from an occupation-based to a more comprehensive political and issue-based organization. In this process of building new communities, as it were, literate practice and general education play very significant roles.

Inipon and particularly Corona, the developmental communities in this typology, are attempting to gain sovereignty over their knowledge, this time in both the oral and written modes, in the context of a new social organization, characterized as in Boheh Umos by equity, solidarity, and communality, oriented towards an explicit and common goal.

These modes of integration are not some sort of return to the original state of the "primitive savage," as is usually the thinking of those who either underestimate or romanticize indigenous knowledge. Underlying these attempts to integrate traditional and literate knowledge is the absence of this illusion, and the understanding that these new forms of integration created by the people themselves are for the explicit political purpose of transforming themselves in order to enter the mainstream which they hope to also transform in the process.

The values embedded in the integration of traditional and literate knowledge are abundantly clear: the importance of literacy, knowledge and rationality, participation, recovery of control over their own knowledge, the value of a real education, a clear understanding of issues, a commonality of interest and community of efforts towards a common goal or a social project.

To be sure, this project has not been without cost, including human lives, for the social project entails changes in structural arrangements involving powerful groups: the control of fishing operations in the lake, environmental degradation of the lake through industrial pollution, regulation of municipal fishing in the country through legislation upholding the rights of small fisherfolk. At the same time, we see the changes in the bases of community life. Where before, family, the practice of Christianity, and elections are separate elements, we now see a more integrated community life where loyalty to family is assumed, but loyalties move beyond family to include a larger social organization espousing a common social purpose in which both religion and authentic political practice are also implicated.

In these two examples, we see very clearly two principal social elements related to social development: the first element is the internal capacity of a community to generate and sustain a development process (in which functional literacy and education are strong elements) (1) by maintaining its focus while expanding its objectives and activities, (2) by protecting itself from co-optation and repression, (3) by continuing to be the authentic voice of the people it represents, and (4) by maintaining the democratic modality of its decision-making process.

The second element is externally generated, and it has to do with the limits of change and development among the marginalized groups, as envisioned by policy-makers and dominant groups.

Some Reflections on the Passage of Marginal Communities to a Literate Tradition

It is evident from the preceding discussion that the discourse on the topic of literacy and development must be framed in a new way: there is only one process at work, and that is the process of development. The passage to a literate tradition of a whole community, and not just of the elite groups within it, is a necessary part of this development, but it cannot happen outside the development process, as previously defined.

The formulation which asserts that literacy leads to development has given rise to policy and practice that are counterproductive to both literacy and development.

At the very least, with particular reference to the Philippine case, it has occasioned the allocation of large sums of public money for basic or simple adult literacy work from which nothing follows and which research has shown as the least sustainable and the least capable of generating literate practice.

At its most cynical, this traditional formulation not only postpones real development work (since individuals must first be made literate) but also leads us away from the critical task of confronting the questions of power relations, redistribution of resources (especially agrarian reform), and access to services and opportunities which, in sociohistorical context, lie at the root of the problem of marginalized communities described as poor, powerless, and illiterate.

The conclusion that usually follows from this formulation is that people are poor and powerless because they are illiterate. At its most extreme, their illiteracy is seen as a pathological condition which must first be cured or removed before development can start, or before they can enter the mainstream of national life.

The lessons to be learned from the examples of marginal communities at different stages of integration into the mainstream suggest that the development process begins from the internal capacity of a community to generate and sustain a development process in which literacy and education are strong elements but not the major defining elements.

Research on poverty in the Philippines is tiresome in its truth and repetitiveness. Urban poverty is rural poverty that has migrated to urban areas. Rural poverty is characterized by a high level of underemployment, limited access to land because of the high concentration of landholding, inadequate access to credit or to modern agricultural technology, little access to social services. Landholding inequality remains virtually unchanged (26 percent in 1980, 24 percent in 1990); 38 percent of families have no access to electricity; road density (the ratio of paved roads to total land area) increased by only 0.02 percent between 1985 and 1991; the income share of the poorest 20 percent of the population dropped from 5.3 percent in 1988 to 3.8 percent in 1991; the average annual reduction of poverty from 1961 to 1991 was dismal compared with neighboring Asian countries (all in Balisacan et al., 1995).

None of these problems can be solved by literacy and education; all of them require the political will to resolve through policy and serious implementation the age-old problems of inequitable distribution and sustaining economic growth.

But in helping marginal communities to develop their internal capacities to generate and sustain a development process, literacy and education are important elements. The following reflections and recommendations from the preceding discussions may thus be considered .

Basic literacy and provision for elementary education

Since the Philippine data show that simple literacy is a function of elementary-school provision, the most obvious policy decision must then be to immediately deliver early childhood and primary education including simple literacy to the most marginal groups, a goal already declared in the UNESCO Conference at Jomtien in 1990.

Basic literacy for adults

Most successful adult literacy programs in the Philippines are those tied to income-generating or other social development projects. The examples given in Inipon and Corona are good evidence of these. For adults, the basic literacy class must be done quickly. We have developed an approach which enables adults to read, write, and do the four fundamental mathematical operations in 50 hours or less.

Choice of script and language, retrieving and writing oral knowledge

In countries without a colonial tradition, the transition from a wholly oral to a literate tradition would involve only the learning of the script. In the Philippines, three elements need to be simultaneously considered: (1) the script (Arabic or roman) in the Muslim areas, (2) the choice of language (mother tongue/regional/national language and/or English and/or Arabic), and (3) retrieving and writing oral knowledge.

The choice of script has both emotional and practical implications as was shown earlier; so has the choice of language to be used for basic literacy.

All Philippine languages are phonetic and therefore relatively easy to transcribe in the roman script; there are only 4 major types of syllable clusters (V, CV, VC, and CVC). Therefore there should be no difficulty in learning to read and write in the mother tongue, and then transfer this learning to the regional language and later to the national language (Filipino). This policy direction will also encourage the writing and publication of materials in at least the 8 major Philippine languages, of which at present there is very little.

There is another good reason for this policy direction – it will encourage the more widespread retrieval and writing of traditional knowledge, which can then be used for literacy and educational purposes on topics which have a direct bearing on people's lives.

The use of Filipino instead of English for teaching science and math in all levels of the formal education systems is still a subject of debate. The University of the Philippines is now spearheading the writing of science and math text-books in Filipino for elementary and high schools, on the assumption that where textbooks are available, there would be fewer reasons for not using Filipino.

Arabic will have to be taught in public schools in the Muslim areas, but it is possible that its use will be limited only to religious instruction. But for practical and integrative purposes, the roman script will probably have to be used in many other instances. It is foreseen that the move to teach Arabic in public schools will minimize people's resistance to the use of the roman script in other reading materials.

Integration of traditional (oral) and literate knowledge

Various modes of integration have already been designed by the people themselves, as discussed in the examples of Inipon and Corona.

The importance of the social project

The reasons given by respondents from the different communities as to why they want to participate in literacy programs and what they have learned in that program vary across community types. More important, the activities that they enumerate vary according to the extent and nature of the literacy skills required by their activities. This functional literacy varies dramatically from culture to culture.

Consider the following sets of activities as they themselves report them (Doronila, 1996). Among the reasons subjects themselves mentioned are to avoid being taken advantage of, to vote, to count and to reason to the more complex goals of analyzing negotiations.

In *Boheh Umos* (land-based Sama): to compute accurately in order not to be taken advantage of; to fill out a ballot for oneself; mat-weaving, sewing, and carpentry.

In *Kala*: knitting, food-processing, dress-making; helping children with assignments.

In *Taka*: to vote; not interested in sectarian literacy program for fear of being Christianized.

In *Magdalena*: raise the level of social awareness; budgeting, recording; understand what is unfair and unjust in the management of the hacienda system; find other income-generating activities; become para-teachers in the literacy program; recruit more participants to the literacy program.

In *Magayon*: read, write, count, measure, compute; give opinions, participate in elections; join community organizations; use a typewriter, vend or sell, have confidence to travel alone; more skills to participate in the political, social, economic life of the community; critical analysis; plan activities, propose projects; write reports and do documentation work; budget, compute income and expenses, loss and gain from production; learn new methods of agriculture production such as organic farming and seed production; develop camaraderie with one another; teach literacy to at least one other adult in community; become para-teachers.

In *Labasan*: negotiate with National Housing Authority for land; subdivide lots ("We are no longer squatters"); organize health programs and family planning seminars.

In *Martires*: no experience in negotiating with government authorities; refuse to join organizations; want to be "invisible" to avoid demolition.

In *Inipon*: write letters to relatives and friends for the post-office-on-the-air; participate in school-on-the-air; participate in programming and production in the radio station; ventilate opinions on issues over the radio, orally, or in writing; participate in mobilization and advocacy on local and national issues (e.g. illegal logging and fishing, corrupt government officials, etc.).

In *Corona*: participate in meetings and seminars; use a problem-posing and problem-solving approach; participate in mobilization, networking, and advocacy on local and national issues (e.g. degradation of Laguna Lake); use and produce multimedia for communication (artworks, music; compositions about current issues, newsletters); use community knowledge extensively in preparing communications; participate in the organization's activities in income-generation, saving, and value formation.

Apart from affirming the close relation between the activities and the rhythm of community life as discussed earlier, the lists suggest dramatic differences not only in the literacy requirements of the activities but also in the integration of both oral and literacy practices, the range of literate and oral skills required by the activities, and the exciting capacity of the community folk in some areas to indefinitely expand the nature and use of literacy skills for their own purposes.

In these senses the meaning of sustainability is demonstrated by the authentic voices of the community folk themselves: how literacy becomes literacy practice in the context of people's lives, and what it means to maintain, reproduce, and expand literacy into literacy practice.

Notes

1 This section originally appeared in Doronila, *Landscapes of Literacy*, 1996.
2 Following ethnographic convention, all names of communities are fictitious; names of provinces are real.

References

Anderson, A. and Bowman, M. J. (eds.) (1965). *Education and Economic Development*. Chicago: Aldine Publishing Co.

Balisacan, A. M., et al. (1995). *If We're So Smart Why Aren't We Rich?* Manila: Congressional Oversight Committee on Education, Congress of the Republic of the Philippines.

Bernardo, A. B. I., Domingo, M. S., and Peña, E. L. F. (1995).*Cognitive Consequences of Literacy: Studies on thinking in five Filipino communities*. Manila: University of the Philippines Education Research Program and Department of Education, Culture and Sports.

Bonifacio, M. F. (1994). *Images of Agriculture: Problems, issues and trends in technology transfer*. Manila: University of the Philippines and the Philippine Council for Agriculture, Forestry and Natural Resources Research and Development.

Cariño, J., et al. (1994). *Preliminary Report of a Study on Rice-Terracing Agriculture*. Up-Education Research Program. (Unpublished)

Congressional Commission on Education (EDCOM) (1993). *Education and Manpower Development Programs: Vol. 1 Areas of concern in Philippine education, Book one. Making education work*. Quezon City, Philippines: Congressional Oversight Committee on Education.

Corpuz, O. D. (1989). *Roots of the Filipino Nation*, vol. 1. Quezon City: Aklahi Foundation.

Cortes, J. (1992). *Explorations in the Theory and Practice of Philippine Education*. Quezon City: University of the Philippines Press.

Cortes, J. and Balmores, N. (1992). *Philippine Education: Promise and performance*. Quezon City: University Center for Integrative and Development Studies, University of the Philippines.

Department of Education, Culture and Sports (1983). *Study on Literacy Retention*. Manila.

Doronila, M. L. (1996). *Landscapes of Literacy: An ethnographic study of functional literacy in Marginal Philippine Communities*. Hamburg: UNESCO Institute for Education.

Doronila, M. L., et al. (1989). *The Limits of Educational Change*. Quezon City: University of the Philippines Press.

Doronila, M. L., et al. (1992). *Education Forum Manual on Basic Literacy and Numeracy*. Manila: Education Forum.

Goody, J. and Watt, I. (1963). The consequences of literacy. *Comparative Studies in Society and History* 5: 27–68.

Gregorio, R. (1980). Chapter 4. In O. D. Corpuz (ed.), *Education and Socioeconomic Change, 1870–1960s*. Quezon City: University of the Philippines Press.

Han, B. A. (1997). *Indigenous Learning Systems (Tawi-Tawi)*. Quezon City: Education Research Program/UCIDS.

Majul, C. (1973). *Muslims in the Philippines*. Quezon City: UP Press.

May, G. A. (1975). *Social Engineering in the Philippines*. London: Greenwood Press.

NSO/FLEMMS (1989). *Functional Literacy, Education and Mass Media Survey*. National Statistics Office: Philippines.

National Statistics Office, Philippines (1992). *Family Income and Expenditure Survey.* Manila.

Ofreneo, R. (1980). *Capitalism in Philippine Agriculture.* Quezon City: Foundation for Nationalist Studies.

Olson, D. R. (1994). *The World on Paper.* New York: Cambridge University Press.

Scribner, S. and Cole, M. (1978). Literacy without schooling: Testing for intellectual effects. In K. King (ed.), *Literacy Research in Developing Countries (Report of the Bellagio IV Workshop on Educational Research with Special Reference to Research on Literacy).*

Stock, B. (1990). *The Implications of Literacy.* Princeton: Princeton University Press.

Wignaraja, P. (1991). Towards praxis and participatory development. In P. Wignaraja et al. (eds.), *Participatory Development: Learning from southeast Asia.* Tokyo: United Nations University Press.

Chapter 14

Issues of Literacy Development in the Indian Context

Chander Daswani

Context

It is often said that India is a "rich" country which is inhabited by poor people. In the context of literacy, too, India presents a paradoxical, and certainly a complicated situation. With a literary tradition which can be traced back to as early as 2000 BC (Whitney, 1964), India is a literate country with the largest number of illiterate people in the world. The educational system in India is comprehensive in its variety, and widespread in its reach. There are over 600,000 primary schools in the country, and over 250 universities. Doctors, engineers, computer scientists, economists, sociologists, and literary scholars from Indian universities have earned distinction worldwide in their fields of specialization. Yet, over 50 percent of all school-age children who enter primary school drop out of school before they reach grade V. The national literacy rate was 52.21 percent in 1991; but while male literacy is 64.13 percent, female literacy is only 39.29 percent. Around 70 percent of all out-of-school children are girls.

Although national literacy programs have targeted traditionally illiterate and underprivileged sections of Indian society, the pace of literacy development continues to be slow.

Literacy in Education

There is evidence that formal (school and university) education was widespread in ancient India (Daswani, 1994a). Budhist literature from the fifth century BC mentions children's games which include guessing the letters of the alphabet (Nanavati, 1973). In some of the documents, there is mention of wooden writing boards and wooden pens. Both the school and university systems of the time were highly structured. Primary education emphasized moral education in addition to the 3Rs. The art of writing was practiced by all classes of people, including the trading and commercial classes. Not much is known about the formal educational system during the Vedic period, but it may be surmised that literacy was practiced in society (Chatterji, 1966). The ancient Indian institution called *gurukul* was built on the age-old tradition of the "disciple–master" relationship between pupil and teacher (Khubchandani, 1981).

Following the advent of Islam, the older educational system was further consolidated. The *gurukul* and the *madrasseh* provided education to the priestly and ruling classes through the study of religious texts in Sanskrit for the Hindus, and in Arabic-Persian for the Muslims. And the *paathshaala* and the *maktab* provided more secular education, emphasizing the 3Rs, for the merchants and administrators, through the locally dominant vernacular languages (Khubchandani, 1981).

The native system of education was replaced in the 1850s by the British system of education, which put an end to the community-owned and community-run school system. In its place came the "official" government-run school system with a salaried teacher who was responsible only to the educational bureaucracy. The school system was given a uniform curriculum and a formal examination system.

Until the early twentieth century, the English language was the only recognized medium of education, as a result of which only the elite classes could participate in the formal school system. In the absence of official support, the native system quickly became redundant, and survived only in isolated pockets of religious orthodoxy – both Hindu and Muslim.

The impact of the British educational policy in India was reflected in the 1901 Census of India, which recorded a national literacy rate of less than 6 percent. A rich and long educational tradition of centuries had been decimated in less than a hundred years, leading to "de-recognition" of any literacy except that acquired through formal education in a foreign language.

In the 1920s, the nationalist movement was able to reinstate school education through the vernacular languages. The policy of providing primary education through the local vernacular languages paid dividends, and the literacy rate rose to nearly 20 percent in 1951, four years after India became free of colonial rule. With the expansion of the formal school system, the literacy rate in modern India has risen from less than 20 percent in 1951 to over 52 percent in 1991.

Literacy and Language

Every school child in India acquires the 3Rs through her/his mother tongue or the regional standard language, which is the official language of the state where the child resides. If the child completes 10 years of schooling, she/he will have learned to read and write in three languages – the mother tongue/regional language, Hindi (the national language), and English (an international language). Of course, the situation is far more complicated. The possible combinations of the three languages turn out to be numerous.

The Indian Constitution recognizes 19 languages (including Hindi and English), termed "scheduled" languages, which may be considered major languages. All but three (Nepali, Sanskrit, and Sindhi) of these scheduled languages are used as official languages in the different states in India. In other words, 16 major languages, including English, are used as languages of education, administration, legislation, and the judiciary by the various states. Each state, of course, has one official language. It is worth noting here that no state in India is monolingual. Indeed, no district in India is monolingual.

Indian Languages

The 1961 Census of India listed a record number of 1,652 mother tongues spoken in the country. However, a total number of 105 languages, each spoken by 10 thousand persons or more, are recognized by the Census (Mahapatra et al., 1989a; 1989b).

Of these 105 languages, 96 languages can be considered as Indian languages belonging to 4 distinct language families: Indo-Aryan (19), Dravidian (16), Tibeto-Burman (48), and Austro-Asiatic (13). Sanskrit, which is classified as an Indo-Aryan language, is considered a classical language, and therefore not included in the list of 96 languages (Daswani, 1994a).

Written Languages

A language may be accorded the status of "written" language if it satisfies at least two criteria, viz., (i) that there should exist printed literature by native speakers of that language, and (ii) that the language should be used as the medium of instruction in primary school. Printed (as against oral) literature ensures continuous literary activity and literacy practice in the language, and being the medium of instruction in the primary school ensures codification and standardization of the language through the creation of school textbooks and other reference materials.

In addition to these basic criteria, other criteria that determine the "written" status of a language are related to the use of that language in domains such as administration, legislation, the judiciary, and the mass media, particularly journalism. The volume of translation into and from a language also adds to the "written" status of that language (Mahapatra et al., 1989a).

On the basis of these criteria, only 50 of the 96 Indian languages mentioned above may be considered as written languages. Of these 50 languages, 15 belong to the Indo-Aryan family, 7 to the Dravidian family, 22 to the Tibeto-Burman family, and 6 to the Austro-Asiatic family. Primary education is provided through these 50 languages, and there is printed literature available in them. Seventeen of these languages (not counting English and Sanskrit) are scheduled languages, as noted above.

The remaining 46 languages are either technically or actually "unwritten" languages. Thirty-two of these are technically unwritten because although they have been alphabetized, they are not used as medium of instruction in primary school, nor is there any printed native literature in these languages. Needless to mention, these 32 languages do not satisfy any of the other criteria listed above. The remaining 14 languages are actually unwritten since they do not even have alphabets (Bhattacharya, 1991). (For a complete list of the 105 languages, see the Appendix at the end of this chapter.)

Writing Systems

The 50 written and 32 alphabetized languages altogether employ 11 different scripts and alphabets. Nine of these scripts are of Indian origin, all having derived from the Brahmi script which has its roots in the Indian writing tradition of the second millennium BC. The 9 Indian scripts have been in use for the last thousand years or more. The other two scripts are the Roman and the Persio-Arabic (Coulmas, 1989; Daswani, 1994a).

A number of Indian languages employ more than one script. For example, before 1947, Hindu Sindhi was written in four scripts, two of them (*Devanagari* and *Gurmukhi*) used for religious literature, one (*Hattai*) for writing accounts, and one, the official script, (*Farsi*) in all other domains such as education, administration, journalism, and creative literature. Not every literate Hindu Sindhi learned all four scripts. Typically, the priests used the Devanagri script. A large number of women read (and wrote) in the Gurmukhi script. Working males, especially businessmen, wrote accounts in the Hattai script, and could perhaps also read and write the Gurmukhi and/or Farsi scripts. And those who had a formal education used the Farsi script. It is significant to note that only the Farsi script was taught in the formal school system. The other three scripts were learned nonformally in places of worship, at home, or on the job. Theoretically, a Sindhi Hindu could use the four scripts interchangeably in all the domains (Daswani, 1985).

A literate Indian who has had 10 years of schooling can read and write at least two scripts. Many Indians read and write three scripts, and some can read and write four or more scripts.

Multilingualism

India is not multilingual only because of the multiplicity of languages spoken by the Indian people. It is multilingual because Indian society is a plural society characterized by multiple cultures, religions, languages, identities, and socio-cultural practices, which co-exist and influence each other. No single individual or group can be characterized by a unique set of attributes, which distinguish her/him or it from another individual or group. People practicing the same religion speak different languages, just as people speaking one language belong to different faiths. Similarly, language preference and language choice also depend on a variety of intersecting variables (Khubchandani, 1981).

Most Indians speak more than one language or dialect. Even if some Indians speak only one language or dialect, they actively understand other languages and dialects, which make up their linguistic repertoire. An average Indian adult employs different languages/dialects in different communicative domains and contexts, often code-switching and/or code-mixing. An individual may use one language/dialect at home, another at work, and a third in other social settings, frequently switching and mixing them all freely (Southworth & Daswani, 1974; Pattanayak, 1981). Even an "illiterate" person uses different dialects and languages appropriately in various communication settings. For both the literate and illiterate individuals switching from one language or dialect to another is an unconscious and natural act, conditioned by the communication setting.

Co-existing Literacies

Even when an individual is literate in many languages, she/he may not use her/his literacy skills equally in all the languages. An average Indian may (be able to) read newspapers in several languages, but she/he may not (need to) write in more than one language. Or, one may be literate in a classical language, yet one may use these literacy skills only rarely when reading religious texts, or deciphering inscriptions on coins or monuments. Indeed, many Indians are able to read many more languages than they are able to write in, although they may speak all of them quite fluently. At the individual level, there are many co-existing grades of literacy that an individual controls and employs.

Within the larger social context, too, several kinds of literacy co-exist. For example, a Hindu priest may be literate only in Sanskrit, which he uses for reading religious texts and drawing up horoscopes. He may be greatly respected for his literacy in Sanskrit, but he may be totally illiterate in any of the other languages which he uses in his day-to-day communication. He may not be able to read official documents or fill in simple forms, but that will not take away his "literate" status. Many older-generation Panjabi speakers learned to read and write their language in the Urdu script, which is no longer employed for writing Panjabi in India. The post-1947 generation writes the language in the Gurmukhi script. Both generations are literate in Panjabi, yet they cannot communicate in writing with each other in the language that they speak natively. Likewise, a number of young Muslims in India do not learn to read or write the Urdu script, although they are native speakers of Urdu. Instead, they learn to read and write other languages of wider communication.

Many Indian parents prefer to send their children to the so-called "English-medium" schools where children are taught English as the "first" language. Although these children are also required to learn three languages at school, they seldom acquire equal literacy facility in other languages. It is another matter that English-knowing individuals in India find better economic opportunities than those who do not have proficiency in English.

On the other hand, it is not difficult to find many craftsmen, technicians, and mechanics who are not literate in the formal sense, but who are able to decode complex technical diagrams and flow-charts entirely on the basis of experience and working knowledge in their fields of work. Many so-called illiterate persons actually pick up rudimentary literacy skills functionally, on the job.

If one were to put the various literacy abilities on a continuum, at one extreme would be the so-called illiterate individuals, at the other end would be those who have multiple literacy, and between the two extremes would be innumerable grades of partial literacy. All these different shades of literacy co-exist in Indian society.

For the purposes of the Census, however, the status "literate" is determined on the basis of formal schooling alone. Consequently, all those persons who have not had any formal schooling are counted as illiterate, even if they have acquired literacy skills outside the school system.

Mass Literacy

Widespread literacy is not the same as mass literacy. In India, even when literacy was widespread, every adult was not literate. For instance, it is well known that literacy was always a male domain. It is only recently that women have begun to participate in education. Traditionally, priests, princes, and high officials alone were entitled to education in the strictest sense. Businessmen, traders, and petty administrators learned the 3Rs. In fact, only those individuals who required literacy in their vocations generally participated in education. For a long time, literacy was seen as a professional skill, and many literate individuals functioned as professional "readers" and "writers" of *texts*.

The concept of mass literacy is a relatively recent phenomenon which has taken on special significance in the postcolonial world. A direct and causal relationship is sought between literacy and development. It is believed by some that the industrialized countries achieved economic development because of universal literacy. The developing countries, therefore, have consciously set themselves the goal of achieving universal literacy through mass literacy campaigns and programs, in the belief that literacy is a necessary (and perhaps sufficient) condition for economic development (Coulmas, 1992; Daswani, 1994b). The developing countries have generally attempted to achieve in the span of a few decades what the industrialized countries achieved over a period of a hundred years or more.

Mass literacy programs have seldom achieved their stated goals. Often, mass literacy campaigns have been overloaded with literacy as well as development components. Most campaigns have attempted quick-fix solutions for mass illiteracy, attempting to impart the 3Rs in the shortest possible time. This also creates a false expectation that literacy skills can be acquired very quickly. In fact, acquisition of stable and automatic literacy skills can take up to four years of constant practice.

In the Indian context, mass literacy programs have not been successful because of the complex linguistic and social factors. Most illiterate individuals belong to language groups whose languages are either unwritten or have been alphabetized recently. Consequently, the mere provision of 3Rs in these languages is never enough, since the neoliterate is not able to practice her/his literacy skills in appropriate social settings.

Literacy and Empowerment

It is generally believed that literacy empowers an individual to perceive and apprehend her/his condition within the sociopolitical realities which control her/his life. Through literacy, an individual is able to access information and knowledge that frees her/him from the exploitative domination of the powerful forces in society. It is also claimed that an individual can achieve economic development through literacy.

There is evidence to show that literacy does enable an individual to order her/his personal and social environment. In the Indian state of Kerala, high literacy has led to an enhanced quality of family life through better health, lower child mortality, lower birth rates, participation of girls in school, and so on (cf. Curtis, 1997). But literacy has not necessarily led to economic development. On the other hand, in another state, Panjab, low literacy has not prevented economic development.

There is no doubt that literacy brings enhanced awareness of one's total environment – physical, social, economic, and political. Indeed, through literacy one begins to understand oneself better. Literacy gives one a deeper understanding of the complexities of the various realities of one's life. It enables an individual to acquire a totally different perception of relationships and responsibilities.

The average nonliterate person perceives her/his existence within the narrow bounds of her/his immediate environment. Literacy enables the individual to relate to situations and events in the larger contexts of society, nation, and the world. How this transformation takes place is not very clear, yet the literate individual demonstrates a deeper understanding of the total environment.

However, this deeper understanding of the objective reality does not happen suddenly. Literacy or education do not influence just the individual, they transform the family and the society. But often one fails to realize that within a family the journey from total familial illiteracy to total familial literacy can take two to three generations.

Literacy also tends to make an individual self-sufficient, and therefore, paradoxically, selfish. Along with deeper understanding, literacy and education seem to generate self-interest in individuals and groups. The Hindi word for "literate" – *saakshar* – can be rewritten as *raakshas*, meaning "a demon." That literacy can turn a human being into a demon is a popular adage in India.

The Making of a Literate Society

Literate societies are characterized by a literate environment which promotes extensive and regular use of literacy in all communicative domains and contexts. The day-to-day life in such societies is literacy sensitive. In such societies, those who do not have basic literacy skills are unable to function optimally. Also, in such societies, illiteracy is considered to be a stigma by both the literate and the nonliterate sections of the society.

In traditionally illiterate societies, on the other hand, societal interaction takes place without literacy. In such societies, illiterate individuals are able to survive, maybe marginally, and participate in economic and social activities. Within such societies, even if illiteracy is considered to be a handicap, it is seldom a stigma.

The goal of a literacy program, then, should be to transform an illiterate society into a literacy using society. Understandably, but unfortunately, most literacy programs place greater importance on individual literacy, giving an illiterate individual the competence to read and write. The emphasis should be on creating and encouraging a literate environment, so that the transformation from an illiterate to literate social culture is both facilitated and accelerated.

Literacy is concerned with the making of and participation in literate culture at the individual, local, and national levels. Literacy and democratic participation at the societal level become mutually reinforcing, enabling individuals and communities to exercise influence over factors that affect their lives. When empowering, literacy practices become self-sustaining. Literacy is not something which is delivered through literacy programs. It is to be employed by individuals in society, in order to explore the world on the individuals' own terms, allowing them to create and engage in diverse worlds of literacy.

In temporal terms, the literate individual is able to conceptualize time in its linear dimension in addition to the seasonal, the culturally cyclical, and metaphysically endless dimensions. The linear dimension of time opens up new vistas for planning one's own life as well as becoming an active agent in the development of the society and the nation.

Spatially, a literate individual finds deeper insights into interdependence of people within a society. In a literate society, interpersonal relationships take on new meanings, leading to a heightened comprehension of one's rights and duties, and participation in personal, local, and national development.

In the national context, literacy not only fosters democratic norms and social networking, it makes the rule of law feasible, ensuring complex and dynamic growth as well as progress of the nation as a whole. Literacy not only enhances exchange of ideas, which make communication of innovations possible nationally, it generates a demand for lifelong education within the society, leading to scientific attitudes, and individual as well as group creativity (Daswani, 1997).

The basic issue of literacy development in India is to promote literate cultures in all the languages, and provide opportunities for both children and adults to participate in the functioning of an egalitarian democracy.

References

Bhattacharya, S. S. (1991). *An Appraisal of the Unwritten Languages of India*. Mimeo.

Chatterji, S. K. (1966). *Brahmi: The mother of Indian scripts*. Delhi.

Coulmas, F. (1989). *The Writing Systems of the World*. Oxford: Blackwell.

Coulmas, F. (1992). *Language and Economy*. Oxford: Blackwell.

Curtis, D. (1997). Literacy is life. In A. Raghuvanshi (ed.), *Spirit of Literacy*. New Delhi: UNESCO.

Daswani, C. J. (1985). Problems of Sindhi in India. In A. K. Biswas (ed.), *Profiles of Indian Languages and Literatures*. Kanpur.

Daswani, C. J. (1994a). The sphere of Indian writing. In H. Gunther and L. Otto (eds.), *Writing and Its Use*. Berlin: Walter de Gruyter.

Daswani, C. J. (1994b). Literacy and development in south-east Asia. In L. Verhoeven (ed.), *Functional Literacy*. Philadelphia: John Benjamins.

Daswani, C. J. (1997). Is literacy really necessary? In A. Raghuvanshi (ed.), *Spirit of Literacy*. New Delhi: UNESCO.

Khubchandani, L. M. (1981). *Language, Education, Social Justice*. Poona: Centre for Communication Studies.

Mahapatra, B. P., McConnell, G. D., Pamanabha, P., and Verma, V. S. (1989a). *The Written Languages of the World: A survey of the degrees and modes of use*, vol. 2. India, Book 1: *Constitutional Languages*. Quebec.

Mahapatra, B. P., McConnell, G. D., Pamanabha, P., and Verma, V. S. (1989b). *The Written Languages of the World: A survey of the degrees and modes of use*, vol. 2. India, Book 2: *Non-constitutional Languages*. Quebec: University of Laval Press.

Nanavati, Jal Jehangir. (1973). *Educational Thought*. Poona.

Pattanayak, D. P. (1981). *Multilingualism and Mother-tongue Education*. Delhi: Oxford University Press.

Southworth, F. C. and Daswani, C. J. (1974). *Foundations of Linguistics*. New York: Free Press.

Whitney, W. D. (1964). *Sanskrit Grammar*. Cambridge, Mass.: Harvard University Press.

Appendix

The following is a list of 105 living languages from the 1971 Census of India, arranged according to written and official status, under the various language families (from Daswani, 1994a).

I. Indo-Aryan: total number – 19
  A. Written languages (scheduled)
    1. Assamese
    2. Bengali
    3. Gujarati
    4. Hindi
    5. Kashmiri
    6. Konkani
    7. Marathi

      8. Nepali
      9. Oriya
    10. Punjabi
    11. Sindhi
    12. Urdu
  B. Written languages (nonscheduled)
      1. Bhili
      2. Bishnupuria
      3. Dogri
  C. Unwritten languages (alphabetized)
      1. Halabi
      2. Lahnda
      3. Shina
  D. Unwritten languages (not alphabetized)
      1. Khandeshi

II. Dravidian: total number – 16
  A. Written languages (scheduled)
      1. Kannada
      2. Malayalam
      3. Tamil
      4. Telugu
  B. Written languages (nonscheduled)
      1. Gondi
      2. Kurukh
      3. Tulu
  C. Unwritten languages (alphabetized)
      1. Coorgi Kodagu
      2. Khond Kondh
      3. Konda
      4. Kui
      5. Parji
  D. Unwritten languages (not alphbetized)
      1. Jatapu
      2. Kisan
      3. Kolami
      4. Koya

III. Tibeto-Burman: total number – 48
  A. Written languages (scheduled)
      1. Manipuri
  B. Written languages (nonscheduled)
      1. Angami
      2. Ao
      3. Bhotia
      4. Bodo
      5. Dimasa
      6. Garo

      7. Hmar
      8. Kabui
      9. Khezha
    10. Konyak
    11. Ladakhi
    12. Lepcha
    13. Lotha
    14. Lushai
    15. Mikir
    16. Phom
    17. Sangtam
    18. Sema
    19. Tangkhul
    20. Thado
    21. Tripuri

C. Unwritten languages (alphabetized)
      1. Adi
      2. Balti
      3. Chang
      4. Deori
      5. Halam
      6. Khiemnungan
      7. Kinnauri
      8. Lahuli
      9. Lakher
    10. Mao
    11. Miri Mishing
    12. Mishmi
    13. Monpa
    14. Nissi Dafla
    15. Nocte
    16. Paite
    17. Rabha
    18. Sikkim Bhotia
    19. Tangsa
    20. Vaiphei
    21. Wancho
    22. Yimchungre

D. Unwritten languages (not alphabetized)
      1. Koch
      2. Lalung
      3. Mogh
      4. Pawi

IV. Austro-Asiatic: total number – 13
  A. Written languages (scheduled)
    None
  B. Written languages (nonscheduled)

    1. Ho
    2. Kharia
    3. Khasi
    4. Mundari
    5. Nicobarese
    6. Santali
  C. Unwritten languages (alphbetized)
    1. Korku
    2. Savara
  D. Unwritten languages (not alphabetized)
    1. Bhumij
    2. Gadaba
    3. Juang
    4. Koda/Kora
    5. Korwa

V. Classical languages: total number – 2
    1. Sanskrit
    2. Tibetan

VI.   Foreign languages: total number – 4
    1. Arabic/Arbi
    2. Chinese
    3. English
    4. Persian

VII. Languages of doubtful linguistic status: total number – 3
    1. Naga
    2. Kuki
    3. Munda

Chapter 15

Women and Empowerment through Literacy

Malini Ghose

Learning to read and write may involve considerably more than the direct acquisition of a skill. For the women in rural India it is a matter of recognizing and in some cases taking power over some aspects of language, literacy, and life. This paper discusses a literacy program[1] based on the collaborative work of Nirantar, a women's collective working in the area of education, and Mahila Samakhya, a women's empowerment program in Banda, a "backward" district in the north Indian state of Uttar Pradesh. The analysis of power structures and dynamics at play in literacy work is based on reports of three teaching/learning environments, a residential literacy camp, a participatory primer development workshop, and a six-month residential educational course for rural women

Goals

As feminist literacy practitioners, we believe that education is not neutral, nor are we in the business of merely delivering certain skills – such as literacy – to women. Our concern has been explicitly with changing power relations at a social and individual level. We are also bound to a pedagogy which sees process and consequence as part of the same continuum, and to a belief that for women to feel empowered as a result of an engagement with education, they must be empowered within the educational practice. How power dynamics play themselves out in literacy programs, which consciously attempt an empowering and participatory pedagogy such as ours, forms the focus of this paper.

Having said this, we should add that the working understanding of power used in empowerment programs such as ours, draws on dichotomous categories like "powerful and powerless," and images of "grabbing power," "redistributing power," and the like, all of which suggest an understanding of power as a finite commodity. We appreciate the limitations of this approach, but we also find it a valid entry point to discussions when we are interacting with women who relate to the concept of power as something lacking in their own lives, and an asset of their oppressors.

On the other hand, our practice is also informed by a view of power at another level of definition: we see power as a phenomenon of structured but mutable social relationships, in patriarchy for example (see Street, 1995). This vision of power is elegantly stated by Isaac:

> the exercise of power is always contingent, it is chronically negotiated in the course of everyday life.... Thus power relations approximate less a model of stimulus and response, and more a model of endemic reciprocity, negotiation, and struggle, with both dominant and subordinate groups mobilizing their specific powers and resources (and for the subordinate solidarity is always the greatest resource). (Isaac, 1986)

This chapter is about just such struggles and negotiation; it is about the reproduction and transformation of power relations in certain literacy learning situations.

Such an analysis of power has of course been at the core of feminism, as have issues of knowledge and representation, control and resistance, authority and subordination, construction of subjectivities, and, above all, a concern for the everyday realities of women's lives. The concept of empowerment too – though now a buzzword – has been crucial in problematizing the issue of power and bringing a theoretical construct within the realm of practice. Our own work, and certainly the Mahila Samakhya program, has its antecedents in this process.

Programs

Mahila Samakhya

As women's issues came to the center stage of the "development" arena in the 1980s in India, a number of empowerment programs for women were formulated. Some were programs mooted by the government. The women's movement in India, through protest, lobbying, and critiquing patriarchal structures and institutions, had created an "alternative space" in the previously forbidden terrain of government programs. Partnerships between women's groups and government agencies, previously unthinkable, began to be forged.

As women's groups attempted to translate feminist constructs into concrete programs of action, there was a shift from looking at power as simply a negative or coercive force to regarding it as a generative, transformative, and productive force as well (Batliwala, 1993). These programs became spaces to introduce a different culture of power. Mahila Samakhya (hereafter MS),[2] originally outlined in the policy document of the Ministry of Human Resource Development (1988), was a product of this period.

The MS program works on issues of women's education and empowerment. Banda, the MS district that is the focus of this paper, is one of the poorest districts in India; it is *dacoit* (bandit)ridden, extremely poor, with a significant tribal and low-caste population, low literacy levels, and a high degree of violence towards women. Over the past six years MS in Banda has addressed a number of issues: struggles against landlords and forest contractors, education, health, and water. A particularly innovative effort has been training illiterate rural women as hand-pump mechanics. It was born out of a need to redress the water scarcity in the region and a nonfunctioning government water department. This intervention has had a number of spin-offs – a growing demand for literacy, the acquisition of new skills like masonry, and a demand for information. All these efforts have been built on a bedrock of women's understanding of their life situation – their subordination, as well as strengths.

Although it is a central government program, MS's broad mandate did encourage the development of a flexible, responsive organizational structure. Autonomous MS societies were set up, a structure that involved the state but also allowed nongovernmental organizations (NGOs), particularly women's groups, to play a role in operationalizing the project. At the core of the organizational structure were village-level women's groups called *mahila sanghas*. Village-level activists or *sakhis* were instrumental in activating the *sangha* of their village, taking up issues, discussing problems, and holding village meetings. They usually were nonliterate, poor, lower-caste women. *Sahayoginis* coordinated the work of 10 villages. They provided leadership and played a catalytic role in building and sustaining the *sangha*, and provided a link with the District Office. They had some formal education. The District Office in turn coordinated, helped plan and oversee the work of the entire district, and was staffed by a district coordinator and resource person.

The education team in Banda initially consisted of a few *sahayoginis* and teachers, called *sahelis*. The formal schooling levels of the *sahelis*, compared to the educational qualifications of teachers in general, were low, though most had completed their primary education. But this is an area where literacy levels for women are abysmally low, somewhere between 8 and 16 percent, and it was often difficult to find even a single literate woman in some villages.

The decision to work with teachers with such low levels of formal education was in part born out of necessity, but also out of programmatic principle. The program decided that it was preferable to train and work with local women, who were culturally rooted, and to create local resources rather than settle for the easier option of getting more qualified women from elsewhere. In fact the education team in Banda today includes some *sahelis* who became literate through the literacy camps organized by MS – an uncommon occurrence as far as education programs go.

Nirantar

Several of the Nirantar[3] members, of which the author is one, have been actively involved in the work in Banda since 1989, with concrete work on literacy beginning in 1991. Our involvement with the gender training and other aspects of the program provided the base for building a common understanding of education and women's empowerment between Nirantar and the Banda team.

The Approach to Literacy Work in Banda

It is important to understand the context of the women's demand for literacy. It grew out of their involvement with MS, an experience which affirmed their own knowledge and skills, and encouraged them to question, critique, and reflect on their life situation. Literacy was gradually seen as a skill that would enable women to deal with their environment from a position of strength. For the *sakhis*, their new roles as village activists demanded that they interact with the bureaucracy, schools, and other mainstream institutions on a regular basis. The women hand-pump mechanics needed literacy for specific reasons: to maintain records of spare parts, other repairs, depths of bores, etc. They expressed a sense of humiliation at having to get their log books updated by the male mechanics of the government department; "*Baar baar un ko poochna padta, achcha nahin lagta*" (We constantly have to ask the male mechanics to write our records for us. We do not like it). The demand for literacy was linked to women redefining their lived realities – which now included learning new skills, interacting with mainstream structures of power, greater mobility and self-confidence, and the desire for information on a range of issues.

Initially, the articulation of this demand compelled the program functionaries to quickly get into the act of "delivering literacy." However, each new intervention has led to an evolution of the team's (and our) perspective on education. The group now considers literacy to be instrumental to the development of a critical understanding of their lifeworld, their experiences of struggle, of joy, as well as their folklore, language, and indigenous ways of knowing. On the other hand, education for many continues to be equated with knowledge, power, jobs, and the path to a better life.

The complexities and contradictions in the approach to literacy closely resemble our understanding of power outlined above. Thus, just as on the one hand we accept power as a concrete asset or a lack, we also find ourselves treating (or being forced to treat) literacy and education as a concrete asset which we must deliver to those lacking it. Then again, we also treat power as a more abstract, contingent, and open-ended phenomenon, and we try quite hard to bring the same openness to our literacy work.

The tension between these two broad perspectives of power and education is probably the most striking feature that emerges in the experiences narrated below. There is, however, another basic thread running through these episodes – the power dynamic between "us" and "them," "teachers" and "participants." This again was an area fraught with contradictions, a situation we both accepted and tried to get past. In truth, we were generally at pains to overcome this divide, but often we reinforced it, as we certainly could not escape it.

An experience from a literacy camp

Literacy camps are residential programs that initiate women into the world of letters. Through the use of locally relevant key words, discussion, and creation of learner-generated texts, these literacy camps provide a supportive learning atmosphere which dispels women's initial lack of confidence about being able to read and write. Since 1990 a number of such camps have been held in Banda. A literacy course consists of a series of three residential camps. Each camp lasts 10 days with a month-long break between each. Nirantar members were involved in evolving an appropriate teaching/learning methodology and training the local team.

What follows is an experience from one such literacy camp. By this time, the Banda education team was familiar with the methodology. This camp was being coordinated by two *sahayoginis*, a group of *sahelis*, and a facilitator from Nirantar.

Durga (a *sahayogini*) began writing the names of the months on chart paper. As she wrote "*Chait*" (approximately corresponding to the month of April) the women in her group read out "*Chaiyat*"; she wrote "*Baisaakh*" they read "*Bayeesaakh*." This continued for a while. I wondered if this was a problem of differences in pronunciation. Or could it be that they were just reading incorrectly.

It soon struck me that the *sahelis* had written the names of the month in standard Hindi and what the women (even some *sahelis*) were reading aloud was in Bundeli – the local language – the language of all oral communication in the area. I posed a question to the *sahelis* – would it not be simpler to write "*Chaiyat*" instead?

There were a flood of protests – "*Chaiyat*" was not "proper" or "correct." "But you speak it?" I inquired. One *saheli* said, "We are teachers, how can we teach them incorrectly? When the women return to their villages their books will be scrutinized by family members and others in the community, like the *pradhan* (village headman). It will reflect badly on us and the program." Said another, "Besides they were learning to read and write to be able to access information. All calendars were written in standard Hindi." I was in a quandary.

If "*Chaiyat*" is how they say it, how they identify with it, they should write it as such. But in the face of such strong protest, could I push my views, it will not be what they want. But then I thought, "*Chait*" for that matter was "incorrect," the "proper" (sanskritized) Hindi word is "*Chaitra*." In fact that is how it is written in most calendars. When I pointed this out to the *sahelis*, they said that while they were familiar with "*Chaitra*" it would be too difficult for the women to learn and pronounce.

On that occasion the women learned to write "*Chait.*"

(From the diary of a Nirantar member, Nov. 1993)

The "*Chaiyat*," "*Chait*," "*Chaitra*" incident might appear trivial to some, especially as the words are so close – *chait* and *chaiyat* do not sound very different – but it threw up a number of issues. Questions of power were central to this. Who decides what is "correct" and what is not? As we had seen, the boundaries between the regional language and standard Hindi were not as clear as we had initially assumed. As "trainers" we could have pulled rank on the *sahelis* and insisted on *Chaitra* being taught. Or we could have ignored their need to access the mainstream and insisted on their learning the months in the local language – the language they identify with.

Decisions on language policies in the formal education system we know, are made by governments on behalf of the people, but the issue of language in the nonformal system is not given serious consideration. Decisions are either not taken, implying that the dominant language is used *de facto*, or at the most a "transitional approach" is adopted where the regional or local language is used as a bridge to ultimately take the learner towards learning the mainstream language.

The *sahelis*, despite the local inflections in their own Hindi, saw themselves as "teachers" representing positions of authority and as providers of information. They were worried that this position would be open to question by other mainstream institutions. They had low levels of education, and would not have been accepted as "teachers" in a formal context. But having become teachers in MS, they had acquired a certain social standing, and they quickly stepped into their roles.

The contradiction lies in the fact that they are aware that in other areas of the MS program primacy is given to women's ways of knowing and forms of expression. Yet when it came to literacy, the *sahelis* became sticklers for formality and purity. They also felt that they needed validation from the community for something as small as writing the names of the months, despite their involvement in processes which question this "authority" in much more direct and visible ways.

This episode forced us to deal with the issue of language in literacy teaching. Then, as now, while the verbal teaching/learning transaction was done in Bundeli, the actual words being taught and the texts being created were in Hindi. Was this instrumental approach to the local language limiting the women's creativity, inhibiting expression and communication of their thoughts and experiences? Was this approach, thereby, making invisible the women's culture and ways of defining and categorizing their lifeworld? If this was so, then it was *our* limitation in not knowing the local language. We were Hindi-speaking people.

However, the situation was not really all that simple. Hindi symbolized the language of power; the *sakhis* themselves perceived their language as inferior. It was, they said, a *dehati* (rustic), *lath maar bhasha* (rough-and-ready language) – a poor alternative to Hindi. Bundeli had no credibility – a reflection of the inferiority they experienced *vis-à-vis* their caste, class, and gender identities.

Three broad categories of power structures came into play in this incident. At a macro level, we see the process through which dominant values, specifically dominant national languages, enforce their hegemony. It is interesting of course that literacy lends itself to this process. That is, the norms of correctness are applied to spelling but not to pronounciation. Second, there is an appeal to the power structures of the educational system. Although this incident occurred in an apparently alternative educational system, expectations of what teachers should teach and learners learn were clearly derived from the mainstream system. Finally, the incident expresses some of the power dynamics between the trainers and the *sahelis*. In this case, the trainers intervened to question the teacher's literacy practice. While we did not enforce any change, the intervention itself opened the issue for negotiation later.

Creating a primer

We decided to develop a new primer for the program. Having a primer that the women identify with, one that reflects the beliefs of the program, was felt to be important, as it is very often the only teaching material that the *sahelis* have. A group of 10–12 *sahelis* and *sahayoginis* and members from Nirantar got together to develop a primer through a series of participatory workshops in 1993. Developing the primer threw up some important power-related issues of a participatory process of materials production. The incidents described below will highlight the issues around language hierarchies and knowledge creation, between oral and written language, literacy pedagogy and participatory processes.

Tackling language hierarchies
At the outset the following exchange occurred:

> Facilitator (F): In what language should your primer be?
> The responses of the participants (P) varied but were unanimously in favor of Hindi:
> P: It should not be in the local language.
> P: We speak our language, there is nothing new in it, so why teach in Bundeli?
> P: If we teach them in their language they will remain where they are.
> P: How will they read other books if they are taught only in Bundeli?
> P: We should teach only the pure and correct form – both in the written and oral mode.
> We felt differently. Language in literacy work was not merely a conduit to pass messages from a group of information providers to passive recipients. While we could not disregard the participants' strong notions of and aspirations for mainstream education, we felt that education work in the local language should at least

be experimented with. Still, their strong articulation in favor of Hindi put us in a dilemma. Could we push our agenda? After all, we were committed to a "participatory" approach. Finally, drawing on the same methodology, we reasoned that it would be unfair if we were not able to find the space to express our views. We thought it necessary to make explicit the issues of power within the question of language.

We decided that a dialogue on the issue was in order. We told the group we wanted to challenge their notions of purity and correctness in the context of language. This proved to be a difficult exercise. We raised with the group issues about the politics of language and the asymmetry of power that exists in the Indian context between the use of standardized (official) languages (like Hindi) and regional languages and local dialects. We tried, through numerous illustrations, to bring home the point that language was a means to exercise control and domination, as well as self-determination, and a strong cultural expression. While they relate to the concept of "power" or "paua" (as they refer to it) and experience it – viz. the landlords (class), by upper-castes, and as women, it was difficult for them to do so within the context of language.

Not having made any headway we decided to explore the issue differently rather than drop it completely. To not make explicit the various dimensions of subordination of Bundeli would have been to perpetuate unequal power relations. We undertook an exercise where we developed word lists in Bundeli in certain categories – items found in the house including architectural terms; kinship patterns; different idioms and qualities related to men, women, and children; adjectives used for different types of personalities; jewelry items, etc. The corresponding words in Hindi and English were written alongside. This exercise generated excitement. Every word brought with it an outpouring of stories – intensely personal, but also humorous and satirical: "they used to tell me not to laugh like that...my mother got these kinds of earrings made when I got married...they used to shout and call him a 'belli' [nut]...the milk used to be hidden in this kind of cupboard..."

Though each story, even around the same word, was different, they all shared a common cultural experience. Experiences, from which we were excluded, but became a part of, in the narration. Our interest somehow seemed to affirm their experiences and the stories kept flowing. (Excerpts from the workshop report)

The process revealed a wealth of indigenous cultural experiences and the richness of the local language while simultaneously inverting the power dynamics between Nirantar members and the *sahelis*. For instance, the group found that there were words in Bundeli that had no equivalent in Hindi. English was able to capture even fewer nuances. In English you have only uncle and aunt, in Hindi there are special terms for every kind of uncle or aunt; your father's sister is *bua*, and mother's sister is *maasi*; and Bundeli is even more nuanced. Each term carries connotations of a unique relationship. In other categories too there were Bundeli words that found no place in Hindi. If these words were not within the mainstream language should they be deleted from our vocabulary as well? Were these words "incorrect"? As the discussion flowed the group decided that they would settle for a mix of Hindi and Bundeli.

This exercise brought into focus the main issues or assumptions. First, that writing, unlike speech, calls for the authorized version. Second, new learners and their teachers are faced with this issue of power and who has the right to say how something will be written.

Participatory writing process: the complexities involved

So far so good. But the next day when we attempted to build on this fruitful exercise we were in for a surprise.

On the basis of the previous day's exercise we asked them to select key words and create reading texts. They wrote: "Minu fetch water," "Ramu go to the fields," "Rita cook the food." Everything was an instruction. The readers were passive receivers. We took their work and read it back to them. They looked unmoved. We asked them, where was the laughter and animation of the previous day? If we had enjoyed the stories so much could that not then form part of their primer? They said, "But then we were 'telling' the story. Those kinds of stories are never in books. We never thought they were worth anything much." "But then you never wrote books before," we replied. "Now you will, so you can put what you want into them."

It is evident from this incident that there was a sharp distinction in the women's minds between what is appropriate for oral and for written communication. While indigenous language and images find reflection in the oral mode, literacy and the written mode is concerned with instructions, development, and informa- tion, and always reflects the images and perceptions of the mainstream language. We felt we had to intervene again to make the group realize that they had the power to shape the primer as they chose, to include their images and content. The conflicting images of that content held by teachers and learners had to be reconciled. It was a realization of the power they would wield, as well as the potential power to change and redefine what counts as knowledge. To make the alternative possible we had to first validate their language and cultural experiences and establish that language was central to knowledge creation. And it was not insignificant that the validation was coming from us – people who to them represented the mainstream.

How did we select what to include in the primer?

In the previous day's exercise they had listed Bundeli words for architectural features within their houses. One such feature was a special cupboard called a *kimaria*, where all the precious "goodies" – like extra milk or ghee or some sweets – would be stored. Numerous stories had been narrated about the *kimaria*. Most of them had to do with women or young girls being denied access to the *kimaria*. One story was slightly different. One of the *sahayoginis* as a young girl was caught stealing milk from the *kimaria*. It was humorous, used the local idiom, and had caused much merriment in its narration. This type of story was finally selected for the primer.

When it came to making a selection a majority of the group suggested one of the denial stories. But we felt very strongly that selecting that story would only reinforce the stereotypical relationship between a mother-in-law and young bride which is usually portrayed as being tense, strained, and one of restriction and denial. Was it not possible to present a more humorous side to women's and young girls' lives? Although many of the books available portray young girls as being burdened with work and discriminated against, we emphasized that every time we present a story (written or oral) we are implicated in a particular way of understanding the world and our place in it (Simon, 1987). Do we then always want to produce narratives that represent women as "victims" – denied, burdened, and discriminated against?

Maniya's story: when real events become material for texts

As we were working on the primer that evening some women from the Mahila Samakhya office rushed into the room saying, "A young woman, Maniya, has been burnt to death by her husband. A group of us are going to Manikpur [a nearby town] to try and catch him."

We all dropped our work and prepared to leave with them. No one needed any prompting.

A group of about 15 women from Mahila Samakhya reached Manikpur. We gathered the women of Maniya's neighborhood and began having a meeting. All of a sudden the dead women's husband appeared – dressed in white, feigning a deep sense of loss at his wife's death. He thought we had come to pay a condolence visit. But the women were in no mood to be taken in by his deceit. We accused him of the crime. He denied having committed it. The women did not relent. He finally admitted that he was guilty, but with no hint of remorse or shame. We were enraged and started beating him. We painted his face black, made him wear a garland of slippers, and paraded him through the town.

On returning to the workshop everyone started writing out the story as a lesson in the primer. There had been no consultation. The key word selected for the lesson was *"chadchatta"* (a deceitful, fraudulent person), a word in Bundeli that had emerged in the previous day's exercise. They were convinced that no other word could describe the man. (From Nirantar's workshop report)

The primer workshop experience reveals an unusual sequence of events. Here the Nirantar members were obviously quite forceful in pushing the women to affirm their local tongue. But after the apparent success in generating a lively discussion on the joys of Bundeli, this momentum floundered the next day on the deeply ingrained association of literacy with the national language. Yet it was finally the intervention of "everyday life" or at least a common tragedy that shook the women into a realization of the virtues of their own language. This episode also reveals to us the virtues and limitations of "classroom exercises." The classroom discussion while creative and important did not seem to have any concrete significance for the women. But after the cathartic experience of punishing Maniya's husband, the women spontaneously drew on their vernacular for the unusual but plainly empowering act of labeling the murderous husband. It is, however, unlikely that this would have happened had the discussions not moved outside the language exercise.

Issues of power emerging from a structured, long-term educational program

The women and adolescent girls who had acquired basic literacy skills at the literacy camps and centers articulated a strong demand for further education. A six-month residential course at the Mahila Shikshan Kendra (Women's Learning Center) began in January 1995 to meet this demand.

The examples below are drawn from the first course at the Mahila Shikshan Kendra (MSK). It was during this period that the curriculum was developed collaboratively by Nirantar, MS Banda, and the 28 participants.

MSK as a "school"

MSK was a long-term, structured educational activity. And it generated a set of power dynamics and negotiations unlike anything in the literacy camps and the primer development workshop. The participants came to the MSK with a fixed set of expectations. For them MSK symbolized a "school" – a school with a difference, but a school nonetheless. This carried with it the entire baggage of notions associated with School as a social institution which define a set of expectations about school and its outcomes. First, a school has a prescribed set of (power-laden) relationships between teacher and learner; teachers have authority over pace and content; they control discipline; the teacher is the "expert"; "knowledge" is what the teacher provides. These notions impacted directly upon the MSK structure and activity in a myriad of interesting ways.

The power of the participants

We know about our forest and trees. We know how integral forests are to our lives. We know what sources of water we have in our village and the problems around it. All you do is listen to us and give back what we have told you. What do you have to give us? Tell us what we do not know. You have not told us anything new in a week! (Participant's reactions a week after the MSK started, Jan. 1995)

We were stunned. We didn't know how to respond. We were all set to explore the possibilities of working on an alternative "learner-centered" curriculum where the learner and her lifeworld would be at the center of the educational experience. Were we free to do this?

We were forced to shift gear, teaching became more information oriented. Learners had an insatiable demand for information. We were doing a session on the movements of the earth – rotation, revolution, and the seasons, and before the session even ended we were questioned: "We want to know about rain and how the monsoons reach us. Why are you keeping this 'hidden' from us?"

They were here at the "school" to learn – learn not what they already knew but what we knew. (Nirantar members' field notes)

As practitioners committed to a learner-centered approach we had planned a curriculum that was not predetermined but loosely centered on issues of land, water, forest, and village and society. The starting-point would be to explore these aspects from the perspective of the participants' own environment, lived experiences, and needs. Around these we would structure new information areas, discussion, critical awareness, gender issues, etc. Texts written and created in the classroom and other informally produced material would be the learning material. This way participants and the local education team, we felt, would have some degree of control over the curriculum. But, as the quote above indicates, the participants clearly wanted otherwise.

The participants certainly had insights and information which we did not, but these were not always precise or comprehensive. It is a mistake, as is the case in many programs, to assume that all local people will be repositories of local knowledge. There certainly existed experts in particular areas of local know-ledge, but these specialists were not at the MSK classroom. We continue to struggle with the issue of how to add substantively to learners' knowledge about the local environment, history, and culture.

This is not to say that we were denying them all mainstream information. The need for MSK to achieve equivalency with the primary school level had been articulated at an early stage of its planning. What we were unprepared for was the intensity and single-mindedness of the demand from the learners.

The demand for equivalency made sense for the girls, some of whom wanted to enter mainstream schools after the MSK. But did the women want main-stream content as well? We knew that rural women reject formal schooling (and have done so for years) precisely because they see it as irrelevant. They don't believe it can change their lives. At the same time many of them were closely scrutinizing the textbooks of their school-going children, probably to make sure that the MSK was not cheating them of mainstream content. This might appear contradictory; it is in fact a reflection of the complex relationships poor rural women have with mainstream education structures. On the one hand, by reject-ing the mainstream, they acknowledge that mainstream curriculum content does not address their needs, and that the teaching methodology of the formal system does not help them learn. On the other hand, the kind of education they desire continues to be influenced by that which is taught in school. This education would give them the knowledge they have been denied; knowledge and informa-tion that allowed the "educated" to remain powerful. Thus, in a sense, while we saw the MSK educational intervention as "providing them with an opportunity," they saw it as "redressing denial."

We gradually found the MSK taking on the trappings of formal education. A Nirantar member wrote in her field-notes: "They are getting too schoolish in their style – sit in straight lines, walk in straight lines, say prayers in the morning, ring bells in between sessions..."

These routines were not initiated by us, but were things the participants wanted at the MSK, even as they admitted that their children learned nothing at school. These seemingly contradictory responses had to be negotiated constantly at the MSK. It was both interesting and ironical that the power exercised by the learners in this process of negotiation was a power given to them by our commitment to a feminist, participatory pedagogy. Certainly a traditional "school" would not have allowed learners to determine the content. Yet this very power was subverting our pedagogy!

It was not as if dialogue, discussion, and critical awareness were abandoned altogether, but it had to be woven in with their demands. Thus began a process of negotiation; a negotiation which forced all of us to change. We altered our approach to include some aspects of more mainstream curricula, not completely at the expense of other subject areas. Consequently the learners, having compared the MSK curriculum with school textbooks, felt satisfied that their education was at par with formal school education. They grew to see that dialogue, discussion, and role-playing of local issues, even if they did not deliver "mainstream information," were not a waste of time, but critical to the learning process. They responded enthusiastically to alternative content and methods. They were excited by debates – on whether large dams are more beneficial than small ones, or whether the Taj Mahal should be protected from industrial pollution by shutting down local factories; and animated discussions took place on the healthcare system, on women, and on violence. Just as we negotiated content we established the validity of dialogues, discussions, and role-playing as important educational tools.

The learners were able to determine the pace and the content of learning because their responses were our only source of affirmation of the entire MSK process. The process was validated when the learners responded, when they asked questions, when interaction took place. And if they chose to be silent, then we were rendered entirely powerless. They could exercise power by simply refusing to learn. Unlike in the formal educational system, where failure rests on the students, in our system it rested on the teachers and us. Because MSK was an "alternative" educational activity it could ultimately only be validated by the learners themselves.

The empowerment of the MSK sahelis

"Everything was new. We have taught in numerous literacy camps but here the process of teaching was very different. We had to teach them things we ourselves did not know and also discuss it with them. We didn't feel competent."

"During a session on eclipses somebody asked how many days does it take for the moon to revolve around the earth? I didn't know, so I diverted the participants' attention and desperately searched for the information."

Why was the diversion necessary?, we asked.

"Otherwise our credibility would be lost. Anyway they are always trying to think of ways to catch us out." (Minakshi, the MSK coordinator, during the review meeting)

Among the defined sets of relationships in a traditional school is that of teacher–learner. The teacher is the expert, the empowered one, the knowledge-giver.

But in the MSK, the teachers were initially the most disempowered group. The *sahelis* who taught at the MSK not only had low levels of formal education, but the quality of education they had received was poor – typical of government schools in rural areas. As the quotation above reflects, they had a limited information base, were not confident of their teaching abilities or their own information levels, nor were they familiar with teaching methodology beyond literacy teaching. To make matters worse they were young, and from the same caste and class as the learners. A traditional, educated, upper-caste teacher would have fitted the bill better. All these factors worked against the teachers being accorded any kind of respect by the learners. In the participants' perception, these teachers simply did not command authority.

The teachers were desperate to establish their credibility. And their position was a constant source of anxiety for us.

> I have been feeling deep anxiety about how the *sahelis* are going to manage . . . their information levels are so low . . . they have forgotten completely what they learnt in school . . . quite a reflection on how ineffective the formal system is . . . but on the 17th they sat down to do their own reading . . . what was good was that they at least were able to grasp what information was being given without us holding their hand – so I guess we have something to be grateful about. (Nirantar, member's diary)

In a traditional school setting we would have been concerned with challenging the all-powerful role of the teacher as the "repository of knowledge." Here, our task was just the opposite. The teaching/learning process had to empower not only the participants, but the teachers as well. Therefore, instead of questioning, we bolstered the teachers' role as "information-givers," allowing them and the participants to feel that the *sahelis* were in control of the information they were giving. On several occasions when some learners were intent on picking out the teachers' mistakes we had to actively intervene and put a stop to it.

It was paradoxical to our pedagogy, that we had to "empower" the teacher by invoking a traditional teacher–student relationship, even as we tried to alter and redefine it. It was a contradiction because it was our participatory approach and MS's philosophy of empowerment which were the source of the power and confidence that led the learners to disrespect the teacher in the first place.

Nirantar's power
During the first few months, as everyone was trying to cope there was little time to reflect. We were all consumed with issues such as: how to teach a particular topic, how to collect the necessary information on such-and-such, and how to prepare the *sahelis* to take the session. In this process a division of roles emerged. As the *sahelis'* own levels of information were so low, it became Nirantar's task to do the research for the sessions, take decisions on what to teach, and plan the lessons as well. The actual teaching, however, was done by the *sahelis*. This role reinforced the notion of the outsider being the "providers of information," a notion we were simultaneously trying to break.

This role also gave us tremendous power over the *sahelis*; for them, we were the "experts" – a role which they began to accept unquestioningly, to the point of total dependence. Breaking free from that role meant disempowering the *sahelis vis-à-vis* the learners. We were caught in a double bind.

Social context of an alternative educational activity
The nature of Nirantar's involvement with the program, the *sahelis*, and the learners left us with no choice but to accept certain problematic power dynamics with the MSK. Among these was Nirantar reinforcing the powerful role of the "outside expert." We were accountable for seeing that the effort was a "success." This must be seen within the context of rural reality.

Those working in literacy are well aware of what it means for rural women to leave their homes for a period of six months to attend an educational program. Behind each woman's presence at the MSK was a story of long struggle and months of negotiations with the family and community. This was an unprecedented occurrence for the area; an effort which, if rejected by the community or learners, would have serious implications for doing education work in the area. That the women should remain, learn, and enjoy their educational experience was uppermost on our minds.

The women's presence at the MSK was not entirely within our control. They were there so long as their community, their families, or rather the men in the families, saw fit for them to be there. Literacy efforts and what happens within them cannot be seen as isolated little conclaves, they must be placed within the realities of the sociocultural context in which they are situated.

The relations between knowledge and power

How do different belief systems and ways of seeing the world impact upon an educational process? This issue came up starkly in certain sessions but was an underlying concern throughout.

Are rivers and the earth living or nonliving?
During one of the sessions in the MSK devoted to looking at different ways of categorizing, the participants were categorizing the world around them into "living" and "nonliving." The lesson progressed smoothly till they came to classifying soil and river. The participants classified both as living. The *sahelis* too believed this. There was a moment of confusion as the MS resource person present had a niggling feeling of doubt. A science textbook she had read had classified soil as nonliving. But the sahelis were not persuaded. Not being absolutely certain, and fearing that the *sahelis'* confidence would be undermined, the MS resource person let it pass and the lesson proceeded without further hiccups.

That afternoon two members from Nirantar reached the MSK. On hearing about the morning's sessions they expressed alarm; it was factually incorrect to classify river and soil as living. A hasty meeting was convened. The *sahelis* defended their position. They eventually referred to the background material that had been given to them by Nirantar, which said, "*Jaise hamare shareer ko hava, pani, aur khana takat badane ke liye zaroori hota hain, vaise hi mitti ko bhi zinda rehne ke liye in sab ki zaroorat hoti hai*" (Just as human beings require air, water, and food to keep alive, soil too requires the above). The lifelike quality attributed to soil was a turn of phrase, and not to be taken literally. For the *sahelis* it only served to reinforce what they already believed. We defended our position by checking both soil and river against the listed characteristics of living things. They did not fit. Science textbooks were referred to. The *sahelis* fell silent. They were uncomfortable about announcing to the class that they had made a mistake. We decided to reopen the discussion and try and rectify things.

Some excerpts from the discussion:

Intervenors (I): Which of you think that soil and rivers are living? [All the learners (except one) raised their hands.] Why do you think they are living?

Participants (P): River is our devi (goddess) and "dharti" (earth) is our mother.

I: Your real mother is living. Earth and rivers are mother images, not your real mother.

P: They both give life – our grain, plants, forests grow in soil. Rivers give us life-giving water. Our mothers give life.

I: It is true that they are life supporting but that does not mean they are living themselves. We eat food and grains to live but the grain itself is not living. They do not grow. They do not procreate.

P: But if soil did not have life it would not produce life. Rivers grow. They grow in the monsoons and shrink in the summers. They do give birth to other rivers.

Chamela, a learner, challenged her colleagues: A river is nonliving because rivers dry up in the summer. Something living cannot periodically live and die.

P: River is a mother and mothers can have many children. If one child dies do we say all others are dead or that the mother is dead? Earth is our mother and earth drinks water.

I: But a piece of cloth also soaks water, it is not living.

I: What is a river made of?

P: Water.

I: Is water living?

P: Water in a glass is not living but a river is living. A river is living because it flows, it moves, it cuts its own course.

I: You are saying that soil is living, but is this (holding up a lump of soil) living?

P: No, in this form it is not living but the earth is living. Gods and goddesses give birth to river. Earth is a goddess. We pray to them.

I: That is a matter of your belief. Your religion. Others religions or belief systems may not accept this. For instance, scientists believe that they are nonliving. Everyone is free to have their own beliefs and that is nice. The logic you put forward holds for the way you look at the world and similarly the logic within the other system is consistent.

This interaction, very early on in the semester, compelled us to reflect on our practice. There was a distinct polarization between the way we categorized the world and their ways of looking or knowing. The interaction described above pitted one belief system against the other. However, the manner in which the interaction unfolded, with us trying to counter every point they made with a different logic, was not fruitful. The two systems really had no basis for comparison. And though we gave value to their ways of seeing, we did try and uphold a scientific, positivist conception of knowledge. Categories such as living and nonliving had been emphasized as "scientific" and "logical," and the task of teaching and learning had to do with the acquisition of "universal," neutral content.

Yet the situation was not simply about imposing our worldview and disregarding theirs. And the episode in many ways was a dialogue among equals. Learners, till the end, were far from convinced that the categorization we were trying to suggest had any value or validity. Their beliefs that earth and river are "goddesses," "life-giving," and "mother" could not be separated or broken down into components such as "river is made of water and water is nonliving." The power and meaning that River and Earth hold in their lifeworld is too great and too integral to their existence. "Humanizing" or giving things human attributes was also integral to the participants' language use – branches are children, sap is blood, when you cut a tree its bleeds, and the rustling of the leaves when a tree or branch is being cut, are cries of pain.

Such an intellectual stance by Western standards exhibits what is called "animism" and is frequently labeled a "misconception" to be overcome. However, Western researchers report the common failure of even systematic instruction to overturn such views (diSessa, 1996; Mintzes, Wandersee, & Novak, 1997). Divorcing this language use when trying to categorize is also not possible. Cultural roots are far more resistant and educational interventions cannot wipe these out so quickly or simply. Furthermore, the dangers of negating the learners' lifeworld are immense. Most education programs pay little attention, as we did on that occasion, to the connections that exist between knowledge and its practical, cultural, and linguistic realities in the learners' lives. Teaching and learning is not simply the acquisition of universal, neutral content; rather, knowledge is an instrument of reflection and insight.

This stalemate was not the last word on the issue of living and nonliving; the dialogue resurfaced on another occasion. The same group of women, when discussing how rivers are formed, unhesitatingly declared that they are formed from melting snow of the mountains. This also brought home the fact that people are products of a complex reality, have different "voices" (Wertsch, 1991), and do not necessarily believe in "one truth." The voice that argues strongly for the river being a mother, living, a goddess, and created by gods, also believes that rivers are born from melting mountain snows. Both voices are equally real.

The interaction also brought out power dynamics in relation to the *sahelis*. The *sahelis* had not really been convinced of our argument but possibly did not feel on strong enough ground to counter our views. In a polarized situation they felt they must team up with us rather than the learners.

Some final questions arise: What made us include this in the curriculum? Why try and teach adult women categories like living and nonliving? They already had well-defined ways of seeing and categorizing. We realized that this decision was unconsciously determined by our own primary-level schooling, and not by any carefully thought-out criteria. And indeed the distinction between living and nonliving is one of the first lessons in most school textbooks. But then, if we did not bring in such topics would we be excluding them from a way of seeing shared with a large section of society? Such questions remain unanswered.

Is there a difference between "forced" and "genuine" sati?
We decided to discuss the issue of *sati* by analyzing the Roop Kanwar Case – a controversial case which brought together women's groups from across the country to protest and lobby for legislative changes. *Sati* is the practice of burning a widow on her husband's funeral pyre. It was widely prevalent in the early nineteenth century in parts of India. Despite legislation against it, some cases of *sati* have been reported in India in the past 40 years. Roop Kanwar, a young widow, was burned alive on a husband's funeral pyre on September 4, 1987, in Deorala village, Rajasthan. When we decided to take up the issue of *sati*, we were aware that many in the group probably believed that women who immolate themselves on their husband's pyre are goddesses and should be revered. They do, however, make a distinction between "forced" and "genuine" *sati*: the latter occurs when women "possessed" by *sat* or truth, after their husband's death throw themselves "willingly" into the fire. It is believed that in this state the widow becomes so powerful that she does not feel pain and can perform miracles. Though *sati* is certainly not a common occurrence, it is integral to their belief system.

> As the *sahelis* were unfamiliar with the case I discussed it with them in great detail – the gender, caste, and political dimensions and the strategies adopted by the women's groups. This was easy as I had been so involved with the case myself. I told them about the family members, how the politicians and police had reacted, and how we had countered all that. The *sahelis* were meant to facilitate the session, and I was to support them.
>
> The discussion had hardly begun when the women made the (expected) distinction between "forced" and "genuine" *sati*. While they upheld genuine *sati* they sympathized with forced *satis*. From this point on *sahelis* were unable to take the discussion forward. They didn't know whether to take on the women and counter genuine *sati* or to elaborate upon the details of the case. The former they were not equipped to do. Some still believed in it themselves.
>
> I had to take over because there was a danger that the discussion would only reaffirm *sati*. I deconstructed the Roop Kanwar Case and discussed the issue of why women should feel the need to commit *sati* in the first place. I linked this to women's status as widows. Many in the group were widows. They shared their experiences of discrimination and hardship. However, they continued to put forward arguments to defend *genuine sati* ... after becoming *sati* women become

goddesses and are revered ... That is the only time women are powerful ... if Roop
Kanwar had been coerced then we oppose it ...

It was at this point that I stated in no uncertain terms that "I believe that *sati* is
murder," and by upholding *sati*, genuine or otherwise, they were participating in
creating conditions to make women believe that. My declaration was met with
silence. (Nirantar member's diary)

Here again we had two positions pitted against each other. But the dynamics
were different. The learners were a group of women who were in the process of
developing a feminist perspective and would instinctively pick up cudgels to fight
cases of rape and domestic violence. Why was there a resistance to questioning
this form of violence against women? As in the previous example, here too we
have a case of women speaking in different voices – hence the distinction between
"forced" and "genuine" *sati*. Their feminist voice allowed them to acknowledge
that there was "forced" *sati*, which was wrong and should be condemned;
and their other voice, which was rooted in religious and cultural beliefs, made
them say "genuine" *satis* were possible and were divine acts. By making this
distinction, they gave themselves the space to hold on to their religious
and cultural beliefs, while simultaneously allowing their feminist voice to
speak.

In an education space like the MSK, such plurality was constantly expressed.
However, upholding plurality could not become an end in itself. Thus it was
important for us to state our position unequivocally and from a position of
power. There is no genuine *sati*. While in the living/nonliving example, we stated
our position, we did it with trepidation, wanting to acknowledge the other belief
system. In this case, we were clear about wanting to state our position and even
replacing theirs with it.

Concluding Comments

The three teaching/learning activities raise important questions for people who
are working in the area of education and literacy. Often by defining education
and literacy as empowering and describing our practice as "participatory," we do
away with the uncomfortable question of power. Participation embodies the
notion of equality – since everyone participated in the activity, they all had an
equal say. We also do away with questions of power by invoking the fact that
we do not work *on* or *for* people but we work *with* people. In this case study
an attempt has been made to unpack the concept of participation and to
demonstrate that we are constantly working in situations that are ridden with
inequalities. An analysis of power in our daily practice becomes critical, as the
teaching/learning situation is not a neutral one. It is a real material site of social
relations.

The other element that runs through all these experiences is the constant
tension that exists between the mainstream and the creation of an alternative.

The experiences demonstrate that neither can we in our practice do away entirely with the mainstream, nor can we simply construct the "other" in opposition to the mainstream. Negotiating between the two becomes crucial to the construction of a sustainable literacy intervention, where there is an integrated "participation" of the two rather than mere substitution. This brings us back to our understanding of power, where the two notions of power – one as a commodity and the other as generated through structured relationships that are mutable – become part of this negotiation with marginalized groups who experience power only as a lack.

Notes

1   A version of this chapter was presented by Nirantar at the International Seminar on Literacy and Power held in Harare, Zimbabwe in Aug. 1995. The field experiences recounted in this paper date from the period between 1991 and 1995.
2   Mahila Samakhya or Education for Women's Equality is an Indian central-government program of the Department of Education, Ministry of Human Resources Development. It was launched in 1989 in the states of Karnataka, Gujarat, and Uttar Pradesh, and has since expanded to cover several other states. Banda is one of the districts in Uttar Pradesh, where the program was first launched. The program was launched in pursuance of the National Policy on Education in 1986, which was the first policy-level expression of the belief that education can bring about changes in the status of women.
3   Nirantar, a Gender and Education resource center, was set up in 1993. Our mandate, very briefly, is to make education an enabling and sustainable process for women. We work in close collaboration with field-based nongovernmental organizations to plan and implement education strategies, produce alternative curricula and reading material for newly literate adults, and conduct gender sensitization trainings. The dissemination of these experiences is an important part of our work. We are involved in action research and various campaigns on women's issues, especially violence against women.

References

Batliwala, S. (1993). *Empowerment of Women in South Asia: Concepts and practices.* New Delhi: Food and Agriculture Organization of the United Nations.

diSessa, A. (1996). What do "just plain folk" know about physics? In D. R. Olson and N. Torrance (eds.), *The Handbook of Education and Human Development: New models of learning, teaching and schooling.* Cambridge, Mass. and Oxford: Blackwell Publishers.

Isaac, J. (1986). *Beyond the Three Faces of Power: A realist critique.*

Ministry of Human Resource Development. (1988). *Mahila Samakhya.* New Delhi: Government of India.

Mintzes, J., Wandersee, J., and Novak, J. (1997). Meaning learning in science: The human constructivist perspective. In G. D. Phye (ed.), *Handbook of Academic Learning: Construction of knowledge*. San Diego: Academic Press.

Simon, R. (1987). Empowerment as a pedagogy of possiblilty. *Language Arts*, 64.

Street, B. (1995). Literacy and power? Paper presented at the International Seminar on Literacy and Power, Harare.

Wertsch, J. (1991). *Voices of the Mind: A sociocultural approach to mediated action*. Cambridge, Mass.: Harvard University Press.

Part III

Conclusion: From Research to Policy

Chapter 16

Literacy and Social Development: Policy and Implementation

Ingrid Jung and Adama Ouane

The authors of the chapters in this volume were concerned with the role of literacy in the activities and institutions of various societies. They were asked to present concrete cases and analyze them from different historical, sociological, linguistic, practical, and political perspectives in order to reveal the relationship between literacy and development. Why revisit such a topic at a time when standard answers are thought to be available? Two reasons: a deep discomfort with the predominant approaches to literacy, and disappointing results obtained by standard practices despite tireless investments and painstaking efforts by individual learners, local communities, and poor states. A simplistic view of the problem, it may be argued, is at the root of inappropriate policy and practice.

The goal of this cooperative, interdisciplinary venture, was to examine the types and uses of literacy in various contexts of social development: to chart the importance of actual and perceived uses of literacy, the relation of literacy to local languages, and the relation to national practices and institutions. Such an examination would, ideally, indicate the conditions under which literacy would develop into an irreversible, indispensable, daily usable tool and an intrinsic part of a viable social structure.

The task of this concluding chapter is to explore the implications of this new understanding of literacy for policy and strategy – to formulate concrete recommendations for policymakers in developing countries and international development cooperation for advancing the uses of literacy in developing countries. The task is not to celebrate the importance of literacy in general terms but rather to formulate the relations between indigenous cultures, societal development, and a literate environment.

We begin by reviewing briefly, the major themes of the papers in this volume including (1) the current assumptions on the benefits derived from literacy, (2) its relations to knowledge and thought, (3) its contribution to democratic participation and social cohesion, (4) its relevance to increasing economic and material wealth and work productivity, (5) its link to the rule of law, and (6) its relevance to the promotion and empowerment of individuals and communities. We go on to advocate and justify more efficient and culturally responsive policies for cooperation for promoting literacy and development.

Understanding Literacy

Widely held beliefs in the transformative power of literacy have resulted in the prescriptive use of literacy as a social instrument of personal and social development, the practice now known to have extremely limited return. The papers in this book describe a great variety of literate practices in a large variety of functional contexts, and indicate that it is impossible to detach the features of these literate practices from their situation and melt them into the general unified conception of literacy. Rather it is essential to see how literacy functions in different social, linguistic, economic, and institutional contexts. Only then can we make useful policy recommendations for different types of actors and stakeholders.

Literacy as a sociohistorical tool

Instead of beginning with a systematic definition, we would recall briefly the history of literacy as a societal practice. With the development of agriculture, whether in Mesopotamia, Meso-America, or China, the management of the division of goods and labor relied increasingly on record-keeping, through the invention of a writing system. Other uses soon emerged. Observation of nature was systematized by calendars, social behavior became subject to codified rules and basic myths were transcribed. Advances in writing soon linked it to oral language, but it went beyond the potential of oral language by facilitating the storage of information and by materializing the culture of a community in artifacts outside the brains of its members. Writing is a technology, shaped over time as a sociohistorical tool (Vygotsky, 1981, p. 137) serving a variety of functions in a variety of cultural contexts. In modern cultures it is used in, among other things, the accumulation, storage, systemization, and distribution of knowledge.

Record-keeping, of course, is quite different from writing which, in most cases, bears a close relation to speech. Just how the characteristics of the writing system influence its uses and its diffusion is under debate, and remains a question for many countries in Africa where people have to choose between the Arabic and Latin script (Taylor & Olson, 1995).

Even if all human societies represent their culture in painting, storytelling, and other forms of representation, writing as a psychological and sociohistorical practice has been invented in only a few societies. It has been borrowed and adapted, however, in many others, which then use it to represent their own societal processes (Diamond, 1997; Olson, 1994). An understanding of the mechanisms of literacy transfer from one culture to another is extremely important for development policy. The most important lesson to learn about the diffusion of technology is that an appropriation of new technologies depends on the needs and possibilities of its application and adaptation to local practices. Literacy was adopted by societies in which economic relations went beyond the basic forms of reciprocity; in other societies it was adopted because it gave personal access to the *Word of God* (Maas, this volume). In yet others it served to circulate letters between members of a larger family and migrants, and yet others used it for the writing of love letters, as in the Tuareg society of west Africa. Other potential uses may not have emerged because the social situation where they could have applied simply did not exist or the institutional structures necessary for enforcement, as in contract law, were not in place.

Literacy is embedded in social practice and, even if this affirmation has become commonplace, it is necessary to repeat it in the context of educational and development policy. Literacy may underwrite democracy in one context, it may underwrite authoritarian rule in another. Similarly, massive educational interventions such as compulsory schooling may be appropriate in societies where reading and writing are, or promise to become, part of daily life. They may be conspicuous failures in societies where it is not. Even though literacy is more likely to emerge in urban contexts, several case studies show how literacy comes to play a role in rural settings where it can be seen as instrumental to some social goal (Maas, Doronila, this volume). Generalizing access in vastly diverse situations in the attempt to create a single model of literacy and society results in statements resembling those characterized as literacy myths. It is impossible to detach literacy from its practice; a better understanding of the role that literacy plays in a range of situations could contribute to the formulation of more adequate development policy. In other words, literacy is not a simple commodity that can be added to any specific situation; it does not have the same consequences in every context. Critical to the uptake of literacy is not the power of literacy itself, but rather the characteristics of the users. Whether and how literacy is taken up and developed depends on the needs and interests of the adopting society, whether in ancient Greece (Thomas, this volume), in Japan (Coulmas, this volume), in German peasants in the sixteenth century (Maas, this volume), in the African Renaissance now underway (Prah, this volume), or in the practices developed by members of women's organizations in India (Ghose, this volume). The conceptualization of literacy as a sociohistorical tool implies the recognition of its potential to do different things in different situations, because literacy is reshaped in every single context of use.

Literacy and its relationships to orality, knowledge, and language

In order to formulate a realistic framework for any literacy policy it is necessary to understand this sign system and its relation to orality as well as its role for knowledge construction in various societies at a given stage of their development.

Orality

The traditional debate about the gains and costs of a transition from mainly oral to a literate society has become more complex. First, it is quite difficult to draw a firm boundary between the two types of cultures today. Mainly oral cultures are paralleled by literate practices in some domains of society, creating what might be called literate subcultures (Triebel, this volume), while in modern literate societies oral discourse mediates written communication (Elwert, this volume). Demands for literacy vary with occupation and class even in highly literate societies. Amongst the costs accompanying the culture change from traditional to modern societies is the loss of the powerful oral culture and the individual knowledge and sensivities of preliterate people, as well as the disappearance of languages that are absorbed by standardized languages or lost by language shift (Coulmas, this volume). Whether this is inevitable or the outcome of colonial or hegemonic practices remains uncertain. Yet literacy is seen as a powerful tool and it is important to determine what it is that learners and societies achieve when they acquire literacy.

First of all, written language is not just a transcription of oral language (Olson & Torrance, this volume). Its grammar is structurally more complex because it is less dependent on situated context and on dialogue than is oral communication and, consequently, is important for the construction of discipline-based knowledge. The first writing systems developed over centuries of borrowing and social change (Olson, 1994, Coulmas, 1989). Once available for borrowing, change can occur quite rapidly. Elwert asserts that 50 years were sufficient to develop standard German within the context of a social movement with utopian claims. In modern times, the written form is one prerequisite for the development, diffusion, and importation of complex technologies. In the industrializing countries, technological innovations between skilled workers and engineers become important for production and productivity. Written language develops accordingly, creating not only new professional languages but also a public discourse on many topics. This discourse penetrates the family context and becomes part of the communication of mothers with their children. Accordingly, themes developed through literate practices and expressed in a more complex language, modeled by the written code, enter the socialization of children (Elwert, this volume). This private communication about different topics and with reference to the written code is important for development because it establishes a link between the more informal content of intrafamily communication and the topics and the discourse of societies undergoing technological and societal change.

If the link between the different realms of oral and written communication is crucial for development, it becomes important to determine the feasibility of developing a written code for local languages and then shaping literate practices to those languages (see below). If literacy must become relevant in developing countries, it is absolutely necessary to provide access to a written code of some sophistication and depth. As several studies in Sahel countries have demon-strated, the quality of technological literacy and historical information available in print is far below that available in the oral tradition. As a result, the gains in terms of knowledge and pleasure are far from commensurate with the time and effort invested in the acquisition of reading skills. Even once literacy is available in a society, people have to learn to distinguish the contexts in which writing is useful from those in which oral speech is most appropriate (Fagerberg-Diallo, this volume). Literacy in the form of adolescent diary writing and books about collective history makes literacy a mirror of as well as a window on the world.

Knowledge

As has been stated before, literacy has been developed as a tool for the storage, systematization, and diffusion of knowledge. Maas (this volume) describes how the involvement of craftsmen in market-related activities during urbanization required new levels of literacy. Today, people in Mali reinvent the same use of record-keeping to keep track of rainfall over a season in order to determine when to plant, what kind of crops to raise, and the corresponding agricultural tech-niques. Literate practices enable people to better understand their production experience, economic exchange, and social relations.

While in oral societies, locally produced knowledge is transmitted from gen-eration to generation through apprenticeship and ritualized oral communica-tion, in literate societies knowledge production and storage depend increasingly on the written mode. A major problem in developing countries – and this constitutes a serious obstacle to development – is that local knowledge is not taken sufficiently into account. Traditional knowledge and practices are inter-rupted (Doronila, this volume) and discarded as not scientific or empirically founded. Knowledge is not simply transmitted from the dominant culture but rather is selected by the borrower. Yet in colonial and postcolonial contexts, Western knowledge systems are simply imposed through formal education, what is called "the Cargo approach" (Farachas, 1998). Development requires both access to nonlocal knowledge and the opportunities to evaluate local knowledge and integrate it into newly literate institutions. Ghose (this volume) shows for the Indian context that empowerment for women means precisely gaining access to relevant spheres of knowledge that have been inaccessible to them.

Development policy should thus take into account the necessity for developing societies to build bridges between local and global knowledge, to get to know and select knowledge inputs from other contexts, and, finally, to help people organize their own processes of knowledge production, storage, and diffusion. Part of this processes is the creation and development of knowledge institutions and education systems.

Language

Another point of great importance in many countries in Africa, Asia, and Latin America is the relation between the language(s) of oral communication and the language(s) of literacy. The question of access to and use of literacy in which languages and for what purpose and under what circumstances is widely discussed. This particular aspect is very pronounced in multilingual and multi-cultural settings and in hitherto predominantly oral societies. There is often a linguistic gap between the language or languages of the community and the language(s) of education. The imposition of foreign languages for written communication within the systems of education and administration creates unnecessary barriers to the participation of a large part, often a majority, of the population (Goody, this volume).

Several contributors to this volume show that the development of personal and social literacy is greatly impeded by the fact that literacy is promoted in an official language that is seldom spoken and even less frequently written, thereby excluding a large proportion of the population from participation in literacy-based social activities and decision-making processes (Fagerberg-Diallo, Goody, López, and Prah). Such conflict has been recounted in a wide variety of situations such as between Latin and vernacular European languages (Maas, this volume); the marginalization of native languages such as Quechua and Aymara in the Andean countries (López, this volume); the English–Tagalog equation confronted by rural communities in the Philippines (Doronila, this volume); the indigenous African languages in relation to the former colonial languages, both continentally (Prah, this volume) and nationwide as mirrored in the struggle for self-identity and self-expression in Ghana (Goody, this volume). On the other hand, an indigenous writing system as in Pulaar can forge a reactive and unifying cultural cement in contrast with French, the official language in Senegal (Fagerberg-Diallo, this volume). Literate practices are closely tied up with linguistic, social, and cultural codes.

The domination and imposition of literate practices is not created only by contact with a foreign, colonial language. Even within national boundaries, within subnational entities and local communities themselves, similar problems of assimilating and interpreting literate practices occur. In all these complex linguistic ecologies, literacy acquisition requires people to overcome and domesticate the existing layers of social practice and sometimes requires members of these communities to learn multiple languages and literacies (Ouane, 1995).

The different case studies reported in this volume give vivid accounts of overt or covert attempts made to internalize, naturalize, or to minimize, neglect, occult, or even negate altogether the implications of such complex linguistic ecologies for literacy and education. Conflicts prevail around the choice of languages for literacy and education relative to the cultural costs involved. What then are the merits and demerits of using small local languages as vehicles for advancing literacy and education (Coulmas, Goody, this volume)?

Daswani (this volume) refers to the bitter language turmoil, provoking violent riots and even bloodshed in India, that led to the current three-tiered language policy based on the mother tongue or regional language, the national language, Hindi, and an international language, English. A number of experiments carried out in India address the problem of dominant language versus regional language, of major language versus minor language, and of language of economic opportunity versus language of cultural identity. Language policies should capture and reflect the existing dynamism, not always evident through the analysis of current situations. As it appears in the case of India, for instance, although a cursory look at publications data clearly points to widespread production in English, a careful look at the data on numerous publishing efforts in various regional languages indicates that the latter publications exceed by a wide margin those available in English.

López (this volume) emphasizes the particular language dynamics prevailing in the Andean countries with almost 400 distinct languages and the paradoxical status of Quechua and Aymara spoken by 63 per cent of the population in Bolivia but still considered as "minority" languages. In all the cases, the struggle is between "nationism" and pragmatism (Doronila, this volume). Coulmas (this volume) urges pragmatism, arguing that giving up social and especially cultural pride is one of the "costs" of literacy especially in contexts such as Japan and China where very old cultural practices and literate traditions are in place. Learning to be literate in a second, international language often at the expense of an indigenous vernacular language is one of the high stakes involved in building a literate society in dense multilingual settings. On the opposite side, Fagerberg-Diallo (this volume) insists that local, indigenous languages are relevant and sustainable by themselves and that it is inappropriate, damaging, and pretentious to assume automatically that every person in the world needs access to an international language in order to be able to be economically productive. Why not allow local communities to solve the problem on their own and to decide about the language(s) of literacy? Perhaps because there are many competing claims which require critical compromise and periodic readjustment to the changing linguocultural and psychosocial relationships. Often real conflict is not between two scientific languages, but between multilingualism and monolingualism in education and literacy (López, this volume). What is required is a recognition of multilayered communication in different languages analogous to the multicode handling of a specific language for different social, cultural, and occupational purposes.

The most positive and constructive policy recommendation within such a perspective is based on principles of inclusivity and integration, valuing both the identity formation provided by local languages and at the same time participation in mainstream literate practices. These are the alternatives to separation and ghettoization. This implies creating an environment in which the learner knows and reads his or her own text, and writes about his or her own experience as well as those of others, thus allowing people to recognize their own mother tongue as a language of identity, thought, and instruction (Maas, this volume). Such an approach offers an alternative to the now common barriers that block cultural and linguistic continuity, and that increasingly push minorities into a separate, artificial existence (Prah, this volume). If literacy should transcend local language, it should at the same time start with and in local languages.

Societal literacy: how societies become literate

For some time, literacy has been considered as an ingredient with the power to bring about social development. This view has led to disappointing results as literacy takes root only in societies where there is a demand for literate practices and competencies (Daswani, this volume). Literacy cannot be conceived of in a social and economic vacuum. It is only part of an equation that optimizes particular aspects of production of a society (Prah, this volume). Literacy and society are linked by literate practices embedded in the functioning of institutions. The development of such institutions is part of growing social complexity (Olson & Torrance, this volume).

Religion and the book(s)
While all cultures recount myths of origin often appealing to abstract gods and other supernatural phenomena, many cultures represent these beliefs in sacred written texts. For the Hebrew, Christian, and Muslim traditions one book is at the center of faith. Yet even within the Christian tradition, the Catholic and Protestant modes of handling scripture had important consequences for the diffusion of literacy and the standardization of folk-languages. Protestantism treated the written text as the word of God, access to which was provided by literacy. Consequently the Bible was translated into vernacular languages such as German, English, and French, and everyone was urged to learn to read (Maas, this volume). The fact that almost the whole Swedish population became literate in the eighteenth century demonstrates the power of religious motivation for the spread of literacy even in the absence of compulsory basic education (Johansson, 1977). On the other hand, the Catholic as well as the Muslim clergy monopolized control over the word of God, the first through the liturgy in Latin, the second through the use of Arabic. The diffusion of the Koran in the Koranic schools emphasizes not so much the reading as the copying of the Koran, a practice that sometimes leads to the use of the Arabic alphabet, Ajami, for representing other languages, e.g. Pulaar or Haussa.

Interest in religion continues to be a major reason for people in several parts of the world to learn to read and write. Religious books rate highly on the scale of interest of newly literates (Fagerberg-Diallo, Daswani, this volume). Finally, it is worth noting that literacy competencies acquired in the context of religious practices have proved to be useful tools in the economic or political context as social institutions become increasingly complex.

Economics
Literacy emerged in agricultural societies where the growing complexity of production and distribution as well as the increasing population made record-keeping necessary. Records for agricultural production, for controlling costs and prices, loans and interest, were fundamental to growing economies. Both individuals and states used writing to gain control over economic processes of

production and distribution, of taxes and of revenues, as well as for communicating commercial and bureaucratic activities. Increasing commercial correspondence between people from different regions in Germany contributed to the standardization of German (Maas, this volume).

Another basic element for economic growth is information about markets, spread first by correspondence and personal communication, later by newspapers, telegraph and radio, and most recently by the Internet. Information technology too is a form of literacy developed to enhance industrial productivity.

Literacy also plays a role in infrastructure in fixing property rights by laws, registering land titles, formalizing wills, and establishing legally binding contracts. Actors in a complex economic field need to know the legal ground of their operations and must feel confident in the stability and justice of social institutions in order to make appropriate decisions. According to Elwert (this volume), this "realm of foreseeability" is necessary for actors in the entrepreneurial field if they are to invest in economic activities involving commitment over the longer period of time required for complex undertakings. This security is linked not only to the existence of laws but also to the knowledge that laws are respected and that the social mechanisms of sanction are effective. The state and its institutions are responsible for the respect of law, in what has come to be called "the rule of law."

The evolution over the last millennium of this type of institutionalized economic sector with its bureaucratic and legal complements can be observed in European countries. The growing towns with their populations of craft and tradesmen required the use of writing for the tasks of record-keeping, corresponding with partners, etc. The administration of the towns increasingly required literate personnel. Hence, the literacy rate during the early modern times grew continuously (Maas, this volume). Even people in rural communities began to integrate literacy into their lives. Yet, with the onset of industrialization, literacy rates decreased. When rural population migrated to towns, child labor ceased to be seasonal and lasted throughout the year, leaving no time for education. Realization that the economic sphere as well as society as a whole needed more educated people came slowly, and compulsory primary education was eventually introduced. The economic complexity of the world today makes literacy an essential part of many institutions. Literacy has thus become part of the environment that creates further demand for literacy acquisition, fueling the demand for education, educational materials, and books of all kinds.

Yet, these literacy practices are not always positive. We must also consider the role literacy plays in contexts where the existing power relations exclude part of the population from access to land, credit, and other resources. The agrarian question is still one of the most important problems in several developing countries (Doronila, this volume). What difference does literacy make in situations where the law may exist but is not respected, where corruption invalidates any social contract, where the economic activity of the majority of the population falls outside the regulated economy, where literacy plays apparently no useful economic role, and people avoid entering into the formal realm of taxes and rules? What role does literacy play when, as Doronila clearly states, to read land registers does not give land?

Democracy and the rule of law

Conflicts between individual members of a community or between groups within a wider population have always existed and probably always will. Can literacy contribute to reduce the level of conflict and violence within and between societies? Social cohesion, equity, and the distribution of wealth do not depend directly on levels of literacy.

Participation in conflict resolution and decision-making in the political affairs of the community or society can take many forms depending on social complexity. In simply structured communities, people can decide upon courses of action in open discussions with everybody knowing and listening to each other. Such consensual means are not uncommon. Participation in more complex social formations depends less upon special competencies of individuals or groups than on the modes of organizing decision-making processes. While consensus is possible in small groups, majority vote, invented first in Greece, forms the basis for democratic decisions. It has been frequently assumed that democracy only emerged on the basis of widespread literacy. A closer look at classical Athens, where democracy for free men was first introduced, shows however that democratic procedures developed well before the introduction of literate practices in the formal proceedings. Literacy became one element of democratic rule without being a precondition for its conception. Participation in public affairs was possible without everybody being able to read and write, as everything that was to be written was also stated orally. People thus participated in a textual community without everyone being literate (Thomas, this volume). Equally important, however, was the presence of written testimonies of decisions in the public sphere which created an idea of political transparency and constituted the beginnings of the circulation of laws.

The fixing of laws and record-keeping were two literate practices embedded in the political organization of democracy in classical Greece, but they do not automatically promote democracy. Highly literate individuals and societies are capable of the most abject crimes, as a glimpse at recent European history tells us. On the contrary, the availability of literacy as a bureaucratic resource contributes equally to standardizing persecution as to providing a defense against it. Literacy, thus, does not necessarily bring with it higher standards of democratic participation, even if literacy is required to participate fully in the bureaucratic institutions of a complex literate society.

Furthermore, underlying any modern complex society is "the rule of law." The rule of law is based on written rules, backed by institutions that guarantee their legitimacy and universal application, that create a realm of security from violence and arbitrariness in which people practice their social and economic activities (Elwert, this volume). The rule of law is built on the ability of citizens to have access to relevant information and to perform legally recognized interactions. The importance of literacy for the legal and other subsystems of modern societies is beyond dispute. Such systems can contribute to social order and social cohesion. But whether this is the case or not does not depend only on the grade of personal literacy but on the formation and enforcement of rules for social order. Even the rule of law does not guarantee social order if the imposition of that rule is perceived as unjust – as in the case of a state controlled by a minority. In such cases laws will not be respected, corruption and wild markets will thrive, leading to the deterioration of civil society and the resort to violence (Elwert, this volume).

Empowerment, identities, and decentralization

Should we thus refrain from linking literacy to empowerment altogether? Should we abandon the hope that the acquisition of literacy can contribute to increased political participation? In societies that are not completely victim to arbitrary rule, and "the barrel of a gun," it has to be acknowledged that literacy can be a tool for social transformation. Literacy can enable people to claim their rights to land or other resources through organizations or community action (Doronila, López, this volume). Indigenous communities in Colombia have secured the property rights of their reservations by appealing to the land titles drawn up by the Spanish Crown during colonial rule. It doesn't protect them, however, from being killed if they actually claim their rights, and only strong community organization prevents them from being completely dispossessed. In these cases literacy is a precondition for getting access to relevant information (laws, archives, history) for social action. But only if the knowledge is backed by a strong social movement can people successfully claim their rights.

With respect to gender relations and literacy, a lack of social development seems to be related to the gap between the literacy levels of men and women, especially when literacy figures are low (Daswani). The participation of women in literacy-related activities seems to contribute to their more active and collective approach to the power relations. Literacy helps them to discover new roles and to contest male monopolies (Ghose, Fagerberg-Diallo, this volume). But even if literacy is an enabling factor, many other social conflicts along the lines of race, class, and caste limit access to an effective share of power. The example of the gender relations in highly literate societies demonstrates that it is not education as such that produces social change; it is social participation and organization that make things change.

Finally, literacy contributes to the creation of collective identities in larger communities. Fagerberg-Diallo (this volume) refers to the cultural movement among the Pulaar population in Senegal that aims at creating common written references to the history of the Pulaar community. People want to become literate in order to read books about their history as well as to understand the concrete situation of their community. It should also be noted that in the process of reconstructing history, even nonliterate people, whose traditional knowledge contributes to the construction of the common text, can play a critical role. Doronila's analysis of communities in the Philippines draws a similar picture of the importance of literacy for the projection of the community identity and for cultural development.

It is noteworthy that it is less costly to create collective identities by means of literacy-structured communication than it is to physically bring together people to perform the necessary integration rites (Elwert, this volume). In fact, the density of communication of people living within the same political entity in societies which are not literate is not very high. It may be argued that a shared written tradition is essential to the development of an effective centralized political system within a developing country.

Historically, as bureaucracies are a necessary element of complex societies, they have been one of the most salient promoters of literate practices, yet their role for political and social development is not always productive. Public administration and bureaucratic rules can constitute a blockade to development, especially in countries where the budget of the state is almost completely consumed by public servants with little impact on the population. Relations between the type of bureaucracy, the operative levels of social organization and of delegation of power are critical. A recent report on education in the Sahel countries has recommended decentralized administration (Yacouba, 1996) because it contributes to the increase of social complexity at the bottom. It can contribute to increased political participation, institutional development, and growing economic activity and cultural development. Decentralization processes also create a demand for the acquisition of literate competencies and give relevance to local languages.

Societal literacy cannot be achieved through imposition from above. It can be achieved only by a policy that focuses on increasing social justice and on promoting access of marginalized populations to resources such as land, credit, and means of production. At the same time, initiatives to strengthen the rule of law have to be given priority ("good governance") as one of the most effective means to prevent violence. From outside, these policies should be backed by international institutions. Further, development agencies should in turn refrain from supporting arbitrary systems. As these policies rely also on the literate competencies and practices of the population, it is extremely important to diffuse the relevant documents in the local languages. Social movements and institutions leading to more participation and communication through creating networks and exchanging and publishing information, are to be encouraged.

Learning to be Literate

Two overlapping and closely interwoven themes dominate discussions of literacy, namely the making of literate societies on the one hand and becoming personally literate on the other. The transformation processes leading to the making of literate societies have been dealt with earlier. Societal literacy is the goal that governments and international agencies are striving for in their pursuit of equality of opportunities, increasing the competencies of the workforce, and a critical, reflective, and creative citizenry. To achieve these goals the common policy initiative is the provision of resources and programs for literacy and learning, it being assumed that the cumulative effect of people being made literate will lead to the creation of literate communities. However, as we have seen, literacy-based competencies and activities must be combined with concomitant developments of complex and transformed literate institutions. Societal literacy is the context that creates the demand for literate skills, hence the futility of divorcing individual literacy acquisition from its social context and social fabric. This section will focus on acquisition and maintenance of literacy by individuals and communities, and their relations to institution-building.

Education

If literacy is viewed as a shared set of ways of interpreting a valued set of texts, then it is important to explore how textual communities are formed (Stock, 1983) and how they function. Such textual communities, whether religious communities, professional societies, or common schools, shape both what is read and how it is read.

Pedagogical theory, especially in developed countries, is focused on the particular understandings that learners achieve in the course of learning to read and write the standard literate forms of the dominant society. Such literate competence is seen as clearly relevant to both participation in the larger society and as a natural extension of ordinary lived experience. None of these assumptions holds in developing countries in which literacy is often seen as irrelevant to the primary concerns of everyday life. While many learners judge the ability to read and write as worthwhile in its own right, the time and effort required for learning often vastly outweigh the minor advantages that literacy brings. Thus, it is essential to assess the social value or utility of the goal and the economy of becoming literate (Paris & Wixson, 1987, p. 46), factors that vary greatly from children to adults as well as from one community to another.

Enabling institutions

Unlike the growth of ordinary language, the spread of literacy depends on specialized and dedicated enabling institutions to promoting the growth of writing as an "autonomous," self-sustained social tool. Several institutions have emerged to promote literacy, the most typical being the school. The understanding given to and the function performed by these institutions were basically identical though inspired and born out of radically different sociocultural contexts. Analyzing this culture of schools, Coulmas (this volume) refers to Japan as a "schooled society" which has now evolved into a "learning and learned society." Traditional institutions were devised very early in Japan to undertake the functions of spreading and consolidating a literate culture by valuing education, knowledge acquisition, cultural growth. Ancient Greece also saw the growth of similar structures and institutions fulfilling the task of disseminating literacy and promoting a national language while building a participatory democracy. In the same vein, Daswani reports that in India as early as 2000 BC there is evidence of highly structured learning institutions promoting initial and higher-level literacy-based learning and education. These institutions were catering for the learning and literacy needs of all members of the society. On this fertile ground, where literacy had been anchored for generations, the Gurukul and Madraseh provided education to the priestly and ruling classes, and the Paathsaala and the Maktab provided more secular education, sometimes using the dominant vernacular languages and targeting merchants and administrators. These traditional functional structures were destroyed in contact with the powerful British colonization.

Elsewhere, especially in Africa, where widespread and mass literacy and literary traditions were missing, the Koranic schools confined literacy to the religious sphere. Attempts to transfer a modified Arabic script, Ajami, to selected African languages (Fulfulde/Pulaar, Hausa, etc.) also restricted their use to personalized and narrow referential purposes. The cultural renaissance movement promoting Pulaar in Senegal (Fagerberg-Diallo, this volume) has broadened the scope of written forms of the language to serve a broad range of historico-cultural purposes. Similar processes have been observed historically in the West (Maas, Elwert, this volume). Both historical and current cases of innovation in the advance of popular literacy clearly point to the importance of social movements adopting literacy as a unifying tool and in giving birth to enabling and normative institutions, a process that Illich and Sanders (1988) call the "alphabetization of the popular mind."

What is required for the teaching of literacy to children is easy to specify but difficult to achieve: (1) suitable pedagogies; (2) comprehensible instruction; (3) available literacy materials and other resources; (4) a skilled and responsible teaching staff. As Goody (this volume) shows, these conditions are rarely met in developing societies. Beyond these, learning requires a supportive cultural environment and, especially for adults, a perception of the value and utility of learning. As long as nations undervalue literacy and underfund enabling institutions, neither literacy nor social change can be achieved.

For adults, in addition to the above, what is required is that literacy be seen as instrumental in allowing them to take charge of their own lives: if literacy is seen as instrumental in any of their valued activities and goals, acquisition is greatly facilitated. Literacy cannot simply be provided but learners must be given scope to select the materials that they find relevant and interesting. For this the market plays a critical role. Publishers' attempts to meet the demands of a growing market lead to the publication of local as well as nonlocal materials, of both utilitarian documents and entertaining fiction, newspapers and religious materials. Publication brings with it standardization and enrichment of language through borrowing and turns literacy into a developmental processes itself.

Cooperating for Literacy and Development: Lessons from the New Paradigm

Development policy aims at offsetting the often detrimental impact on developing countries of the economic, social, cultural, and political policies and practices of industrialized countries. At the core of development policy lies the conviction that it is both possible and morally desirable that less-developed societies build social and economic structures that enable them to attain at least a degree of autonomy. Development is not to be imposed but rather is built upon available material and intellectual resources through the promotion of education and literacy. At issue here is the role of literacy in enhancing the economic, social, and political processes in developing countries. The goal is not to use literacy as a means of central domination but as an instrument that individuals and groups can exploit in the pursuit of specific social, cultural, economic, and political goals.

Certainly, the analysis of the history of literacy as a sociohistorical tool reveals it to be as often a tool of control and oppression as a means of democratizing knowledge and power. Consequently, we can no longer simply treat literacy as an input into the development process, producing as an output an increase in production, equality, democracy, and justice. Literacy is not a magic wand that will transform poverty into wealth or ignorance into knowledge. Although an investment in education and literacy is an investment in human resources, we must see literacy from the perspective of the user, how literacy enables persons and groups to achieve their own rights and goals.

The historical perspective of this volume helps us to conceptualize literacy as one element of increasing social organization. The PADLOS study and Doronila (this volume) describe how literacy-related activities become part of social interaction in contexts in which the local society becomes more autonomous by taking over political and administrative responsibilities, and, at the same time, develops more and increasingly diversified economic operations. The overall process is embedded in local culture. This process could be described as growth of complexity in the differentiation of activities, roles, and attributions in which literate practices become essential. Within such a dynamic system, input of literacy and output in terms of development become indistinguishable. Such grassroots programs frequently require assistance from national or international agencies which may provide consultants and resources for teaching literacy, bookkeeping, and the like. Thus, in terms of development strategy, the approach should be interdisciplinary and integrated, searching to increase and diversify local activities in the economic, political, administrative, and cultural spheres. Obviously, this cannot be the fruit of the arbitrary decisions of sponsoring agencies. Such a decentralized approach to literacy stands in marked contrast to the universalized and decontextualized properties of national literacy campaigns. The provision of literacy, especially to adults, must not be separated from demand and from the ongoing social practices.

Literacy is also part of cultural development. In every case we should analyze the role literacy may play in reflection on and the development of the indigenous cultural resources of a given community. Literacy is not only to be considered as a medium of access to so-called global, disciplined knowledge, but also an important medium for the conceptualizing of local knowledge and local experience. A common theme in this volume is the importance of relating local knowledge and "global" knowledge. Currently economic incentives drive research in biology and genetics to literally eat up the local knowledge which has been produced over centuries, giving nothing in return but dependence on Western genetic technology and expensive medication. The ethical responsibility of cooperative development is to assist local societies in processes of systematizing and securing their own cultural resources. In this endeavor, literacy plays a vital role.

These examples show how the demand for literacy is a function of locally based transformation processes. Educational and cultural policy can both foster and support such local institutions and also create conditions for an increased demand for literacy. In fact, Fagerberg-Diallo (this volume) shows how the availability of attractive reading materials contributes to increasing the demand for literacy courses and for access to materials that are seen as linguistically and culturally embedded and locally relevant. Small investments to support the emergence of a local publishing industry could contribute importantly to both the formal education sector and individual development. The existing policy in educational cooperation, as expressed by the World Bank policy, impedes the development of a local publishing industry by imposing international bidding procedures leading to reinforcement of the already powerful publishing houses in developed countries; a policy that is counterproductive *vis-à-vis* increasing local literacy. The flow of material as well as cultural resources from the developing world to the most industrialized countries in the name of liberal economics and free markets constitutes an overwhelming obstacle to the achievement of the goals of cooperative development.

Finally, what is at stake regarding the realm of education is the relevance of education itself. The education systems in many countries fail to provide relevant knowledge, to create mechanisms of social integration, or to set the basis for personal development. We should explore ways to transform formal and non-formal education into local, grassroots movements by organizing learning processes rooted in local culture. The content of education, the pedagogical organization of teaching and learning, and the type of relations created through interaction, as well as the choice of the medium of instruction, should build on prior individual competence and collective experience. Of course, this starting-point doesn't set any limits regarding where the process may lead to; this will depend on local dynamics and on the evolution of knowledge, institutions, and relations on an international level. Investment in the education sector can contribute to development and the spread of literacy only if the education provided is competently executed and socially relevant. The debate about the role of education in society is not new but has to be reconsidered, especially in the context of development policy where its effectiveness cannot be measured only by its success in the reproduction of elite minorities.

In conclusion, we do not suggest that social evolution will resolve the problem of literacy by itself. But literacy as an instrument of growing social complexity is a necessary component of the development process. And, even if there is no simple causal link between literacy and development, without adequate support for the acquisition of literate competencies, social development will not be possible. Consequently, for historical as well as for ethical reasons, we plead for investment in civil society, the creation of participation processes, and relevant education systems.

References

Archer, D. and Cottingham, S. (1996). *The Experiences of Three REFLECT Pilot Projects in Uganda, Bangladesh, El Salvador.* London: Overseas Development Administration. Education Research Serial, Action Research Report 17.

Bhola, H. S. (1984). *Campaigning for Literacy: Eight national experiences of the twentieth century with a memorandum to decision-makers.* Paris: UNESCO.

Bhola, H. S. (1988).*World Trends and Issues in Adult Education.* Prepared for the International Bureau of Education. London/Paris: Jessica Kingsley, UNESCO.

Coulmas, F. (1989). *The Writing Systems of the World.* Oxford: Blackwell.

Dave, R. H. (1976).*Foundations of Lifelong Education.* Hamburg: UNESCO Institute for Education; Oxford: Pergamon

Diamond, J. (1997). *Guns, Germs and Steel: The fate of human societies.* London: Jonathan Cape.

Easton (1989). *Structuring Learning Environments: Lessons from the organisation of post-literacy programs. International Review of Education,* 35(4).

Elwert, G. (1998). Wie ethnisch sind Bürgerkriege? *Entwicklung und Zusammenarbeit,* 39(10): 265–7.

Farachas (1998). Development, power and identity: The challenge of indigenous education. In L. King (ed.), *Reflecting Visions: New perspectives on adult education.* Hamburg: UNESCO Institute for Education.

Freire, P. (1970). *Pedagogy of the Oppressed.* New York: Herder and Herder.

Freire, P. (1975). *Cultural Action for Freedom.* Harmondsworth, UK: Penguin.

Freire, P. (1985). *The Politics of Education: Culture, power and liberation.* Basingstoke, UK: Macmillan.

Freire, P.and Macedo, D. (1987). *Literacy: Reading the word and the world.* London: Routledge & Kegan Paul.

Gillette, A. and Ryan, J. (1983). *Assignment Children: Eleven issues in literacy for the 1990s.* Geneva: UNICEF. (No. 63/64.)

Gintis, H. (1984). The political economy of literacy training. *The UNESCO Courier* (Paris), 37(2).

Habermas, J. (1981). *Theorie des Kommunikativen Handelns.* Frankfurt a.M.: Suhrkamp.

Illich, I. and Sanders, B. (1988). *The Alphabetization of the Popular Mind.* San Francisco: North Point.

Jarvis, P. (1987). *Adult Learning in the Social Context*. London: Croom-Helm.

Johansson, E. (1977). The History of Literacy in Sweden. *Educational Reports Umeå*. No. 12. Umeå: Umeå School of Education, University of Umeå.

Olson, D. R. (1994). *The World on Paper*. Cambridge, UK: Cambridge University Press.

Ouane, A. (1989). *Handbook on Learning Strategies for Post-Literacy and Continuing Education*. Hamburg: UNESCO Institute for Education. (UIE studies in Post-literacy and Continuing Education, no. 7.)

Ouane, A. (1995). *Vers une culture multilingue de l'éducation*. Hamburg: UNESCO. (UNESCO Institute for Education Study no. 3.)

Paris, S. G. and Wixson, K. K. (1987). *Literacy and Schooling: The development of literacy: Access, acquisition and instruction*. Norwood, NJ: Ablex.

Resnick, D. P. (ed.) (1983). *Literacy in Historical Perspective*. Washington, DC: Library of Congress.

Rogolf, B. and Lave, J. (eds.) (1984). *Everyday Cognition: Its development in social context*. Cambridge, Mass.: Harvard University Press.

Stock, B. (1983). *The Implications of Literacy*. Princeton, NJ: Princeton University Press.

Stock, B. (1984). Medieval history, linguistic theory, and social organization. *New Literary History* 16: 13–29.

Taylor, L. and Olson, D. R. (1995). An introduction to reading the world's scripts. In I. Taylor & D. R. Olson (eds.), *Scripts and Literacy*. Boston: Kluwer Academic Publishers.

Yucouba, M. (1996). *Project d'appui au developpement local au Sahel (PADLOS)*. Bamako, Mali: Canadian Centre for International Studies and Cooperation (CECI).

Vygotsky, L. S. (1981). *The Instrumental Method in Psychology*. Cambridge, Mass: MIT Press.

Name Index

Page numbers in italics indicate reference list items.

Abadzi, H., *176*
Acevedo, M. L., 212, *222*
Acosta, J. de, 202, 207
Adams, M. J., 8, *16*
ADEA, 126, *140*
Afolayan, A., *199*
Ahohounkpanzon, M., *65*
Aigner-Foresti, L., *51*
Ake, C., *140*
Akoha, J., 12, 144, *151*
Albó, X., 203, 212, *222*
Alidou-Ngame, H., *79*
Almond, G. A., 24, *46*
Anderson, C. A., 25, *46*, 254, *282*
Appiah, K. A., 129, *140*
Archer, D., *176*, *335*
Assmann, A., 31, *46*, *51*
Assmann, J., 31, *46*, *51*
Astington, J., *47*
Astle, T., 3, *16*
Azikiwe, N., 136, *140*

Balisacan, A. M., 278, *282*
Ballara, M., *176*
Balmores, N., *282*
Bamgbose, A., *199*
Barton, D., 10, *16*, 22, 40, 44, *46*, 225, *245*

Batliwala, S., 297, *315*
Bauman, R., 228, *245*
Baurmann, J., 47, *51*
Bening, R. B., 189, *199*
Bennett, J. A., 198
Berding, E. H., *47*
Bergen, T., *18*
Bernardo, A. B. I., 7, *16*, 248, 257–8, 282
Bernstein, H., 61, *65*, 124–5, *140*
Bhattacharya, S. S., 287, 292
Bhola, H. S., 24, *46*, *335*
Bhola, J. K., *46*
Bloch, M., 11, *16*, 226, *245*
Blyden, E., 129, 130
Boeren, J. M., *176*
Bonifacio, M. F., 262, 270–1, *282*
Boone E. H., 5, *16*, 209, *222*, *246*
Boring, T. A., *80*
Bourdieu, P., 26, 41, *46*
Bowman, A. K., *80*
Bowman, M. J., *46*, 254, *282*
Box, L., 60, *65*
Boyarin, J., 14, *16*, 225, *245*
Braudel, F., 41, 45, *46*
Breier, M., 4, 8, 14, *17–8*, 54, 62, *67*
Brice-Heath, S., 62, *65*

Briggs, C., 228, *245*
Brill. E. J., *119*
Brookfield, S. D., 150, 151
Bruner, J. S., 61, *65*, 194, *200*, 225, 228, *245*
Brunner, O., 37, *46*
Bubba, C., 208
Bull, B. H., 46
Buraku kaihōkenkyūsho, 113, *119*
Burke, K., 45, *46*
Burnaby, B., 14, *16*
Busia, K. A., 131, *140*
Byrne, R. M., *16*

Calder, R., 137, *140*
Calvo, J. 223
Capo, H. B. C., 148, 151, *151*
Cariño, J., 262, *282*
Carroll, J. B., *16*
Carruthers, M. J., 6, *16*
Cartledge, P., 79, 80
Casley-Hayford, J. E., 129–30, *140*
Cavallo, G., *246*
Cenoz, J. 223
Chall, J. S., *16*
Chambers, R. *176*
Chartier, A., 225, *245*
Chartier, R., *16*, 225, 226, 243, *245–6*
Chatterji, S. K., 285, *292*
Chi, M., *16*
Cipolla, C. M., 38, *46*
Clanchy, M. T., 5, 6, 8, *16*, 40, *46*, 79, *80*
Clark, H. H., 196, *199*
Claure, K., 221, 222
Cole, M., 4, 7, *18*, 33–5, 45, 52, 56, 61, *67*, 225, *245, 246*, 249, 258, *282*
Coleman, J. S., 24, *46*
Coler, J., 60, *65*
Condorcet, M. de, 3, *16*
Coombs, P., *176*
Cornfield, M., 44
Corpuz, O. D., 250, *282*
Cortes, J. 254, *282*
Cottingham, S. *176, 335*
Coulmas, F., 14, *46*, 102, 104, 113, *119*, 287, 289, *292*, 322, 324–5, 331

Crummell, A., 128, 129
Cummins, J., 198, 129
Cummins, T., *246*
Curtis, D., 290, *292*
Curtis, L. R., 24, 29, *46*

D'Emilio, L., 216–17, 220, 222
Damerow, P., 35, 37, *50*
Daswani, C. J., 80, 284, 286–9, 291, 292, 324, 326, 329, 332
Dave, R. H., *335*
Davidson, B., 129, 132, *140*
Davis, N. Z., 226, *245*
deFrancis, J., *16*
Dei, G., 124, *140*
Delors, J., 24, 27, *46*
Diamond, J., 321, *335*
Diop, C. A., *176, 177*
diSessa, A., 8, *16*, 312, *315*
Dixon, J., *177*
Domingo, M. S., 7, *16, 282*
Doronila, M. L., 6, 8–9, 12, 14, *16*, 63, 70, 77, 79–80, 143, 150–*1*, 171, *177*, 196, 216, 249, 252, 255–7, 259, 268–9, 280–2, 321, 323–5, 327–9, 333
Drecoll, F., *51*
Dutcher, N., 212, *223*

Easton, *335*
Edmonds, L., 79, *80*
Ehlich, K., 45, *46*
Eisenberg, P., 33, *47*
Eisenstadt, S. N., 104, *119*
Eisenstein, E. L. 4, *16*, 30, *47*
Ekeh, P. 125, *140*
Eller, W., *48*
Ellis, A. W., 52, 80
Elwert, G., 12, 14, 20, 31, 32, 37–42, 45, 47, 55–64, 66, 79, *80, 177*, 322, 327–30, 332, *335*
Emenanjo, E. N., *151*
Engelsing, R., 37, 38, 45, *46–7*, 86
Englund, R. K., 35, 37, *50*
Epskamp, K. P., 30, *47, 176*
Estienne, C., 60, *66*
Etzioni, A., 21, *47*
Ezzaki, A., 198, *199*

Fabre, D., 225, 227, 242, *245*
Fagerberg-Diallo, S., 9, 12, 14–15, 145, 173, *177*, 196, 198, 217, 323–6, 329, 332, 334
Fagerlind, I., 25, *47*
Farachas, 323, *335*
Farr, M., 227, 228, *245*
Faye, A., *176*
Feldman, C. F., 38, *47*, 225, *245*
Fergusson, S., 143, *151*
Ferreiro, E., 5, *17*
Fiedrich, M., 176, *177*
Finnegan, R., 6, *17*, 79, *80*, 227, *245*
Flusser, V., 19, 29–31, *47*
Foley, D., *246*
François, E., 38, 45, *47*
Fraser, H. G., 130
Freire, P., 7, *17*, 23, *47*, 149, *151*, 335
Fryer, G., 16
Furet, F., 226, *245*

Gaden, H., 174
Gaur, A., *17*
Gee, J. P., 4, *17*, 225, 226, *246*
Gelb, I. J., 5, *17*
Genesee, F., *223*
Gentili, B., 79–*80*
Geva, E., 64, *66*
Ghose, M., 80, 195, 196, 321, 323, 329
Giere, R., *16*
Giese, H. W., 44, *47*
Giesecke, M., 32, 37, 38, 40–2, 45, *47–8*, 57, 61, 62, *66*
Gillette, A., *335*
Gintis, H., *335*
Ginzburg, C., 38, *48*
Gläss, B., 20, *43*
Glave, L. M., 206, *223*
Glück, H., 27, 44, *48*, 56, 64, *66*
Gode, A., *18*
Godenzzi, J. C., *223*
Golte, J., 207, 221, *223*
González, M. L., 202, *222*
Goody, E., 9, 12, 14, 64, 146, 183, 185, 194, 196, *199*, 324, 332
Goody, J., 4, 7, *17*, 29–31, 38–40, *48*, *51*, 54, 56, 62, *66*, 74, 79, *80–1*, 125, 133, *140*, *151*, 225, 227, *245–6*, 273

Gottlieb, N., 104, *119*
Goudsblom, J., 35, *48*
Graff, H. J., 4, *17*, 25, 44, *48*, 87, *100*, 225, *246*
Gregorio, R., 269, *282*
Grillo, R., 45, *48*
Grunzski, S., 227, *246*
Gumperz, J. J., *65*
Günther, H., 44, *47–8, 51, 100, 292*
Gutmann, M., 208
Gwam, L. C., 129

Habermas, J., *335*
Haggis, S., 24, *48*
Hahn, F. H., 125, *140*
Hale, J., 154, *177*
Hama, B., 149
Han, B. A., 261, *282*
Hanson, A. E., 80, *81*
Hardmeier, C., *46, 51*
Harman, D., 20, *48*
Harris, W. V., 79, *81*
Havelock, E., 4, *17*, 29, 44, 45, *48*, 56, *66*, 227, 243, *246*
Heath, S. B., 40, 45, *48*, 62, 65, 227, 229, *246*
Hébrard, J., 225, *245*
Heine, B., *51, 67,*
Herington, J., 79, *81*
Hill, J. H., 231, *246*
Hill, K. C., 231, *246*
Hinzen, H., *66*
Hirsch, E. D. Jr., 29, *48*
Hirschman, A., 64, *66*
Hladczuk, J., 44, *48*
Hladczuk, S., *48*
Hobart, M., 132, *140*
Hocquenghem, A. M., 207, *223*
Hodder, B. W., 137, 138, *141*
Holland, D., *246*
Homann, K., *49*
Hopf-Droste, M. L., 87, *100*
Hopkins, K., 80, *81*
Hornberger, N., 203, 212–15, 220, *223, 246*
Horowitz, R., 60, *66*
Hubertus, P., 83, *100*
Humbert, C., 62, 63, *66*

Hutchinson, J., *177*
Hymes, D. H., 45, *49, 65*

Iliffe, J., 134, *141*
Illich, I., 6, 30, 31, 38, 44, *49*, 134, 332, *335*
Imhof, K., 45, *49*
Innis, H., 28, 29, 44, *49*
Isaac, J., 297, *315*

Jackson, H., 35, *49*
James, W., *66*
Jarvis, P., *335*
Jaynes, J., 35
Jennings, E. H., *52*
Johansson, E. 326, *336*
Johns, A., 6, 58, *66*
Johnson, H. G., 124, *141*
Jones, S., 20, *49*
Jung, I., 15, 62, *66*, 216, *223*
Jungeblut, A., 19, *49*
Justice, S., 227, *246*

Kaestle, C. F., *52*
Kartunnen, F., 227, *246*
Katz, M., 4, *17*
Kees, P., *176*
Khubchandani, L. M., 285, 288, *292*
King, K., *282, 335*
Kirsch, I., 19, *49*
Kitta, H., 106, *119*
Kittay, J., 6, *17*
Knoop, U., *47, 51*
Kocka, J., 37, *49*
Koselleck, R., 45, *49*
Kozol, J., 19, *49*
Kraft, R., 182, 187, *199*
Kuenzi, M., 155, 162, 166, 170, 171, 175, *177*
Kullmann, W., 45, *49*

Lambek, M., 57, *66*
Langley, J. A., 128, 129, 131, *141*
Latour, B., 39, *49*
Lave, J., *199, 336*
Lefevre, L., 30, *49*
Lema, J., *246*
León-Portilla, M., 227, *246*
Lerner, D., 24, 25, *49*

Leschinsky, A., 45, *49*
Levine, J. M., *199*
Levine, K., 10, *17*
Levinson, B., *246*
Lévi-Strauss, C., 31, 38 *49*
Levy-Bruhl, L., 6, 7
Lilley, S., 30, *49*
Lloyd, G. E. R., 5, *17*, 71, 79, *81*
Lockhart, J., 227, 240, *246*
Lockheed, M. E., 20, 24, *50*
López, L. E., 12, 14, 196, 203, 210, 212–13, 217, 221, 223–4, 324–5, 329
Lord, A. B., 45
Lornezen-Schmidt, K., 87, *100*
Lucy, J., 10, *17*
Ludwig, O., 44, *48, 100*
Luhmann, N., 59, *67*
Luria, A. R., 7, *17*, 30, 45, *50*
Lüsebrink, H. J., 19, 20, 30, 39, *50*
Lutz, B., *47*
Luykx, A., 213, 220, *223*
Ly, M. A., 164, 169, *177*

Maas, U., 87, 92, 99, *100*, 321, 323–7, 332
Macedo, D., 23, 47, 238, *335*
Madden, N., 154, 155, 168, 169, *171*
Maddox, B., *67*
Mahapatra, B. P., 286, *292*
Majul, C., 266, *282*
Malinowski, 55, *67*
Mannheim, B., 203, *223*
Markoff, J., 45, *50*
Martin, H. J., 30, *49*
Mateene, K, 144, *151*
Mathews, R. C. O., 125, *140*
May, G. A., 264, *282*
Maybin, J., 33, 42, *52*
McConnell, G. D., *292*
McKitterick, R., 40, *50*
McLuhan, M., 19, 29, *49, 50*
Mercado, R., 238, 244, *246*
Mignolo, W. D., 5, *16*, 205, 206, 208, 209, 220, *222–3*
Mintzes, J., 312, *315*
Molema, S. M., 129
Montemayor, C., *246*
Moran, J. H., *18*

Morsy, Z., 21, *50*
Moscovici, S., 7, *17*
Moya, R., *223*
Müller, U., 19–21, *50, 51*
Munguía, I., *246*

Nanavati, J. J., 284, *292*
Nascimento, G., 19, 20, *50*
Neu-Altenheimer, I., *50*
Neustupný, J. V., 104, *119*
Nguessan, M., *177*
Ngugi wa Thiong'o, 149, *151*, 168, *177*
Nissen, H. J., 35, 37, *50*
North, D. C., 41, *50*
Novak, J., 312, *315*

Obote, M., 130, 131, *141*
OECD, 18, 25, *50*, 82, 99, *100*, 201
Ofreneo, R., 251, *282*
Olson, D. R., 4, 7, 10, *16–17*, 24, 30, 32,
    41, 44, *47*, *50*, 58, 61, *65*, *67*, 79, *81*,
    93, *100*, *151*, 196, 198, *200*, 205,
    209, *223*, 225–7, *245–6*, 273, *282*,
    315, 320–2, 326, *336*
Ong, W. J., 4, 29, 30, 35, *50*, 56, *67*, *151*,
    171, *177*
Otto, L., *292*
Ouane, A., 15, 20, *50*, 324, *336*
Oxenham, J., 30, *51*, 170, *177*
Oyelaran, O. O., *151*
Ozouf, J., 226, *245*

Pamanabha, P., *292*
Paris, S. G., *49, 50*, 331, *336*
Parris, K., 21, 143, *151*
Parry, M., 45
Parsons, T., 38, 39, 42, 43, *51*
Patrinos, H. A., *223*
Pattanayak, D. P., 288, *292*
Pellicer, D., 227, 228, *246*
Pemagbi, J., *177*
Peña, E. L. F., 7, *16*, *282*
Peters, J., 87, *100*
Phillipson, R., 142, *151*
Phye, G. D., *315*
Pike, K., 33, *51*
Platt, G. M., 38, 39, 42, 43, *51*
Postman, M., 19, 29, *51*

Poulsen, B., 87, *100*
Powdermaker, H., 55, *67*
Pozzi-Escot, I., 203, *224*
Prah, K. K., 12, 14, 80, 126, 128–9, 132,
    141, 321, 324–6
Prinsloo, M., 4, 8, 12, 14, *17, 18*, 54, 62,
    67, 181
Probst, P., 22, 31, *51*, 57, *67*
Psacharopoulos, *223*
Purves, A. C., *52*

Raible, W., 39, 44, *51*, *100*
Ramírez, J. D., 244
Reh, M., 37, *51*, 64, *67*, *100*
Reichel, M., 45, *49*
Rennel of Rodd, Lord F., 56, *67*
Resnick, D. P., *336*
Resnick, L. B., *199*
Reuter, Y., *245*
Rix, H., 37, *51*
Robins, S., 8, 12, *17, 18*
Rockwell, E., 226, *246*
Rodas, R., 221, *224*
Roeder, P. M., 45, *49*
Rogers, A., 20, *51*, *177*
Rogolf, B., *336*
Romano, G., 45, *49*
Ross, G., 194, *200*
Rostorowsky, M., 221
Rostow, W. W., 43, *51*, 124
Rousseau, J. J., 3, *18*
Rubinger, R., 104, *119*
Ryan, E. B., 64, *66*
Ryan, J., 27, *51, 335*

Saenger, P., 30, *51*, 227, *246*
Saha, L., 25, *47*
Said, E., 138, *141*
Sampson, G., 5, *18*
Sanders, B., 30, 31, *49*, 332, *335*
Sanhaas, B., *50*
Scheerer, E., 35, 45, *51*
Schenda, R., 37, 45, *51*, 86
Schlaffer, H., 31, 45, *51*
Schlieben-Lange, B., 39, *51*
Schmandt-Besserat, D., 35, *51*
Schwöbel, H., 24, *52*
Scott, J., 226, 227, *246*

Scribner, S., 4, 7, *18*, 33–5, 45, *52*, 56, 61,
    67, 225, *246*, 249, 258, *282*
Seeley, C., 102, *119*
Séhouéto, L., *58*, 59, 61, 66, 142, 144–6,
    149, *152*
Selznick, P., 21, *52*
Senghor, L. S., 130, *141*
Shor, I. I., 149, *151*
Siegenthaler, H., 41, *52*
Silverstein, M., 99, *100*
Simon, R., 305, *316*
Skutnabb-Kangas, T., 142, *151*
Small, P., 79, *81*
Smith, F., 9, *18*
Sougou, O., 168, *177*
Southworth, F. C., 228, *292*
Sow, A. I., 143, *152*
Spratt, J. E., 198, *199*
Stock, B., *18*, 33, 40, *52*, 58, 67, 258, *283*,
    331, *336*
Stone, L., 45, *52*
Street, B. V., 4, *16*, 18, 23, 33, 40, 42,
    44–*5*, *52*, 54, 62, 67, 79, *81*, *177*, 226,
    246, *247*, 297, *316* Sum, A. M., *52*
Sumon, T., *177*
Sylla, Y., *176*, *177*

Tannen, D., 225, 227, 234, *244*, *247*
Taylor, G., *224*
Taylor, I., 104, *120*, 320, *336*
Taylor, M. M., 104, *120*
Teberosky, L., 5, *17*
Thaer, A. von, 60, 67
Thomas, R. P., 5–6, 12, *18*, *41*, *50*, 79, 80,
    81, 194, 227, 232, *247*, 321, 328
Tollefson, J. W., *223*
Torrance, N., 32, *50*, 225, 245–6, *315*,
    322, 326
Triebel, A., 4–5, 9, 42, 44, *52*, 54–5, 61–2,
    67, 86, 198, *200*, 322

Trillos, M., 221
Twine, N., 106, 200

Ullmann, H.-P., *47*
UNESCO/UNDP, 24, 45, *52*, 55, 67
Unger, J. M., 104, 113, 117, *120*
United Nations, 148, *152*
Urban, G., 99, *100*

van den Berghe, 212
van Lancker, D., 35, *52*, 60
Venezky, R., *52*
Verhoeven, L., *52*, 119, 292
Verma, V. S., *292*
Verspoor, A. M., 20, 24, *50*
Vico, G., *18*
Vollrath, H., 39, *52*
Vygotsky, L. S., *200*, 225, 320, *336*

Wagner, D. A., 19, 20–1, 23, 25–6, 33, 38,
    43, *52*, 54, 67, 198, *199*
Wallace, R. W., 79–*80*
Wandersee, J., 312, *315*
Watt, I., 29–30, 40, *48*, 79, *81*, *151*, 273,
    373
Weber, M., 26, *53*, 60, 63 67,
Wehler, H.-V., 45, *53*
Wertsch, J., 244, 312, *316*
Whiten, A., *16*
Whitney, W. D., 284, *292*
Wiegelmann, U., 20, *53*
Wignaraja, P., 250, *283*
Winterowd, W. R., 23, 44, *53*
Wixson, K. K., 331, *336*
Wolf, F. A., 44
Wood, D., 194, *200*
Woolf, G. 80,
Woolgar, S., 39, *49*

Zboray, R.J., 34, 37, 39, *53*

Subject Index

academic, 22, 39, 42, 66, 150, 188, 228, 243, 244, 255, 257, 315

accountability, 75, 78

Acropolis, 73

adult education, 14, 51, 83, 144, 149, 159, 161–2, 253–4, 335

Africa, 3, 6, 12, 18, 50, 56, 58, 80, 123–42, 144, 147–51, 164, 177, 199, 320–1, 323, 332

African
  dialects, 128
  languages, 126–31, 139, 141, 144, 157–8, 168, 324, 332
  scholarship, 124, 137–9
  voice, 138

agriculture, 34, 50, 55, 60, 66, 190, 263, 270, 281–2, 320

Ajami, 133, 332

alphabet(ic), 5, 12, 30, 31, 38, 57, 70, 72, 76, 93, 101–2, 106–15, 117–19, 143, 157, 172, 181, 192, 202, 205–9, 211, 213, 219, 226, 230, 250, 284, 326

alphabetization, 20–4, 27, 30, 42, 46, 48–9, 52, 335

Amerindian, 202–5, 216, 221

analytic, 30, 236

ancestral land, 266

Andean, 202, 203, 207–9, 211, 216, 324–5

Arabic, 34, 154, 156–7, 160–2, 174, 198, 251, 253, 265–7, 279–80, 285, 287, 295, 320, 326, 332

archive, 68–9, 71, 74, 79, 234–5, 242

art of persuasion, 75

assimilation, 143, 211

Athenian control, 73

Athenian democracy, 74–5

Athens (classical), 18, 68–79, 195, 247, 328

authoritative texts, 69

authority, 6, 13, 56, 63, 90, 96, 128, 134, 179, 182–3, 194, 234–6, 241, 243, 272, 281, 297, 301, 306, 309

authority and power, 12–13

authorized version, 304

basic literacy, 279

Benin, 66, 142–51

Bible translation, 184

bilingual, 83, 85, 199, 201–4, 211–19, 221

Bolivia, 202–4, 207–8, 212–18, 221–3, 325

bookkeeping, 37, 84, 86–7, 275

bureaucracy, 63, 71, 73, 77, 80, 146, 193, 234–5, 241, 285, 299, 330

bureaucratic, 3, 4, 6–15, 70–1, 74, 77–9, 124, 178, 188, 243–4, 327–8, 330

Burkina-Faso, 142, 144, 148, 150, 152

Caliban, 135
capital letters, 91
capitalism, 37, 41, 53
catechism (school), 85, 88
Chile, 202–4, 216
Chinese, 101–6, 111–12, 119–20, 137–8,
    260–1, 295, 320
choice of script, 279
classroom, 14, 165–7, 183, 199, 233, 305,
    307
codification, 143, 286
collective identity, 23, 41–2
Colombia, 202–4, 220, 329
colonial(ism), 6, 11, 20, 120–44, 155, 157,
    189, 203, 206, 209, 216, 222, 250–1,
    253, 261, 263–5, 269, 279, 285, 289,
    322–4, 329
community knowledge, 269
compulsory schooling, 88–9, 98, 321
computers, 16, 92, 101, 114–18, 120, 245,
    284
consciencization, 7
constitutional government, 74
creole, 127, 210–11
culture
culture traditional, 1, 14, 261
cultural identity, 78, 154–5, 158, 160–1,
    266, 325
cultural institutions, 125, 129
cultural practices, 6, 204, 225, 226–7,
    230, 243–4, 258, 287, 325
cultural production, 142, 149, 223, 246
cultural subordination, 212
culture-cognition model, 34

decolonizing (the mind), 168
democracy, 6, 13
democratic institutions, 148
democratization, 93, 142, 146, 148, 333
    see also literacy and democracy
desktop publishing see publishing
development
    social, 5
    of writing, 5, 102, 204, 216
dialect(s), 38, 84, 97–8, 128, 153, 157–8,
    162, 187, 191–2, 221, 288, 303
dialogue, 56, 60–1, 155, 303, 308, 312,
    322

direct democracy, 12, 72, 75
diversity, 68, 202, 207, 225–6
document(s), 6, 68, 70–1, 79, 91, 170,
    229, 234–5, 239, 241, 297
documentation, 87–8, 99, 235, 243, 256,
    281

economic growth, 26, 65, 124, 140, 254,
    279, 327
education
    ancient India, 284–5
    structural adjustment in education, 188
education policy, 178–9
elite(s), 76, 106, 124, 132, 156, 253
emic, 33, 42
emigration, 162
empowerment, 315–16, 329
English law, 73
Enlightenment, 3, 5, 15, 86
eurocentricity, 3
everyday life, 23, 26, 31, 33, 35, 125, 207,
    214–15, 217, 219, 231–2, 234, 297,
    305, 331
evolution
    of economic sector, 327
    of institutions, 4
    of knowledge, 334
    of literacy, 83
    of literary tradition, 7
    of new ways of life, 40
    of rationality, 4
    of scripts, 5, 102
    social, 335
    of writing systems, 6, 119
expert, teacher as, 38
    accountability, 78
    decentralization, 204
    feminism, 296–7, 314
    financial see bookkeeping
    resources, 145, 156, 166, 178
    support, 165

folk knowledge, 7–8, 267, 275
formal education, 20, 34, 63, 89, 147,
    149–50, 153, 159, 161, 165, 175,
    196, 203–4, 210, 212–13, 253–5,
    257, 261, 266, 268, 274–5, 280, 285,
    287, 298, 301, 307, 309, 323, 334

formal logic, 10
functional literacy *see* literacy: functional

global(ization), 22, 26–7, 41, 51, 127, 143, 147, 218, 258, 323, 334
government, 5, 9, 11, 14–15, 35, 37, 63, 74, 80, 92, 104, 134, 146, 149, 155, 158–9, 164–5, 178–80, 183–4, 186–91, 193, 201, 204, 207, 215, 220–1, 227–8, 231–9, 243, 253, 255, 260, 262–3, 266, 271, 281, 285, 297–9, 309, 315
graffiti, 70, 76
graphic representation, 205–6, 208, 219, 221
grassroots movement(s), 153–4, 156, 161, 167, 334
great divide, 28–9, 31, 39
Greece, 17, 24, 30, 44–5, 68–77, 79–80, 321, 328, 331
Greek culture, 56, 72
Guarani, 216–19, 222

hegemonic, 124, 131, 201–2, 210–12, 214, 217, 219–20, 302, 322
Hellenic tradition, 68–9
Hindi, 80, 285–6, 290, 292, 300–3, 324

idealogical, 173
identity, 9, 12, 23, 37, 41–2, 78, 154–5, 158, 160–1, 165, 179, 194, 212, 263–6, 324–5, 329, 335
illiteracy, 13, 19–21, 23, 27, 40, 43, 48, 50, 55, 77, 80, 82–3, 113, 153, 169, 251, 255–6, 275, 278, 289–91
illiteracy rates, 21
immigrant
  language learning, 96, 198
  languages, 98
  population in Germany, 82
Indian languages, 286–7, 292–5
  Devanagari, 287
  Farsi, 287
  Gurmukhi, 287
  Hattai, 287
  Persio-Arabic, 287
Indian writing, 287, 292

indigenous
  knowledge, 64, 135–6, 220, 277
  languages, 6, 128, 134, 142–50, 201, 203–5, 211–13, 215, 221–2
  societies, 220, 226
  ways of knowing, 299
industrial revolution, 43–4, 133
inscriptions, 70, 74–6, 102, 288
institutional
  arrangements, 40, 44, 58–9, 65
  contexts, 4, 5, 15, 62, 320
  diversity, 160
  embedding, 36, 57, 59, 62
  environment, 56
  forms, 11, 57
  framework, 26, 41, 62
  library, public, 69
  stabilization, 62
  structures, 3, 65, 321
institutions, 3–7, 9, 10–15, 19, 26, 28, 32, 41, 45, 55, 57–62, 65, 83, 93, 96, 125, 129–30, 132, 136, 144–6, 148, 166, 174, 191, 203, 212–14, 226, 269, 272, 297, 299, 301, 319, 323, 326–7, 328, 330–4
instrumental conceptions of literacy, 4
instrumental role of literacy, 5–7, 11, 15
interpretation, 7, 12, 14, 28, 41, 52, 57, 93, 209, 239, 243

Japan, 101–20, 130, 137, 141, 157, 321, 325, 331
Jomtien, 21, 26–7, 44, 53, 279

kana, 101, 104–7, 113
kanji, 101–14, 119
knowledge, 114, 127, 135, 221, 249
  access through literacy, 290
  acquisition, 135, 323, 331
  alphabetic, 118, 192
  ancestral, 217
  construction, 211, 302, 304, 322
  democratization of, 333
  documents, 235
  and domination, 150
  and empowerment, 299, 307
  and feminism, 297
  formal, 264

knowledge (*cont.*)
 functional, 289
 global, 323
 indigenous, 136, 163, 202, 215
 institutions, 323
 and language, 321
 literate, 263–4, 266, 270–1, 273
 local (community), 219–20, 232, 307,
   323, 334, 265, 269, 281
 Mochica, 207, 221
 oral and written traditions, 249, 270,
   273, 275–7
 oral mode, 260, 262, 323
 and power, 236, 310
 and practice, 260
 pre-literate, 322
 production, 135–8, 323
 received, 135, 270
 reproduction, 138
 scientific and technological, 139
 and social status, 160
 and thought, 320
 traditional, 168, 220, 259, 261, 263–4,
   270–1, 279, 323, 329
 western, 132, 251, 323
 and wisdom, 260

L1 (first language), 146, 178–9, 182–98
L2 (second language), 146, 151, 178–98
language(s)
 instruction, 147, 187, 189
 national language(s), 6, 45, 96, 126,
   130, 143–5, 148–50, 153, 157,
   159–60, 174–5, 187, 204, 220–1,
   253, 279, 285, 302, 305, 324, 332;
   choice(s), 249, 267, 279, 288; policy
   (ies), 37, 103, 126–7, 142–3, 146,
   150–1, 203–4, 221, 301, 324
Latin, 3, 8, 12, 39, 83–5, 87–93, 97–9,
   111, 130, 174, 199, 201–2, 204, 211,
   219, 221–3, 268, 320, 323–4, 326
Latin America, 221
law, 4–6, 11, 13–14, 26, 41, 58, 63–5, 70,
   73–5, 78, 149, 204, 221, 236–7, 291,
   305, 320–1, 327–30
liberation, 31, 132, 141, 151, 154, 268,
   335
libraries, 39, 69

linguistic extinction, 217
linguistic unification, 84, 144
literacy
 access to, 3, 12, 85, 88, 9
   3, 96, 133, 209–10, 218, 233, 262,
   322–3
 and access to: another language, 64;
   communities/institutions, 15;
   education, 249, 253, 255; knowledge
   (information), 3, 7–9, 56, 60–2, 114,
   135, 146, 148, 173, 212, 251, 290,
   300, 323, 328, 334; L2 literacy,
   178–9; linguistic knowledge, 196;
   literate structures, 96; literature, 207;
   power, 329; print, 273; records, 86;
   resources, 146, 148, 155, 162, 178–9,
   191–4, 249, 278, 321, 327, 330;
   schooling, 238; state bureaucracy, 64;
   subculture(s), 179, 191; to the word
   of God, 326
 acquisition of, 10, 12, 23, 43, 93, 96,
   199, 324, 327, 329, 331
 adult, 9–10, 15, 17, 25–6, 54–5, 64,
   146, 150, 165, 176, 184, 190–4,
   197–8, 217, 219, 248, 278, 279
 bureaucracies, 69
 camps, 298, 300, 306, 308
 classes, voluntary, 166; *see also* teachers
 and democracy, 6, 12, 22–3, 30–1,
   68–78, 131, 140, 147–8, 190, 259,
   292, 321, 328, 332–3
 development, 5
 documents, 14, 55, 68, 73–4, 77, 80, 84,
   86, 109, 146, 156, 174, 195, 227–8,
   232–44, 284, 288, 330, 332
 feminist, 296
 functional, 52, 55, 62, 67–8, 75, 104,
   119, 145, 149, 177, 195, 254, 256,
   259–60, 262, 264, 270, 272, 274–5,
   277, 280, 292
 grassroots, 153, 157–8
 initial, 179, 182–6, 195
 insular, 35–6, 71
 mediating effects of, 28
 metaliteracy, 192, 198
 and orality, 6, 21, 31, 72, 79, 227
 policy, 142
 popular literacy, 71, 332

and poverty, 13, 26, 27, 135, 147–8, 223, 251, 254–5, 259, 264, 271, 273, 278, 333
  practices, 19, 39, 87, 249, 257–8, 291, 327
  public access, 74
  rates, 43, 63, 82, 104, 119, 327
  schooling, 4
  and social development, 11–15, 22, 48, 63, 125, 132, 148, 151–2, 226, 246, 248, 250, 254, 274, 277–9, 289, 319–20, 326, 329–30, 333, 335
  societal, 12, 54–5, 62–5
  subcultures of, 178–9, 193, 196–7
  teaching, 12, 165, 168–9, 182, 186, 194, 254, 301, 309, 333
  vernacular, 7, 33, 36, 39–40, 64, 119, 130, 178, 183–5, 188, 190–4, 198, 210–12, 216–19, 221, 285, 305, 324–6, 332
literate
  communities, creation of, 331
  culture(s), 28, 36, 38–9, 48, 55, 57, 61–2, 94, 242, 245, 291–2, 331
  environment, 10, 62, 64–5, 68–70, 72–4, 78–9, 142, 146, 156, 160, 205, 212, 215, 219, 291, 319
  institutions, creation of, 9
  practices, 4, 10, 12, 40, 226, 228, 248, 258, 320–30, 333
  society, 12, 14, 16, 59, 79, 119, 219, 291, 322, 325, 328
  subcultures, 179
  tradition, 6, 54, 151, 216, 227, 248–50, 258–9, 270, 276, 278–9
literature, 4, 6, 8–9, 11, 31, 37, 39, 49, 52, 69–70, 72, 77, 83, 85, 105–6, 130, 137, 142, 144, 148–51, 154, 161, 163, 177, 193, 206–7, 218, 221, 284, 286–7
litigation, 230, 236, 240, 243
living things, 311
local language(s), 14, 130–2, 142, 144, 148, 150–1, 183, 185–7, 192, 250–1, 253, 266–7, 270, 300–3, 319, 322, 324–5, 330

magic(al), 28–30, 38, 43, 127, 134, 206, 264, 333

mainstream content, 307
mass literacy, 9, 36, 144, 248, 289–90, 332
media, 19, 24–5, 43, 45, 47–8, 60, 62, 65, 84, 98, 102, 147, 164, 173, 203, 212, 214, 253, 255, 261, 265, 268, 275, 281, 286
metalinguistic, 10, 32, 211
metascript, 112
Mexico, 201, 204, 211, 220, 222, 225, 227, 229–31, 237, 244, 246
misconception, 125, 273, 312
modernization, 22–7, 31–3, 35, 40, 60, 106, 129, 143–4
modes of representation, 205, 227
mother tongue, 90, 93, 128, 143, 187, 210–11, 217, 279, 285–6, 324
mother tongue literacy, 64, 85, 93, 96, 187, 195, 210–11, 217, 220, 279, 285, 324–5
motivation, 9–11, 59, 155, 162, 164, 182, 192–5, 326
multilingual, 32, 64, 69, 151, 223, 230, 287, 324–5
multiple literacies, 289, 324
myth(s), 8, 31, 48, 52, 67, 87, 123, 320–1, 326

Nahuatl, 222, 230–1
narratives, 228
nation state, 12, 41
national identification, 268–9
nation-building, 24, 272
negotiation and conversation, 236
neo-colonial, 125
New education, 76
NGO(s), 145–6, 149, 158–9, 165, 167, 272, 274, 298
Nirantar, 296, 299–315
non-formal education, 20, 153, 159, 165, 183–4, 188, 190, 192
non-literate cultures, 4
norms, 13, 37, 42, 54, 59, 63, 92, 176, 249, 271, 291, 302

oral
  culture, 6, 9, 29–30, 55–6, 61, 72, 77, 133, 245, 322
  mode, 260, 262–4, 302, 304

performance, 76, 243–4
presentation, 60, 72, 237, 242, 244
skills, 72, 77, 227, 230, 244, 281
oral-literate, 6, 96, 246
orality, 17, 27–31, 35, 39–40, 47, 49–51, 60, 67, 72, 76–7, 79–80, 93, 96, 133, 201, 208, 218, 220, 225, 227, 230–2, 242–7, 321
orthography, 9–10, 14, 47, 57, 89–92, 95–7, 99, 101, 106, 120, 146, 150, 157, 165, 175, 215, 219
ostracism, 75

participatory, 13, 283, 304
partnerships, 297
pax Europa, 135
persuasion, 75–6, 235–6, 238–9, 243
Peru, 201–4, 214, 216, 221, 223
philosophical view, 33
Phoenicians, 70
picture writing, 5, 209
pidgin, 97, 127–8
political
  image, 64
  satire, 72
postindependence, 144
postcolonialism, 123, 126
postindependent, 142
poverty see literacy and poverty
power relations, 28, 44, 59, 63, 278, 296–7, 303, 327, 329
praxis, 124, 139, 150, 283
primer, 157, 176, 275, 296, 302–6
primitive, 5, 30–1, 67, 136, 209, 212, 277
printing plants, 145–6
printing press, 16, 29, 36, 47, 83
property relations, 249, 261, 263
Protestant, 39, 85, 99, 128, 251, 261, 326
Protestantism, 29
public education, 3, 15, 254
public policy, 13, 153
publication, 60, 82, 144, 146, 163, 165, 242, 279, 332
publishing, 60, 75, 156–7, 159, 160, 162, 165, 325, 330, 334
Pulaar, 153–77, 324, 326, 329, 332
pupil teachers, 183–4, 188–9, 197

Quechua, 203–5, 208, 210–11, 215–16, 222–3, 324

rationality, 4, 6, 23, 30–1, 42, 70, 133–4, 277
reading aloud, 209, 300
reading comprehension, 185–6, 195
record keeping, 3, 73, 207, 320, 323, 326–8
records, 8, 11–12, 14, 68–73, 75, 78, 87, 130, 156, 185, 261, 299
  bureaucratic lists, 71
  publicly inscribed, 73
regional languages, 36, 38, 84, 85, 303, 325
reinscription, 204, 211, 215, 217, 220–1
Renaissance, 158, 160, 164, 168, 174, 208–9, 223, 321
representation, 13, 32, 34–5, 90, 92, 106–7, 118, 127, 205–11, 219, 221, 225, 244, 297, 320
revolutionary movements, 144–5
rhetoric, 31, 72, 75–7, 80, 131, 227, 233, 269
rhythm of community life, 259, 281
rhythm of production, 88–9
rice-terracing agriculture, 261–3, 269, 282
ritual, 214, 229, 236, 243, 245, 263
rote learning, 10, 251, 267
rote memory, 186, 194
rules, 11–14, 25–6, 34, 40–1, 54, 77, 136, 146, 162, 195, 199, 227, 229, 260–1, 263, 271, 320, 328–30
rural life, 135

Sahel, 153, 323, 330
Sati, 313–14
savage, 3, 30, 126, 136, 277
scheduled language(s), 286
schooling, 3–4, 7, 10–12, 20, 27–28, 34, 37, 69, 88–9, 98, 119, 162, 167, 170, 186, 192, 211, 213–14, 217, 226, 231–4, 238, 257, 285, 287, 289, 307, 313, 321,
scribal caste, 73
scribes, 37, 77, 102, 125, 142, 226, 233, 235, 256
segmentation, 40, 107, 109–10, 267

self-consciousness, 170
self-teaching, 88
Senegal, 20–1, 39, 53, 153–66, 173–5,
    324, 329, 332
social
    change, 4–5, 21, 32–4, 40–1, 43, 46, 49,
        52, 173, 248–9, 261, 267, 322, 329,
        332
    development, 5, 11–15, 22, 63, 65, 125,
        132, 148, 220, 226, 248, 250, 254,
        274, 277, 279, 319–20, 326, 329–30,
        335
    embedding, 35, 47
    mobility, 127–8, 146, 149, 212, 253
    reproduction, 143
    transformation, 54, 135, 249–50, 329
sociocultural, 125, 155–6, 159–60, 225,
    263, 276, 287, 310, 331
speech registers (keys) 57, 59, 93, 133
standard language, 9–10, 34, 36–7, 91, 285
standardization, 40–1, 57, 61–2, 143, 157,
    286, 326–7, 332
study, 11, 13, 15, 32, 136, 162–73, 195,
    202, 234, 251
subordination, 297–8, 303
Swidden agriculture, 263, 269
syllabary, 35, 71
syllabic, 70, 109

teachers, 10–11, 21, 23, 86, 92, 96, 136,
    150, 154, 156, 158, 161–9, 172,
    180–98, 210, 213, 218, 226,
    229, 231–4, 242, 280–1, 298,
    300–9
technological determinism, 4
technology(ies), 4–5, 11, 24, 28–9, 31, 34,
    36, 47, 58, 71, 102, 114–16, 136,
    149–50, 155, 165, 170, 176, 249–50,
    261–2, 270–1, 276, 278, 319–21, 327,
    334
testimonies, 74, 232, 240, 328
textiles, 207–8
textual community, 58, 78, 328
textuality, 205, 207, 209
time/space, 40, 145, 209
town schools (*dudesche scholen*), 84
traditional knowledge, 8, 12, 168,
    220, 259, 261–5, 270–6, 279, 323,
    329
transcription, 10, 93–4, 107, 157, 322

UNESCO, 5, 19–21, 24–5, 27–8, 45–6,
    48, 50–3, 55, 67, 69, 143, 145, 152,
    157, 176–7, 198–9, 262, 279, 335–6
UNICEF, 27, 53, 145–6, 168, 221, 335
universities, 13, 37, 59, 62, 136–7, 194,
    274, 284
urbanization, 24–5, 38, 84, 99, 230, 239,
    323
Uttar Pradesh, 296

Vai, 33–4, 45